Where in the World Is God?

Humanity as Mirror

For Valerie —

*With hope for
the future of our planet —
Hope Raymond
August, 2023*

Where in the World Is God?

Humanity as Mirror

HOPE RAYMOND

PALO ALTO, CALIFORNIA

ReadersMagnet, LLC

*To the Millennial Generation
who have within themselves
all that is needed
to play their part well*

CONTENTS

Part Three

CRITIC'S REVIEW

APPENDICES

ILLUSTRATIONS

ACKNOWLEDGMENTS

As incomplete as this listing is, I want to acknowledge the following individuals and groups of people who, in their own unique ways, contributed far more than they suspect in helping shape this book. My profoundest thanks go out to them all!

— The countless individuals, unknown to me personally, who lived the stories that shaped this book through their actions, words and ideas.

— The many newspapers, news services, journalists and editors who provided the research and stories that formed the core of this book. Their choice of news coverage, in response to human interest, largely determined what was included.

— The extraordinary patience of those who accepted insufficient answers when they asked me, "What is your book about?" I am grateful for their interest, even though I was unable to convey a satisfying answer until I reached the end of the book.

— Diane Pendola and Teresa Hahn at Skyline Harvest, whose solitary cabin provided space for my thinking through the meaning of the data I had collected, without interruption.

— My brother, Jack, who gifted me with a month of uninterrupted time in his home to put my thoughts about the meaning of the data in writing.

— Betty Howell, for her accompaniment throughout the entire gestation period of collecting data and writing this book, and for her consistent encouragement and support with insightful comments. She was invaluable to me throughout the whole process.

— John Petroni, who was enormously helpful in keeping me on track, offering unending encouragement, prodding and support, and eliciting insights that enabled me to grow along with my book. Without his tutelage, this Work would never have come into being.

— Steve, who so generously shared his computer expertise, and exercised unending patience in working with his digitally-challenged mother.

— Family and friends, for tolerating the long process that kept me from being as present to them as I would have liked. They showed remarkable resilience in accepting my need for space to think and write, which included the barrier of my answering machine while I was writing, and tolerating long delays in my responding to e-mails. Thank you for hanging in there with me!

— And Nikki, who faithfully lay by my side as I wrote, and whose uncanny canine sense knew exactly when I needed to take a break— and insisted I do so!

PREFACE

This morning I have been overcome with a sense of gratitude and amazement that I am living in the particular time frame that spans my life. I have felt this way about my *own* life for some time, since I first began to sense that these latter years were drawing my life together as a whole and giving meaning to it. But what I am seeing this morning is the life of *humanity*, with that same sense of gratitude and amazement. Many times it has occurred to me that the development of humanity follows the same course as the development of an individual human being, but today I see it in a much clearer way. The course of development falls into three distinct periods:

1. In the earliest eons of humanity's development, people were animists, seeing themselves as an integral part of a world filled with magical spirits that portend good or evil. Gradually these omens became detached from the natural world, through which they manifested themselves, and took on a life of their own up in the heavens. These heavenly gods created their own colony there, looking down on, and controlling, human activity. In response, humans sacrificed offerings to appease them and curry their favor.

   This follows closely the pattern of an individual's development. At first an infant makes no separation between herself and the world outside herself. Then she sees her mother as something other, something magical that can bring food or warmth or dry diapers—or withhold them— depending on the infant's actions. If she cries out, her mother may answer her needs. If she lies there quietly, possibly nothing will happen. The child learns how to work with the uncertainty of her needs being met.

2. When the figure of Jesus came on the scene, his vision of the kingdom of God being "within" persons brought a new consciousness. No longer did God live up in the heavens, according to Jesus, but down here within us and within the world. Humans were not only of collective value to God as "his children," but each human being was of value; each person mattered. The individual had emerged from being lumped together with all of humanity, and assumed a uniqueness and value that mattered to God.

   This second period also followed the course of individual human development. Psychologically we would call this period the development of the ego in the teenage years. The child who has been dependent on her parents to meet her needs now strives to become independent. She is trying to shake off that tie to her parents that keeps her from becoming a unique individual in her own right. She struggles with the question: Who am I? Who am I apart from being my parents' daughter?

3. Humanity is now in the process of emerging from the second period into a third period, which draws together and embraces the first two periods but shifts the focus to the life that an individual encompasses. The first period made no distinction between the individual and the rest of life. The second period saw the separation of the individual from the collective and began to value the uniqueness of the individual. The third period lifts life to a higher level of being. Now that the individual has separated herself from her parents, or her "Parent" in heaven, and has embraced the uniqueness and value of her own life distinct from others, she is able to engage in true relationship with the universe and with all of creation. She has become an adult.

   Humanity has arrived at adulthood. The focus has shifted from the individual to the life the individual embraces. This includes humanity as a whole, inasmuch as each individual life is part of the same larger life. In the process of humanity's growth, the individual has developed the capacity to step outside herself into the realm of this larger life, and to view herself and the rest of life from that perspective. She has not lost her individual identity—it is still invaluable as a unique human life. In fact, it is her primary responsibility, as no one else can bring her life into the fullness of being. But even as she is living that life into its fullness, she is seeing it as one of countless expressions of life, each of which must be lived out fully if life is to flourish in its evolutionary movement through humanity.

Humanity is back where it started, as an integral part of life itself. But now humanity stands at a more evolved level, in which every human being embraces the entire universe within herself. In fact, the individual and the universe have become one. At the same time, humans have the maturity to carry full responsibility for developing and living out their own unique expressions of life.

This is the task and goal of the third period, which is the focus of this book.

INTRODUCTION

S ome people look to music, poetry or drama as conveyors of the depths of life. I look at humanity directly.

Humanity, of all living creatures, has been given the unique capability of developing higher consciousness, the point at which the seen and unseen worlds meet. In this book I observe the life of humanity in the culture of today's world and assess what is going on behind the scenes, that is, the most energetic movements of the universe being lived out through humanity. These movements reflect the current consciousness of humanity.

This book is compiled of three sections, each having its unique style and purpose. Part I is background for the rest of the book. It traces the development of religion, its encounter with science, and the later merging of both with psychology at the point of consciousness. This is the headiest part of the book, more technical and academic in style, but important for proper reading of the rest of the book.

The largest body of the book is Part II, which examines the most energetic movements being lived out through humanity today. Material for this section was drawn largely from print (and, in the past few years, online) newspapers, plus other forms of media. I made this choice based on the belief that humanity has been given the role of consciousness for the universe, parallel to the mind being given the role of consciousness for an individual human being. As a species, humanity fleshes out the "living ideas" (Appendix A) of the universe through events and processes in the world. These phenomena are reflected most widely in mainstream media—not necessarily the most erudite and elite media, but those that reveal the lives of the average person, as consciousness of the average person determines the level of consciousness of humanity as a whole.

How did I select the most energetic movements? By observing repetitious themes or living ideas, especially those that appeared over and over in totally different contexts. As a rule, frequency of appearance and number of different contexts determined the most energetic movements. Part II is more journalistic in style, easiest to read and probably of greater general interest. Because the information is largely from daily newspapers over the last several years, much of it will sound familiar, though some examples cited will almost surely be new to most readers.

Part III, a single chapter, is proof of the pudding. Though it is relatively short, it culminates the entire study, drawing together the findings explored in Part II, but presenting the information differently. The arrangement of chapters in Part II is largely topical, whereas Part III is organized thematically, teasing out the main living ideas that appear throughout the chapters. The style of this section is more philosophical and reflects on deeper movements within the ideas, choices, actions and processes of humanity as a whole.

The years of gestation for this book unfolded like a mystery story. At any given moment I knew only where I was and the next step I needed to take. Beyond that, it was all a mystery. This element of not knowing where it was headed and where it would end up kept me interested throughout. The day I reached "the end" of Chapter 22 in Part III, I made the following entry in my journal:

> It happened so quickly when the time was right. Suddenly, as I was fitting pieces together, I began to realize that this is what I've been working toward all these years. It was so numinous I was afraid the spell would be broken if I allowed myself to think about it. So I just kept on working very deliberately, not rushing, just doing what I knew I needed to do. And then... there it was! The gift I had been waiting for. And I had no idea until that very moment what the whole gift would look like. It boggles my mind that I could

work on something for such a long time and not know until it has totally come together what it would look like. But there it is—so simple, really, but absolutely authentic. It is beautiful—and I feel so much gratitude. (March 26, 2011)

* * * * *

Shakespeare was right: "All the world's a stage; and all the men and women merely players… " Every human being is an actor creating the drama on the stage of life.

But we are not the only ones with a part to play. Fish, birds, animals, creepy, crawly things, thunder storms, tsunamis—even stones and hills, deserts and jungles, mountains—everything has a role. Whatever and whoever enters time-space contributes to the events. Everyone and everything is part of the great drama of life.

Events happen, but stories are made. Without humanity, events would still occur, but no stories would be told about them. Only humans can create stories. We entertain ideas and experience events and processes— inside and outside ourselves, directly and vicariously—and weave stories from them. Though our story may be labeled "true" or "fictional," in either case, it is our own particular way of telling the story. It carries our unmistakable DNA, if we are being true to ourselves. That is part of the beauty and interest of life: each of us makes a unique contribution to the larger story we are creating together.

This book is about the larger story, the one to which we all contribute every day of our lives, whether or not we are aware of it. We are always on stage, from the moment of birth until death. There is no way around it.

The larger story is comprised of events and processes and, where humans are concerned, ideas. Each of us is free to weave these ideas, events and processes into whatever stories we choose to tell, offering meaning as we fit them together.

What follows is a record of how the events we are acting out together on the world stage today are seen through the eyes of Hope. The story you would tell is necessarily different, but hopefully some touchstones along the way are yours, too.

Because of the unique patterning within each of us, the reader may find greatest value from this book by approaching the story as an observer. Only Hope can fully inhabit this book's viewpoint, though the drama as a whole belongs to us all.

You would write and direct the drama differently. You might choose other themes to highlight; different actors to play leading roles; include scenes I have omitted, and cut some of mine. That is your story, which also needs to be told. I invite you to share with me **(mshoperaymond@ gmail.com)** what *you* see in Section Two as the strongest energy coming from the universe, as well as the questions that arise in you from each chapter of that section.

Now, on with the show!

All the world's a stage,
And all the men and women merely players:
They have their exits and their entrances;
And one man in his time plays many parts...

—William Shakespeare

PART ONE
DRAMATURGY NOTES

To the Reader:

In Part One (chapters One to Three), there is space at the end of each chapter for you to record three questions that come to you as you read the chapter. You may find these useful for general reflection, discussion groups, or to mull over with a friend.

"For Reflection" is designed to probe perplexing questions and deepen our thinking. None of the questions has a right or wrong answer, so risk giving candid, deeply personal responses.

CHAPTER 1
COLLAPSE OF HEAVENS

"The material world, the world of matter,
runs like a clock and resists change, while the unseen
world of the spirit calls it forth. The choice is
which world to live in."
—What the Bleep Do We Know? (p. 190)

JUDEO-CHRISTIAN TRADITION

The point in development of consciousness at which the Judeo-Christian tradition began was during the mythological era, when monotheism began to share the stage with polytheism. Humanity had entered a childhood state in which people depended on parental figures—human or divine—for security and help with living their lives, as well as for giving meaning to their existence. In this stage humanity projected authority, power, decision-making, wisdom and other attributes often associated with God, onto divine figure(s). The Bible tracks the development of Western monotheistic belief through stories of human experiences of God.

The overarching story begins with a small band of tribal people, *habiru* (or Hebrews), who were called by a god, Jahweh, to enter into a covenant with him: he would be their god, if they would be his people. This was unique at the time, as most religions in that eastern Mediterranean area were polytheistic, believing in multiple gods and goddesses, as in the Roman and Greek worlds. To be sure, each city had its own god or goddess, but Jahweh claimed to be God beyond the boundaries of any city. Jahweh was God of all.

When the *habiru*, having become known as "Israel," were slaves in Egypt and cried out for help, God heard their cry and responded by approaching Moses in the land of Midian. Speaking from a burning bush, God called him to lead his people out of slavery in Egypt and into freedom. Moses, feeling skeptical about his ability to convince the people to leave their present circumstances, asked God what he should respond if the people wanted to know the name of the god who sent him. Jahweh responded: "I AM WHO I AM… [Say] 'I AM has sent me to you.'" (Ex. 3:13-14) With this response, we learn that Moses is to become carrier of "I AM" to the Israelites, thus paving the way for their future.

Moses accepts God's call and leads the people safely out of Egypt, through the desert, and into the Promised Land under God's guidance as a "pillar of cloud" by day and a "pillar of fire" by night. God remains with them throughout a variety of experiences in the "land of milk and honey," as well as into exile in Babylon, and back again.

Centuries later "I AM" is carried forward in the book of "Daniel" through Daniel's vision of the future, in which humanity arrives at adulthood and achieves its full maturity. At that time, according to Daniel's dream, the reins of God's kingdom will be handed over to humanity. The human being will assume total, universal responsibility for the affairs of the world:

> And the kingdom and the dominion and the greatness of the kingdoms under the whole heaven shall be given to the people of the saints of the Most High; their kingdom shall be an everlasting kingdom, and all dominions shall serve and obey them. (Dan. 7:27)

This vision is punctuated by Ezekiel's vision of Yahweh on the throne in "the likeness, as it were, of a human form." (Ezek. 1:26) No longer will the I AM need to be deliberately carried forward in time, as was Moses' charge, because *then*, according to these visions, humanity will have incorporated the power, authority, and wisdom of God into itself and will have assumed the role of God in the world. The human being will have essentially become god.

The theme of I AM is picked up again in the gospel of John in the Christian scriptures. There we encounter the man/God, Jesus Christ, assuming the attributes of God in saying: "I Am… the Truth… the Life… the Light." (John 14:6; 8:12) For the first time we see the character of God being shared by another. The accomplishment of what began with Moses, and fleshed out by Daniel, had reached halfway to its goal. The last step is the point at which God becomes dissolved within all humanity, bringing humanity to fully adult status, and humans assuming total responsibility for choices regarding planet Earth and its inhabitants.

Yet this is not how the "I Am" statements in the gospel of John are generally understood. Usually they are conflated with Pauline thought and regarded as statements that form the core belief of the Christian community of faith: that Jesus was God, the long-awaited Messiah. He had been sent from heaven by God into the world to save mankind from its sins through his crucifixion, resurrection, and ascension back into heaven, where he rules the world forever with God the Father. Tradition has held that he will remain there until the "end of the age," when he will come into the world a second time to separate the faithful from the wicked, redeeming the faithful and taking them up to heaven with him, while punishing the wicked and sending them down into the bowels of the earth to burn forever in the flames of hell.

Many still hold to these core beliefs of Christianity. But regardless of whether one accepts or rejects them at a conscious, rational level, these beliefs are still within us Westerners at an emotional level, the cellular level of our being. They have become part of a deep split in the Western psyche between faith and reason, causing dis-ease in soul. Reason tells us one thing; faith says something else.

The dilemma of the post-modern soul is expressed poignantly in the following excerpts of a poem:

… In my life, the tide and waves
of the church are ebbing,
going out, leaving me on the shore.
I'm glad to see them going,
Leaving me behind and to myself.
At least that's how it seems…

The wind is raw and briny, the foaming surf
Even further from me now.
I resolve, as I have before,
To leave the beach…

The waves are coming in again,
Lapping at my ankles and feet.

The tide of the church is coming in again,
The waters of the Spirit

I thought I had wanted to go.
But still I am here.

("*Scavenging the Tide of Church*", Ann Keiffer, January 2007)

THREE-TIERED UNIVERSE

In the mythology of biblical times, the world was seen as a three-tiered universe: good God in heaven (more specifically, a whole series of heavens, with God in the highest of them), evil Satan in the underworld, and humanity stuck on earth in between, where the cosmic struggle between good and evil was being played out. A variation of this, held by many native traditions, connected (God the) Father with the heavens, Mother with the earth, and humans sandwiched in between our two Parents.

In both views, God the Father is in the heavens, which form the canopy overhead: the sun moving across the sky and giving us bright light during the day, and the moon, stars, and planets quietly offering their soft light at night. That's it. What we see is all there is; the heavens end with that canopy in a simple, contained universe.

And we are at the center. Father Sky protects us and spews his semen into Mother Earth in the form of rain. She, in turn, supports us from below by giving birth to seeds, grains, and other fruits of the earth that we need in order to live.

In biblical thought there is an additional dimension of rewards and punishment. Father rules the whole world, using a punishing hand when necessary to keep his children faithful to his purposes, and intervening on our behalf when he chooses to. Because we never know what God's mood will be, we need to play it safe by coming together as his people and offering him praise and thanksgiving, prayer and offerings, to appease him and try to abate his wrath. Sometimes it works; sometimes it doesn't.

God's punishment for unfaithfulness might take the form of giving parents a deformed child, sending a grave illness, causing a drought, killing someone with a lightning bolt, sending an army to defeat your people—anything God chose. Whether it was retribution against an individual or against "the people," the entire nation was held responsible. Therefore, everyone had to be kept in line to avoid contamination of the whole tribe. One never knew what this capricious God might do to his people when they were unfaithful.

These beliefs remained in play for most people in the Western world for centuries and formed the unquestioned worldview, the paradigm that shaped every thought and action. We knew the rules of the game, and it was up to us to abide by them. Though God was unpredictable and often seemingly unfair, at least we knew that someone was in charge, had a plan, and we were at the center of it. That was enough.

> **"If it's personal, we call it an attitude;**
> **if it's cultural, we call it a paradigm;**
> **if it's universal, we call it a law."**
> —*What the Bleep Do We Know?*

FALL OF THE HEAVENS

Then came a bombshell—a slowly detonated one.

In the sixteenth century an astronomer named Copernicus conjectured that the Earth revolves around the sun, that we are not at the center of the universe. However, he lacked scientific data to support his findings, so people largely ignored him. Nevertheless, he opened up the way for successors in various scientific endeavors—especially Galileo in astronomy, Newton in physics, and Darwin in biology— to corroborate his speculation.

Galileo Galilei, following shortly after Copernicus, based his own work on empirical observation and mathematics, which provided solid support to Copernicus' convictions.

A century later Sir Isaac Newton formulated an entire scientific worldview, which envisioned the world as a machine within which events take place in time. There are laws of nature, like gravity, that apply to all levels of creation from small particles to galaxies, with behavior of the smallest parts determining behavior of the whole. Although his findings left no room for miracles or an interventionist God, Newton never questioned the dominant worldview of religion.

Charles Darwin's *Origin of Species*, published in the nineteenth century, opened up a can of worms. It set forth an evolutionary view of the world, a view that shattered the prevailing idea that human beings were "the crown of God's creation." We were merely part of the animal kingdom.

With sufficient data from their respective disciplines, these scientists fully exploded the bombshell of truth that Copernicus had fired. People could no longer see themselves as the center, which is no one place. For the first time, Earth had become a place. The whole structure of the universe as people had known it had collapsed.

**"In all living systems,
that which doesn't move and change
and evolve becomes stagnant and dies."**
—*What the Bleep Do We Know?*

It is difficult for most of us to imagine the shock such discoveries had on the people, with mounting evidence that there is no God in the heavens guiding operations of the world. Life had been blown to bits and pieces, and humanity's psyche was thrown into a tailspin. The universe had been shattered, and nothing was left to grab hold of.

Where in the world was God if he was no longer up there in the heavens to protect us and inseminate Mother Earth so she could feed us? What are we to do if we have lost our Parents? If Earth is just one of many objects moving around the sun, does this mean we have been totally rejected and forgotten by God? What are we to do? How do we conduct our lives without God to show us the way?

Robert Russell encapsulated our situation in "Bridging Science and Religion": "With Copernicus our universe was inverted, the earth cast adrift... into the unending night of a vast and trackless universe."

Some have kept on clinging to the debris from the bombshell, pretending (as we do with Santa Claus) that things have not really changed, never fully accepting the implications of Copernicus's findings. This has provided some people with a sense of peace, while having to expend enormous amounts of energy—either consciously or unconsciously—to hold down what the deepest level of their psyche knows to be true: that God is not up there in the heavens—even astronauts can verify that. If God is not there, where in the world is God?

For Reflection:

1. How does your body (your heart, your pulse, your breath, etc.) respond when you take in the following two phrases?

   a. "Humanity will have incorporated the power, authority and wisdom of God into itself and will have assumed the role of God in the world. The human being will have essentially become god."

   b. "God becomes dissolved within all humanity, bringing humanity to fully adult status, and humans assuming total responsibility for choices regarding planet Earth and its inhabitants."

3. What words would you use to describe your feelings?

4. Do you ever feel "the tide and waves of the church" (or synagogue, temple, etc.) ebbing from your life? If so, what's that like for you? If not, what might you say to a friend who does feel that way?

5. How do you respond to the fallout from the "bombshell" (the implications of Copernicus' findings)? Ignore it? Let yourself be "cast adrift... into the unending night of a vast and trackless universe"? Address it directly (such as expressing the shattering in art, dance, writing, etc.)? Another way?

6. How can I know if I am living with the world (and myself) as it is, rather than living in a Dreamworld? What might help me most to live in reality: living with, and responding to, what *is*?

CHAPTER 2

COLLAPSE OF MODERN SCIENCE

"The material world, the world of matter,
runs like a clock and resists change,
while the unseen world of the spirit calls it forth.
The choice is which world to live in."
—*What the Bleep Do We Know*

CHALLENGE TO THE OLD ORDER

After humanity had moved through childhood and into teenage years, we began to rebel against parental authority. We distanced ourselves from our Parents by developing science, which essentially said—deep within its more pedantic style, mathematics, and words: No more of this giving authority to heavenly Parents, to something unseen, which we don't even know for sure exists. Let's explore what is *real*, what can be proved, the substantial world we live in. Everything else is merely speculative.

Scientific findings began to seep into religious consciousness and dissolve it, even though the prevailing worldview remained unconscious in the minds of most Western people. That hidden worldview, carried over from medieval times, envisioned a hierarchical cosmos, with Earth at its center. God ruled over all creation and ordered the structure of society. The purpose of life was to prepare for the next life, striving always to bring about the triumph of good over evil.

Discoveries of science challenged that view and led to a paradigm shift[1]. Attributes traditionally applied to God were now seen as laws of nature:

- Universal: laws of physics are assumed to be valid at every place in the universe
- Absolute: natural laws do not change with time
- Eternal: all known fundamental laws have mathematical form, which is infinite
- Omnipotent: nothing can be held to be outside the scope of natural laws[2]

Assumptions about the universe became more rational. Nature was a machine that could be explained without reference to a God; mechanical causes, not purposes, determined material events. Each person was a mere cog in the machine, with mind and body being separate entities within it. Structuring of the world was seen as "reductionistic," that is, behavior of the smallest parts determined behavior of the whole. The same laws applied from small particles to galaxies.

Through the years scientific insights came with startling new data. For instance, the DNA of chimpanzees and humans is more than 98% the same, and there are more bacterial cells in our intestinal tract than the total number of people who have ever lived.[3] The simple, contained world of the religious Middle Ages had been blown apart, almost like a second Big Bang.

The findings of science led to a "two world" view, with no overlap between science and religion, between the material world and the unseen world. The wholeness and comfort of a world overseen by God was replaced by a fractured, scientific world that operated as a machine without God. Everything, including humans, had been reduced to bits and pieces, to particles that determined the shape of the whole.

Deism attempted to provide an answer to the startling claims of physics by declaring that God created the world and then let it operate on its own; but longing for an involved God remained in the hearts of the faithful.

As painful as the scientific worldview was for many people in the Western world, the extreme separation between science and religion enabled scientists to discover that the universe is a single organism[4].

THE NEW PHYSICS

"Classical physics… was based on the promise that only by knowing the separate parts could you eventually understand the whole. The new physics is more organic and holistic; it is painting a picture of the universe as a unified whole, whose parts are interconnected and influence each other."[5]

STRUCTURES AND LEVELS

The shift from classical physics to the new physics began in the 20th century. Since the days of the Enlightenment, technology had developed to the point where sophisticated experiments could be conducted in both the macro- and micro- worlds. These experiments revealed a hierarchical universe that has many different levels and structures of reality. Levels comprise enveloping regions of depth, each level surrounding the next deeper one.

When a process at one level gets new properties, it has to move to a new level. When it moves to that new level, it can be understood only at that level. For example, a flock of birds is not the same as a few birds. The level of a flock of birds has its own inner structure that is not present in a few birds hopping around in your back garden. They represent two different levels of reality. What determines the various levels of reality is not the composition, but the structure. (See Appendix C)

MICRO WORLD

Joel Primack succinctly describes the human's place in the universe: "The universe is not outside us, and we are never outside it. We are it on our scale."[6] It is moving to note that, of the 60 orders of magnitude of the visible universe, humans are at dead center of all the size scales, halfway between the micro world and the macro world. Half of the levels are below us in size, half are larger.[7]

Particle-Wave

New discoveries gradually shifted the focus of much scientific interest from the macro world to the sub-atomic world of particles and the vast area between particles—the area of space, of "nothingness."[8] In speaking of the electromagnetic field of particles, Albert Einstein had said it may not be the behavior of particles, but the behavior of something between them, i.e., the field, that is essential for ordering and understanding events. A number of scientists, guided by Einstein's insight, began to focus more closely on what held particles together and their relationship to each other. Other scientists, of course, continued to experiment with particles and matter.

During experimental observations of the micro world, scientists' curiosity was aroused by some weird behavior. Each time they tried to observe a wave, it instantaneously shifted to becoming a particle[9]. Perhaps the most mysterious part of this phenomenon was that the shift from wave to particle was determined by nothing that is part of the physical universe, but by human observation.

Through further study scientists came to understand that the wave they were attempting to observe contained multiple *possibilities*, but the wave had not become an *actualized* reality. With human observation it collapsed into one particular (note its derivation from "particle") form of reality[10] at the level of the particle world, the world in which we live.[11]

In addition, they noticed "particles seem to communicate instantaneously over any expanse of space."[12] This has led scientists to conclude that particles are intimately linked on a level beyond time and space. They exhibit the amazing ability to shift from wave to particle and back again with ease. They can also take a "quantum jump," disappearing in one location and appearing in another. In fact, "particles may be in two or more places at once... The same object may appear to be a particle, locatable in one place, or a wave, spread out over space and time."[13]

Much of the time they are poised somewhere between wave and particle in a state of multiple possibilities.

A startling conclusion from all this was the instability of matter, the fact that matter is not a permanent state. It can—and does—shift back and forth from matter to energy, from particle to wave, in the blink of an eyelid.

It also suggests the amazing power of the human mind to determine reality at the level of our everyday world. Scientists followed up on this with experiments to determine the extent to which the human mind can actually affect reality. Observations of experimental subjects supported findings from the particle/wave experiments that "determining reality," i.e., creating reality, which had previously been attributed to God, was a function of the human mind.[14]

MEMES

When scientists noticed "particles seem to communicate instantaneously over any expanse of space" and take "quantum jumps," they may have been encountering memes.

As long ago as 1976 Richard Dawkins, evolutionary biologist, wrote in *The Selfish Gene*:

"A new kind of replicator has recently emerged on this very planet… It is still in its infancy, still drifting clumsily about in its primeval soup… That 'soup' is human culture; the vector of transmission is language, and the spawning ground is the brain."[15]

He named these bodiless replicators by which ideas travel, "memes."

"The meme is not the dancer but the dance."
—James Gleick, *Smithsonian*

More recently Nobel Prize winning biologist, Jacques Monod, put Dawkins' insight into perspective. He said that just as the biosphere (an entity composed of all the earth's life forms) stands above the world of non-living matter, so an "abstract kingdom" of ideas rises above the biosphere.

These ideas are to be regarded as organisms rather than particles because they tend to perpetuate their structure and to breed. Furthermore, they evolve as complex units and "infect" human culture like a virus, leaping from brain to brain and competing for brain time.

The nature of memes led philosopher Daniel Dennett to ask, "Who's in charge... we or our memes?" He then answered his own question: We are seldom in charge of our own minds.

SDIC and chaos

Not only the human mind, but also seemingly insignificant happenings in the world can have profound effects in distant locations. A significant finding of scientists today has been their discovery of the effect of any variation in the initial state of something. Scientists call this "Sensitive Dependence on Initial Conditions" (or SDIC). No matter how small or insignificant the variation may seem, it is sufficient to cause a system to evolve into a different state. A familiar example of this is the flutter of butterfly wings in Beijing affecting weather patterns in North America.

> **"The inner depths of each being in the are activated by the surrounding universe."**
> **—Brian Swimme, *The Universe Story***

A variation of this phenomenon is the chaotic nature of reality. During periods of predictability, a system may respond more readily to a chaotic attraction. As with non-linear equations, in which solutions reflect missing information, the changed system reveals the missing information through which changes have taken place. An example of this was the chaotic fluctuation of the stock market during the recession of 2008. Suddenly the stock market became wildly unpredictable. A chaotic attractor carrying missing information threw it into a tailspin, and no one knew what it would look like from week to week—or even month to month.[16]

MACRO WORLD

Expansion of the universe

In the opposite direction from the sub-atomic world, macro-scientists were observing that the universe has been expanding at an accelerating rate ever since the Big Bang more than 13 billion years ago.[17] To scientists, expansion means the movement of galaxies away from each other— and from us. When one considers that light travels 186,000 miles per second, and the universe has expanded from its original pinprick to its current diameter of 93 billion light years, the size of the unbounded universe is literally mind-boggling. In trying to imagine its size head-on, our psyche today becomes as dizzied and confused as the psyche of the Middle Ages when scientists observed that the heavens above do not form a container, but are merely part of farther reaches of space. The vastness of the universe is, indeed, staggering.[18]

Discovery of the continual expansion of the universe, which has no outer edge, or limits, has presented a challenge for theologians as well as for particle researchers. If there is no "outside" of the universe, then deism no longer works. To be in accord with post-modern science, there can be no "transcendent" God, no God "outside" the universe. God can be only "immanent", or "within" the universe—if God exists at all.

Time-Space

Expansion of the universe is closely related to another important area scientists are probing, time-space[19], which dates back to the initial Big Bang of the universe.[20]

When the Big Bang occurred, the tiny pinprick of cosmos 'exploded' and its pieces kept on expanding[21]. Its energy initiated two opposite dimensions, 'space' and 'time', the only two dimensions of the newly formed universe[22].

Space—of which there is only one—has attracted special attention from scientists. They have verified Einstein's prediction that it is the vast amount of space between particles that provides the glue for particles to relate to each other across great distances.

An analogy for the relationship of "one space" to particles might be a river and a boat. It's not the boat that enables us to go to another landing place; it's the river. The boat merely keeps us afloat while the river carries us to our next landing place. And it's all the same river.

It may be surprising for some of us to think of there being only one space, as our language divides up space artificially into spaces. Using words such as inner and outer, here and there, East and West, upper and lower, make it seem as if there are different spaces. In reality, these terms are merely useful ways of handling the concept of space in everyday situations. The danger is that it can lead us into a less-than-truthful vision of reality.

Joel Achenbach has drawn together some insights about space with other major insights of the new science:

"Matter bends space; space directs how matter moves. Light is both a particle and a wave. Energy and mass are interchangeable. Reality is probabilistic and not deterministic."[23]

Gravity

Even as the universe is driven to expand, gravity is driving against it. Gravity is like a poised bow that pulls back as the arrow is released. In fact, the arrow can be released only by the tension caused by pulling back in the opposite direction. Such is the taut relationship between gravity and anti-gravity.

All four basic forces of the universe, of which gravity is one, cause separation as they exert their force. While there is great pressure in the universe toward pulling together and aggregating, gravity and other forces are working almost as hard to separate, which leaves the world in a state of unceasing change of loose aggregations.

Aggregations and novelty

A directly observable example of the tendency to aggregate is iron filings being attracted to a magnet. We can see the irresistible pull of the magnet, drawing bits and pieces of iron filings together as one. In later chapters we will encounter numerous examples of this driving force pulling toward oneness (think "globalization")—even as gravity is pulling to separate.

One familiar biological process that illustrates the drives of aggregation and separation is the process of cell division in human development. Humans develop by a series of cell divisions forming various parts of our body, and the parts being drawn together, i.e. aggregated, into one human being.

Although the process of cell division works the same way in the formation of every person, there is also uniqueness, a novelty in each individual. Life is always changing and developing new forms, new combinations, new aggregations of particles. This element of novelty is inherent in each emerging level of the universe, which contains something genuinely new, something that is not present at lower levels. In later chapters we will see how novelty is being lived out today.

In order for novelty to occur, existing combinations must separate, even though separation is counter to the strongest drive of the universe, which is toward unity, oneness, and wholeness. In all structures of the universe, wholeness has the final word. It supersedes bits and pieces. As we observe events, processes, and relationships in our world today, we will see these fundamental, opposite forces pulling for and against oneness. They work simultaneously as we shape history.

The tendency of particles toward aggregation has led particle scientists to probe more deeply in their research to discover how fundamental particles at the core of matter acquire mass. Specifically, they are hoping to find what is sometimes called the "God particle," or the Higgs Boson, which would explain this. Because the primary investigation is being conducted with a huge particle accelerator in Europe, the center of particle physics has shifted from the United States to Europe.[24]

Complexity-Simplicity

In the section on gravity, we noted that gravity's force against expansion is causing separation of aggregates of particles. The particles, in response, are seeking to re-combine in other aggregations, causing greater and greater complexity. This process of recombination of loose aggregations of particles is unceasing, making the world more and more complex.[25]

Scientists measure the degree of complexity of an object by its fractals dimension. They are interested in the *qualities* of patterns, events, and relationships rather than a *quantitative* measurement. ("Fractals" normally refers to patterns of replicating self-similarity, which is a quantitative measurement.)

Matter is fundamentally relational. One might even call the relatedness "gregarious," as particles tend to aggregate into larger and more complex structures (think: iPad). Darwin had a sense of this when he noted that the goal of evolution is diversity, which occurs with novelty and complexity. Because of this tendency toward greater complexity, we could say that matter is constructive, that it builds and develops.

At the same time, matter also destroys.[26] We are familiar with this concept in events such as a fire, which creates room for new growth even as it destroys a forest.

This pattern of destruction/creation also occurs in psychological growth. Traditionally complexity, disequilibrium, and chaos have been seen as signs of sickness. Today they are often seen as preparedness for reorganization of the self at a higher level. Periodically disequilibrium and chaos destroy the structure of the human psyche to make room for an expanded structure that can incorporate more of reality. This enables movement to higher levels of consciousness, which is requisite for a world destined to become more and more complex. The use of "thought" energy for growing consciousness is a singular contribution of humanity to the universe.

"Studies of chaos and complexity… demonstrate the astonishing ability of nature for self-organization and the temporal and historical character of all natural processes."
—Robert J. Russell, "Bridging Science and Religion"

This shift in understanding psychological growth revises our concept of mental health, which now includes knowing that complexity is a fundamental drive in nature. Chaos, entanglements, and uncertainties are realities of the universe that underlie the orderly way we try to live our lives. Masterpasqua affirmed the growth-inducing nature of this reality when he said, "Individuals most capable of adaptation and growth are those poised at the edge of chaos."[27]

The human brain is one of the more intricate examples of complexity. It is like a map of the United States that, at first, has just bare markings of the states, but then more intricate and complex markings are added—state highways, local roads, and even little cul-de-sacs. This aspect of the nature of the world is so common that we tend to accept it without being aware of its being a primary characteristic of the way the universe is structured.

OTHER CHARACTERISTICS of the NATURAL WORLD

Though the Big Bang should have yielded equal amounts of matter and anti-matter, it in fact produced more matter than anti-matter—not too much, just enough. Without that imbalance, matter and anti-matter would have cancelled each other out and reverted back into energy.

Experiments have revealed that the Big Bang provided a "single energetic event."[28] The matter that was generated through that event was all the same—then and now. Celestial bodies comprise the same matter as everything here on Earth; we are truly made of stardust.[29]

Though energy, nothing but energy, is within all levels and structures of the universe, it manifests itself in a variety of forms, from physical energy, to seemingly solid energy, to thoughts. A basic structure for many forms of energy is "opposition." Two examples are the oppositely charged particles that balance one another by electromagnetism[30] and the opposite spirals of the double helix structure of the DNA molecule.

An even more dramatic example is the universe itself, which began and will end (if it ends) with opposites: "Billions of years ago the universe was too hot for life to exist. Countless eons hence, it will become so cold and empty that life, no matter how ingenious, will perish."[31] David Schramm says: "The alternative to this big chill is a big crunch. If the mass of the universe is large enough, gravity will eventually reverse the expansion, and all matter and energy will be reunited."[32]

A general belief of scientists today is that behavior is what counts most. The fundamental realities of the universe are relationships, processes, and events, not bits of physical matter. As long as physical matter was seen as the foundation of the universe, science and religion could not be reconciled. "It was that extreme separation from the spirit world that enabled Western science to discover that mind and matter are the same thing."[33]

For Reflection:

1. The beginning of this chapter read: "The material world, the world of matter, runs like a clock and resists change, while the unseen world of the spirit calls it forth. The choice is which world to live in."

    What, for you, might be the pros and cons of living in each of these two worlds? Might there be a way to live in both simultaneously? If so, how? Which world(s) do you choose to live in?

2. Try thinking these thoughts:

    *   Life occurring at the intersection of space and time (the two basic dimensions that formed out of the Big Bang)
    *   Material things as different *forms* of energy (i.e. waves that collapse into particles when we observe them)
    *   Soul† (See Appendix B) *actualizing* particul-ar forms of energy (at its intersection with the created world) at a given moment in history.

    How might these thoughts affect the way you relate to the world?

3. How, if at all, might reported phenomena of distant healings through prayer, or viral infections of memes, or a fad that suddenly appears in several places in the U.S. at once, be related to "quantum jumps"? Or to the universe's being "a unified whole, whose parts are interconnected and influence each other"?

CHAPTER 3
COLLAPSE INTO CONSCIOUSNESS

"Psychology... has left both science and religion beneath itself, and at the same time it contains them as sublated moments within itself... It is their successor."
—**Wolfgang Giegerich,** ***The Soul's Logical Life***

HUMANITY'S DEVELOPMENT

Today humanity teeters on the brink of adulthood. It has moved through the magical childhood years of religion, has weathered storms of the rebellious teenage years of science, and is now poised to plunge into the scary world of adulthood, where it must fend for itself. Humanity can no longer look to heavenly Parents for rescue from the travails of life, and the elephant brought into the room by science cannot go unnoticed much longer. Humanity is now on its own to make choices that will affect the whole future of the universe.

It is no wonder that many people still cling to the safety of religion and refuse to face the truths of science. The power we hold is daunting to admit, and even more daunting to exert. Yet that is the task that faces us today. The sooner we accept the challenges it offers, the more fully we will be living out humanity's fundamental role as consciousness of the universe.

At this point in the evolution of consciousness (Appendix B), psychology receives the baton handed down from religion to science.

Religious figures knew intuitively all along that the unseen world (of consciousness) holds the key to life and all of creation. Scientists discovered the relationship between the unseen world of particles and (consciousness at the level of) human choice making. Humanity in its new psycho-logical state contains all the understandings of both religion and science, now raised to a higher level of consciousness.

The stream of consciousness continues to wend its way and evolve through events, relationships and processes in our world today. Humanity is now prepared to enter that stream consciously and move with it as it continues to evolve.

When Humanity Was a Child

As we saw in Chapter 1, the psychology of humanity in pre-modern history resided in belief that people are within the protective sphere of Heavenly Parents. The sixteenth century ushered in the modern age, when Copernicus floated the idea that Earth is not at the center of the universe. If we were not at the center of the universe—increasingly seen as vast beyond comprehension—we were no longer comfortably sandwiched between Heavenly Father and Mother Earth. We had suddenly become a mere blip on the unlimited screen of a mind-boggling universe. Startled as people were by the unfolding data, Copernicus' idea gradually took root in humanity's psyche.

It has been difficult not only to accept the loss of meaning provided by Heavenly Parents, great as that loss is, but also to know that we stand alone carrying the burden of responsibility for the world. We recoil at the "alarming possibility of being able," and many of us have chosen to deny this new state. Instead, we continue to cling to the safety and comfort of the past, often with evangelical fervor.

In noting this, Micael Ledwith[34] said, "The greatest problem we as a human race have is accepting our own questions. We run screaming from anybody who would suggest that we are all-powerful in ourselves."[35]

Though some people have courageously accepted our new situation and look squarely at "what is," many people have chosen to live only biologically, as animals, while denying themselves psychological growth beyond childhood.

Animals are not split between the biological and psychological. They are largely adults at birth, wearing their own blankets and having active instincts to guide them in caring for their own needs. Soon after they are born, they are thrown out into the world to fend for themselves.

Humans are different, requiring several years before being able to care for themselves. Many never grow beyond the point of self-maintenance. Instead, they continue to seek parental figures outside themselves—heavenly parents, political parents, or some other idol—in whom they place their hope, security, and meaning for life.

To be sure, we engage in initiation rites of various groups to help us move beyond home and our need for being parented, but these rites of passage merely substitute as metaphysical parents for our biological ones. The new metaphysical community keeps us in a childlike state by providing us with a sense of "in-ness," meaning, and belonging. Now modern science has removed the safe uterus of in-ness, so we are forced to become adults.

It can be scary to suddenly be thrust into the world of adulthood, with its heavy burden of responsibility, and without parents to care for us and provide security. On the other hand, emancipation from in-ness frees us to engage in the human task of giving birth to new consciousness, enabling it to evolve at a comparable pace to the physical evolution of the universe. Consciousness-work is the greatest gift we can offer to the universe, as it supports natural patterning and helps keep our planet from destruction.

Prior to the modern age, the *concept* (of God, of heaven, of good and evil, etc.) was the true reality. With the collapse of Heavenly Parents, and the individual emerging as its own center, the only true reality became what actually occurs in the individual. To speak of it in a larger context, the singular had wrested itself free from the universal (concept of religion) and became the all- powerful one, formerly attributed to God. We are left holding responsibility for the world, as no one is "out there" to carry that weight for us. Without our knowledge, or our choosing, we had taken back the heavy burden we had previously laid on the shoulders of "God."

Birth of Humanity's Adulthood

We are now alone, with no gods to look to. We know that the images and ideas of religions, formerly seen as actual substances, exist within the human psyche, so religions—and Religion itself— have become obsolete. All their former contents have become integrated into human consciousness "like a sugar cube dissolves in coffee."[36] Religion's task— to provide meaning—has been fulfilled and born out of it. It is now present as a quality within humanity in the form of consciousness.

Religion has been shed like a dead snakeskin, no longer useful, and God has dissolved from substantial Father or Son into spirit. Therefore, to preach religion as substantially real, instead of treating it as an *historical* reality, is "like squeezing an adult into a crib."[37] There is no way back.

This new status of humanity accords with evolution, which is always changing and moving into something new. It never goes backwards. Yet nothing has been lost in this shift into metaphysical adulthood. The contents of religions are within us as historical presences and can still be drawn upon as sources of inspiration. Only the substantiality of them is missing.

We are left with no higher being to solve our problems; we have only ourselves. The good news is that we have within ourselves, and in our relationship to the rest of creation, all that is needed. Nothing is lacking. The only question is whether or not we will accept our adult role and support the workings of the universe as it is.

The death of God has been the birth of humanity's adulthood.

WHAT IS CONSCIOUSNESS?

The birthing of humanity's adulthood is also the birthing of consciousness at a higher level. When we speak of consciousness, we are speaking about something that has no agreed-upon definition. Rather, the word elicits a whole range of differing ideas about its meaning.

Psychology and Consciousness

Humans view the world through the eyes of the ego (the usual way) or of soulf, but it is not possible (from within the actualized world) to see with both at the same time.

However, the threshold between the ego and soulf encompasses both, providing a way of seeing that includes the ego and soulf at the same time, without identifying with one or the other. This way of seeing is possible because it exists only in *thought.*

To be with life's movement today, we must engage in a fundamental shift from ego-centered, either-or thinking to thinking from within the threshold between ego and soulf. This involves letting the opposites of ego and soulf collapse into each other, so each one has its opposite fully present in itself within consciousness.[38]

Science and Consciousness

Modern science does not have the framework to understand consciousness[39] because the scientific method makes a sharp distinction between things and no-things, believing that everything can be reduced to just matter or just energy. Traditional science has viewed consciousness as "just energy," belonging to the realm of psychology, not science.

Many post-modern physicists reject this notion, saying that it is illusory to think that there is a separation between things and no-things[40]. Both are energy at different levels of reality. "Everything is really energy," said Ed Mitchell, "with matter a form of energy."[41]

Other Views of Consciousness

Some religious traditions have carried Mitchell's thinking a step further, saying that there is nothing more basic than consciousness, and energy-matter is a product of it. Maharishi Mahesh has spoken of the universe as being "one unbounded ocean of consciousness in motion."[42] It has even been suggested that celestial beings—angels, archangels, seraphim, etc.—are "classification systems for… consciousness."[43] Others say that consciousness is "as fundamental as space, time, and matter, perhaps even more so."[44] It has also been described as "a sequence of discrete events."[45] Perhaps the point of closest agreement about consciousness is its basic threefold structure comprising observer, observed, and process of observation.[46] Beyond that, concepts of consciousness vary greatly.

William Tiller attributes the emergent level of scientific thinking about consciousness to the split between science and religion:

> "It was very important that a long time ago, we made the decision to separate spirit from science. And so we were able to learn how to do science. But now we've learned, and we can take on the richer task of learning to do science when consciousness is part of the experiment."[47]

This new way of scientific thinking has ushered in the convergence of religion, science, and psychology at the level of consciousness.

LEVELS OF REALITY

Levels of reality span the range from things to no-things—from subatomic particle-waves to concrete pavement, from consciousness to the war in Ukraine. Everything is part of the same reality—at different levels of being.

Our actions are connected to the universe at the vibration level. Everything of the same frequency responds to these actions, helping to shape our reality. In fact, all levels of vibration are affected to some extent by our choices of action, as "quantum [i.e. non-local] computations in our brains connect our consciousness to the 'funda-mental' universe."[48]

Quantum uncertainty underlies the operating system of the human brain, opening the possibility for choice. With free will, we can train ourselves to make smart choices— even for a quick response from a myriad of choices—and to be conscious of what we are choosing.

The discovery of a continuous particle-wave process in the subatomic world sheds light on this process of quantum uncertainty. In conjunction with human choice, a particular particle-wave collapses into itself and becomes a particle; that is, it becomes an actualized reality in our world of substance. Before that, as a particle-wave, it had been merely one possibility among many, still in a world of non-existence. Human choice decided which of all those possibilities to actualize, and the particle-wave responded accordingly.

Depending on our choice, cell connectors retain, or let go of, old patterns by hooking or unhooking other nerve cells. This process either retains old consciousness or generates a new form of consciousness. If we let go of old patterns, the new living idea released by our choice jumps from one level to another without experiencing anything in between… And all this is engineered at the quantum level of particle-waves!

"From the stance of new consciousness, our personal world is but one thread of a universal web. Focusing solely on our own inner world can cause us to miss that indispensable connection with the energy that enables us to be fully human… To engage with reality, we must see our connection to each other biologically, to our world chemically, and to the universe atomically." (Source unknown)

EMOTIONS

Each emotion that arises within us is associated with a particular chemical. Emotions chemically reinforce beliefs into long-term memory, so they will be retrieved first by the brain when needed quickly. If we act without thinking, our brain reacts automatically according to its past programming. When we discard a stimulus of the moment, seeing it as just the same old thing, the emotion triggered by the situation often blocks our seeing reality.

Humanity usually reacts that way, succumbing to the lowest, automatic response in choiceful situations, which often translates into finding pleasure and avoiding pain. This accounts for many of the destructive actions—or inaction—we see in the world around us. For example, some people repeatedly try to touch the pleasure center of the brain through addictions, triggering the *same* chemical in the brain over and over again. The brain is not made for that purpose. It is for dreaming *new* dreams and realities[49], and for experiencing *new* emotions.

Despite our predisposition, humans are capable of choosing at a higher level, which includes unconditional love, deep new understanding, and cosmic consciousness. A basic human task in this regard is to transform our emotions and "own them into wisdom"[50] for the sake of higher consciousness. Choices made at a higher level of consciousness can be life changing—not only for the individual, but also for the world.[51] At such times "consciousness is moving through the brain, and using the brain to examine its options and possibilities."[52] This leads to the collapse of all possibilities into the chosen one, a function of the particle-wave phenomenon underlying choice. If it seems difficult to believe in such a close mind-body connection, consider the fact that one sexual fantasy can trigger an erection.

MORPHIC FIELDS

It appears that nature is comprised of a hierarchy of non-locally connected systems. Rupert Sheldrake has developed a hypothesis that these systems are shaped by "morphic fields" at all levels of the hierarchy.[53] A morphic field is like a blueprint or template that, "when impressed upon the random nature of quantum [i.e. non-local] events, [it] changes those events into some of a higher order. It is like an invisible hand guiding which property of many possible ones emerge into the physical world.[54]

Another way of looking at this is in terms of self and soul. Their relationship is like the process of stitching a living idea into cloth with a sewing machine. Think of the self as the needle holding potential patterns (thread). Soul moves along the field (cloth), informing the self when a choice is made, and of the new form needed to bring it into reality (to be stitched). The self releases the form of patterning (as thread) designated by soul, and the new living form is stitched into reality (onto the cloth). No actualization happens without the joint work of self and soul.

During this process of actualization, information is shared among the systems at all levels. Dr. Laszlo adds: "And the information that in-forms them is as physically real as… particles: mind as matter."[55] (This sounds remarkably like the functioning of the Internet.)

Experiments performed on highly sensitive gauges by Roger Nelson[56] during public ceremonies for Princess Diana after her death and immediately after attacks on the World Trade Center showed that collective reaction [spread by memes] to stirring public events have a common effect. That is, morphic "fields generated by individual consciousness can combine during moments of like-mindedness."[57] The same phenomenon precipitated the Arab Spring uprisings.

This has raised questions about extreme moments in human history, such as Hitler's atrocities, the Spanish inquisition, and the Salem witch trials. Perhaps depression (spread by memes) following World War I affected the Germans on a quantum level, making it easier for Hitler to constellate a negative collective consciousness. Similar constellations may account for the Spanish inquisition and the Salem witch trials.

Scientists hypothesize that a "Zero Point Field" (similar in function to the God particle, or Higgs Boson) is the underlying force that unites morphic fields. The experiments regarding Princess Diana and the World Trade Center were "the first inkling that group consciousness, working through a medium such as the Zero Point Field, acted as the universal organizing factor in the cosmos."[58]

Scientists regard the Zero Point Field as "the Rosetta Stone of human consciousness." It merits this description by its properties that run through all levels of being. As the substructure that underpins the universe, the Zero Point Field provides means for cell communication at every level in the universe. Similar to soulf's being the pulsating wave between possibilities and actualization, the Zero Point Field exists as a pulsating frequency. It encodes information and provides instantaneous communication. This property may explain physical synchronicities such as the coming together of menstrual cycles among women in close proximity.

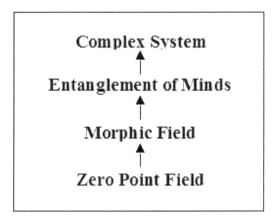

Zero Point Field

WHAT IS SOULF?

Self and Soul as "Soulf"

Self and Soul are presences in the unseen world that combine as soulf to become "thoughts" in our everyday world. Self provides the patterning and Soul designates the structure of actualization. Together, as soulf, they actualize thoughts in and through humanity. (See Appendix C)

Soulf in Historical Situations

In every major historical situation, the particular form that the relationship of humanity and the world takes is enlivened by soulf and becomes a living idea or thought.[59] But something more is needed. Soulf is dependent on humanity to be *thinkers* of soulf to allow soulf to live (in thought) in and through them.[60]

"A thought is actually a structure in which reality is patterned. It is the architecture of reality."
—*What the Bleep Do We Know?*

Soulf as Secret Known to All

Soulf can be imagined as a secret known to all, even though it cannot be seen, or known through any of our sensory functions, or proved. It has resonances with the childhood game of Sardines, in which a secret hiding place becomes the secret known to all. It may also lie behind the tradition in some African tribes that forbids anyone from announcing with words that the king is dead. When a king dies, his death is "told" through a series of unique African drumbeats, a secret known to all. This reluctance to use words is also present in the Jewish tradition of never speaking or writing the name of God. Yet even in the silent absence of the word, the name is the secret known to all Jews. The secret is our key to knowing humanity's role vis-a-vis soulf in the evolutionary process of the universe.

Soulf as Independent Agent

Sometimes we experience soulf as an independent agent, moving in us but not generated by us. Soulf is "not the life of a being, it is movement, fluidity as such, without a being that performs that movement or is in motion."[61] As with a meme, soulf is not the dancer but the dance.

Soulf can feel like a surging team of horses to which we are holding the reins—or not holding them. For this reason, it could be called a "living idea." It produces itself and has its own life the way a particle-wave actualizes itself as a particle on its own initiative. Particle-wave, soul-self and memes may all converge at the point of "living ideas" or "thoughts," or perhaps they are one and the same.

Soulf and Layers of Consciousness

Soulf encompasses all the layers of consciousness development that humanity has ever experienced, similar to the Zero Point Field moving through all levels of existence. These layers extend all the way from core living ideas, which shaped the entire created world, to the human experience of poignancy, in which soulf pulsates between opposites.

Feelings and images

Between those extremes are other layers, or dimensions. Two layers commonly experienced by humans are feelings and images. Feelings are closest to the surface, with images just beneath them. Living ideas underlie images, on the bottom layer. Nothing is deeper.

Images are *visible thoughts* that arise within humanity from a pool of images in the unseen world. These images remain unconscious unless we *consciously think* them. For example, in order to catch up with the dissolution of Religion within humanity, we must transform our envisioned images of Religion into conscious thought.

Nothing lost

In making images conscious, we can be assured that nothing is lost. Each time one form of thought supplants another, the previous form becomes dissolved within the new one and remains a presence there.

Wolfgang Giegerich succinctly describes this process within consciousness: "Notion [read: "thought"] is sublated image; image is sublated emotion; emotion is sublated behavior or physical condition."[62]

SUBLATION AND HIGHER CONSCIOUSNESS

In the real world, one thought or its polar opposite can be actualized in any given moment, but not both at the same time. However, it is possible to include both opposites simultaneously if they are held only in *thought*, not in *actuality*.

In the sublation process, a pair of opposites (comprising a "thought") collapses into each other, resulting in each having its opposite fully present within itself. When this happens, the "thought" is catapulted into a higher level of consciousness, preserving the full, unique distinctions of both opposites as one. When sublation is applied to consciousness, ego and soulf collapse into each other as one, while preserving their unique distinctions.

Most of us have had experiences at the feeling level similar to sublation, though perhaps not consciously. When we are deeply "moved" by something—for instance, the simultaneous birth of a longed-for child and death of the child's mother—we are in touch with the "move"-ment of soul between opposites, shimmering like light on the crest of a wave. We are "moved" to tears as a process of "sublating" the moment, dissolving the sharp division between life and death, which *must* be split in the "actualized" world.

Sublation applies to other polar opposites as well. For instance, imagine yourself looking at a balloon, and then someone turns it inside out. Are you looking at the "inside" or the "outside" of the balloon? The question can't be answered because the notion of "inside" and "outside" has dissolved, or collapsed, respective to the balloon itself. It is just "balloon."

To be fully in accord with soulf today, we must transform our usual ego-centered, either/or way of seeing life into a soulf-centered view, entering the "abstract sphere of 'pre-existence'."[63] This involves letting ego and soulf collapse into each other, so that each is fully present in the other. (This is not the same as introducing a third point to include both opposites. A third point neutralizes the opposites.) Sublation preserves the full, unique distinctions of both within consciousness at a higher level, where ego and soulf have become one. (See Appendix D)

SUMMARY OF PART ONE

Perhaps the earliest signs of human consciousness came in the form of religious rituals. *Homo sapiens* has engaged in various kinds of rituals since first starting to roam the Earth—up to the present. Though originally the behavior was largely instinctual, through time collective consciousness developed and, much later, what we would call "individual consciousness." Only in the past century or two has consciousness taken a further step, in which humanity has become conscious of consciousness. Yet throughout its history *homo sapiens* has had an innate sense that the core of life exists in an unseen world.

The rise of modern science enabled humanity to become conscious of consciousness. This began as a correction to our perceived place in the universe, countering the tenets and creeds of organized religion. As scientists explored the innermost regions of life at the subatomic level, they found an amazingly close relationship between thoughts in humans at the macro level and the behavior of particle-waves at the quantum level. This has led scientists to see the crucial role of human consciousness for evolution, the primary process of life.

This insight of scientists has required them to rethink their previous attitude toward psychology, which has long held (in psychology's relatively short life) the highly significant role of consciousness. Science and psychology have now moved closer together, where psychology's role has changed from inferior stepchild to wise crone. However, this new role is not always openly admitted in the scientific community.

The stream of living consciousness has been working out is own development in human history by moving through religious thought, to scientific thought, and now to psychological thought. Finally—at least for humanity—consciousness has made its present home within *homo sapiens*, through whom it can now further its own development until humanity has carried it as far as it is able. At that point a new species will develop to carry the stream of consciousness onward.

For Reflection:

1. What might be meant by: "The death of God has been the birth of humanity's adulthood"? What feeling(s) does this statement evoke in you?

2. Let a world event, a personal relationship, or a process in your everyday life emerge from your depths.

    See if you can identify the image, or physical condition, or emotion underlying it. (If you have difficulty doing this, let it express itself through crayons on paper.)

    What might be the "living idea" embedded in the image, or physical condition or emotion?

    (The embedded thought is at the core of soulf.)

3. In reflecting back on your own life (or on the life of someone else), when was there a situation in which opposites were sublated within you? What does it feel like to experience sublation? How would you express this in music? dance? poetry?

4. Earlier in this chapter was written: "The Zero Point Field exists as a pulsating frequency. It encodes information and provides instantaneous communication."

    How, if at all, might this be related to Internet communication? If you see a relationship, what similarities do you see?

PART TWO
THE PLAY

WHERE IN THE WORLD IS GOD?

CHAPTER 4

RELIGION TODAY

**"The era of Christianity as a Western religion is
already over. Instead of 'Western Christianity,'
we now witness a post-Christian West (in Europe)
and a post-Western Christianity (in the global South).
America is somewhere in between."
—Harvey Cox, *The Future of Faith***

Despite the advent of scientific knowledge of the universe and the movement of life toward new consciousness, religions persist in varying forms in today's world. People cling to the notion that our deepest longings are necessarily tied to religious beliefs and practices, and they fear letting go of the known. Like a first-time acrobat swinging from one high bar to another, people find it scary to release their grip on one bar—and hover alone over nothingness—in order to grasp the bar of reality out there in front.

Yet soulf remains undeterred, simultaneously working through the final throes of Religion and moving forward.

REGRESSIVE PULL IN THE CHURCH

Baptism has been an area of significant change. Until the fourth century C.E., baptisms were conducted in rivers or "baptisteries," large rooms able to accommodate full immersion of adults. After that time, baptism faded into a formality rather than a central sacrament of the church. In the 1960's Pope Paul II brought a renewed interest in the ways of the Early Church, including full immersion in baptism.

In recent years, baptism has taken a step forward—and backward. Not only are Catholic bishops strongly encouraging full immersion of adults in baptism (infant baptism is never performed with full immersion), but also the U.S. Conference of Catholic Bishops has prescribed architectural guidelines on how such structures should look and be used. Some dioceses even require that all new churches include designs that provide for full immersions.

Each one of these baptismal structures costs in the $100,000 range, yet they are admittedly used only at the Easter Vigil when adults are baptized. Infants are baptized almost weekly during the rest of the year with water carefully poured on their heads, but the baptistery pool is rarely used for those baptisms.[64]

Something is amiss in this picture. Why would a church spend $100,000 for a structure that is fully used only once a year? The irrationality of this suggests the strength of resistance to today's reality. The Church's hope is that the desperate move to copy the Early Church might magically revive religious faith today. In the eyes of the church, it is well worth the $100,000 if it works.

But the attempt is futile. Soulf's evolutionary edge has moved on and is now found in the secular world.

UPDATING RELIGIOUS TRADITION

Jewish Tradition

A ritual from the Jewish tradition suggests acceptance of today's reality, while reluctant to let go of tradition altogether. A centuries-old Blessing of the Sun occurs just once every 28 years, when the sun returns to its exact location at the time of creation. In hundreds of places throughout the world, people gather to celebrate this moment, as the sun passes by their location.

An expert on this holiday, Rabbi J. David Bleich, is quick to point out that the Blessing of the Sun is not an honoring of God as creator, a strong Jewish tradition that occurs every Friday evening in the lighting of the Sabbath candles. Rather, it affirms God as sustainer of energy (through the sun). As he puts it: "He's like a generator of electricity: If it doesn't keep on working, the lights go out."[65]

This celebration, as interpreted by Rabbi Bleich, combines knowledge of the sun's role in providing energy, while attributing it to God as part of continuing Jewish tradition. The original understanding of the ritual was closely connected with God as creator and the dawn of creation.

Christian Churches

Updating of religious tradition is not unique to Jews. Many Christian churches reinterpret the Bible and Christian rituals to fit today, while clinging to vestiges of tradition to stay connected to the past. However, parishioners are finding this cumbersome. Life and cultural changes make the vestiges seem more remote and removed from their everyday lives. Re-interpretation can go only so far. Eventually traditions outlive their era and fade away as new ones, relevant for the current times, supplant them.

HEALTH AND DEATH

Attitudes toward health and dying is another area in which soulf is pushing away from the past to allow for newness.

Common thinking says that religious people are more accepting of illness and death than others, but this is not the case. A study published in the *Journal* of the American Medical Association shows that terminally ill cancer patients who are religious want more aggressive treatment and life-prolonging care in the week preceding death than less religious patients. "11.3 percent of the most religious patients received mechanical ventilation during the last week of life, compared with only 3.6 percent of the least religious." In addition, the most religious patients are less likely to do any advance care planning such as end-of-life decisions, preparing a will, or appointing a health care proxy.[66]

When death is knocking at the door, fear is suddenly aroused and looms large in the dying one. Doubt breaks through their lifelong trust in God, revealing a discrepancy between what they have been saying they believe and what they truly believe at their deepest level. Out of fear they demand that everything be done to forestall the inevitable. Or perhaps they fear going to hell, suspecting they have not lived a good enough life to merit heaven. Therefore, they want to postpone death as long as possible—and not think about it.

Some people, however, have an unshakable faith that keeps them faith-blind, another common phenomenon. A study conducted in 2005 showed that more than half of the randomly surveyed people believed that divine intervention could revive the dying. This is true even when doctors have declared that treatment would be futile. Moreover, nearly 20 percent of doctors and other medical workers said that God could reverse a hopeless outcome.[67]

Again, fear apparently sets in and triggers wishful thinking. Theistic belief, which asserts that God intervenes from time to time in people's lives and events of the world, died with Copernicus and his successors in science. In affirming divine intervention, people are avoiding the realities of soulf and the universe.

Of course, what appears to be hopeless according to medical science may not be hopeless. The difference is that the revival in a "hopeless case" comes from within the laws of nature, not from a God intervening from outside of nature.

RELIGION AND THE STATE

In a different arena, desperation sometimes paves the way for religion to move into, and use, the state.

The Texas Legislature passed a bill mandating that all public high schools offer an academic course on the Bible, a requirement that no other state has ever made. The bill passed the Texas House with a vote of 139-1, and the Senate with a vote of 28-2. The governor signed the bill into law in 2007.[68]

The church was once again grasping for straws. If the church were alive and well, high school students would have been studying the Bible in church, and there would have been no need for the secular world to be involved. When this kind of tactic becomes necessary, it is a sign of desperation.

SOULF SHEDDING THE SHACKLES

Response of Laypersons to Pope Benedict XVI

While churches as a whole are searching for changes that will work in the post modern world, Pope Benedict XVI and the Roman Catholic Church are encountering more severe challenges by clinging to ancient church dogma.

An image that captures this reality is that of a juggler frantically struggling to keep numerous balls in the air at the same time. Another image is that of a fire fighter striving to put out multiple fires all over the world simultaneously. The Pope's single intention—and hope—is to hold together the tenets of the Church as viable and necessary. To this end he is enforcing the Church's stance on social issues with dogmatic statements.

Many parishioners are drifting away from the Pope's dogmatic stance. A poll conducted for U.S. bishops in 2008 showed that few young Catholics go to confession. Only 35 percent of the younger Catholics attend mass at least once a month, compared with 64 percent of the older generation. Most young Catholics, and an astounding 68 percent of all Catholics surveyed, believed they could be good Catholics without going to weekly Mass. Also, an increasing number of Catholic Latinos are converting to evangelical Protestantism.[69]

During a trip to Spain in 2006, the Pope denounced legalization of gay marriage and the "rapid secularization" of Europe. Gay issues, along with loosened laws on divorce and medically assisted fertilization, have deepened the rift between the Church and Spain, which was once solidly Roman Catholic. Like much of Europe, Spain has recently been moving away from the Church. Though 80 percent of Spaniards still consider themselves Catholic, only 18 percent attend mass regularly on Sundays or religious holidays. Even the Prime Minister opted out of attending an outdoor Mass that the Pope led while in Spain, despite the fact that a million or more people attended it.[70]

The Pope's strong desire to uphold church dogma has exposed his hypocrisy on some social issues. An astute reader of the *San Jose Mercury News* wrote a letter to the editor about the Catholic Church's conflicted stance on flu and HIV. He wrote: "How hypocritical that the Catholic Church goes to such great lengths to halt the spread of swine flu, even suspending the taking of holy communion, yet the Vatican continues to vehemently oppose the distribution and use of condoms in Third World countries to curtail the pandemic spread of HIV."[71] Social issues may account for the fact that no American faith group has lost more adherents than the Catholic Church.[72]

When in Brazil in 2007, the Pope responded to a question about Mexico's recent legalization of abortion by saying that he would support Mexican bishops if they were to decide to excommunicate lawmakers who voted for the law. (Excommunication is the harshest form of punishment in the Roman Catholic Church.)

His tough message sparked a fiery debate across the world over the Roman Catholic Church's efforts to influence politicians. A Mexican legislator, Leticia Quezada, who voted for abortion rights said, "I am religious. I am Catholic... I continue believing in God but not the institution of the church."[73]

Response of the Priesthood to Pope Benedict XVI

Opposition to Pope Benedict XVI does not stop with Catholic laypersons. His rigidity has cost him trouble with the priesthood as well.

In South Carolina a priest acted as local firefighter for the Pope, telling his parishioners that they should not receive Holy Communion if they voted for Obama as president because he supports abortion, which "constitutes material cooperation with intrinsic evil."[74]

A renegade movement is ordaining women as Catholic priests in defiance of the Vatican. In response to a celebration of Mass by one of these women, the Diocese of San Jose warned parishioners that the sacraments offered would be invalid. The ordination of women is a sticky issue that Catholic dioceses will be forced to address at some point, as increasing numbers of women join the ordination movement.[75]

As women are joining the priesthood, some priests are leaving it. Father Alberto Cutie left the Catholic Church and became Episcopalian in order to be with his girlfriend, in defiance of church law. He said that the church is about seeking God, and "the spirit of God has been with me... God is the only one we follow."[76] Having just moved away from the Roman Catholic Church, it is telling that he does not mention Jesus Christ, but only "God" and "the spirit of God" as the one to follow.

In Latin America Pope Benedict XVI has a different problem with Catholic priests. Many are deeply engaged with liberation theology, a rival theology to traditional Roman Catholicism that promotes a "preferential option for the poor." It is thriving even without hierarchical support from the Catholic Church. Eighty thousand "base communities," Bible circles that meet regularly to discuss scripture from the viewpoint of liberation theology, are active in Brazil alone.

When queried about liberation theology, the Pope's anachronistic and tradition-bound response was: "It seems to me we need not theology of liberation, but theology of martyrdom."[77]

The number of converts in Latin America, where nearly half of the world's Catholics live, is striking. In Brazil, the most populous Catholic country, the number of Catholics dropped from 89 percent in 1980 to 64 percent in 2007. During that time period Protestant denominations grew to 22 percent of the population, with Pentecostal congregations seeing the biggest gains. Brazil has lost multitudes of followers not only to Pentecostal denominations, but also to secularism and apathy. Ninety-four percent of Brazilian Catholics support contraception, and more than 70 percent support the right to divorce, both of which church policy opposes. Brazil's free distribution of condoms to combat AIDS, a rise in second marriages (not recognized by the church), and Mexico City's legalization of abortion all add to the Pontiff's overwhelming challenge in Latin America.[78]

Even the personal visit of Pope Benedict XVI to Brazil did nothing to shore up "threats to the church." His pontifications, signifying dedication to guarding and purifying the faith, seemed archaic and totally out of touch with the people. As a result, he had little or no impact on the relatively few who came out to hear him speak.[79]

Compromises of Pope Benedict XVI

Signs of the extent to which both the priesthood and parishioners are squeezing the pope are the compromises he has made from time to time, unable to stem the tide of change.

Pressure has been building for years for the Vatican to change its stance on limbo, a place regarded as somewhere between heaven and hell. The Roman Catholic Church has taught that children who die without baptism go to limbo rather than to heaven. To change this stance has been problematic. If there is no limbo for unbaptized infants, the Church could go only two ways: declare that those infants go to hell or, by implication, they—and all people—are born in the state of grace instead of original sin. To make such a change would be chipping away at a foundation stone of the Roman Catholic Church.

In 2007 the Vatican attempted to get around this dilemma through a document prepared for the Pope by their International Theological Communion, which said they have "serious" grounds to hope that babies who die without baptism will go to heaven rather than to limbo. It still holds to the Church's doctrine of original sin but says that the exclusion of innocent babies from heaven does not seem to reflect Christ's special love for "the little ones."[80]

Another area in which the Pope has been squeezed into softening his dogmatic stance is Christian-Muslim relationship. One of the tenets of Catholicism has been that Roman Catholicism is the only way to God, but on a visit to the Holy Land in 2009, Benedict XVI denounced "the ideological manipulation of religion" and called for greater understanding between the Christian and Muslim faiths. He said that both Christians and Muslims should "strive to be seen" as faithful worshipers of God.[81]

In relations with China, too, Pope Benedict has shown pressure from the state. The Vatican's need to renew relations with China has officially reversed the Church's policy of resisting governmental role in religion. In 1988 his predecessor, Pope John Paul II, gave priests in Communist China special powers to operate secretly and independently without the mandate of the Vatican to avoid persecution and danger. In reversing that policy, Pope Benedict XVI said it is time for the underground and state-sponsored Catholic churches in China to reconcile.[82]

SOULF'S WRESTLING IN CHURCH AND STATE

This bedfellow relationship of church and state is not unique to the Vatican. During the administration of George Walker Bush, Paul Krugman wrote of the "infiltration of the [U.S.] federal government by large numbers of people seeking to impose a religious agenda." He pointed out the Texas Republican Party pledged to "dispel the myth of the separation of church and state." Accordingly, the Bush administration hired unqualified people because of their religious connections. Many of these were graduates of Regent University, founded by televangelist Pat Robertson to provide "Christian leadership to change the world." The university boasts that 150 of its graduates worked in the Bush administration.

With this infiltration of religion into governmental affairs during the George W. Bush administration, the GOP became the first religious party in U.S. history. The White House adopted agendas stemming from a biblical worldview that included a national security defined by patriotism; a simplistic, crusading Christianity; and a reckless, credit-feeding financial complex that has in recent years played itself out to the max in our financial markets. Oil, fundamentalism, and debt slowly merged as the GOP became captive of biblical inerrancy, dismissing modern knowledge and science.[83]

A cozy relationship between church and state has also developed at the state level. In the last section we noted that Texas mandated an elective course on the Bible in all Texas high schools. A more subtle— yet outward—intrusion of the church into state matters took place when President Obama arrived at Roman Catholic Notre Dame University to deliver the 2009 commencement address. More than 100 protesters greeted him, saying he should not be allowed to speak because of his support of abortion rights and embryonic stem-cell research. Local Bishop D'Arcy even skipped the commencement exercises because of Obama's presence. Although 23 protesters were arrested, notably none of them was a student.[84]

Some conservatives took a forceful stance in Texas, where the Board of Education had upheld teaching evolution as accepted mainstream science. In the face of this, several social conservatives succeeded in requiring biology teachers to evaluate critically a variety of scientific principles like cell formation and the Big Bang.[85]

Though a less frequent occurrence, the state has occasionally injected itself into religious matters. A District Judge in Minnesota said that a 13-year-old, whose parents had refused chemotherapy for him on religious grounds, had been "medically neglected." He ordered re- evaluation of the boy's Hodgkin's lymphoma and that he undergo chemotherapy, if it would still be helpful. (Considerable time had elapsed before the court made its judgment.) Doctors had said that the boy had a 90 percent chance of cure with chemotherapy and radiation treatment.[86]

Perhaps most reflective of soulf's wrestling with the relationship of church and state comes through people's expectations of political candidates. People today expect political candidates to be religious, but not too religious. Though Americans do not object to political candidates mixing religion and politics, they do not want them to be ruled by the tenets of their religion in decision-making. People want to know "if your religious beliefs give you the capability to adapt to changing circumstances or whether they are so rigid that you can't adapt."[87]

A survey conducted during the 2004 Presidential election showed that 70 percent of Kerry supporters said they worried more about political leaders who "are too close to religion" than about those who "don't pay enough attention" to religion. At the same time 52 percent of Bush supporters said they worry more about political leaders who "don't pay enough attention" to religion than about those who "are too close to religion."[88]

Islamic cultures are split on the issue of the role religion plays in state affairs. Unlike fundamentalist cultures such as Iran, where "fativas" (religious edicts) on how to be a good Muslim can be a life-or-death matter, most Indonesians shrug off the judgments of the Council of Ulema. "Who cares?" people ask. Because the edicts usually have little to do with what really matters to them, most Indonesians just ignore the rulings.[89]

Struggle to keep church and state completely separate is most evident in the choice for a new Dalai Lama. A serious conflict looms in selecting the 15th Dalai Lama, spiritual leader for the Tibetan people. The current one, exiled with his followers to India by China, fears that two Dalai Lamas may be chosen, one by Tibetans and the other by the Chinese government. A showdown may occur sooner rather than later, since the current Dalai Lama turned 84 in July of 2009 and has had some ill health in recent years.[90]

In the midst of internal struggles working out the relationship between church and state, President Obama transcended them and carried the issue to an international plane and a higher level of discourse. In covering President Obama's visit to Egypt in 2009, the Washington Post wrote about "historical mistakes made over centuries in the name of culture and religion that he said are now overshadowed by shared interests."[91] Though possibly unintentional, it is telling that the President spoke of shared interests of nations taking precedence over religion. In the last century a U.S. president would never have openly expressed such a view. With this leap in consciousness, President Obama correctly pegged where the world now is.

SOULF'S MOVE AWAY FROM RELIGION

As we have seen, a considerable number of mopping-up exercises are still needed as soulf sheds itself of the encumbrances of the religious past. However, even more energy is being exerted in soulf's actual move into the secular world. Surveys point to the state of flux that is taking place because of this shake-up and to a move away from religious tradition.

In early 2009 the American Religious Identification Survey, conducted by researchers at Trinity College in Connecticut, showed that the number of Americans who call themselves Christians has dropped to 76 percent of the U.S. population, down from 86 percent in 1990. Those who do call themselves Christian more frequently use "nondenominational," "evangelical," or "born again" to describe themselves.[92]

An extensive Religious Landscape Survey, one of the largest polls ever conducted, with 35,000 adults interviewed in 2007, showed that Protestants had slipped to 51 percent of the U.S. population. Americans increasingly dismiss the importance of denomination and church membership, while forging a more bottom-up, individualized concept of faith.

The survey also showed that people who call themselves "unaffiliated" rose to 16 percent. Significantly, less than half the "unaffiliated" were raised that way. The "unaffiliated" group, including those who call themselves "atheist" and "agnostic," has grown the most and is growing fastest of all groups surveyed.[93]

"When it comes to religion, there is believing, belonging, and behaving, and they don't always correlate," says Barry Kosmin, co-author of the 2001 American Religious Identification survey. Her statement points to the controversy among scholars as to what is happening in American religion. Some think that secularism is underreported because people sometimes check a box correlating to a faith group without actually believing its tenets or following its practices. Others think the growth of "unaffiliated" disguises the 25 percent who consider themselves "spiritual but not religious." Some trends show less support for organized religion but rising support for personal religious beliefs. Wherever the truth may lie, an incontrovertible feature of religious surveys is the fluctuation of identity, with all groups constantly gaining and losing members.[94]

Supporting evidence of the current shift in religious interest is the number of doctorate level programs now being offered in "spirituality." This reflects both a growing cultural interest in the subject, as well as a growing disinterest in organized religion. "Religion" focuses on beliefs and practices from an academic, objective, or detached position, whereas "spirituality" delves into people's personal experience and practice of their faith.

Professors report that, starting in 2007, there has been an increasing demand from students for courses on biblical spirituality, "and those classes are packed," said Diane Traflet, founder of the Institute for Christian Spirituality at Seton Hall University. "People are very, very interested in them."[95]

Countries in other parts of the Western world are experiencing a faster move away from organized religions, though it is sometimes eclipsed by a seeming desire to remain loyal to one's religious institution of origin. An extreme example of this is a notation made by Spiegel Online. According to that group, 80 percent of Sweden's citizens are registered as members of the (Lutheran) Church of Sweden. Yet a 2006 survey revealed that Swedes ranked "religions" 14th on a list of institutions in which they placed their trust, or very much trust. The institution trusted most by Swedes was Ikea, the Swedish furniture chain, with 80 percent of the people having trust in it. Among other institutions ranking higher than "religions" were Volvo, Ericsson, and Saab. [96]

In nearby England another factor points to the rapid decline of religion in Europe in general. According to a British Broadcasting Company survey, 56 percent of British children are unaware that Christmas is a celebration of the birth of Jesus.[97]

This move away from religion carries over to the war-torn area of Iraq. After several years of warfare, and experiencing the violence of religious extremism and restrictions that have come with it, many young Iraqis have become disillusioned with religious leaders and what they preach. Graduate students are not enrolling in religion classes, and attendance at weekly prayers appears to be down, even where there is little violence. A 19-year-old from a heavily Shiite neighborhood in Baghdad said: "The religion men are liars. Young people don't believe them. Guys my age are not interested in religion anymore."[98]

Back here in the United States religion has become sidelined enough to make it feel relatively safe to call oneself an atheist. Representative Pete Stark was the first member of Congress to state publicly that he doesn't believe in God. Some affirm his openness in "coming out of the closet." Others say, "A Christian worldview is proper for a politician to have." Although there was no public outcry with Stark's claiming to be an atheist, only 14 percent of Americans believe we are ready for an atheist as president.[99]

"God didn't make man; man made gods."
—J. Anderson Thomson and Clare Aukofer, *Los Angeles Times*

Atheism is taking hold more openly in Europe. Although more than three of four people in the world consider themselves religious, a high-profile atheist campaign that started in London spread around the globe. Nonbelievers raised $200,000 to place an anti-religious advertisement on 800 London buses that read: "There is probably no god. Now stop worrying and enjoy your life."

This prompted Christian groups to counter with ads of their own. The ongoing dialog gained ground in many of the world's richer nations, stirring up debates about God and fostering an increasingly vocal nonreligious movement.[100]

An everyday marker of the shift away from religion and into the secular zone is the area of wedding ceremonies. Many couples are opting for courthouse weddings instead of churches. In Los Angeles County, civil weddings were up 17 percent in 2008 over 2007. By 2009, civil wedding ceremonies had increased nationally by 60 percent in the first quarter over the same period a year earlier. Shane McMurray, chief executive of a research company named Wedding Report, said, "Those types of ceremonies are certainly on the increase."[101]

To meet the demand in Contra Costa County, California, the clerk-recorder's building has replaced counter-side weddings with two wedding rooms, the largest holding 25 people. An appealing feature is that weddings can be seen on a live video-feed from a county Web-site.[102]

A Los Angeles wedding site, the Norwalk Registrar-Recorder's office, was "recently so mobbed that the line was out the door and down the sidewalk." Couples waiting to be married were not even allowed to see ahead of time where the wedding would take place.

"Inside the Registrar-Recorder building, the tiny waiting room for about-to-be-married couples was packed with brides and grooms and friends and family. The deputy commissioner had to squeeze through the crowd and yell to be heard when she called their names.

'Santiago Miranda?'

Miranda took Bracamontes' hand. Bracamontes screamed. Their friends hummed, 'Here comes the bride,' as the couple headed into the chapel."[103]

Paralleling this move away from religion, and integral to that move, is a shift in thinking from "modern" to "post-modern."

In an article written for the newsletter of a Presbyterian church, Bruce Reyes-Chow said that churches are dying because they cannot handle the complexities of being church in the shifting worldview from modern to postmodern. Although much of the world has been in post-modernity for some time, the church lags behind. He points out the obstacles that confront the church:

- Modernity says that we can overcome the chaos of life.
- Post-modernity says that chaos is life… Believing that the chaos of life in today's time of globalization and technology is *ever* going to go away or be conquered is downright irresponsible.
- Modernity says that there is one way, the old way.
- Post-modernity says that new ways must flow FROM the old ways.
- We value the DOing of the institution over the BEing in relationship.
- Modernity says that community is in the methodology and ways we DO church.
- Post-modernity says that community is about BEing church.
- Modernity says that there is one and only one "Big Story" or meta-narrative and truth.
- Post-modernity says there is not ONE meta-narrative or truth… [104]

Boyung Lee, a Korean professor at Pacific School of Religion in Berkeley, tells the story of how she came to "reach" young people of today.

One day she went shopping with her church's youth group for toys for children in shelters. As they entered the mall, Joan Osborne's "One of Us" was blaring on the loud speaker.

"All of a sudden these kids were very animated and singing along: 'what if God is one of us / Just a slob like one of us…'

The next time we met, I played that song and asked them to discuss its theology. It became a rich conversation."

In that experience, Lee realized that popular culture is not just an appendage for young people. It is a "vital core" for them. This is borne out in her course on media culture and theology, which has been one of the most popular courses at Pacific School of Religion.

Lee wrote: "Post-modern ideas gave me language to name what I had been doing in Korea: challenging the dominant culture and its meta-narratives."[105]

The final push beyond Religion has been most fully accomplished by a relatively small number of individuals—people like Reyes-Chow and Lee—who have found their home in a new consciousness, riding the wave with soulf. These individuals have incorporated into themselves contents of Religion that still have value for our post-modern world, but these contents have become so integrated that they are no longer separate entities in everyday consciousness. Religion's contents are now part of who they are.

> This shift from "modern" to "post-modern" thinking is required if we are to enter into today's movement of soulf. In the days of scientific modernism, we oversimplified life, thinking there is one answer, one way. We thought that life was fully rational and predictable, which would give us a handle on the universe and allow us to figure out life's deepest secrets.

We have just seen how this form of thinking is taking a battering, and have witnessed the gradual struggle to move away from Religion. Rituals that were formerly meaningful have revealed themselves to be empty shells, and the Pope's tenacious hold on Church doctrine has become a losing battle in the face of soulf's forward movement through the masses of humanity. The Church is still occasionally pressing for entrance into affairs of state, but the wave of new consciousness is relentlessly washing over such movements. Bobbing up from time to time within the wave are those striking out against Religion, part of the final throes of its demise and of humanity's slow movement into post-modernism.

This move into post-modernism began to happen when scientists probed more deeply into the microworld, and it became incontrovertibly evident that chaos and unpredictability are basic structures of the universe. These irrational elements have thrown our "modernist" thinking into a tailspin. Life's complexities have suddenly become obvious to the average person. We can feel the chaos, as if something is spinning out of control. We are aware of never being able to catch up with life, as soulf's wave moves faster and farther ahead of us. Soulf is always on the forefront of the wave, which *is* chaos and uncertainty—akin to whitewater at the front of an ocean wave with its unpredictable foam and bubbles.

Who can predict the crazy zigzagging of the stock market? Does anyone know where the worldwide economic crisis is headed? How can we possibly sort out the complexities of international trade, and relationships, and security? Should I buy the latest iPhone? Or i-Pad? Or Kindle? Or wait for the next generation, since I know that anything I buy now will be updated in just a few weeks, or months? Can I ever catch up with technology, or will I be left behind? What about the doomsday picture of global warming, which scientists keep battering us with?

The list of questions goes on and on. These all indicate our movement into a post-modern world. Yes, it is disconcerting. But seen from the perspective of soulf, it is a moment of emergence, a time for humanity to shift to a new level of consciousness. This shift is so deep and so widespread that we are caught in its dizzying chaos, and are thrown off balance by its unpredictability.

Furthermore, there is no "other" God to turn to for comfort. We have only ourselves; yet, if we look inside ourselves deeply enough, we will find *all* the values we have attributed to God and Religion because now they are part of us. We have become our own god.

All that is required for this scenario to fully take its course in us—though it can seem like an impossible task—is to trust that we individually, and humanity as a whole, have within us all that is needed to ride the wave with soulf into the next evolutionary structure—and the next, and the next, and the next. . .

**"I have found that losing faith is not a cataclysmic event. It's more like watching mist rise off a river in the morning. You can't say exactly when it disappeared, but you know it is gone for good."
—Erik Reece, *An American Gospel***

For Reflection:

1. ....

....

....

2. ....

....

....

3. ....

....

....

CHAPTER 5

THE NATURAL WORLD: COSMOS

"There is neither spirit nor matter in the world;
the 'stuff of the universe' is spirit-matter."
—Teilhard de Chardin

EXPANSION

The desire to expand our knowledge of the universe has been unstoppable. From the time of early explorers of our planet, to first explorations of outer space and the moon, to the launching of a spacecraft to track down other Earths, humanity's imagination and vision have always drifted to what is beyond. Although the planet-hunting spacecraft launched to explore the distant regions of the Milky Way up to 3,000 light years away cost $700 million, it is not surprising we place such high value on expanding our horizon in space, given that expansion is at the heart of the created world.

It becomes increasingly evident that soulf is pushing relentlessly to know and be known, relying on humanity's ever-complexifying computer-brain to become more conscious. Humanity acts out soulf's pressing desire to search the depth and breadth of life, exploring both the macroworld and microworld as far and deeply as possible. Even at times when a significant portion of society balks at spending billions of dollars for space exploration while human needs here on Earth remain so great—such as at the time of the first moon landing—soulf trumps that thought and drives us into deeper exploration.

DARK MATTER AND DARK ENERGY

On the forefront of cosmic exploration today is dark energy, discovered in 1998. Often paired with dark matter as its repulsive, or negative force, dark energy drives galaxies apart at an ever- increasing speed, acquiring its nickname of "negative gravity." Because dark energy is a little stronger than dark matter, expansion and newness supersede gravity's retraction.

Dark matter and dark energy together comprise 95 percent of the mass and energy of the universe, leaving just 5 percent for atoms we are familiar with—such as hydrogen, carbon and iron.[106] A report of the Dark Matter Search Project at the University of California-Los Angeles said:

> "Dark matter played a crucial role in the past by causing galaxies to form, and dark energy will play a crucial role in the continuing evolution of the universe. Understanding what dark matter and dark energy are, are among the most compelling scientific questions of our time."[107]

More recently another role for dark energy has been discovered: "It prevents the biggest clusters of galaxies from getting too fat... from essentially overeating." In other words, it governs the growth of the universe.[108]

THEORIES OF COSMOLOGY

Other voices from the scientific field are expounding on a variety of ideas about cosmology, searching for answers to perplexing questions about the universe.

Joao Magueijo

In 2008 a special program on the Science Channel, "Joao Magueijo's Big Bang,"[109] presented a radical (but legitimate) theory of cosmology developed by Dr. Magueijo, a theoretical physicist at Imperial College, London. He attempted to explain what he sees as inconsistencies in the theory of relativity. He calls this the "fatal flaw" of the Big Bang theory and attributes it to the hypothesis of the varying speed of light.[110]

Joel Primack

Another voice comes from cosmologist Joel Primack in a book he wrote with his wife, Nancy Ellen Abrams, *The View From the Center of the Universe*. In speaking of humanity's place in the cosmos, Primack said the center of the universe is right where you are, countering the worldview shaped by Copernicus and Newton. A profile of Primack in *Smithsonian* magazine pointed out that the physical size of human beings is about halfway between the microworld and macroworld of the universe. "Much smaller creatures than we are could not develop the complexity necessary for intelligence; much larger ones would be limited by the time it takes information to travel across their brains."[111]

In the final chapter of their book, Primack and Abrams addressed the question of where they stand relative to belief in God. They "believe in God as nothing less than the process of opening our personal lines of contact with the unknown potential of the universe." Jerry Adler, author of the profile, adds to their words: "a sentence that the word 'unknown' transforms from merely insubstantial to, well, empty."[112]

At New Year Primack and Adler engage in an unusual and amusing ritual:

> "They celebrate New Year's Day with a confection they call the Cosmic Dessert, symbolic of the distribution of mass energy in the universe: 70 percent chocolate cake, representing dark energy; 25 percent chocolate ice cream (for cold dark matter); and the rest other stuff, including a tiny pinch of cinnamon, which stands for heavy elements forged in stars, in other words, most of what constitutes life."[113]

CLOUD FORMATIONS

Observations of the heavens that are easier to relate to are happening close to home. In June 2006, strange-looking clouds appeared in different parts of the world. Dark undulating clouds with greenish-yellow backdrop "looked like Armageddon," according to Jane Wiggins, an amateur photographer in Cedar Rapids, Iowa, who was on the scene and captured a photo of the odd phenomenon.

Weather authorities are now being pushed to create a new cloud category, which has not happened since 1951. As we learned in school, there are three main groups of clouds: cumulus, cirrus and stratus. However, the clouds seen on that special day in 2006 defy categorizing. "When we put pictures [of clouds] up online we list the category, and I wasn't sure how to categorize it," said Pretor-Pinney, author of "The Cloudspotter's Guide."[114] Perhaps basic cloud formations are complexifying, along with other things in the universe.

SPACE MISSIONS

Asteroids

Several years ago, when all attention was focused on the Indian Ocean tsunami, astronomers were sweating an asteroid that could well have collided with Earth. "It was very scary," commented Rusty Schweickart, an astronaut who is not an alarmist, and who has had many years of experience with the world of space. The event prompted scientists to urge experts who study asteroids to hurry up and learn how to deflect them. Their possible threat to our planet is all too real.[115]

Scientists were already concerned about that threat. In July 2007 a National Air and Space Administration (NASA) mission, Dawn, visited Vesta and Ceres, two of the largest asteroids in the solar system, with the specific intent of increasing our limited knowledge of asteroids. Are they clumps of solid rock? Are they piles of rubble held together by gravity? The mission was designed to probe these kinds of questions. Planetary scientists are keeping a careful watch over asteroids and are determining ways of nudging them off the path of damaging our planet.[116]

Mars and the Moon

A few other missions went into space in 2007. Among them was the Mars mission, Phoenix, which sent back valuable data to NASA for five months after its landing.[117]

Two other missions are of special interest because they remind us of the distant reach of soulf's intense urging. Japan sent a spacecraft to orbit and map the moon's surface, and a few months later India followed up with an extended two-year mission of its own, with the same purpose. Both missions were intended to pave the way for future lunar exploration.[118] That will be even more complex and expensive than previous missions, so pooling resources of several nations will be a necessity. Collaborative research is becoming the only way to investigate the world's most complex problems.

International Space Station

Missions to provide ongoing maintenance for the international space station have taken place intermittently and have become almost routine. Although the United States has now cancelled its involvement with maintenance of the International Space Station, other countries are continuing to provide for it. Now that people are living there, regular maintenance is required, as well as addressing particular needs, such as the replacement of an old camera the size of a baby grand piano on the Hubble Space Telescope.[119]

The Telescope is indispensable for cosmic research, as it enables scientists to take pictures of asteroids that may threaten our planet, as well as other phenomena behind the curtains of space. In 2008, for instance, scientists captured the first pictures in history of planets orbiting stars other than our sun. One of these is a giant planet that orbits the star Fomalhaut, located 25 light-years from Earth.[120]

INVOLVEMENT OF THE AVERAGE PERSON

Google Earth

Technology has helped the average person observe cosmic action. Through Google Earth, millions of people have become virtual stargazers along with the experts. Google's service called "Sky" shows detailed imagery of about 100 million stars and 200 million galaxies. "These are really the images of the sky. Everything is real," said Carol Christian, an astronomer with the Space Telescope Science Institute.[121]

Brian Malow

The average person is also being brought into the world of science via people like Brian Malow, who considers himself a science comedian. He is on the comedy-club circuit regularly, with his shows centering on scientific topics that range from infectious disease and technology to quarks and quantum physics. He jokes about attending a magnet school for bipolar students, and quips that he used to be an astronomer, "but I got stuck on the day shift." Perhaps the greatest value of a science comedian is making complex science topics entertaining to anyone and making science "cool" in the eyes of the public.[122]

Space exploration is on the cutting edge of today's interest in physics. Two recent Nobel Prizes in physics were awarded to scientists engaged in cosmic studies. American astrophysicists George Smoot and John Mather received the 2006 prize for their measurements of early cosmic light that strongly suggested a gargantuan explosion gave birth to the universe and everything in it.[123] Three theorists of Japanese heritage received the prize in 2008 for their work with "broken symmetry," which helps to explain the asymmetrical behavior of certain elementary particles.[124] Through these prize-winning explorations, and all explorations into the cosmos, humanity is drawing closer to nature, reflecting soulf's drive in today's world.

For Reflection:

1. ....
   ....
   ....

2. ....
   ....
   ....

3. ....
   ....
   ....

CHAPTER 6

THE NATURAL WORLD:
ENVIRONMENT AND ECOLOGY

"People have begun to realize that we could win
every other battle and it would be meaningless
if we lost the fight against climate change."
—Bill McKibben, *The End of Nature* **[125]**

GLOBAL WARMING

The move toward climatic disaster began near the end of the nineteenth
century. For most people science and religion were unrelated, so the
environment became a ready target for human exploitation. What had
started as humans taking on the biblical role of respectful responsibility for
creatures of the natural world morphed into "domination over" the natural
world. This shift provided a wide-open invitation for western materialism,
and for technological power to step in and (unknowingly) lead the way to
the ecological crisis that now engulfs the world.[126]

Nature's Urgency

At an energy conference sponsored by *Newsweek* in 2009, Steven
Chu, U.S. Energy Secretary and Nobel Prize-winning physicist, brought
conference members face to face with the imminent threat of global
warming: "Earth is like the great ship Titanic," on a collision course with
disaster unless action is taken. "Off in the distance is an iceberg, so how

do you turn the ship so there is only a glancing blow?... And the good ship Earth takes time to turn."[127]

A classical image also warns of impending disaster. In Greek Mythology Phaeton, son of the sun god, raced his father's chariot across the sky, despite his father's warnings. Not having the maturity to handle so much power, Phaeton and the sun chariot were struck by a thunderbolt, fell to Earth, and burned up.

Humanity, too, has taken the reins of power and used it as unconsciously as Phaeton. We have acted like a teenager driving at break-neck speed just because he can. He loves living at the limits of what he can do, regardless of the irresponsibility of his actions. Humanity is still in process of developing the consciousness needed to use responsibly the power vested in us.

A sobering fact is that until recently the United States was the worst culprit in paving the way to greenhouse gas emissions, which have been largely responsible for the climate change the world is now experiencing. The ignominious number-one position has now shifted to China.[128]

Effects of Climate Change

The onrushing disasters of climate change are global in scope and pernicious in their invasiveness. Recognition of this has brought about a steady morphing of the environment movement into the climate movement. Following in the footsteps of Al Gore and his "inconvenient truth," countless voices are now pointing to the urgency of the global warming situation. Thomas L. Friedman wrote in a column for the *New York Times* in 2009:

"The pace of global warming is likely to be much faster than recent predictions, because industrial greenhouse gas emissions have increased more quickly than expected and higher temperatures are triggering self-reinforcing feedback mechanisms in global ecosystems... We are basically looking now at a future climate that's beyond anything we've considered seriously in climate model simulations," [said] Christopher Field, director of the

Carnegie Institution's Department of Global Ecology at Stanford University.[129]

That insight had already begun to shape our thinking in 2006. Ross Gelbspan, author of *Boiling Point*, wrote a front-page piece for the *San Jose Mercury News* headlined: "Why we need to worry about global warming *now*: With climate-related changes occurring faster than expected, scientists say we have 10 years to slash carbon fuel use—or else." In his article Gelbspan pointed out that the Kyoto Protocol barely touched the problem of global warming with its mere eight percent reduction of emissions.[130] Even California's seemingly bold step—cutting emissions 25 percent by 2020 and 80 percent by 2050—are not nearly drastic enough to meet the accelerated pace of global warming.[131]

Problems humanity faces

The volatile, changing and extreme weather patterns we are already experiencing underline the problems we face. In 2006 the snow-pack of California, which constitutes 75 percent of the water supply in the West, was at 172 percent of average, the second-wettest in the northern Sierra Nevada since 1921.[132] Yet the snow-pack has declined by almost a third in the northern Rocky Mountains and more than 50 percent in the Cascades since 1950.[133]

Both the Arctic and Antarctic have experienced ice shelves breaking away at an alarming rate, a dramatic indication of how warmer temperatures are changing the polar frontiers. One chunk that broke away in northern Arctic, the 4,500-year-old Markham Ice Shelf, was nearly the size of Manhattan,[134] and an even larger chunk, Wilkins Ice Shelf, suddenly collapsed in western Antarctica. It was nearly seven times the size of Manhattan, about the size of Connecticut.[135]

Australia suffered its worst drought on record in 2005. The Prime Minister called the situation "unprecedentedly dangerous" for farming and the economy as a whole due to lack of water for irrigation.[136] In 2007 northern Alabama endured the most severe drought in more than a century, rendering a "poor to very poor" classification for a high percentage of their corn, soybean, and cotton crops.[137]

Rising temperatures are affecting wildfire behavior as well. Fire seasons have become longer and more severe, raising fears among scientists that fragile ecosystems will be disrupted, putting native plants and animals at risk of extinction. The wildfire season in the United States in 2006 was the most severe and expensive one on record. More than 89,000 fires scorched 9.5 million acres, according to the National Interagency Fire Center.[138]

In the winter of 2009-2010, Washington, D.C. chalked up the heaviest snowfall on record since at least 1884, shutting down federal offices in February for the better part of a week. Closing the agencies cost the government $100 million a day. Only 230,000 employees were affected, however, as the rest of the 2 million workers of the federal work force are spaced throughout the country. Many essential government services are performed in those outlying offices, so anything that is essential gets done, even in the worst of circumstances.[139]

In general, however, higher temperatures are causing warmer winters, earlier springs, less snow and more rain. That, in turn, has raised the risk of floods in winter, droughts in summer, and higher incidents of famine and violence. All this is added to its devastating effects—including death—on millions of people around the world, as well as on plants and animals, birds and fish. [140]

Famine and disease

Along with temperature increases often come new waves of disease, in addition to drought and famine. This is especially true in Africa.

Christian Aid reports that 162 million people in sub-Saharan Africa could die of disease due to global warming by the end of the century. The organization urges sub-Saharan Africa to do its part in curbing global warming by using renewable energy sources, which would be possible for less money than burning oil during the next decade.[141]

Malaria-bearing mosquitoes have found a new home at 6,243 feet in Kenya's uplands, which has become hospitable for them because of global warming. For a long time Africa's highlands had been spared this serious, ancient malady.[142]

Most currently we have seen the devastating effects of global warming played out in East Africa—especially Somalia—where the population has been ravaged by drought, hunger and disease.

Human Choice and Climate Change

Adding to the plight of the environment are human choices about how and where to build structures. The U.S. government chose to build a 360-mile fence along its southern border with Mexico, endangering the habitat of jaguars, ocelots, and long-nose bats among other species, from the Lower Rio Grande Valley in Texas to Arizona's San Pedro Conservation Area.[143]

Another example, which is duplicated nationwide, is Louisiana. Though it is well known that the State is slowly sliding into the Gulf of Mexico, we continue to re-build on the Mississippi River Delta, inviting disaster as we counter natural behavior patterns. Everywhere we choose to build on deltas, we are courting catastrophes similar to the one experienced during and after Katrina.

However, nature's resiliency offers hope for recovery from potential environmental disaster. In Cambodia, four decades after relentless bombing raids by U.S. warplanes, the Ho Chi Minh Trail is once again overgrown and becoming a haven for endangered wildlife. At least 42 formerly threatened species now roam its jungles, including tigers, elephants, and rare apes.[144]

Loss of biodiversity

It was not until May of 2008, when polar bears were finally placed on the endangered species list, that the federal government first identified climate change as the driving force behind a species' potential demise.[145]

However, such a view had become mainstream ever since Al Gore's wake-up call in 2006.

At least one quarter of the world's mammals are threatened with extinction, due to loss of wildlife habitats caused by climate change, plus hunting and poaching. The risk of extinction for marine mammals is even higher—perhaps as much as one third. In their case, however, the cause is largely due to their becoming entangled in fishing gear or being struck by ships. Almost one half of the world's apes, monkeys and other primates are seriously threatened by the destruction of forests to make way for farming, as well as by hunting. Scientists are especially worried about mammal extinction because nature relies on a diversity of species for stabilization of the planet. Each extinction disrupts stability, sending a rippling effect throughout the food chain and making survival more difficult, even for humans.[146]

GREENING THE PLANET

> **"I think that the most important thing to happen this past year was that living and thinking 'green'— that is, mobilizing for the environmental/energy challenge we now face—hit Main Street."**
> —*Thomas L. Friedman, December 2006*

High-Profile Involvement: Individuals

When the tide turned, and it became generally accepted that global climate change was something that needed to be addressed yesterday, some people in high positions stepped up to the plate to help.

One of these was former president Bill Clinton, who drew a coalition of 22 of the world's largest cities into his "Clinton Climate Initiative" to limit global warming. The group planned to expand its number to 40 cities with area populations of three million or more, which account for 15-20 percent of the world's emissions. The international consortium was designed to bargain for cheaper energy-efficient products and share ideas on cutting greenhouse gas pollution.[147]

Another leader in the climate movement has been former Governor Arnold Schwarzenegger, who enacted several pieces of legislation in his home state of California to address global warming. He also joined with former British Prime Minister Tony Blair in sharing clean energy technology.

Thomas Friedman cites five "green" suggestions offered by Hal Harvey, CEO of Climate-Works:

"Energy-efficient buildings and appliance codes now save Californians $6 billion per year... The European Union's fuel-efficiency fleet average for new cars now stands at 41 miles per gallon... power utilities needed to produce 15 or 20 percent of their energy from renewables by 2020... power utilities [can and need to] make money by helping homeowners save energy rather than by encouraging them to consume it... we need a price on carbon."[148]

Perhaps Chevron was responding to this plea to save energy rather than consume more of it when they ran a promotional series coupling persons that would normally be regarded by the public as being on opposite sides of the issue saying, "We agree!"

High-Profile Involvement: Constituencies

Some cities, including Washington, D.C. have bought into that line of thinking. Washington now requires private buildings, in addition to government buildings, to be certified as "green." Steven Chu, U.S. Energy Secretary, pointed out that merely the inclusion of smart sensors can reduce energy consumption in office buildings by 80 percent.[149]

In 1998, 195 nations ratified the United Nations' Montreal Protocol, an ozone treaty that eliminated chlorofluorocarbons (CFC's) and replaced them with hydrofluorocarbons (HFC's). The Obama administration carried the action a step further. Recognizing that even HFC's damage the atmosphere, though to a lesser extent, the Administration decided to ask the same 195 nations that ratified the Montreal Protocol to enact mandatory reductions in (HFC's) to totally eliminate ozone-depleting materials.[150]

Kofi Annan, former Secretary-General of the United Nations, was very concerned about carbon emissions. In fact, he spent most of his time in office getting companies worldwide to sign on to a "Global Compact," which set international environmental standards for carbon emissions and other disturbances in eco-systems, such as ballast dumping and infectious diseases borne on jets. [151]

Involvement of Average Persons

Ideas and actions for addressing global warming come from less well-known individuals and groups, as well as from high profile people and organizations.

An insightful reader of the *San Jose Mercury News* wrote a letter to the editor in which he said: "Unless somebody wakes up and looks at the real problem, we are doomed to fail. The world's population is doubling every 50 years, and if our efforts to reduce carbon-dioxide emissions by 50 percent are successful, 50 years from now we will be back at square one. [We must] persuade the world's population that they must start working to slow its growth."[152]

Some people have banded together to "borrow, barter, and buy used."[153]

Silicon Valley held a "Greenfair Silicon Valley" to help people green their business, home, and life.[154]

Organic cotton clothing is now considered chic, and it shows up at Wal-Mart as well as in Hollywood. Concern about the dangers pesticides pose to the environment is largely behind this change in attitude. Global organic cotton sales increased 119 percent between 2001 and 2005. [155]

Recognizing the environmental impact of transporting and disposing of bottled water, some upscale restaurants now serve only filtered tap water.[156]

Wangari Maathai, who was awarded the 2004 Nobel Peace Prize for founding a movement that planted 30 million trees in Kenya and throughout Africa, inspired citizens of depressed East Palo Alto in northern California to plant a minimum of ten trees for each person living in their town. Out of this, a regional effort sprung up to beautify historic El Camino Real in Palo Alto.[157]

These are just a smattering of individual projects that are contributing worldwide to the green movement.

Involvement of Industries

Various industries, too, have joined the bandwagon.

In 2007 Silicon Valley venture firms invested $1 billion into clean-tech technologies, a sizable portion of the $5 billion total venture capital investments into the energy sector of our economy. [158] This set a new record: the $1 billion investment in clean tech in that single year equaled the combined amount invested in clean tech from 2000 to 2005. What was the driving force behind this? "The clean-tech sector is being driven by two massive engines—the industrial rise of China and India, and the environmental changes being caused by global warming."[159]

Cisco Systems collaborated with an organization called Metropolis, a group of 106 large cities (mostly outside the U.S.) aiming to help leaders use technology to be more efficient and less polluting. This step took Cisco beyond its core products of routers and switches to markets still on the horizon that demand greener, cleaner technologies. "For example, Cisco is working on technology that will automatically adjust lighting and air conditioning based on when employees arrive for work. If an employee badge is swiped across a censor early in the morning, only power systems for his or her office and corridor will be turned on."[160]

Microsoft has addressed global warming by developing the Bay Area's largest solar energy system. Their action was part of a "slow trickle of facilities to embrace solar panels."[161]

One of the largest national homebuilders, Lennar, planned to install solar power systems as part of its standard inclusion in all new homes in the San Francisco Bay Area. This is part of California's Solar Initiative, which is dedicated to installing 400 megawatts of solar power in the next decade.[162]

Even as the housing market was crashing, developer Warmington Homes built a cluster of environmentally-friendly town homes with a range of standard water-and energy-efficient features from solar panels to very low flush toilets, drought-resistant landscaping, and tankless water heaters. Furthermore, these homes proved to be so popular the developer was able to increase its initial offering price.[163]

Banking, too, hopes to benefit from the growing demand for green industries. New Resource Bank was the first commercial bank to be founded with the purpose of loaning money to businesses developing environmentally friendly products and seeking depositors who want their money used for projects that create jobs and profits by reducing global warming. Their bank building in San Francisco is "gold certified" under green building standards, and the bank offers up to $60 a week to employees to take public transit.[164]

Cashing in on the green movement's ever-increasing popularity, Wal-Mart started working on an "eco-rating" for hundreds of thousands of products in its stores. Their plan was to develop a green index for Wal-Mart products similar to the nutritional label found on the packaging for food products. Many suppliers of Wal-Mart have already taken steps to become more eco- friendly, such as Levi Strauss now recommending that jeans be washed in warm or cold water, as opposed to hot water, which uses more energy.[165]

Thomas Friedman expanded on Wal-Mart's role in the green movement:

"Wal-Mart has earned its black eyes for labor practices. But the world's biggest retailer lately has gotten the green bug…

"Wal-Mart has opened two green stores where it is experimenting with alternative building materials, lighting, power systems and designs… From the big wind turbine in the parking lot and solar panels on key walls, which provide 15 percent of the store's electricity, to the cooking oil from fried chicken that is recycled in its bio-boiler and heats the store in winter, to the shift in LED lights in all exterior signs and grocery and freezer cases… you know you're not in your parents' Wal-Mart.

"The more energy-saving bulbs Wal-Mart sells, the more innovation it triggers, the more prices go down. That's how you get scale. And scale is everything if you want to change the world."[166]

Could it be that soulf is moving on a course of least resistance, as water does in a stream, to restore the health of the entire planet?

For Reflection:

1. ....

....

....

2. ....

....

....

3. ....

....

....

CHAPTER 7

THE NATURAL WORLD: ANIMALS

CHANGING ATTITUDE TOWARD ANIMALS

Before the 18th and 19th centuries, humans saw themselves at the pinnacle of existence. Philosophically and scientifically they placed animals on a much lower rung of existence than themselves. Kathryn Shevelow, author of *For the Love of Animals*, wrote of how animals were regarded: "Animals existed to provide humans with food, clothing, implements, labor, and, in the case of science, knowledge."[167]

This led to cruel and brutal treatment of animals throughout the centuries. They were used and abused as labor, food and sport. Dog fighting, painful laboratory experimentation with animals including vivisections, and abusive training of performing animals were common practices.[168]

At some point people's hearts began to soften in their attitude toward animals. Monkeys and apes demonstrated in performing acts that they could dance, bow, calculate sums, and read, which blurred the lines between human and animal. At the same time, domestic pets were growing in popularity and bonding intensely with their household members. Gradually, the role of animals increased from providing labor and food to include companionship.[169]

The world's first national animal-protection law was passed by the British Parliament in 1822 to protect cattle, and later extended to include all domestic animals. This type of legislation could pass through Parliament because revulsion over slavery had enabled people to see the injustices being inflicted upon animals.

This changing attitude toward animals was not limited to England. Americans, too, began protecting animal welfare. Domestic pets had become firmly entrenched in the homes and hearts of people, and the horrific plight of work animals and animals in slaughterhouses had entered their consciousness.[170]

ANIMAL WELFARE

Sport Animals

A persisting sport that has needed animal protection laws is *charreadas*, Mexican rodeos. Legislation in California now requires that a veterinarian be on call during competitions, in case rodeo animals are injured.[171]

Big game hunting has been illegal in the United States for a number of years, but hunters still chase trophy animals in the West. Poaching of elk, deer, antelope, bighorn sheep and other big- game animals continues and has alarmed state and federal wildlife officials in several Western states. Their concern is not only for illegal killings, but also for organized rings of poachers that are trading their bounty on Internet auction sites and submitting pictures to hunting magazines. [172]

Lead bullets

Another concern of wildlife officials is the use of lead bullets, which are less expensive than copper and steel shot, and therefore more widely used. Ranchers consider the thousands of ground squirrels and wild pigs that roam their property as vermin. They turn to lead bullets, as the cost of copper and steel shot to control them would be prohibitive.[173]

The California Legislature has banned lead bullets in condor country, where lead poisoning is the leading condor killer. The Arizona Game and Fish Department has gone so far as to give hunters non-lead bullets, hoping to stem the use of lead bullets.[174]

Circuses

Circuses, too, are being watched to ensure humane treatment of animals. In one incident, animal rights groups banded together to sue the Ringling Brothers and Barnum and Bailey Circus to stop them from using elephants in their shows. They argued that the elephant handlers harm the company's 54 Asian elephants (protected by the Endangered Species Act) when they strike them with metal-tipped prods. The circus company rebutted that the prodding is necessary to keep the elephants under control, and it does not harm them.[175]

Laboratory Animals

Animal rights proponents have also kept an eagle eye on the treatment of laboratory animals. When Japanese researchers created the first genetically modified monkeys that were able to pass on new genetic attributes to their offspring, their research was condemned by animal rights proponents. Activists said it paved the way for primates to be conceived expressly for suffering cruel illnesses and enduring painful and dangerous medical experiments. Previously, scientists had genetically engineered mice and other species to be used as research tools, but they were so genetically different from humans, it had not caused such alarm.[176]

Food Animals

Part of the raging debate about humane treatment of animals is the welfare of food animals. "In 1982, there was close to zero public awareness about this issue," said Joy Mench, a University of California-Davis professor who studies animal welfare issues.[177]

By 2004 California had become the first state to ban making or selling *foie gras*, which is created by force-feeding geese until their livers swell. The ban took effect in 2012.[178]

Illinois became the last state to make it illegal to kill horses for human consumption. Prior to the legislation, the last slaughterhouse had been shipping horsemeat overseas, where it was sold for people to eat.[179]

Two sides of the issue

As consumers caught up with the technology of raising modern livestock, they started demanding more space for animals to turn around and stretch their limbs. In California, concern took the form of an animal welfare ballot initiative in 2008, following the path of four other states that already had similar legislation. It focused primarily on California's 19 million egg- laying hens that were caged in crowded wire boxes.[180]

Farmers claimed it is not more humane to house hens in cage-free barns or to allow them free roaming. That kind of freedom costs 70 percent of chickens a broken bone, as continuous egg- laying requires a large supply of calcium for eggshells, making their bones more fragile. Furthermore, cannibalizing each other becomes more of a problem, and eggs become more expensive and less safe.[181]

ANIMALS vs. HUMAN CONCERNS

Controversies surround the treatment of animals *vis-à-vis* human concerns. In one example, an injured mountain lion strayed into a retirement community and was hiding in the bushes. Animal control officers had no tranquilizer that works on mountain lions, so police said they had no choice but to shoot and kill the animal. Some residents at the retirement community questioned whether police overreacted. "There was no need to shoot it like they did," said one resident.[182]

Another example concerns a new animal antibiotic to treat a pneumonia-like disease in cattle. The drug, cefquinome, belongs to a class of powerful antibiotics that are among the few choices for defense against several serious human infections. The American Medical Association fears that giving the drug to animals would speed the development of resistant strains, which could spread to people. However, Carl Johnson, director of product development for the pharmaceutical company seeking to market cefquinome, says, "There is reasonable certainty of no harm to public health."[183]

ANIMAL RIGHTS PROTESTS

Animal rights protests have turned more violent in recent years. In 2008 two research scientists at University of California-Santa Cruz became targets of firebombs. Santa Cruz police labeled the incidents as "acts of domestic terrorism" because one bombing required hospitalization of a family member, and the other destroyed a car belonging to a researcher. [184]

One animal rights activist, Daniel Andreas San Diego, has been added to the FBI's "Most Wanted Terrorists" list for the 2003 bombings of two Bay Area biotechnology companies. This is considered significant because it equates animal rights extremists with people who terrorize nations. The FBI said San Diego is "as great a threat to the peace and security of the United States as any foreign terrorist."[185]

Because of the rise in violence among animal rights protesters, the Food and Drug Administration has encouraged companies to find ways to assess their products without animal experimentation. Animal researchers say they would like to, but it is easier said than done. So far they have been unable to find few practical alternatives to gauge the safety and usefulness of products. However, scientists are making concerted efforts to find new test methods and are hopeful that they will reach that goal over the next several decades.[186]

MEDIA COVERAGE OF ANIMALS

While controversy rages over animal welfare, media are giving increasing coverage to animals as news items as well as "human interest" stories.

One story reported that lifeguards in Long Beach, California, responded to an emergency call to rescue a baby Caspian tern that was found drowning in a harbor. Tourists on a nearby boat cheered when lifeguards scooped up the bird from the water and took it to a local bird center. [187]

Another story concerned pack animals being rescued after falling into a canyon: "The horse was injured in the fall, and a small group of vets and others spent the night in the canyon with the animals… Early Saturday rescue workers hoisted the donkey and the mules up the side of the canyon. A helicopter airlifted the injured horse a few miles for treatment."[188]

A half-page spread in *The Washington Post* featured an animal Birthing Center at the Maryland State Fair. With carefully timed breeding, fairgoers could watch farm animals being born every Saturday and Sunday during the fair. "And on Labor Day, of course."[189] A telephone tape recording supplied information as to which cow or sow was due when. Describing one birth, the article said a veterinarian reached inside a cow, wrapped a pair of chains around the calf's front legs, and started pulling. "A nose came out, then a tongue darted around. The calf tumbled out, black and white and gangly. The crowd—several hundred strong—cheered."[190]

Associated Press covered the story of new tracking equipment for tiny birds that allows scientists to follow their migration patterns, something previously done only with large birds such as geese. A surprising finding was that little songbirds like purple martins or wood thrushes cover more than 300 miles a day on their migrations, rather than the previously estimated 90 miles per day.[191]

These animal stories, though relatively minor in overall importance, are capturing human interest.

PETS

Even more media coverage—considerably more—is given to pets. From minor stories such as one on the world's tallest dog[192] to a Public Broadcasting System documentary on the "Evolution of friendship between humans and animals,"[193] to the mega-business of catering to dogs and other pets,[194] to regular pet columnists and a regular special section on pets,[195] newspapers today include a raft of stories about pets.

Up until recently, household pets were seldom mentioned in news items about home fires. Yet today it is not unusual to read "Firefighters were also able to safely remove two dogs, two birds and a snake" or to see a headline that mentions pets first, "Pets, family escape bedroom blaze."[196]

Sometimes pets move to center stage. After a headline, "Firefighters rescue dog from fire that ruins house," the news item included "The first crew went in with water hoses [to search for people] and found a 'very affectionate' but frightened dog in a bedroom. It appeared to be a terrier... Four people had escaped from the house before or during the fire."[197]

In August/September 2007, a special supplement to the *San Jose Mercury News* ran a cover story that featured "The Pet Effect: How the creatures who live with us boost our well-being in so many ways."[198] Given that more households in the United States have pets than children, this attention to pets is not surprising.[199] A 2007-2008 National Pet Owners Survey showed that 63 percent of United States households own a pet—approximately 71.1 million homes.[200] In addition to boosting our general well-being, interacting with a pet "can actually lower blood pressure, lighten depression, alleviate asthma, enhance self-esteem and even decrease the risk of heart attack."[201] Until recently, however, these advantages were underestimated or unrecognized.[202]

Some people will recall seeing a video on YouTube of Snowball, a cockatoo that bobs his head and kicks to the rhythm of music—especially to The Backstreet Boys. Snowball enabled scientists to document for the first time that some animals actually "dance" to a musical beat, which supports a theory for why the human brain is wired for dancing. Some animals actually feel the beat of music they hear and have the ability to mimic those sounds. The brain circuitry for that ability is precisely what lets people learn to talk—and dance or tap their toes to music. The video of Snowball bobbing and kicking has been viewed on YouTube more than two million times since it was posted in 2007.[203]

Despite Snowball's wide publicity, chickens are the chic new pets in the United States. A resurgence of keeping chickens in the backyard—and in some city condos—has swept the country, as chickens are no longer relegated only to rural settings. Many United States cities permit—or are being hounded to permit—homeowners to have pet hens in their backyards. "Chickens are America's cool new pet," said Dave Belanger, publisher of the magazine *Backyard Poultry*. The publication has a bi-monthly print run of 100,000, five or six times the number of subscriptions originally anticipated.[204]

With an increase in diversity and numbers of household pets, veterinarians are seeing more rodents and reptiles coming for office visits, along with chickens and exotic birds like Snowball. And, of course, dogs and cats.[205]

Dogs and Cats

Humanity drawing closer to nature

Dogs and cats still head the list of pets, with households averaging 1.7 dogs per dog household, and 2.3 cats per cat household. What is most striking, however, is not the numbers, but the changed relationship between humans and their pets. Dogs used to be considered "Man's best friend," but today they are "members of the family." In fact, "people" names have become popular for pets, overtaking the popularity of Fido, Snoopy, or Lassie. Max is the most popular name for both dogs and cats, and Lucy and Bella make both lists of names. Most telling is the fact that the top ten dog names are also names for people.[206]

This shift in relationship is borne out in legislation in some parts of the country, where reference to those who have pets is being changed from "owner" to "guardian."[207] Substantiating the closer relationship between humans and their pets, an Associated Press-Petside.com poll found that 67 percent of pet owners say they understand their pets' barks, purrs, and other sounds. More women than men make such claims, as well as older and lower-income people.[208]

With their new status as family members, dogs now have special advocates to pave the way for their freedom and rights. "Guardians" have been successful in lobbying for dog parks, often carved from territory for human parks, so dogs can run about off-leash within a fenced-in area. The new push for Max's freedom is allowing him to roam freely on human parklands and fields early in the morning.[209] New regulations such as microchipping and sterilizing dangerous animals, spaying and neutering loose pit bulls, and limiting the number of hours a day a dog can be chained in one place have also been put into effect.[210]

Effects of Economic Downturn

One in seven pet owners said they were forced to make cuts in spending on their pets during the recession,[211] but some seniors have bridged the budget gap by feeding their own meals to their pets instead of themselves. Other seniors have had to make the wrenching choice of paying for medication and food for themselves or food for their pets. Meals on Wheels responded to this repeated scenario by including donated pet food in its deliveries.[212]

Mickey Rourke movingly summed up the situation of many seniors in his acceptance speech for a Golden Globe Award as best actor in "The Wrestler". He thanked the dogs in his life, ending with, "Sometimes when a man's alone, all you got is your dog."[213]

The American Society for the Prevention of Cruelty to Animals estimated between 500,000 and one million cats and dogs in the United States were at risk of becoming homeless as a result of the 2008 downturn in the economy.[214] Many pets were dumped at shelters in areas with too few would-be owners. Pilots N Paws, a volunteer group of private pilots, stepped in to help. They transported pets—not only dogs and cats, but also snakes, lizards, chickens, and pigs—from overwhelmed shelters to communities where they would stand a better chance of adoption, often those with a higher median income.[215]

Pampering pets

At the same time, Americans were spending more than 43 billion dollars for goods and services for their pets, according to Pet Sitters International and the American Pet Products Association. One of many pet services that spread like wildfire is pet sitting.[216] Canine day care chains have been popping up all over the country. One of these, Camp Bow Wow, became one of the fastest-growing businesses in the pet industry. Dogs come to play during the day, or board while their owners—oops, guardians—are on vacation.[217]

Some lucky dogs get to play and sleep and eat in more upscale environments, such as hotels. Wag Hotel in San Francisco offers 239 rooms and suites for dogs, plus 20 two-story condos for cats. Rooms include air-filtration system, closed circuit TV monitoring, a 10,000-square-foot rooftop dog park, and industrial kitchen for food preparation.[218] Overnight rates range from $30-$85 a day, including premium bed, plasma TV, sofa, painting and classical music—and play groups for all. If more pampering is wanted, the hotel offers blueberry facials, massages, full grooming services, and an indoor swimming pool.[219]

Ritu Raj, owner of Wag Hotels in Sacramento and San Francisco, pointed out how much closer the relationship between people and their pets has become, and therefore the demand for more pampering: "In the last three or four years, an animal that was a good friend or a guard dog has now become a member of our family," he said.[220]

Other entrepreneurs have incorporated pampering services for dogs into the facilities of people hotels. Although pet-friendly hotels have been popular for several years, they are now climbing another rung on the upscale ladder for dogs.[221] The Cypress Hotel in Cupertino, California, sends out a welcome letter to arriving pets, and provides beds and bowls on request. Loews Hotels offer a learning program, where dogs can take singing lessons and cut a CD, take a surfing lesson (more than 500 dogs have taken advantage of this), or go on an off-leash guided hike.[222]

The Benjamin Hotel in New York provides bathrobes for their canine guests, a choice of orthopedic beds, and a consultation with a pet psychic. At the Ritz-Carlton Sarasota, dogs can enjoy massage therapy, choosing between therapeutic Swedish massage to full-body relaxation, for $130 an hour.[223]

Vacations

Times have fast-forwarded. In the mid-nineties it was nearly impossible to find a place that allowed pets to stay overnight. "Now you'd have a difficult time finding a hotel that *doesn't* accept the family dog or cat. In fact, the competition to lure guests and their pets has almost become a dogfight as hotels try to one-up each other."[224]

Chain stores such as PetSmart are also getting a share of the pie. In their hotel rooms dogs can lounge on hypoallergenic lambskin blankets, watch videos of "Lady and the Tramp" and "101 Dalmatians" on their own TV, and snack on lactose-free, fat-free ice cream. Because pet services are twice as profitable as selling pet toys and food, PetSmart has set a goal of opening 435 PetsHotels, a sevenfold increase from its current 62 locations.[225]

Dog guardians on business in New York might want to consider staying over for the weekend— and flying Max in to join her. [NOTE: As of April 2021, the Pet Airways website indicates that the airline plans to resume flights after the COVID-19 pandemic, hopefully mid-2022.] The Big Apple was named the pet-friendliest destination of 2008 by the magazine, *Animal Fair*. Not only will Max be pampered at hotels, but he can also be treated to "dining at canine-cuisine restaurants."[226] And how to get Max there? Pet Airways has aircraft designed expressly for the purpose of transporting pets all around the country. Because their aircraft have no passenger seats, there is room for 50 dog and cat carriers that are checked every 15 minutes by an attendant.[227]

Staycations

Fun abounds for dogs and guardians who prefer staying home, too. Social groups for dogs and their guardians are springing up everywhere. One group called Society Dog enjoys outings together, such as riding on a steam train, followed by a barbecue with live music; sharing "Yappy Hour"; Canine Christmas Karaoke; and "Whine Tasting." They also promote responsible dog ownership and help pave the way to increase the number of eating establishments that allow dogs on the patio. [228]

Even if restaurants are not responsive, bakeries such as Five Paw Bakeries in California's Silicon Valley cater to pooches' culinary tastes. Their bakers use human-grade ingredients in cookies, cakes, and pastries for dogs. Conscious of healthy eating, the pastries do not contain salt, sugar, chemicals, artificial colors, or preservatives, and carob is substituted for chocolate. Their popular peanut butter bones sell for fifty cents each, and bone-shaped "Oreo" sandwiches, which are carob cookie sandwiches filled with cream cheese, cost one dollar. They even sell soft treats for dogs with teeth problems, and Allergy Stars for dogs allergic to wheat flour. Cakes are ordered for birthdays and graduations from obedience school, plus an occasional cake for a dog wedding. For birthday parties celebrated at the bakery, customers are, of course, encouraged to take home leftover cake in doggy bags.[229]

Boutique items are for sale in all Five Paw Bakeries, and they offer pet CPR and first aid classes through Adult Education programs. Paul Callary, founder of the bakeries, grew up in a home in Scranton, Pennsylvania, where the first slice of roast—not the leftovers—was given to the dog. "These are family members," he said.[230]

Dog-less people

Some people would like to have a dog, but for a variety of reasons cannot care for one full-time. No problem. They can now satisfy their desire by buying into "shared pet ownership," based on the model of a vacation time-share or a gym membership. In other words, a company such as FlexPets contracts out dogs—only those with social temperaments—by the day. Ideally, no more than two or three guardian-members share each dog. Part-time dogs can be had for an annual fee of $99.95, a monthly payment of $49.95, and a per-visit charge of $39.95 a day. Aspen Animal Shelter in Colorado goes a step farther, allowing residents and tourists to take dogs out for a few hours or overnight for free.[231]

The United States pet industry expanded 36 percent to $45 billion between 2000 and 2006. In fact, pet-item sales and services have the second-fastest growth for United States retailers after consumer electronics, according to the American Pet Products Manufacturers Association.[232]

Pets and Cyberspace

Dogs and cats entered into cyberspace along with their guardians, as content-focused, social- networking Web sites became a growing trend. Many dogs and cats have Facebook accounts and followers in Twitter. They now have their own site, Doggyspace.com, which is "a crossbreed between MySpace and YouTube." Dog guardians from all over the world create profiles of their dogs, get advice, and share photos and videos with each other. Those who live close to one another arrange play dates for their dogs, and the dogs exchange messages with other doggy "friends."[233]

"One profile is for a chocolate Labrador retriever named Guinness, who said her mom 'couldn't resist naming me after her favorite beverage' and said she is shy around other dogs and scared of small, furry creatures because she lives with a 'VERY MEAN CAT.' Postings on Guinness' profile include a message from Chico, a Chihuahua mix who offered to help with the shyness problem."[234]

Max Goes Green

The green trend, too, has enveloped the world of dogs and cats. After the massive recall of tainted pet food in 2007, customer demand for holistic food or pet food with human grade ingredients suddenly mushroomed. "The lifestyles of the animals are starting to parallel the lifestyles of the humans," said Sam Blackford, owner of a feed and pet supply store. Pet stores now sell Earth-friendly toys, all natural pet bedding, and completely organic, biodegradable bedding for hamsters and gerbils. They even carry a line called "Deli Fresh," refrigerated meals that look like stew.[235]

An ad in the April 2008 issue of *San Francisco* magazine featured "Petchitecture Goes Green," a benefit for Pets Are Wonderful Support (PAWS), held at the posh St. Francis Hotel in San Francisco. It lured supporters with "a night of cocktails, culinary delights, and live and silent auctions where leading architects and designers use the best in renewable resources to create custom pet habitats that are yours for the bidding. Dogs on leashes are welcome (accompanied by well-mannered humans, of course)."

Health Issues

Unfortunately, an unhealthy human trend has invaded the dog world: obesity. Veterinarians say it has become an epidemic and appears to be increasing in this country. Five percent of dogs in the United States are obese, and another 20-30 percent are overweight.

Veterinarians place most of the blame for it on humans. "People are treating their dogs like children. They overindulge them, they get them heavy," said Hal Taylor III, a veterinarian in Columbus, Ohio. He says obesity is one of the biggest health issues dogs face.[236]

In addressing the issue, the Food and Drug Administration (FDA) has approved the first prescription drug to treat obesity in dogs. Pfizer, maker of the drug, called Slentrol, estimates that four million American dogs are obese. In clinical studies of the drug, dogs on Slentrol lost about three percent of their weight in a month, without changing their diets.[237]

Another drug called Palladia was the first cancer drug to be approved by the FDA for the treatment of dogs. In clinical studies, it shrunk mast-cell tumors, the second most common form of cancer in dogs. The tumors usually appear as lumps on the skin but often spread elsewhere. [238]

Although only one percent of pets in the United States are covered by health insurance, the number is expected to increase, as CAT scans, MRI's and chemotherapy have made veterinary care very costly. The largest pet insurer in the United States, Veterinary Pet Insurance, has about 465,000 pets enrolled. Americans already spend about $9.8 billion a year on veterinary services, and billions more on health supplies and over the counter drugs for pets.[239]

With pets being treated like children rather than possessions, more and more people are making provisions for their pets in their wills. Between

12 and 27 percent of people provide for their pets in estate planning, which often includes a "pet trust."[240]

Tender Loving Care, a program at University of California-Davis, takes a different approach. They arrange for private adoptions of pets—even horses—after the death of their humans. Richard Timmins, a veterinarian at the University said, "Most people today consider their pets part of the family." This is substantiated by studies showing that two-thirds of pet owners consider their pets as family members, and 37 percent carry pictures of them in their wallets. [241]

Is soulf once again choosing a path of least resistance to draw humanity closer to the natural world?

For Reflection:

1. ....

   ....

   ....

2. ....

   ....

   ....

3. ....

   ....

   ....

CHAPTER 8

THE NATURAL WORLD: PLANETARY AND HUMAN HEALTH

**"We cannot have well humans on a sick planet…
Human health is derivative. Planetary health is primary."**
—*Brian Swimme and Thomas Berry*

As we have already seen, humanity has struck an imbalance with the environment at the point of global warming, so now humanity must scramble to help the universal body as it struggles to heal itself.

The disease that needs healing does not stop there, however. Humanity is experiencing a boomerang effect in the form of human health hazards from its actions since the time of the Industrial Revolution. When the environment is sick, so are we, as we are inextricably a part of the world in which we live. There is no escape.

Consistent with the way the universe works, disease and good health are both growing at the same time. Whatever affects the world around us affects us, and vice versa. Physical and mental problems are inseparable. Our human task is to work with the real situation as holistically and effectively as possible in order to foster planetary health.

HAZARDS TO ENVIRONMENTAL AND HUMAN HEALTH

Chemicals

In the past few decades' environmentalists have been biomonitoring chemical health hazards, which cause cancer, lung diseases, miscarriages and other health-related problems in humans, as well as foster a sick environment.

Ground water often contains dangerous chemicals that have leached into the soil from contaminants poured on the ground or into drains, sewers, or creek beds. Carbon dioxide is a major player in terms of air pollution, though other chemicals in smaller amounts also contribute to dis-ease of the air, the very same air we breathe to sustain life.[242]

One large arena for biomonitoring is the ocean, which carries hazardous chemicals due to tanker spills, ocean dumping, or shipwrecks. The shipping industry exacerbates the situation when goods are delivered from port to port around the globe. Carbon dioxide emissions from international shipping, now around four to five percent of the global total, is estimated to rise to about 72 percent by 2020 if the current rate of emissions continues. In addition, ships take on ballast water in one place and discharge it at the next port of call, contaminating foreign ports with non-native species that damage the aquatic ecosystems. All this has contributed to a huge garbage dump twice the size of Texas that swirls around the Pacific Ocean, harming sea life and causing them to become extinct at a faster rate than other living species.

Urban Living

Another hazard to the environment is urban sprawl. When humanity spreads itself over vast areas of land, it ruins natural systems and displaces species that are needed to keep Earth balanced and healthy. Many of the displaced species are becoming extinct, diminishing natural diversity and sickening the planet.

Yet living in large city clusters, which most of humanity is already doing, often leads to increased poverty, religious extremism, as well as spread of disease. Unless we give serious attention to addressing the needs of urban populations, these hazards could be exacerbated.[243]

A University of California-Irvine study shows that suburban living is better for people's social lives than city dwelling. Residents become friendlier in less-crowded neighborhoods.[244]

Addressing public health concerns

Former governor Arnold Schwarzenegger addressed environmental/human health concerns on a large scale. Aware of potential health hazards within his state, he planned as early as 2006 for a major epidemic or bioterrorist attack by instituting a Department of Public Health in California.[245] Other states and the federal government have followed suit since then.

OBESITY

Beginning in the early 1960's, we as a nation gradually started gaining weight until our stomachs suddenly ballooned in the 1980's. In just ten years Americans had collectively gained more than a billion pounds. "If this was about tuberculosis, it would be called an epidemic."[246]

Food and Drink

Cost

A contributing factor to the obesity epidemic is that food—especially fattening foods—became cheaper relative to other commodities. This affected people just above the poverty level most because the cheapest food is the unhealthiest.

Portions

One of the greatest culprits in fostering obesity has been the increasing size of "one serving." Newer editions of *Joy of Cooking* include identical recipes from previous editions, but the predicted number of servings has been lowered. Jumbo-size boxes of popcorn are promoted at movie theaters, while bagels have grown over the years from 140 calories to 350 calories each.

This has taken root because people judge food amounts on external cues, namely units. They will not buy two boxes of popcorn because that seems greedy, but they will buy a jumbo-size since it is "just one." The same is true for fries, or Cokes, or hamburgers. If it is packaged as one, people will buy it and eat it—the larger the better for our increasingly "elastic" appetite. McDonald's sodas have, accordingly, grown from the original 8 ounces to a 16-ounce "small" soda and a 32- ounce (300 calories) large soda.[247]

Overweight and malnourished

Unlike earlier days of our history, today a person can be both overweight and malnourished. Whereas soft drinks used to be reserved for special occasions, they now comprise seven percent of the average American's diet. "If, instead of sweetened beverages, the average American drank water… he or she would weigh fifteen pounds less," calculates Eric Finkelstein, a health economist at a research institute in North Carolina.

Hypereating

Fat, sugar, and salt are the crucial ingredients for what has become known in the food industry as "eatertainment," which fosters "conditioned hypereating." David A. Kessler, author of *The End of Overeating*, said: "Conditioned hypereating works the same way as other 'stimulus response' disorders in which reward is involved, such as compulsive gambling and substance abuse."[248]

Contributing to over-eating are so-called "functional foods," foods dressed up with healthy- sounding additives, such as vitamins, folic acid, and Omega-3 fatty acids. The SmartChoice check-mark compounds the problem when it marks even such "nutritional culprits" as Fruit Loops with their seal of approval. Consequently, people are consuming too much of certain nutrients, plus too many calories and fats. Functional foods now account for about 5 percent of the U.S. food market.[249]

Effects in Everyday Life

Children

The epidemic rate is high in young children, especially boys of immigrant families. Thirty-four percent of kindergarten-age immigrant boys are obese or overweight, compared with 25 percent of the sons of native-born Americans. By eighth grade, those numbers swell to 49 percent for immigrant boys and 33 percent among natives. Girls show no similar discrepancy.[250]

Although the obesity rate in children and teens has tripled since 1980, we lived in denial until it reached epidemic proportions. Michael Moore's pointedly revealing movie, "Super-sized Me," may have brought the whole issue to a head, as he laid out a strong case for the central role fast food plays in the obesity epidemic. At that point the elephant in the room could no longer be denied.[251]

Other areas of society

The United States military reported that 40 percent of young women and 25 percent of young men weigh too much to enlist. Hospitals have had to buy special wheel chairs and operating tables to accommodate the obese; revolving doors have had to be to be widened; undertakers now offer triple-wide coffins; and airlines fork over an extra quarter of a billion dollars annually for jet fuel because of the added weight.[252]

Obesity also affects our overall economy and health-care system. It is estimated that the extra pounds carried by Americans add 90 billion dollars a year to the country's medical spending.

"Obesity is inescapably confirming itself as one of the biggest drains" on national health-care budgets worldwide.[253]

Over-population

As the number of humans on Earth passes the 7 billion mark, obesity in the form of over- population is taking a heavy toll. The runaway population growth plays a crucial role in both societal and natural problems: human health, food, clean water, encroachment on natural habitats through urban sprawl, climate disruption leading to loss of biodiversity, increasing risk of pandemics, encroachment on natural habitats through urban sprawl etc.

**"Population and consumption are no more
separable in producing environmental damage
than the length and width of a rectangle can be
separated in producing its area—both are equally important."**
—*Paul Ehrlich, population biologist*

Other Nations

Yes, worldwide. It may not be just coincidental that obesity has spread to other nations. U.S. corporations have been investing 55 billion dollars a year in food-processing and distribution facilities abroad. In fact, the point has been reached where the proportion of overweight adults is higher in Cyprus, the Czech Republic, Finland, Germany, Greece, Malta, and Slovakia than in the U.S., and obesity is on the rise in Asia, Africa, and South America.[254]

Obesity and Lack of Activity

Pediatricians have become especially alarmed by the obesity epidemic. They say, in addition to making changes in food consumption, we must raise the activity level of children, as statistics show that youths are more sedentary and unhealthy than ever.[255] Just as dark energy forces dark matter to "move outward" to keep the galaxy from getting too fat, parents are advised to turn off the TV and send their kids outside.

For many children, the virtual world is more familiar than the natural one. Children can recognize hundreds of TV commercials, but they know almost nothing about the world that surrounds them. If they go outdoors, they do not know what to do unless an activity has been scheduled for them.

Between 1997 and 2003 there was a decline of fifty percent in the proportion of children aged nine to twelve who spent time in outside activities (organized sports not included). What engages them for six and one-half hours a day are video games, computers, texting, music, and other electronic media—with many of them multi-tasking.[256]

Raising "indoor children" may have long-term consequences that will affect their emotional well-being, physical health, learning abilities, and environmental consciousness. encroachment on natural habitats through urban sprawl Richard Louv, author of *Last Child in the Woods*, said that indoor kids are more prone to obesity, depression, attention disorders, stress and "nature deficit disorder," all of which are major concerns regarding children and youth today.[257]

Another author and associate professor of psychiatry at Harvard, John Ratey, noted that researchers have studied the powerful connections between exercise and improved memory, academic performance and executive functioning. He said, "As our kids mature, improving their ability to remain focused for learning is critical; exercise has a role. As our schedules create more stress, achieving mental calmness is needed; exercise has a role."[258]

But it is not an easy task in this day and age to get kids to put aside their mesmerizing electronic gadgets and go outside to make their own fun. Older physical education teachers are seeing the effects of that difficulty in their classes, compared with a few years ago. They say a higher percentage of children today have less ability in the most basic physical skills. Football coaches, too, have noted this, reporting that children are not ready to play football. They connect their shrinking player pools with childhood inactivity.[259]

Environmentalists are quick to agree and chime in with suggestions to lure children outdoors. They have observed how disconnected children have become from their relationship to nature and a sense of place. Without children feeling that they belong to our home planet and to the universe as a whole, the future of both environmental and human health is endangered.

Other Factors

Although curbing food intake and spending time outside are widely recognized as important factors in addressing the obesity epidemic, we know that even more is needed. Agricultural policy must be revised, as it fosters poor health in our population. "The food system promotes high pesticides and overuse of antibiotics, which… [is] promoting antibiotic resistance," said the food coordinator for Health Care Without Harm.[260] In recognition of this fact, the 2007 Organizing Committee for the Beijing Olympics provided athletes with organic meat, fearing that regular meat could lead to false-positive results in anti-doping tests.

Of course, other factors contribute to the problem, too. "One in ten people carry a common genetic variation that may make it particularly tough for them to keep their weight down."[261] In preschoolers, obesity may be largely due to iron deficiency, caused by not weaning them and feeding them iron-rich foods.[262]

Addressing Obesity

Efforts are being made to counteract destructive patterns leading to obesity. Farmers' markets have doubled in number in the last decade, and planting backyard gardens or participating in community gardens has become a trend.[263] Michelle Obama contributed greatly to raising awareness of healthy eating when she developed an organic garden at the White House. Many children plant and tend gardens at school, while learning the benefits of eating healthy foods. Hospitals, too, are promoting good health with more appealing menus that include locally- produced organic foods for in-patients, staff, administrators, and their cafeterias for the general public. An obstetrician at Kaiser Permanente Hospitals started a movement to put farmers' markets outside thirty Kaiser hospitals. Some hospitals in Northern California are even sprouting on-site organic gardens and raising free-range chickens.[264]

Clearly we are becoming wiser about good health and are recognizing the role healthy eating plays in both environmental and human health.

MENTAL HEALTH

An integral part of the health picture is mental health. Whatever is going on physically in a person is reflected in the person's psychological health, and vice versa. Though the two are inextricably woven together, it is only during the past few years that insurance companies have been required to give equal coverage for mental and physical illnesses. Dr. Steven E. Hyman, former director of the National Institute of Mental Health, has said it is impossible to justify insurance discrimination when scientific evidence overwhelmingly shows that "mental illnesses represent real diseases of the brain."[265]

Psychiatric Disorders

Role of stress

A survey conducted in 2001-2002[266] showed a stunningly high rate of psychiatric disorders in young adults, precipitated by stress. One-half of the individuals surveyed met the criteria for at least one psychiatric disorder, including substance abuse, nicotine addiction, personality disorders or other mental-health conditions. According to the survey, the most common disorder among college students was alcohol abuse, whereas personality disorder and nicotine dependence were the most frequent disorders among those not attending college.[267]

Mahjong epilepsy

Mahjong epilepsy is a specific condition induced, surprisingly, by the game itself, not by the stress or exhaustion associated with it. In fact, most patients never suffer seizures other than when playing mahjong.[268]

Bipolar disorder

Bipolar disorder, characterized by an excess of energy with severe mood swings between depression and mania, affects about two percent of American adults and one percent of children. Among adults, the disorder occurs mostly in women, but among children nearly two-thirds are boys.

Bipolar children usually become depressed rather than manic, making the disorder more common among children than even clinical depression. Adding to the distress of some, half of bipolar children have other mental difficulties as well, most often Attention Deficit Disorder. [269]

Autism and ADD/ADHD in children

The greatly increased pace and complexity of living today is taking its toll in the lives of many children (mostly boys) in the form of autism, Attention Deficit Disorder (ADD) and Attention Deficit Hyperactivity Disorder [ADHD].

Autism affects over four percent of today's children in the United States and is growing each year, and ADD/ADHD affects up to 12 percent. The brains of these children may have genetically enlarged too quickly and gone out of control, manifesting in these different forms. In some cases, regulatory therapy may be needed to help them grow into their prematurely-large brains.

Inattention, hyperactivity, and impulsiveness characterize typical ADHD behavior. Although many children exhibit such behavior occasionally, the behavior is constant in those with ADHD. [270]

It is interesting to note that inattention, hyperactivity and impulsiveness are also characteristic of soulf. Perhaps they are suffering a severe case of living with soulf.

Pathological gaming

Most young people play electronic games, but some become addicted to them. When this happens, it has a devastating effect on their lives. Pathological gamers do worse in school, lie about how much they play, struggle unsuccessfully when they try to cut back, and spend increasing amounts of time and money on video games to feel the same level of excitement.[271]

Although adults as well as youths suffer many of the same symptoms, they do not have true ADD and are not pathological gamers. Psychiatrist Edward M. Hallowell calls their situation "a severe case of modern life," noting the upsurge since the mid-1990's of people being disturbed, distracted, disorganized, overbooked, and suffering memory loss from data overload. People do everything faster because speed is fun, rivets your attention, and "blasts you out of boredom." He sums up life today when he writes:

> "Today's world, with its energy, excitement, and excess, its novelty, chaos and confusion, its dust storms of data, its creative spirit and irreverence, its speed and its incoherence, looks much like another world I know well: the world of attention deficit disorder or ADD."[272] (And perhaps the world of soulf as well.)

Compulsive buying

Compulsive buying is considered by some scientists to be a mental disorder. They say it is really no different than addiction to gambling or sex. A Stanford University study showed that about one in twenty Americans—men and women—are compulsive buyers, most of whom are young with lower incomes, and are four times less likely to pay off credit card balances in full. Men shop mostly for tools, electronic gadgets, books and CD's, whereas women overspend on clothes, jewelry, makeup, craft paraphernalia and items for the home. Shopping addicts of both genders are so obsessed that they may go deeply into debt, wind up divorced, or even consider suicide.[273]

Depression

Perhaps the greatest mental problem of our time is depression, which runs rampant in various forms throughout our society today. Most disturbing is its effect on young people. In California alone, 8.5 percent of high school sophomores attempt suicide. Three California students from the same (upscale) high school committed copycat suicides at the same railroad crossing in a three- month period, despite many preventative measures taken by the school and city in which they took place.[274]

Search for Answers

Ecotherapy

Some psychotherapists believe that much depression and anxiety throughout our society today stem largely from our lack of connection with the Earth. They are convinced that "ecotherapy" is needed to address the problem.

Craig Chalquist and Linda Buzzell have edited a book of essays called *Ecotherapy: Healing with Nature in Mind*. The writings urge therapists to face environmental concerns and disasters in therapy sessions, as "eco-anxiety" over environmental catastrophe underlies much of the depression people are experiencing. An equally important element for healing, which is also highlighted in the book, is forming a deeper connection with the Earth and nature. As people draw closer to nature and see themselves as an integral part of life, healing can take place.

Buzzell, a marriage and family therapist, said the fact "that we're living so unnaturally and so disconnected to nature is, I believe, the root of depression and anxiety for many people that are flooding into doctors' offices right now… The nature connection is essential to human health."[275]

Pills

Even as addictive behavior is breaking out like flu throughout our society, scientists are struggling to find new solutions for addressing it. For some time they had hopes that new pills would help people quit smoking, lose weight, and perhaps curb other tough addictions like alcohol and cocaine. However, the pills seemed to raise the risk of depression and suicide. Since addictions and depression often go hand-in-hand, restricting the drugs' use deprives the very people who need help the most.[276]

Vaccines

Another approach to addictions may prove more successful. Vaccines to end nicotine and cocaine addiction are in process of development by the National Institute on Drug Abuse. These new vaccines construct antibodies that lock onto nicotine and cocaine molecules, preventing them from reaching the brain. This diminishes the pleasure normally derived from drug use, thereby decreasing desire for the drug.

Meanwhile, a major obesity vaccine trial is underway in Switzerland. In this study, antibodies attach to the hunger protein, preventing it from reaching the brain and stimulating appetite.

Healthy ways of working with addictive behavior are much needed, as the problem appears in many different forms and is widespread. In the United States there are 50 million cigarette smokers, 5 million drug addicts, 60 million obese adults and 9 million overweight youngsters between the ages of 6 and 19. The one thing they all have in common is a desire to quit, but they cannot.[277]

GENERAL HEALTH AND HEALING PRACTICES

Alternative Healing

Besides traditional Western medicine, demand for alternative healing practices is on the rise. More than one-third of American adults use alternative medicine, including massage therapists, acupuncturists, chiropractors, and herbal remedies, as well as meditation and yoga. These practices consume about one-quarter of what is spent on visits to mainstream physicians.[278]

In response to the demand, our nation's first degree-program in herbalism is now being offered at Minneapolis Community and Technical College. This two-year clinical program uses medicinal plants to promote healing, though this is not unique. A number of health practices subscribe to a similar mode of thinking.

Dr. Karen Lawson, who teaches a course on shamanism at the Center for Spirituality and Healing at the University of Minnesota, says many complementary practices "have core philosophies that acknowledge the role of spirit or unifying energy or life that explains how these things are connected… It's based on the understanding that all things are alive, all things are connected, all things are impacted by worlds both seen and unseen."[279]

Human Biological Needs

We Americans tend to downplay our biological needs as animals, seeing them as signs of weakness. For instance, unless illness is serious, most people in the United States try to overlook it. Almost everyone admits to having gone to work when feeling sick. Most report that the reason is either feeling guilty for calling in sick or their workload is too heavy for them not to work. [280]

Another biological need, sleep, is also underplayed. Sleep problems have reached almost epidemic proportions, as our culture lives actively 24/7, overlooking the importance of nighttime and sleep. Round-the-clock television, texting, open stores, the Internet, and pressure to fit more work and play into every day are large contributors to our sleep disorders. Yet sleep deprivation is seen as a badge of honor.

The biological need for sleep cannot be sidestepped, but medical research has revealed new ways of dealing with conditions like sleep apnea, as well as complex sleep disorders that can raise the risk of hypertension and stroke.[281] At the same time research has uncovered other less-critical findings. For example, they have found that taking in familiar fragrances during sleep helps performance on memory tests by almost fifteen percent.[282]

Daylight Savings

Even seemingly insignificant happenings such as the shift in the fall from daylight savings time to natural time helps our health. A five percent drop in heart attack deaths and hospitalizations occurs the day after clocks are reset each year to standard time, according to the New England Journal of Medicine. Its counterpart, the onset of daylight savings time in the spring, appears to increase the risk of heart attacks.

Use of E-mail

For routine health matters, such as scheduling a doctor's appointment or getting a prescription refill, most Americans like the convenience of e-mail. Some insurance companies are trying to build on that idea by compensating doctors for making virtual house calls via the Internet. Doctors, however, are reluctant. They fear that communicating with patients electronically will lead to a deluge of e-mails.

Despite their fear, most studies show that patients do not abuse e-mail. One health care study made by Kaiser Permanente found that patients who used its secure Web system were seven to ten percent less likely to schedule an office visit. They also made 14 percent fewer phone calls than those who did not use the online services.[283]

Improvement in Human Health

Although new health problems are always rising to the surface, overall we are experiencing gains in understanding and improving human health. For example, for the first time since the U.S. government began compiling records, the rate of cancer has declined.[284]

A possible boost to the improving record is a recently developed "vaccine," a new way of addressing cancer in addition to surgery, chemotherapy, and radiation. Though not truly a vaccine, since it treats the disease rather than preventing it, it uses the body's natural immune system. The "vaccine" has kept a common form of lymphoma from worsening for more than a year.[285]

EVOLUTION IN HUMANITY

Changes are also taking place in the larger picture of humanity as a whole. When agriculture became widespread, it provided the necessary support for increasingly large societies. Researchers examining variants of DNA found that the more the population grew, the faster human genes evolved. Among the fastest-evolving genes are those related to development of the human brain. Today the rate of human evolutionary change has risen to more than 100 times historical levels.[286]

Another change in humanity is our general health and longevity, which greatly surpass those of our ancestors, offering nature more time to evolve the human brain. One of the most striking differences is the change from small, relatively weak and sickly people, to people who are so big and robust that our ancestors almost appear to be from a different strain of humanity. (Recently this has been pushed to the extreme in our becoming a nation of obese people.) Scientists attribute this to a change in human form, like greater heights, longer lives, and different appearance, rather than to genetic change.[287]

Whatever lies behind them, these changes are a boon for the evolution of natural patterning, which requires larger, more complex human brains for ongoing development of consciousness. [288]

For Reflection:

1. ....

   ....

   ....

2. ....

   ....

   ....

3. ....

   ....

   ....

CHAPTER 9

PERSONAL RELATIONSHIPS
PART ONE

Relationship is basic to structuring of the natural world, as we know it. Therefore, it is also a key element in understanding most human endeavors, interactions, and events at all levels—personal, social and corporate. Chapter 9 explores these three levels of relationship as they are being acted out in today's world.

A phenomenon particularly worthy of note is "abstraction," a new component to the complexification of language, which has been happening ever since earliest times of human communication. Basic words and concepts whose meanings have always been "known" unquestionably—mother, father, marriage, family—are now being abstracted back to their roots and called into question.

Does "mother" refer to the woman whose DNA matches that of a particular infant? If so, does that mean that an adoptive mother—or stepmother—is not really a "mother?" Does "father" refer to the hunter, the breadwinner? Where does that leave a woman who may also be a breadwinner, or the *only* breadwinner in the family? Who is the "mother" in a gay family of two men and a child? Or two women and a child? What does "marriage" mean if gender no longer defines it? What defines a "family" when all members are male, or female?

These human questions in the forefront of our society today reflect deeper "living ideas" in soul. We are concerned about these relationships because soulf is concerned. We are "thinkers" for soulf's evolving patterns of relationship.

SEX

A clear indication of the depth of change and turmoil we are experiencing in virtually every sector of society today can be seen in sexual relationships. Expectations we have held for generations around sex and actual sexual relationships are greatly at odds with one another. The gaping distance between expectations and reality has elicited vast amounts of energy—and media coverage—in examining issues connected with sex. Soulf is in the midst of it all.

Our fascination with sex is, of course, as old as sex itself. Yet it was only as recently as the 1950's that the sex life of college students was first studied. What has changed drastically since then is our openness about sex, our "undressing" before the public, as it were. News media no longer blink an eyelash at blowing the whistle on sexual escapades of political figures, writing unabashedly of oral sex, and calling an orgasm an orgasm. Prudishness is "so yesterday."

Abstinence Only

During the George W. Bush administration, the federal government spent $1.3 billion dollars on abstinence-only sex education programs in public schools. Although many experts testified before a House committee that the idea that "one size fits all"[289] does not work, funding for abstinence-only programs persisted for eleven years. By 2006 the teenage birth rate had started rising again.[290]

A study ordered by Congress found no change in the sexual behavior of students in abstinence- only education programs. Students in these programs had similar numbers of sexual partners as those who did not attend the classes, and they first had sex at about the same age (14.9 years) as other students.[291]

Yet abstinence-only persists in the minds of some school authorities. In 2009 a girl whose mother approved her prescription for birth-control pills was suspended from school for two weeks for inadvertently bringing a birth-control pill to school. In comparison, only one week's suspension was required for bringing heroin to school. "Officials told the Washington Post that birth-control pills are particularly objectionable because they countermand the school system's 'abstinence-only' sex education classes."[292]

Sex as Living Reality

Countering this view of sex, society and science have been exploring sex as a living reality.

Librarians

Librarians in Santa Clara County, California, were incensed when, with no notification, the publishers of *Sports Illustrated* failed to send 21,000 public institutions, including theirs, a swimsuit issue[293] that showed a model wearing nothing but an iPod. They said this was an assault on free speech, was paternalistic and patronizing. "It's not their job to decide what we have on our shelves," said Anne Turner, director of the neighboring Santa Cruz County library system. Furthermore, it is pointless, since the images in *Sports Illustrated* are available at any library Internet terminal.[294]

TV

HBO pushed the boundaries of sex in its 2007 fall series, "Tell Me You Love Me," "the most sexually explicit-show to ever air on mainstream TV."[295] The intention of the series was to explore "real intimacy, and sex happens to be a part of real intimacy between people… We're having sex where you're trying to get pregnant, which is not hot," said Ally Walker. [296] It was the most talked-about new series among TV writers at the Television Critics Association press tour in 2007, and DVD's of it became "hot property" in Hollywood even before its first episode aired. "Even by premium cable standards, it's fairly startling."[297]

Scientists

Scientists are looking from an objective stance at the biology of romantic love. Findings show that brain images, hormones, and genetics provide most of our understanding of it, and that "love works chemically in the brain like a drug addiction."[298]

"People kill for love. They die for love," said Helen Fisher, a researcher and professor at Rutgers University. Another researcher at Einstein Medical College added, "The brokenhearted show more evidence of what I'll call craving. Similar to craving the drug cocaine."[299]

Columnist Dennie Hughes' response to a reader's inquiry about sex addicts included thoughts from a psychotherapist, Tina B. Tessina. She asserted that people with true sex addiction become so obsessed with their need for sex they become dysfunctional in everyday living. "The need to have sex is stronger than any of their relationships, their career, their health or their reputation," she says. And addictions are never completely cured.[300]

Sexual behavior

A study examining how sexual behavior before marriage has changed over time showed that nine out of ten Americans—both men and women—have sex before marriage. The study's author, Lawrence Finer[301] said, "Premarital sex is normal behavior for the vast majority of Americans, and has been for decades." In Finer's analysis of more than 38,000 people (mostly women) interviewed in 1982, 1988, 1995 and 2002, 99 percent had had sex by age 44, and 95 percent had done so before marriage. He said the likelihood of Americans having sex before marriage has remained stable since the 1950's. This data "calls into question the federal government's funding of abstinence-only-until-marriage programs for 12- to 29-year-olds."[302]

The strong inner drive toward sex often transcends morality or cultural expectations, even to the point of abusive behavior. One of countless examples—including many well-known, esteemed figures in our society—is that of a former swim coach who started sexually abusing girls who were hoping for a chance at the Olympics. They were all nationally ranked swimmers who relied on him to help them make Team USA and attain Olympic fame. He chose those who were especially vulnerable at the time.[303]

Sex Internationally

Chile

In Chile, youth have been experiencing a sexual awakening in striking contrast to the country's history of being one of Latin America's most sexually conservative nations. Young people are having sex earlier and testing the limits of sexual conduct. Describing a disco bar in Santiago, a reporter[304] wrote, "[It] is a tangle of lips and tongues and hands, all groping and exploring. About 800 teenagers sway and bounce to lyrics imploring them to 'Poncea! Poncea!'—make out with as many people as they can."

Their behavior stems from the Internet. Websites like Fotolog connect young people so they can organize parties drawing as many as 4,500 teenagers. With the explosion of explicit content and social networks on the Internet, societies throughout the world are grappling with this new source of sexual awakening in youth.[305]

Great Britain

One area of Great Britain has an answer to raging teenage hormones. The National Health Service of Sheffield issued "guidance" to schools, encouraging them to suggest alternatives to premarital sex, including masturbation. A leaflet sent to the schools likened health benefits of eating fruits and vegetables, and exercising, to the benefits of masturbating twice a week. A catchy slogan in the leaflet read: "(A)n orgasm a day keeps the doctor away."[306]

Egypt

A furor arose among conservatives in Egypt when the Artificial Virginity Hymen Kit became available through the Website of Gigimo, a Chinese mail-order company.

"The kit allows a bride who is not a virgin to pretend she is on her wedding night. A pouch inserted into the vagina ruptures and leaks a blood-like liquid designed to trick a new husband into believing that his wife is chaste."[307]

Although conservatives condemn the Kit as technology that will promote promiscuity, some Egyptian women see a double standard. One young woman said, "Sex is a right for every woman but unfortunately we started turning to products like these because men—even nonreligious ones who have sex before marriage—wouldn't marry a girl if she's not a virgin."[308]

South Korea

A double standard also exists in South Korea in terms of jail sentences for adultery. A famous actress was convicted of adultery under a law prohibiting extramarital affairs. She was given a suspended eight-month jail term, while her lover received a six-month suspended term. The actress filed a petition to have the adultery ban ruled an unconstitutional invasion of privacy, but the Constitutional Court upheld the ban.[309]

Sex trade

Sex trade is the most pervasive of illicit sex practices worldwide. Each year 800,000 people are trafficked around the world, according to the U.S. State Department. Characteristically, these people are from desperately poor families, who make the easiest prey for traffickers. Many of them have been eking out a living sorting through garbage dumps. When an opportunity arises to go to a city and earn real money, many people jump at the chance. Most are not aware that they are being sold into prostitution, and little do they know the high cost ahead for them in terms of health, shame, and self-esteem.[310]

MARRIAGE

Marriage as a Religious Concept

Nancy D. Polikoff, [311] author of *Beyond (Straight and Gay) Marriage: Valuing All Families under the Law,* makes a compelling argument for marriage becoming solely a religious term and concept, leaving room for many different forms of partnerships between human beings. She cites precedents for doing so throughout our country's history.

For years slaves, interracial couples, and same-sex couples were excluded from marriage, and married women had no separate legal identity. Although much of that has changed, the word "marriage" has not. Since many people consider marriage to be tied to religious doctrine, the argument that marriage be relegated to the religious realm seems logical.

Breaking family law terminology also has precedent. In about a dozen states "divorce" has been replaced by "dissolution," a process regularly associated with the ending of a "partnership." This has by-passed one person being "innocent" and the other "at fault." "Alimony" used to be a sex- specific term, referring to a man's support of his wife after divorce. Some states have switched to using the words "maintenance" and "support," which are gender-neutral and less value-laden, rather than the term "alimony." "Custody" and "visitation" have been abandoned in some states, too, with "parenting time" and "parental responsibility" being substituted. This terminology suggests equal importance of both parents, thus avoiding a win/lose situation.

If "marriage" was solely a religious institution, and "partnership" referred to the commitment that two people make to each other, there would be room for various types of partnerships. People would still be free to speak of being "married" or "divorced," but the shift in thinking would allow fresh air into rigidly defined relationships and would more truly reflect modern ideals.[312]

Opponents of Same-Sex Marriage

Opponents of same-sex marriage also use history as the basis for their viewpoint, but some of those claims are demonstrably untrue.

First, they claim that marriage as the union of one man and one woman goes back thousands of years. Yet polygamy was the most common form of marriage in the first five books of the Old Testament.

Second, they claim that marriage has always been regarded as a sacred relationship in our Judeo- Christian tradition. In fact, the Judeo-Christian tradition did not have a single viewpoint on such matters. Polygamy, divorce and concubines all appear in the Old Testament.

In the New Testament, Jesus broke with older religious traditions by prohibiting divorce for men as well as for women, in addition to challenging the right of a man to take a second wife if the first wife could not bear children. Though Jesus rejected divorce, Christianity did not even sanctify marriage until the year 1215.

Third, they claim that marriage has endured for thousands of years without change. However, in the early 1800's, those years of tradition were overturned when the older generation insisted that young people must choose their own mates on the basis of love rather than to further the economic and political ambitions of their parents.

Another monumental change in marriage was the power of a man over his wife. Until just before the 20th century, a husband legally owned all his wife's property and earnings, along with the right to "correct" her, and even imprison her in the house, for disobedience. It was not until the 1980's that the courts redefined marriage as a union of two people with reciprocal, not complementary, duties.

"Once marriage came to be seen as an institution bringing together two individuals based on mutual affection and equality, without regard to rigidly defined gender roles or the ability to procreate, it is no surprise that gays and lesbians said, 'That now describes our relationships, too, so why can't we marry?'"[313]

GENDER

Homosexuality

Argument over gay marriage raises the inevitable question: Is homosexuality innate or is it a choice? Research on sexual orientation has found common biological traits among gay men, including the likelihood of their being left-handed, being the younger siblings of older brothers, and their having hair that swirls in a counter-clockwise direction. This data and other scientific findings have led to a growing consensus that a person's sexual attractions are largely decided before the person is born, and that sexual orientation is an inborn combination of genetic and environmental factors.[314]

In examining 83 studies on sexual orientation conducted since 1960, the American Psychological Association (APA) reinforced these findings. They repudiated "reparative therapy," urging mental health professionals not to tell gay clients they can become straight through therapy or other treatments. Some research suggests this could induce depression and suicidal tendencies. Where sexual orientation and religious faith conflict, they recommended helping clients with "acceptance, support and identity exploration and development without imposing a specific identity outcome," according to the APA report. A deep rift currently exists between religious conservatives, who believe in the possibility of changing sexual orientation, and the many mental health professionals who reject that option.[315]

Two sides of the gay issue

A heated debate over homosexuality and its ramifications has elicited deep emotions on both sides of the issue.

In a letter to the editor of the *San Jose Mercury News*, a woman[316] expressed her fear of removing the "limits" of marriage by opening it up to gays and lesbians. "We couldn't draw a picture of it anymore, and that terrifies me."[317] She is right; marriage is not concrete. It is now being abstracted back to its source, which is relationship. We are terrified of reality being beyond the material realm because we cannot get a handle on it.

On the other side of the issue, former New Jersey governor James McGreevey, who resigned after revealing that he was gay, called his decision to come out "one of the most painful but honest decisions of my life." He said that culture is outpacing politics in the acceptance of homosexuality and denounced Marine General Peter Pace's policy of "don't ask, don't tell" because it "encourages people to be less than honest, less than open, less than transparent."[318] That policy has since been overturned.

Homosexuality and the church

The split over homosexuality is also painful within religious communities. Tension has been building for years within the Episcopal Church, which is the Anglican province in the United States. In 2003 when Episcopalians consecrated their first openly gay bishop, V. Gene Robinson of New Hampshire, it caused uproar in the Anglican Church. To ease the tension, the Episcopal General Convention that met in 2006 urged restraint by dioceses considering gay candidates for bishop.

Despite their attempt, the rift deepened. In 2009 Episcopal conservatives formed a rival Episcopal Church called the Anglican Church in North America. A month later, the legislative assembly of the Episcopal General Convention declared gays and lesbians eligible for "any ordained ministry," sending a shock wave to the Archbishop of Canterbury, who had been struggling to prevent consecration of any more gay bishops and a permanent Anglican split.[319]

The largest grouping of churches, the Roman Catholic Church, has been in turmoil over legalizing same-sex marriage. Archbishop Donald W. Wuerl of Washington, D.C. sent a reminder about the Church's opposition to same-sex marriage to 300 local Catholic priests in an effort to bring about a public vote on whether same-sex marriage should be legalized. On the same day as his reminder, eight other opponents of same-sex marriage filed a proposed initiative with the D.C. Board of Elections and Ethics that read: "Only marriage between a man and a woman is valid and recognized in the District of Columbia."

In opposition to the church's stance, D.C. Council member David A. Catania said he would not be deterred from introducing a bill legalizing gay marriage in the District. "We have a long tradition in this city of evolving toward equality and a better, more expansive view of human rights, and in 2009 this includes marriage equality for same-sex couples," said Catania.[320]

Same-Sex Marriage

Legalization of same-sex marriage

Elsewhere several states were also grappling with the issue of same-sex marriage, and six of them have now legalized it: Massachusetts, Iowa, New Hampshire, Connecticut, Vermont, New York, plus Washington D.C. and the Coquille and Suquamish Indian tribes. Other states have had encounters—some repeatedly—with legalizing same-sex marriage, but it has not become permanent law.[321]

Winning strategy against same-sex marriage

On every front against same-sex marriage that has been successful, a tried-and-true approach has been used. The message is: If you approve gay marriage, children will be taught homosexuality in school.[322]

The method was first used in 2008 in the successful effort to ban same-sex marriage in California by passing Proposition 8. Developed by the "public affairs team of the year for 2009,"[323] advertising images of what would supposedly happen if same-sex marriage were legal contributed heavily to its success: "students going on a field trip to a lesbian wedding, elementary school kids reading books featuring gay couples, kindergartners learning about homosexuality from their teachers—all without any say from parents."[324]

Voters were swayed by the message, and since then it has become the strategy of preference in most of the 31 consecutive statewide ballot measures against the issue of gay marriage.[325]

Rising support for same-sex marriage

Despite many successful challenges to same-sex marriage, a sharp increase in the number of gay and lesbian couples has occurred since 2000 in some areas, according to the U.S. Census Bureau. [326] More perplexing is a poll conducted by Washington Post-ABC News, which showed rising support for same-sex marriage. This is striking, as it was a sharp shift in public opinion on same- sex marriage. Whereas in 2006 a large majority said same-sex unions should be illegal (36 percent legal to 58 percent illegal), by 2009 forty-nine percent said gay marriages should be legal, and 46 percent said it should be illegal.[327] More recent polls show support above 50 percent.

Same-Sex Relationships in Other Countries

While states have been hashing out disagreements over same-sex marriage, gay relationships have moved ahead in the rest of the world.

In 1989 Denmark became the first nation to legally recognize same-sex relationships, soon followed by other Scandinavian countries and Iceland. By 2006 twelve thousand Canadians, 7,000 Dutch, 2,500 Belgians and 1,300 Spaniards had same-sex marriages with full benefits.

In South Africa a law recognizing same-sex relationships passed by an astonishing 230-41 vote in Parliament. Israel's Supreme Court took the step of requiring the government to officially register gay couples that had married in Canada as they would any other foreign marriage.[328]

When the Spanish government approved same-sex marriage in 2005, the Prime Minister proclaimed: "After us will come many other countries, driven, ladies and gentlemen, by two unstoppable forces: freedom and equality."[329] At the heart of these "unstoppable forces" are soulf's "living ideas" driving through outgrown patterns of relationship.

Other Gender-Neutral Developments

Other arenas of life also reflect progress in differing sexual lifestyles.

Hollywood

One area where progress has been made is Hollywood, where acting opportunities for gays has been broken open. Gay story lines have become more prominent in movies, and lesbian, bisexual and transgender characters have become almost commonplace on television.

In fact, Hollywood's influence has extended beyond the entertainment field to play a key role in making gay men and women part of mainstream American life.

A gay Hollywood publicist[330] remarked, "We've gone from the revolution to the evolution."[331]

Textbook revision

Another sign of mainstream acceptance of gays and lesbians is the approval of a bill in California requiring history textbooks to include discussion of the contributions of gays, bisexuals, and transgender people to the state's and nation's history. The executive director of Equality California, sponsor of the legislation, said the invisibility of gays contributes to the fact that two of three gay students are verbally harassed and one of six is physically harassed.[332]

Religious freedom vs. anti-discrimination

Areas of conflict continue to arise. In one case heard by the California Supreme Court, religious freedoms collided with state and federal anti-discrimination laws. The case involved a doctor who denied infertility treatment to a gay couple based on his religious views about same-sex relationships. This raised the question of whether doctors can selectively choose patients based on their religious views.[333]

Deportation issue

In another situation deportation was part of the issue. A lesbian couple that had been together for 23 years were married in San Francisco during the brief window of opportunity in 2004 when the Mayor opened marriage to gay and lesbian couples.[334] They are parents of twin sons. Because they are a same-sex couple, Tan, a native of the Philippines, is not eligible for legal permanent resident status the way a heterosexual spouse would be. She also is denied legal status for the purpose of international travel or immigration under the federal Defense of Marriage Act,[335] which limits marriage to a man and a woman.[336]

Fighting the Wrong Battle

Some people argue that gay activists have been fighting the wrong battle. While acknowledging that health decisions, inheritance rights, and tax benefits have been limited to only one kind of partnership, they think it makes no sense to try to make the marriage-shoe fit gay partnerships. After all, half of first marriages, and nearly two-thirds of second marriages, fail. Why get involved in something like that?

Instead, gay activists should be fighting a larger battle, one that strives to catch up with human behavior. Government needs to recognize "the legitimacy of a range of consensual, nonexploitative romantic partnerships."[337]

Highest priority should be given to "cohabitation" (which is really renewable short-term marriage) since it is increasing, while married households are now in the minority in the United States. To take this step would begin to stabilize relationships as they actually are in 21st century America.[338]

BIRTH AND DEATH

As the world has complexified in recent years, so has our relationship to birth and death. No longer are there simple answers to complex questions:

When does the life of a human being begin? Who can make decisions about an embryo before its actualized birth, such as whether or not to terminate the pregnancy? Under what circumstances is abortion acceptable, if at all? At what stage of pregnancy is it acceptable to abort the fetus, if at all? What does it mean to be a "parent"?

Not only birth sparks controversy, but death does as well, the two ends of human life.

When does life end? Does one have the right to end his/her own life at choosing? Does society have the right to end a person's life at society's choosing? Does an individual have the right to end, or assist with the end of, another individual's life?

What about the rights of groups or societies in regard to the same issues? If an individual or group, or society, does have a right to end a life, under what conditions is it applicable?

These are some of the thorny issues that underlie suicide, murder, euthanasia, the death penalty, group cultic suicides, war, and suicide bombers. None of them have easy answers.

BIRTH

Birth Options

Perhaps no single news item incorporates more of the complexity of issues stemming from birth options than the pregnancy of Mary Cheney, the former vice president's openly lesbian daughter. Traditional taboos abound in her status: 1) she had a sperm donor rather than a husband's sperm, 2) she was pregnant out of wedlock, 3) she has a lesbian partner and lives in Virginia, where voters banned same-sex marriage and civil unions, and 4) her partner may not have full legal rights as a parent of Cheney's child, according to the laws of Virginia. In addition, as daughter of a former Republican vice president, her situation complicated issues for the Republican Party. [339]

Births out of wedlock

Out of wedlock births reached an all-time high in the United States in 2005, accounting for nearly four in ten newborns.[340] However, those numbers pale compared to Northern Europe, which leads the world in births to unwed mothers. With declining birth rates in some European countries, people are more concerned with a newborn's health than the marriage status of the parents. This may contribute to men and women in northern Europe often living together in unmarried, long-term, stable relationships. In Iceland, six in ten births occur among unmarried women, and half of all births in Sweden and Norway are out of wedlock. France, Denmark, and the United Kingdom also have higher percentages than the United States, according to the U.S Centers for Disease Control and Prevention.[341]

Despite the growing trend in the U.S. of out of wedlock births, the teen birth rate has dropped to its lowest level on record. At the same time, births among unwed mothers has risen dramatically among women in their 20's, especially Latinas. Experts attribute the overall rise in out-of- wedlock births to the number of people who were putting off marriage or living together without getting married.[342]

The trend may also be due to greater social acceptance of having children outside of marriage. Carol Haub, a demographer at the Population Reference Bureau in Washington, D.C. said, "The values surrounding family formation are changing and women are more independent than they used to be. And young people don't feel they have to live under the same social rules that their parents did."[343]

Ready-made embryos

With advances in biotechnology, more options have opened up for women who wish to have children. One option now on the market for single women and infertile couples is ready-made embryos that can be purchased through the Abraham Center of Life, a mail-order company in Texas. The company's goal is to provide embryos for unspecified recipients that match their preferences such as race, education, appearance, and personality.[344]

In vitro fertilization

Another option is giving birth at an advanced age. In 2008, a 56-year-old grandmother gave birth to her triplet granddaughters. Her daughter, who already had two children, was unable to have more children with her husband due to a hysterectomy, so her mother became a surrogate for the embryos from in vitro fertilization. The grandmother gave birth two months prematurely by Caesarian section to identical twins and their sister.[345]

Premature Births

Giving birth prematurely occurs in ten percent of births worldwide, according to a study made in 2009 by the World Health Organization and the March of Dimes. The study also showed that more than one-quarter of the deaths that occur in the month after birth are the consequence of preterm birth. The highest rate of premature births occurs in Africa (11.9 percent), followed by North America (10.6 percent). Australia and New Zealand have the lowest rate of premature births.[346]

Abortion

A lawyer representing supporters of a proposed amendment to the Colorado Constitution giving legal rights to fertilized human eggs directed attention to the core question underlying abortion. "The whole issue centers on when does life begin.[347]"[348]

This very question sparks deep emotion in both pro-life and pro-choice adherents. Sometimes it boils over in rage, causing violence and even death.

The most prominent provider of late-term abortions in the United States, Dr. George Tiller, was shot and killed in the lobby of his church in Wichita, Kansas in 2009. While many activists on both sides of the issue denounced the attack, some said abortion procedures are "homicide," and they called Tiller "a mass murderer."[349]

Tiller's performing late-term abortions drew desperate women from all over the country. "What made Dr. Tiller unusual was that he specialized in seeing women who found out late in very wanted pregnancies that they were carrying fetuses with anomalies that were incompatible with life," said Vicki Saporta of the National Abortion Federation, the largest group of abortion providers. Such devastating news late in pregnancy makes many women desperate to end their pregnancy.

One typical response from a woman who chose abortion in a doomed pregnancy was: "It was very difficult, but I knew it was the most humane thing I could do for my baby."[350]

While it is clear that late-term abortions account for a tiny fraction of the 1.2 million U.S. abortions each year, data about them are scarce.[351]

Birth and Abortion Internationally

Amidst the large number of abortions worldwide, unsafe abortion kills 70,000 women a year. More than half of those are in sub-Saharan Africa, which has the lowest rates of contraceptive use and the highest rates of unintended pregnancies. Though increased contraceptive use has led to fewer abortions worldwide, and abortion is safe and legal in most developed countries, "in much of the developing world, abortion remains highly restricted, and unsafe abortion is common[352]."[353]

Nicaragua

Sexual violence is rampant in Nicaragua, where half of reported rapes are of girls under 18, and most of those who get pregnant are under 15. Yet in 2006 Nicaragua joined a group of only three percent of the world's nations where abortion is not allowed under any circumstance. In responding to this total ban of abortion in Nicaragua, Amnesty International launched a campaign to repeal the law, pointing out that it is not only a violation of human rights, but it is killing a growing number of women and children.[354]

Colombia

Around the same time that Nicaragua legislated a total ban on abortion, Colombia's high court overturned their country's complete ban. The Constitutional Court ruled that abortion was to be permitted when the life of a woman was in danger or the fetus was expected to die, or in cases of rape or incest.[355]

India

Abortion does not always fit into those categories. In India, for example, abortion is legal except for the purpose of sex selection. Yet the law is rarely enforced. As a result, the aborting of female fetuses by women who want sons[356]is a growing problem. About 250,000 female fetuses are aborted each year in India.[357]The effect of sex selection was evident in the 2001 census, which showed 93 girls for every 100 boys in children under the age of seven.[358]

Vietnam

Vietnam, too, is tipping the balance between the sexes in Asia, which could lead to increased trafficking of women, according to a United Nations report. Vietnam logs about 110 boys born to every 100 girls. According to the United Nations Population Fund, the sex rates should equal about 105 boys to 100 girls.

"The consequences are already happening in neighboring countries like China, South Korea and Taiwan. They have to import brides," said Tran Thi Van of the United Nations Population Fund. In China, more than 120 boys are born to 100 girls—and, in several provinces, it spikes to more than 130 boys to 100 girls.[359]

DEATH

Choosing One's Death

Dignitas and assisted suicide

An eminent British musician, who had been knighted by Queen Elizabeth II, and his wife decided to end their lives together at a Zurich clinic run by the assisted suicide group Dignitas. Sir Edward Downes had conducted world-renowned orchestras, including years as head of the BBC Philharmonic. When he became almost blind and was growing deaf, and his wife had been diagnosed with terminal cancer, they chose to die together, hand in hand, at Dignitas.[360]

Some months earlier, another Briton who was almost completely incapacitated by motor neurone disease, had chosen to end his life at the same clinic. 59-year-old Craig Ewert laid out his options: "If I go through with it, I have death. If I don't go through with it, my choice is essentially to suffer and inflict suffering on my family, and then die."

It is illegal in Britain to "aid, abet, counsel or procure" suicide. Though Ewert's wife broke the law by helping him travel to the clinic in Zurich, she was not prosecuted, as application of the law is murky. About 100 Britons have committed suicide at Dignitas in past decades, but their cases have never ended in prosecutions.

What was unusual about Ewert's case was that his death was broadcast on British television, the country's first broadcast of voluntary euthanasia. The film showed how he traveled to the Zurich clinic in 2006 and took a fatal dose of barbiturates.[361]

Rejected legislation

In 2006, the same year as Ewert's death, Britain's House of Lords rejected a bill allowing doctors to prescribe lethal drug doses to terminally ill patients. This reflected opposition to assisted suicide among the public, government, and church in Britain. The proposed bill had been based on legislation in Oregon, the only state in the United States with legalized assisted suicide.[362]

While suicide is the choice of some people with terminal illness, others choose to fight to the last breath. These two poles define the debate over physician-assisted suicide, an issue that has erupted six times in California. The topic is so emotion-laden and controversial that experts agree there is no neutral term to describe it. Unlike England's population that is largely against doctor-assisted suicide, 70 percent of Californians support it, and at least 18 states are debating the idea.[363]

Capital Punishment

Taking one's own life is surely an agonizing decision, but taking the life of others is equally difficult. We encounter this decision as a society in the form of war (which will be discussed in a later chapter) and of capital punishment for individuals. Both are highly charged areas of decision-making.

The debate about capital punishment often centers on the question of whether or not the death penalty deters murders. As important as this information is, there are deeper questions that need to be addressed.

On what ground(s) will we ultimately base our decision about the death penalty? Moral/religious grounds? Economic grounds (financial burden on society)? Legal precedents? Pragmatic grounds (what works best for the prison/justice system)? Total number of lives lost or saved by its use? A combination of the above? Other grounds?

Until society decides on the bottom line of decision-making about capital punishment, heated arguments will continue to rage.

Movement to repeal the death penalty

A movement to repeal the death penalty in California started to grow in early 2007, largely because of rising costs, though the state's greatest concerns were wrongful convictions and moral objections. Because capital punishment is so costly, carrying out death sentences has dramatically slowed. The number of executions has decreased from about 300 death sentences annually in the 1990's to 128 in 2005, according to the Death Penalty Information Center, a group that lobbies against capital punishment. Despite the movement to repeal the death penalty in the 37 states that have it, public opinion polls consistently show majority support for capital punishment.[364]

Later in 2007, a few highly respected economists highlighted recent studies, showing that the death penalty deters murders. Since this has been a central justification for capital punishment, their announcement created an uproar. The findings flew in the face of the movement to repeal the death penalty, which had been gaining momentum. Scholars, lawyers, and economists all chimed in with arguments of their own, showing the validity, or invalidity, of the studies on which the economists had based their conclusion. For the most part, they talked past one another because they work in different disciplines.

Economists citing the studies pointed out that executions save lives. For each inmate put to death, three to 18 murders are prevented. "To economists, it is obvious that if the cost of an activity rises, the amount of the activity will drop."[365] Therefore fewer murders will take place as the likelihood of execution rises.

An argument to counter that viewpoint is the situation in Canada, where no one has been executed since 1962. "Yet the murder rates in the United States and Canada have moved in close parallel since then, including before, during and after the four-year death penalty moratorium in the United States in the 1970's[366]."[367]

For Reflection:

1. ....

....

....

2. ....

....

....

3. ....

....

....

CHAPTER 10

PERSONAL RELATIONSHIPS
PART TWO

CHILDREN AND FAMILIES

Marriage and Children

American society has divided itself into two groups. Marriage and children can no longer be lumped together in the same package.

Living together and having children out of wedlock is the living pattern of the working class and the poor. Marriage without children is being relegated to the college educated and the affluent, and it has become the norm for the elite. Although some of these folks continue to have children, married couples with children now occupy less than one in every four households, the lowest ever recorded by the census.

"The culture is shifting, and marriage has almost become a luxury item, one that only the well-educated and well paid are interested in," said a senior fellow at the Brookings Institute.[368] This "new" patterning is actually a reversion to an historic pattern, one in which elites married, with a far larger number of people cohabiting and having children.

In a further separation of the two groups, college educated women and men are increasingly less likely to choose mates who have less education and professional standing than they do. They are also less likely to divorce. [369]

Importance of children in marriage

In a 1990 World Values Survey, 65 percent of the respondents said children were "very important" to a successful marriage. By 2007 a dramatic shift had taken place. A Pew study of nine factors that Americans associate with successful marriages showed that children ranked eighth, well behind the importance of "sharing household chores." By a margin of nearly 3-to-1, respondents said the "main purpose of marriage is the 'mutual happiness and fulfillment' of adults rather than the 'bearing and raising of children.'" Blacks and Hispanics place a higher value on the importance of children to a successful marriage than whites.[370]

Parenting

Parents today spend more direct time with their children than ever before—nearly 14.1 hours a week for mothers. Yet half of mothers say they do not spend enough time with their children. "It's almost like it doesn't matter how much they do, they feel they do not do enough," said the lead author of a University of Maryland study.[371] After pointing out that mothers' perception is colored by an increase in expectations, the author continued: "This is part of the burden of this generation of parents: enormously high expectations for how children develop, how they feel about themselves, how they achieve and how successful they are in the world."

Sharon Hays of the University of Southern California summed it up: "Ours is a "culture of intensive mothering."[372]

Survey findings

Mothers' qualms about their parenting may be calmed by the results of a 2007 survey.[373] When asked, "What makes you happy?" the top answer given by nearly three-quarters of young people ages 13-24 was "Spending time with family." Almost half also mentioned one or both of their parents when asked to name their heroes.

Additional findings of the survey include: whites are happier, across economic categories, than blacks and Latinos; many young people feel stress, especially middle class females; having highly educated parents is more important than income in predicting happiness; being sexually active leads to less happiness among 13 to 17-year-olds; simply belonging to an organized religious group makes people happier; school makes young people happy; young people think marriage would make them happy, and they want to be married someday and have children.[374]

Other research shows that those who make us happy are much wider spread than our parents or family, important as their influence is. The Framingham Heart Study found that our emotional state stems not only from our *own* choices, actions and experience, but also from those of others, including people with whom we have no direct connection—as much as three degrees of separation. This 20-year study is the first to find that happiness can spread across groups for up to a year. Although unhappiness can also spread from person to person, its infectiousness appears to be far weaker than happiness. The same study found that obesity and the likelihood of quitting smoking also appear to spread from person to person.[375]

Another study,[376] conducted in 2009, was the first to connect teen behavior to dishonest activities in adulthood. It found a steady increase in high school students admitting to cheating, lying and stealing, which is of special significance because those who cheat on exams in high school are considerably more likely to be dishonest later in life. The study showed that teens are more likely than adults to believe lying and cheating are necessary to succeed (ten percent vs. five percent) and to think it is okay to cheat to get ahead.[377] Given that many successful adults appear in headlines for cheating, perhaps dishonesty spreads like happiness.

Camp life

In an article written for *The Washington Post*, Ruth Marcus captured the camp life of children in the 21st century, reflecting parents' fragmented mode of living and parenting.

Most camps are short-term, ranging from as few as 3 ½ days to a week. "All the fun in half the time!" as one short-term camp promotes itself. Most are specialized (with an eye on college admission)—tennis camp, computer camp, art camp, etc., and even the more traditional camps have children sign up for individual activities. Marcus says her daughter mapped out a program for herself that created "the world's first fully air-conditioned summer camp"—indoor soccer, "pompoms," and yoga.

"The Camping Alone phenomenon reflects a number of strands of 21st century childhood: not only the atomized nature of the modern condition but also the frantic pace of life today, the pressure to specialize early and the indulgent, child-centered nature of the contemporary family[378]."[379]

Separation anxiety of parents

Modern technology now provides a way to ease over-protective parents' separation anxiety. They can now be almost intrusive in the private lives of their children, which raises the question, "How much is it good for us to know?"

Online data systems make it possible for parents to track nearly everything their children do at school, from checking on homework, whether or not they cut class, grades they got, even how many cookies they had for lunch. If parents disapprove of their children's choices at lunch, they can restrict what items they can buy, examine everything they order for lunch each day, and set limits on how much money they can spend daily.[380]

Safety of children

We have become a nation of hovering, over-protective parents, who are hyper-anxious about the safety and well-being of our children, requiring an adult to supervise all their outdoor activities. Some students in grades K-4 may not even ride their bikes to school—forbidden not only by parents, but also by written rules of their school.

Child abduction and sexual abuse

Flying in the face of such caution, rates of child abduction and sexual abuse have moved steadily downward since the early 1990's. Even Megan's Law web site says stranger abduction is rare, and someone known to the child commits 90 percent of sexual abuse cases. Yet our perception of crime and its statistical reality remains disconnected.

One alarming result of this false perception is often overlooked. As child abduction and abuse decreases, Type II diabetes, hypertension and other obesity-related ailments in children increase.

"Which scenario should provoke more panic: the possibility that your child might become one of the approximately 100 children who are kidnapped by strangers each year, or one of the country's 58 million overweight adults?[381]"[382]

Generation Gap

Vietnam era and today

American adults today disagree increasingly on social values and morality, creating an even larger generation gap than during the Vietnam War era. According to a survey conducted by the Pew Research Center, the difference in points of view of the two generations became evident after the election of President Obama.

Younger people report disagreements over lifestyle and views on family, relationships and dating, while older people cite differences in a sense of entitlement. Both groups feel differences in views of morality and work ethic.[383] Today's generation gap, however, is far "gentler" than that of the 1960's, causing little angst. Boomers and their children merely agree to disagree.

Another difference between them is in education. Baby boomers enjoyed a level of education that was sharply different from that of their parents—especially for women. The gap is much less significant between the boomers and their children.

Today the strongest divides in American society are between immigrants and the native-born, the poor and the rich, and blacks and whites. Woodstock youth of the sixties were more homogeneous in terms of race and national origin. At that time about 90 percent of 20-to-24-year-olds were white, contrasted with 60 percent in that same age group today.[384]

Challenges in the workplace

Today's generation gap has presented a challenge for workers in the workforce. Often four distinct generations find themselves working together in the same organization: traditionalists, baby boomers, Generation X and Generation Y. This can cause problems unless their differences and stereotypical views of one another are dealt with.

Older workers tend to see the youngest employees, Generation Y, as lacking a work ethic. They are inclined to dress too casually or revealingly for most workplaces, find it difficult to take criticism and are hesitant to ask for help when they need it. They also hold expectations of instant gratification, expecting to have a fancy office on their first job out of college and to draw a six-figure salary. In addition, they feel entitled to make their own flexible work hours and leave work early. Finally, they lack communication skills outside of texting, instant messaging and social media. They expect everyone to communicate in their shorthand language and think it can be used across the board in place of face-to-face interaction. So say the older workers.

Generation Y workers, from their vantage point, see older workers as slow, not having a clue about technology, and strongly resistant to change. Older workers need to appreciate the technological skills of younger workers and ask for their help in updating their own tech skills. They ought to be open to the fresh perspectives of younger workers, embracing innovation, and not cling to the way things have always been done. If a younger worker offers a suggestion that would negatively affect quality, customer service or safety, the older worker needs to point it out clearly or it will be regarded as mere rigidity.[385]

EDUCATION

Americans' relationship to education is in a state of flux, too. Awareness has arisen of the need for big changes in our educational system, but actual changes are hard to come by. With the world rapidly evolving, questions surrounding education have complexified dramatically, making decisions more difficult. Following are some of the perplexing questions that continue to nag us:

What educational basis does the U.S. need to have today? Do we educate our children to regain America's #1 position in the world (which is the apparent focus)? Do we educate them from the viewpoint of America as part of a global community? Do we educate them according to perceived needs of the universe—Soulf's needs? Should our educational basis include a combination of the above or be something else entirely?

Is it more important to educate specialists or generalists—or both? Do we educate for the type of world we have known, the world we live in now, or the world of the future? What are the differences? What methods are most successful in educating today's children and youth?

Preparation of Students

Effects of the Recession

When the recession OF 2088 struck a severe blow to the American economy, the need for budget cuts raced through school districts across America. Superintendents scrambled to meet the needs of their students, while feeling pressure from government and industry to compete educationally with other countries. America was losing its standing in the eyes of the world, and some nations were all too ready to replace its venerated position. Education was key to catching up with those nations, and school districts needed to do something to raise America's educational standards. Because of the dire situation, school districts welcomed help from whatever sources were available.

American students, compared to students from other developed countries, ranked 25th out of 30 in math literacy, and 21st out of 30 in science literacy. To address the situation, President Obama proposed "Educate to Innovate," a call to corporations, nonprofits and other groups to partner with schools in an intervention program. The summer program, which zoned in on the critical years of middle school, showed promise after its first year, with a 20 percent increase in math skills after four weeks.[386]

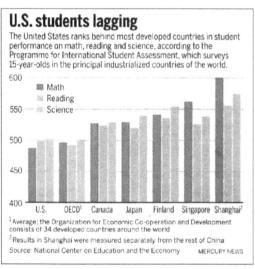

U.S. students lagging

The United States ranks behind most developed countries in student performance on math, reading and science, according to the Programme for International Student Assessment, which surveys 15-year-olds in the principal industrialized countries of the world.

- Math
- Reading
- Science

U.S. OECD[1] Canada Japan Finland Singapore Shanghai[2]

[1] Average: the Organization for Economic Co-operation and Development consists of 34 developed countries around the world

[2] Results in Shanghai were measured separately from the rest of China

Source: National Center on Education and the Economy   MERCURY NEWS

Foreign language instruction

Foreign language instruction received help from an unexpected source. While tight budgets forced thousands of public schools to stop teaching foreign languages,[387] the demand for learning Chinese was so great[388] that the Chinese government decided to help. They sent teachers from China ¬to teach Chinese in schools in America[389] and paid part of their salaries. "It's really changing the language education landscape of this country," said Nancy Rhodes, director of the Center for Applied Linguistics in Washington, D.C.[390] As a result of China's help, Chinese was expected to become the third most-tested Advanced Placement language in 2010, after Spanish and French.[391]

Though the study of Chinese has, indeed, changed the landscape, such as attracting 400 students to the Chinese American International School in San Francisco, "only 24,000 students study Chinese in the United States… [whereas] 200 million Chinese students are studying English," said Andrew Corcoran, head of the Chinese American International School.[392]

Arts education

Budget cuts have affected areas of school curricula besides foreign languages. Arts education took an early hit, though it, too, is now receiving help, thanks to a program started by the John F. Kennedy Center for the Performing Arts in Washington, D.C. Linking local arts groups with schools, a pilot project called "Any Given Child" helps teach music, theater arts and visual arts to students in grades K-8. Michael Kaiser, president of the Kennedy Center, thinks that schools need a comprehensive way of teaching the arts in order to have the skills needed for the U.S. economy, which is increasingly driven by creativity.[393]

Expanding Horizons

Individuals

Individual adults are also reaching out to broaden and enrich children's education in ways that reflect the 21st century and the expanded world of globalization. For example, a principal dancer with Ballet San Jose took her kindergartner with her to China for the last few weeks of the school year, using it as an independent study. Her daughter was required to complete some assignments during the trip, so she sent pictures of her homework, taken with a digital camera, to her teacher. [394]

Schools

Some schools have an equally far-reaching vision of educational needs in the 21st century. At one private girls' high school in California,[395] every student spends ten days of her junior year in either Bangalore or Shanghai studying international relations, women's rights, and possibly competing on a robotics team.

Back at school, they are introduced to a broad and creative view of technology through special presentations tailored for them. They see, for instance, how power is becoming decentralized between men and women on the Web, with Wikipedia being a prime example. Traditional, male-dominated corporate structure does not necessarily apply to the field of technology, they discover, though gender inequality is still an issue.[396]

Universities

Universities have also pitched in to help with educational needs. For instance, Stanford University now offers its Education Program for Gifted Youth online, the first of its kind. The program provides a full curriculum for 10th through 12th grade students, leading to a high school diploma. Although any gifted student may apply, leaders of the program are making a special effort to reach out to gifted students from disadvantaged schools. "That's one of the most underdeveloped pools of gifted students in the country," said Patrick Suppes, director of the program.[397]

Charter schools

In recent years charter schools have taken root in the United States, widening the possibilities for public school education in the 21st century. Ever since 1993 when the first charter school was authorized, charter schools have mushroomed. They have become popular as an answer to parents' increasing frustration with the quality of their local schools, since parents, rather than the State, make most decisions about curriculum and the use of State money.

Originally charter schools were organized and operated mostly by parents, teachers and community leaders. But through the years some local school districts have chosen to develop "conversion" schools (schools that convert from being a public school to a charter school), which now comprise a third of the total number of charter schools.[398]

When President Obama took office in 2009, he opened the door to charter schools throughout the nation, giving a huge boost to their development. They are especially effective for poor and limited English-speaking children in failing schools because the curriculum and use of funds can be tailored to the particular needs of local children.[399]

Schools and Technology

As laptops became commonplace in most classrooms in the United States, one laptop per child drew close to the norm. Teachers began to discover new and creative ways to integrate them into the curriculum, utilizing technology to support learning goals.

One major way is through use of the Internet. Students build on each other's findings in cooperative searches for school projects, thus modeling their future collaborative work style as adults in a complex maze of specialized work.

Online communication also leads to new relationships and communication between classrooms. For instance, an art class may post their work online for an English class down the hall to evaluate.

One-on-one programs have become popular with younger children. ST Math, an online enrichment program of individualized learning, teaches mathematical concepts without the use of words. Through trial and error, children are guided to think about what is needed to allow Ji-Ji, the penguin, to overcome an obstacle he has encountered so he can continue his journey.[400]

Language arts

While many adults are concerned that the Internet is destroying the reading habits of young people, a national survey conducted by Scholastic publishing house in 2008 indicated that the Internet is reinforcing some children's interest in books. It is true that the time children spend reading books for fun declines after age eight, but children who are frequent users of the Internet are more likely to read books for fun every day. One in four of high-frequency users of the Internet read books daily for fun, and over half of that group read books for fun at least two or three times a week.[401]

Yet the debate about language and learning in a high-tech age rages on. One criticism focuses attention on the change in vocabulary that children are exposed to. A 2007 revised edition of the *Oxford Junior Dictionary*, widely used by children between the ages of eight and 11, has dropped numerous nature terms and replaced them with terms such as "MP3 player," "blog" and "cut and paste." Words missing in the new edition include "dandelion," "acorn," "beaver," "moss," and "fern." Certain Christian terms, too, have been removed, such as "chapel" and "saint". Oxford University Press, which published the dictionary, said their selection of words was based on "language children will commonly come across at home and at school."[402]

Education for high-tech

As the debate continues, technology companies are reaching out to students, encouraging them to consider careers in the high-tech industry.

A group of high-tech companies[403] offers a three-day program, "High-tech U.," to orient high school students in 11 states to the high-tech industry. Though open to all students, the program reaches out especially to girls and minorities, who are underrepresented in math, science and technology. Even B and C students are encouraged to participate. Professionals in the high-tech industry teach the lessons and share their experiences in jobs ranging from solar technology to nanotechnology.[404]

Despite statistics showing that girls are falling behind in math and science at lower levels of education, the situation at the doctoral level is less pronounced. California higher education trends, analyzed by the *Sacramento Bee*, show that the men-to-women gender gap shrunk during a decade to 3.5 to 1. Though these numbers outstrip figures from the rest of the United States, California is usually the bellwether state, indicating future national trends.[405]

Measuring Schools and Success

Use of technology for assessment

Some educators think that technology should be used not only for the learning process but for the testing process as well. This may require going back to Square 1, as the types of tests teachers have traditionally used may not be appropriate for today's world.

This raises the question: What kinds of tests will measure what is needed for today's world? Perhaps there is "a role for tests that measure a student's ability to quickly acquire and interpret information through mobile devices, even if they know nothing about the subject prior to sitting down for the test."[406] Most situations in the workplace require the ability to acquire information when you need it, and to understand it. It does not matter where the facts are stored. Interpretation is what counts.

Peggy Sheehy, a library media specialist, puts it simply and directly: "We can't teach 21st century literacy and assess with 19th century methodology. We have to look at what we really need students to be able to do when they leave us.[407]"[408]

Drop-outs

Many students of high school age are lost, despite myriad programs to keep teens interested and in school. Data suggest that almost a quarter of teens in California drop out of high school— more than 50 percent in some school districts. The reasons cited are fear, poverty, boredom, failure, and addiction.[409]

Exit exams

Of those who stay in school, tens of thousands have been failing high school exit exams, causing some states to rescind the requirement.

California was one of those that revoked the requirement, but it turned out to be more complicated than simple revocation.[410] State Superintendent Jack O'Connell submitted an appeal to have the exit exam reinstated as a requirement for graduation, and the issue ended up in the California Supreme Court.[411]

In studying California's exit exam, the Institute for Research on Education at Stanford University found no evidence that exit exams have improved overall academic achievement. The study points out that diversity and individualism, which are regarded as virtues in California, require a broad curriculum to meet the needs of a diverse student population. The existing one-size-fits-all policies, including the "exit exam," undermine the very essence of education. In addition, the current educational policies place extra stress on female and nonwhite students to do well on tests, fearing that failure would reinforce negative stereotypes[412]. [413]

Academic performance of boys

Although it was touted in the media in 2006 that boys were falling behind in academic achievement and graduating from high school at lower rates than girls, this was largely a "manufactured crisis," according to a senior scientist at Brandeis University. Poor and working class boys do lag behind girls in reading when they get to middle school, he said, but boys in the wealthiest schools do not fall behind, either in middle school or in high school. This is borne out in statistics compiled by the National Education Association, which showed that the sex composition of colleges was fairly well balanced: 51 percent female and 49 percent male.[414]

Other professors said that men cluster disproportionately at both ends of the spectrum, "students who are the most brilliantly creative, and students who cannot keep up[415]."

Higher Education

Gender factor

By 2010, men constituted only 42 percent of college enrollment, and they were said to be laggards. They were less likely than women to get bachelor's degrees,[416] and of those that did, fewer completed their degrees in four or five years. Both male and female students agreed that men studied less, socialized more, and got worse grades than women. Accordingly, women took the lion's share of honors degrees.[417]

Digital divide

Professors note that "rudeness" has seeped into college classrooms. Much of this is due to the digital divide. Students find professors' e-mails an old-fashioned way of communication. They want to text, and to have their professor be their friend on Facebook. Professors complain that students are disengaged, as they are constantly diverted during lectures by laptops, phones, and iPods. Some say this reflects American society in general, where 70 percent of the population (in 2005) said people are ruder today than 20 or 30 years ago.

Lee Shumow, educational psychology professor at Northern Illinois University, expressed her frustration with student behavior: "I literally cannot imagine having addressed any teacher I had in my career as 'Hey' and then their first name. I love them… But man, the world has really changed from when I was a student."[418] Experts say that the attitude professors are pointing to is more than entitlement. It often is: "I don't need you, I have the Net."

"These are students for whom the computers are the training wheels of their knowledge since early childhood… the prestige of the teacher and the professors as providers of knowledge and wisdom has decreased as the importance of the information technology has increased."[419]

Education Internationally

The illiteracy rate worldwide has decreased from 44 percent in 1950 to 16 percent today.[420] This means that one in six men and women around the Earth today cannot read or write a simple message. Sub-Saharan Africa accounts for eight of the 210 countries with highest illiteracy rates, while much of the progress in literacy has come in south Asia.

Surprisingly, India's illiteracy rate is 34 percent, despite the country being a high-tech center for global outsourcing services. It has nearly four times as many illiterate adults as China, where the illiteracy rate is 7 percent, significantly below the 20 percent illiteracy rate for developing countries as a whole.[421]

In seeking to address the overall problem, a coalition of governments, charities and United Nations agencies have pledged $4.5 billion to eradicate illiteracy worldwide and provide universal primary schooling by 2015.[422]

By 2021, the global literacy rate for all people aged 15 and above was 86.3%.

For Reflection:

1. ....

....

....

2. ....

....

....

3. ....

....

....

CHAPTER 11

EMERGENCE OF THE AVERAGE PERSON

YOU

When *Time* magazine named You as "Person of the Year" for 2006, it captured the essence not only of the digital revolution, but also of the Millennial Generation itself. The editors recognized how the average person was taking charge of directing the course of new digital media, but they were perhaps less prescient of its aptness in describing, in general, those born into a digital world.

Time's pronouncement was one more step in the movement from groups to individuals, a process that has been evolving since the beginning of *Homo sapiens*. Each successive era has carved out finer definition of the human being, much as a stone artist chisels away at ever-finer features of a bust. In following the lead of *Time*, one could say that the average human being is finally emerging from the shadows into the light, or perhaps more truly, from the teenage years into young adulthood. For the first and only time, some individual human beings and humanity as a whole are entering adulthood simultaneously.

Community and collaboration are now possible on a scale we have never before known, as the Internet, with its social websites, has opened the way for users to bypass gatekeepers. The everyday person has surged ahead and taken both technologies and content out of the hands of their creators to control them themselves.[423]

Time's Leo Grossman believes "an explosion of productivity and innovation" is *taking* place, as "millions of minds that would otherwise have drowned in obscurity" are now participants in "the global intellectual economy."[424] The 21st century could be called "the century of emergence of the individual."[425]

Narcissism

Some people feel that the "century of narcissism" is a more appropriate name. Everyone is entitled to create content for the Web, which is not controlled by law and, some would say, is not in good taste. As a result, we amateurs are so busy celebrating ourselves through the Web we may well miss great books or great ideas when they come along.

Others carry this way of thinking beyond the Internet. Jean Twenge[426] believes that youth of the Millennial Generation are narcissistic, with a rising ego rush and an inflated sense of self. They have unwarranted self-esteem, since they have accomplished little to earn it. Moreover, narcissism is toxic for our society because people take more for themselves and leave less for others.[427]

In addition, narcissism fosters an entitlement mentality, which has been formed by permissive parenting, self-esteem programs adopted by many elementary schools, and a culture that builds self-esteem by giving everyone a trophy. Some researchers also blame the Internet, where you can shape your own image, post your own opinions, and become your own publicist.

Twenge and her fellow researchers point to a study based on responses to the Narcissistic Personality Inventory. Among the statements for students to respond to were: "I think I am a special person" and "I like to be the center of attention." 30 percent more college students showed elevated narcissism in 2006 compared to 1982[428].[429] These researchers are countering some others who say college students are more civic-minded and involved in volunteer activities than their predecessors.

"Our history has always been the sum total of the
choices made and the actions taken by each individual
man and woman. It has always been up to us."
—President Barack Obama

WHO ARE THE MILLENIALS? (Generation Y)

The Millennial Generation, people born between 1982 and 2003, are
a unique generation that will shape a vastly new landscape of American
life for the foreseeable future. Graduating high school students in 2009
described themselves and their generation as "plugged-in," "globalized"
and "competitive."

The dominant theme of all these designations is technology. Millennials
recognize that they are the first generation to grow up entirely with modern
technology, which has put them in constant communication with one
another through Facebook and other social websites, cell phones and other
forms of electronic media. Because of the speed of communication and the
"availability of constant interruption," they are learning how to cope with
distractions. Their challenge is to "apply this vast amount of information
to the ever-mounting number of social, political and economic problems
the world faces," said Amy Wipfler, a 2009 high school graduate.[430]

The global perspective of the Millennial Generation shows up in many forms. Some students have scholarships to attend international meetings, such as the G8 Summit in Italy. Others take a "gap" year between high school and college to travel abroad or to work with international nonprofit organizations. Some of those going directly to college seek special college programs related to a global perspective. Georgia Tech, for instance, offers an "international plan" option with any major. The plan includes a global perspective in all departments and substantial time abroad.

One student expressed the impetus behind the choices of many students: "It seems as though the United States is becoming less of a global power and foreign governments are having increasing influence on the global community… I think it's important that people have at least a background in international relations.[431]"[432]

A trait of the Millennials—one they fail even to mention because it is so integral to their makeup—is an acceptance of people for who they are. Morley Winograd, co-author with Michael Hais of *Millennial Makeover: MySpace, YouTube, and the future of American politics*, said: "With Millennials, racial, ethnic and gender distinctions are much less important than they've ever been."

Millennials are also civic-minded problem-solvers, tech savvy, and optimists, believing that the United States can do some good in the world.

"They're not only the most diverse generation in U.S. history; 40 percent of them are people of color. They're also the largest, numbering roughly 100 million. By the sheer strength of their numbers, the Millennials will leave their mark."[433]

MILLENNIALS SURFING THE WAVE

Personal Identity

Tattoos

One form in which Millennials are expressing their uniqueness is through tattoos. Tattoos used to be associated with "jarheads" and "jailhouse residents," but reality shows have helped raise the level of their acceptability to the point where they have now become mainstream. People turn to tattoos as a way of celebrating the birth of a child, the death of a war buddy, or victory over cancer, to name a few uses.

At a deeper level, people may also be using tattoos as a way of playing with fringe identities without sacrificing middle-class status or jeopardizing their jobs. Moreover, it is their passport into a special community, while saying, "I'm unique!"[434]

Casual dress

On the job scene, casual dress has been making inroads for several decades, with Friday becoming almost universally a "dress down" day. It has now reached the level of job interviews. In a survey conducted by YahooHasJobs and Banana Republic, more than 25 percent of the human resource recruiters interviewed said wearing a business suit to an interview at their company could be too formal.

Along with casual dress, a new generation of companies has come to believe that comfort equals productivity, so they are fostering a casual environment in their workplaces.[435]

Trends in comfortable and informal living

Comfort and informality had already been prized since the 1950's, when domestic architecture sought to humanize modern housing. The "Good Life" that Americans were enjoying included a master bedroom and family room, two brand-new rooms for a home.

By the 1990's, public taste had become extravagant, and people were offered easy credit to spend far beyond their means. Historical houses became demolished to make room for large, luxurious homes set far back from the street, with tall gates and security systems. The comfort and informality of the 1950's had become supplanted by the desire for a conspicuous display of wealth. Freedom of expression morphed into "the right to do whatever you want, to be totally self-absorbed.[436]

Today we find some people at the other end of the spectrum. They enjoy consuming less and living as simply as possible, while saving money and saving the planet. It is not about being frugal, but of making life choices that "get the best bang for the buck," says Peter Lawrence, a retiree at age 44 who lives happily as a minimalist.[437]

Homebuilders are aware of a new uniqueness in buyers' taste and are catering to it. New homes are built to accommodate what residents want, wherever they want it. For instance, small refrigerators and pantries may be located in entertainment rooms and children's playrooms, and laundry rooms may be upstairs among the bedrooms.[438]

At the same time decorating is becoming much more personalized and eclectic. People no longer decorate with a single style throughout the home.[439] Instead, they combine whatever furnishings appeal to them or have sentimental value.

Gifts

Uniqueness in personal taste carries over to gifts. People have become more consciously aware of their desires and are not reluctant to let others know exactly what they want in the way of a gift: money, or a gift certificate. While brides have "registered" their hopes for gifts for the past several decades, with the advent of the Internet the average person can register their wish list online.

Now gift-giving has become farther removed from the giver, with 70 percent of people saying they would rather receive a gift certificate than a present. They know better than anyone else what they want.

Control over oneself

Today people want control over their own health care, and some health care plans are facilitating this. Kaiser Permanente uses Health Vault, a free web site for storing personal health information. A Kaiser spokeswoman[440] said, "Our whole goal is to make health care patient-oriented and give people the online tools that they need to manage their health."[441]

An extreme case of a college student taking control over his own body, erasing all privacy, and drawing attention to himself occurred in 2008. Abraham Biggs ended his life by taking a drug overdose in front of a live web cam. Watchers were stunned with disbelief until 12 hours later when police arrived with the web cam still rolling.

He was not the first person to commit suicide with a cam rolling.[442]

Food

People want to be in charge on the home front, too. When cooking, they want to decide for themselves or learn from others like them. Forget the experts.

Starting around 2006, people turned aside chefs like Mario Batali in favor of home-cooking Paula Deen and Rachael Ray. They wanted recipes from real home cooks, "home-style," "country" and "everyday" meals. Bloggers from all over the globe contributed recipes. Home cooks responded similarly to Amy Cisneros of San Antonio who said, "When you have the Internet, who needs cookbooks? I look at all the different recipes, and then I make it my way."

This trend toward plain home cooking and doing it my way is reflected in the media. Television's cooking shows now feature home cooking rather than chef food; *Taste of Home*, the most popular food magazine in the United States, has more subscribers than *Gourmet*, *Food & Wine*, and *Bon Appetite* combined; and not one of the top 10 best-selling cookbooks of 2006 was written by a professional chef.[443]

Penny Fersko of New York's Staten Island said: "I never had any interest in cooking chef food. If I want fancy, I'll go to a restaurant."[444] She speaks for many others.

Restaurant food is no longer critiqued only by experts. Many newspapers and other media now invite "You" to review the restaurant you go to.[445] As the *San Jose Mercury News* issued the invitation: "We want you to have your say about some of the restaurants we review… Contribute your thoughts… We will print a selection of reader comments with [Aleta] Watson's review."

Entertainment

American Idol

The average person also has a say about the immensely popular "American Idol" and other reality TV shows. In fact, text-votes from viewers decide the winner of the singing contest.

"It says to the whole entertainment industry, "You are not in control; we are."" commented Neal Gabler, a cultural historian.[446]

"How We First Met"

An acting version of "American Idol" has taken place in San Francisco for the last decade. Each Valentine's Day couples in Silicon Valley compete with true confessions of their courtship, hoping their personal story will snag a starring role in "How We First Met."

Winners are interviewed before a live audience, while actors re-create their first meeting in skits and songs. Jill Bourque, creator and host of the show, said: "Transparency and openness are cool right now. It's sort of like reality TV and social networking sites. People want to tell their stories."[447]

Creating their own web stars

Jill Bourque is right. People are being brought into the limelight through social networking sites, the new conduits for celebrities. While more traditional sources—recording companies and movie studios—are busily scanning the Internet for possible celebrities, kids are creating their own Web stars though text-messaging and sound files. When you have YouTube and Facebook, there is no need for a major label to become famous.

Teens are "tired of being force-fed the latest studio creation" and are waiting for an artist of their own choosing. When they find one, they will spread the word within minutes throughout the social websites.[448]

Advertisers and amateur videos

The advertising world has given still more exposure to creative young artists. A growing number of companies have sought out real people to produce—or supply ideas for—TV ads, capitalizing on the public's strong interest in amateur-produced videos. In 2007, submissions were solicited from amateurs for the TV SuperBowl coverage, exposing the winners to tens of millions of viewers.[449]

YouTube Video Awards

YouTube encourages amateur videos by having YouTube Video Awards to recognize the best user-created videos. Who decides the winners? You, of course. Winners chosen by the community members are prominently featured on YouTube and receive a trophy.[450]

Bum Rush the Charts

Podcasters have organized to hoist certain preferred tunes to the #1 spot on iTunes. Bum Rush the Charts is a movement that seeks to show the power of new media by encouraging 50,000 purchasers to buy particular songs at 99 cents each. This, they hope, could make the song #1 at iTunes for one day.[451]

More music choice

With the demise of record stores and depleted CD sales, average people have carved out the music world of their choice: one in which they can select the particular artist and song they want without having to buy someone else's predetermined collections of songs. "Digital downloads allow consumers to order exactly what they want at the very moment they want it."[452]

Once again, "You" are in charge.

The Internet and Self-Expression

The growing influence of digital self-expression raises many questions.

Blogging

Perhaps the thorniest question for the blogging world is the role of blogging: To be a trusted source of insight and information, or an Internet version of an infomercial?

Marketers know how powerful and well-connected some of the 12 million plus American bloggers are, so they seek to drive a wedge between them and their readers by luring bloggers to promote their product in blogs.

Blogger Seth Godin writes: "If your blog is remotely influential, people will attempt to influence you. The more often a blogger accepts the temptations, the less influential her blog will become."[453]

Wikipedia

Another way that people are directly affecting Internet content is through Wikipedia, the free Internet encyclopedia that anyone can edit. Here the driving question is centered on professional expertise. To what extent must a person have verified professional credentials, and reveal them, in order to be a contributor to the Wikipedia website? This is a central question because anonymity is considered responsible for Wikipedia's astonishing growth, riveting a reader's attention on the substance of what people have written rather than who they are.[454]

Other questions have arisen, too, around who should be allowed to contribute articles to Wikipedia. Gregory Kohs, a market researcher, launched a service called MyWickiBiz, a service that offered to write Wikipedia entries for businesses for $49 to $99. But a few days after putting out a press release, his account on Wikipedia was blocked, and he was told that MyWikiBiz was "antithetical" to Wikipedia's mission. Why is it so bad to pay someone to write something on Wikipedia? Kohs wanted to know.[455]

When Wikipedia barred the Church of Scientology from revising articles to reflect a pro- Scientology viewpoint, some bloggers claimed that Wikipedia was stifling free speech. Wikipedia bans hundreds of users every day to keep people with an agenda from propagandizing.[456]

Work

Before the recession of 2008 took hold, employees were becoming less satisfied with their jobs. [457] One in six workers sampled in 2006 intended to quit a job in the next year because of their dissatisfaction—*not* for better pay. This was a strong indication that workers were disengaged with their companies.[458]

Satisfied worker

Among workers who *are* satisfied with their jobs is Jim Buckmaster, CEO of Craigslist. He is not interested in dragging in a boatload of money through advertising; his interest is in the user.

"The impetus for everything we do comes from users," said Buckmaster. Because users are not suggesting they run text ads, they don't. Instead they happily rely on revenue from small fees charged (mostly) for job postings and real estate. In 2006 he was planning to keep growing the business by hiring more people and adding foreign sites in local languages.

As for charitable giving, Buckmaster prefers pursuing philanthropy from within the business model, rather than make money and then donate it to charity, as many companies do.[459]

Photo business

An online enterprise that has been drawing hoards of consumers is the production of merchandise containing photos. With myriad possibilities generated by Snapfish and Shutterfly, sales in photo novelties jumped 50 percent between 2005 and 2006 and were predicted to nearly double 2006 sales by 2008. Photos appear on calendars, greeting cards, china plates, and clothing—even on Jacuzzi tiles, furniture and tombstones.

"There's a big trend that people don't want to just have the same generic jewelry or the same generic card," said Jeffrey Housenbold, CEO of Shutterfly.[460]

Social entrepreneurs

Nicholas Kristof, *New York Times* columnist, made interesting observations about social entrepreneurs today relative to other generations.

In the 60's, students became civil rights workers and anti-war protesters, movements that transformed our country. Then in the 80's, entrepreneurs such as Steve Jobs and Bill Gates started companies that revolutionized societal problems in a new way, social entrepreneurship. This field has become so popular that universities now offer classes in it, and many students today are becoming social entrepreneurs to reach out and address the world's problems. Social entrepreneurship has clearly entered the lives of many average individuals, who strike out on their own to do what they can to help the world.

Kristof offers several examples of young entrepreneurs. One college student started Orphans Against AIDS, an organization that pays for schooling for children who have been affected by AIDS in poor countries. Another student founded an organization that collected old reading glasses while she was in college and shipped them to poor countries. Within just a few years Unite for Sight had provided eye care to 200,000 people.

The CEO of an organization that supports social entrepreneurship says that such people "neither hand out fish nor teach people to fish; their aim is to revolutionize the fishing industry."[461]

Government and Politics

When Arnold Schwarzenegger arrived at the swearing in ceremony for his second term as governor of California, he made his entrance to the soaring notes of Aaron Copland's "Fanfare for the Common Man." This was an especially timely tribute, which lifted up a new focus that was gaining momentum in the political realm during the early years of the 21st century.[462]

2008 election

The Web took a bold new step into politics in the 2008 election, when traditional sponsors faded into the background and CNN emerged as sponsor of the presidential debates. As candidates and parties successfully reached out to engage young people, online political activism became especially hot.[463]

That election became known as the YouTube election because video clips from average Americans supplied most of the questions to the candidates. Nearly 5,000 video clips were submitted for the Republican debate, from which CNN chose about two dozen.[464] The public at large was even given a chance to view and rate potential questions before the debate, though CNN made the final decision on which clips to use.

According to the Pew Internet and American Life Project, 14 million users created or shared political content during the 2006 campaign,[465] and 21 million users had watched political videos by February 2008.

Web interaction between presidential candidates and average Americans had started long before the debates. Hillary Clinton had an ongoing relationship with Yahoo that included contributing to a blog on Yahoo Health, in which she solicited ideas from users about ways to help prevent and eradicate breast cancer. It drew 4,890 responses. Julie Barko-Germany of the Institute for Politics, Democracy and the Internet at George Washington University said Clinton was showing that the Internet is the new town hall.

"So many people are used to politicians telling them what they think. In this case, it's the politician asking voters what they think and actually listening to the answers."[466]

War casualties

In a different way, certain individuals have stepped in where they felt the government was lacking. A number of Americans were frustrated by the U.S. Department of Defense tally of U.S. casualties in Iraq on its website. The numbers were updated slowly and showed different fatality counts from those in the media. Pat Kneisler, an anti-war protester, posted on the Web her own self-researched tally of troop casualties to show what she considered a more accurate count.[467]

We are bringing the world into ourselves—or, more accurately, finding the world within us— where we are envisioning the transformation it needs, and some are being moved from within to carry out their unique vision into the world. This may be one of the most energetic movements of soulf in the world today: the emergence of the average individual in shaping the course of human history.

For Reflection:

1. ....
....
....

2. ....
....
....

3. ....
....
....

CHAPTER 12
GLOBAL RELATIONSHIPS

"Now here, you see, it takes all the running you can do,
to keep in the same place. If you want to get somewhere
else, you must run at least twice as fast as that."
—Lewis Carroll, *Through the Looking Glass*

Twice as fast. This is the challenge of globalization in today's world. Just to stay where we are as a nation requires all the running we can do.

We see a focus on speed, with increasing momentum, in longer workdays; the highly scheduled lives of our children; societal pressure to make every moment count by multi-tasking, and prizing those who do most; fewer hours of sleep for both adults and children; 24/7 connectivity with others through Facebook and Twitter; and the consequent rebellion of the body in the form of widespread depression. We can't keep up with all we have to do.

No longer is there time to just "be." Instead of eating together as a family, we grab a bite of fast food on the way to the next soccer game, or meeting, or play rehearsal, with SUVs racing to deliver each family member on time and scattering them to the four winds. Quiet evenings at home watching TV together has been gobbled up by increasing amounts of homework, texting, scrambling to wash uniforms for tomorrow's game, checking Facebook, talking on cell phones, packing lunches, trying that new computer game—the list goes on and on. And not just one activity after another, but several at the same time.

Even that is not enough, we are told. If we are to remain #1 in the world, we must run at least twice as fast. Education has fallen way behind other countries, IPO's need to sizzle, and China is outpacing the U.S. while Uncle Sam runs up higher and higher deficits. We must do more!

This is the frantic world we are desperately trying to control. Even as the horses are running as fast as they can, we must crack the whip and urge them to go faster. Twice as fast!

ROOTS OF GLOBALIZATION

With our beginning as a species now traced back to a particular woman, "Ardi,"[468] in Ethiopia 4.4 million years ago, we could say that globalization also began at that time.

From Africa, we spread around the globe, some humans migrating westward into what has become Eastern Europe, and others migrating eastward and later forming nation states in Asia and Australia.[469] People lived as hunters and gatherers as they migrated until 10,000 years ago, when agriculture was developed. This enabled them to choose where to live and settle down in one place, managing their environment by planting crops rather than having to move around according to nature's whims.[470]

The new lifestyle was accompanied by a massive population explosion, as the number of offspring was no longer limited by the amount of available food. People could simply plant and harvest more crops to feed more mouths.[471]

Forward Leaps

Exploration and colonization of areas outside of Africa have been called the first "leap forward." The second great leap, agriculture, thrust us into the modern age. The current-day abstraction of life into cyberspace, fostering international communication and trade on a scale never before possible, is the third great leap. (This leap will be developed in subsequent chapters.)

GLOBALIZATION OF THE U.S. TODAY

If you planned an overseas trip in 2008, the chances are you were not going to Africa—and probably not to Europe. Your most likely destination would have been Mexico or Argentina—or maybe India or Japan. The only European countries that made it to the top ten list of hot vacation spots that year are Spain and France, both of which sneaked in under the wire at numbers nine and ten.[472]

These vacation choices are part of the phenomenon of globalization: humanity's horizon has expanded.

Global Trade

"A colleague of mine recently needed a new bicycle light. He flipped on his computer, searched for a few minutes and found a good one for the right price. Using his PayPal account, he paid for the light and shipping costs, shut off his computer and went back to his day. It wasn't until later that he realized he had logged on in Berkeley, bought the light from an online company in Hong Kong, which had the light assembled in inland China with parts made in the United States, and he had paid for it all thanks to a company head-quartered in San Jose.

"We suddenly live in a truly global world."
—*Jim Wunderman, president of the Bay Area Council of CEO's*

Outrunning competitors

Globalization in the San Francisco Bay Area rooted itself in megacompanies like Google and Intel over a period of years. In 2006 it spread to an astonishing 26 percent of companies with one to 49 workers. Trying to keep up this momentum and outrun U.S. competitors, the Bay Area Council[473] proposed a three-part plan:

1. Attract creative, innovative people
2. Support their innovative ideas by providing research facilities and a supply of risk capital; and
3. Increase global connectivity to spur trade capacity[474]

By 2007, the top five companies in Silicon Valley were taking in an average of 62 percent of their sales from overseas.[475]

Outsourcing

Outsourcing to Asia is another way companies were hoping to remain competitive on the world scene. The first jobs to be hit by outsourcing were in U.S. manufacturing, then technical support, airline reservations and tax preparation.

By 2007 it had started to claim even local journalism.

Publisher James MacPherson said small newspapers that could not afford additional staff in today's economy could improve their journalism by outsourcing reporting. He hired two reporters in India for about $21,000 to cover city news in Pasadena, saying that weekly Pasadena City Council meetings could be watched over the Internet.[476] "Whether you're at a desk in Pasadena or a desk in Mumbai, you're still just a phone call or e-mail away from the interview[477]."[478]

But outsourcing had its problems. Americans needing customer service complained that they had difficulty communicating with overseas employees who had learned English as a second language. Some companies responded by requiring employees to improve their American accent.

Near-shoring

Other companies found a different way to address customer service complaints—and cut costs at the same time. Instead of outsourcing, they switched to "near-shoring," that is, enlisting the services of people in Costa Rica, Mexico and other countries in the Western hemisphere. There they found knowledgeable, low-paid workers who spoke the customers' language fluently and understood their cultural nuances.[479] By 2008, language had become such a crucial factor in global trade that Craigslist added pages in French, German, Portuguese and Italian.[480]

Cultural differences

Language was not the problem of MySpace when it entered the Japanese market with its website. Instead the company was surprised by a challenging clash of cultures. Japan's counterpart to MySpace, "Mixi," had prim, organized columns and stamp-size photos instead of the flashy text and in-your-face photos of MySpace. A vice president[481] at Viacom International Japan[482] commented: "MySpace is about me, me, me… In Mixi, it's not all about me. It's all about us." The 31-year-old Mixi president Kenji Kasahara said the two websites merely reflect cultural differences. "I feel people speak their mind on MySpace. Japanese tend to like peaceful communication."[483]

Signs of Globalization in the U.S.

Air pollution

Scientists engaged in a 25-year study detected one of the earliest signs of globalization in the U.S. Their research showed that during the spring, ozone from Asia wafts into Washington, Oregon, California and other states west of the Rocky Mountains, impeding attempts to clean up the air in western United States. At the same time, emissions from the United States drift across the Atlantic and reach Europe. Air pollution is truly a global problem.[484]

Japanese car sales

A more overt sign of globalization was evident by 2006, when Japanese car sales in California surpassed domestic models. Although the state had developed a reputation for loving Toyotas and Hondas long before that, 2006 was the first year Japanese cars took the lead, grabbing a 44.8 percent share of the California market.[485]

Legal disputes

As the world economy began to play a larger role in the U.S., foreign countries started winning disputes in U.S. courts. One of the largest claimants, a Hong Kong conglomerate, won a $2.8 billion judgment against a company that provides interactive video technology.[486]

Linguistic diversity

In 2007, languages other than English began overtaking the homes of Silicon Valley, making it one of the most linguistically diverse places in America. Residents were challenged to see how living in a community of many languages could bring them together rather than divide them. [487] One of many responses was teaching earthquake readiness, a necessity in California, in Mandarin throughout Silicon Valley.[488]

Global stock trading

The impact of globalization hit the financial market, too. E-Trade Financial became the first U.S. discount brokerage to make it possible for customers all across America to trade foreign-listed stocks online. Seeing that U.S. investors were clearly ready for global stock trading, the company envisioned expanding to 42 international markets.[489]

"Nobody can deny the world is becoming more interconnected, a more global community," said Jarrett Lilien, president and CEO of E-Trade Financial (a timely comment in 2007). Since then, other brokerage firms have followed E-Trade Financial's lead.

Asian imports

Another sign of globalization was the explosion of imports from Asia. Imports from China alone increased 101 percent between 2000 and 2005. In addition, goods were arriving in America from Thailand, South Korea, Taiwan and Japan.

Suddenly huge shipments of arriving goods needed to be shipped to different parts of the United States. This spearheaded a railroad boom.

Boxcars, many of which had not seen the light of day for years, were rushed to ports in Los Angeles and Long Beach. There, goods were unloaded from container ships and sent by rail to their final destinations all across America.[490]

Chinese home buyers

People, too, began arriving. By 2009, wealthy Chinese had started signing up for home-buying tours to the U.S., hoping to snag a good deal as the U.S real estate market continued to plummet. Oriental Horizon, a popular TV program in China, recognized the trend and dedicated half an hour of prime time to the topic of house-hunting tours to the U.S. Luo Jie, a tour organizer from Beijing, explained: "You can buy a much better home in America for $400,000 or $500,000 than you can buy here."[491]

Co-opting people's cultures

McDonald's reached out to the ever-expanding Asian population in southern California by renovating its Hacienda Heights restaurant with the consultation of experts in feng shui, the Chinese practice of creating harmonious surroundings. A sociologist[492] at Pomona College called McDonald's experiment "a perfect example" of global capitalism co-opting people's cultures. "Hacienda Heights is a microcosm of a changing United States," she said.[493]

Racial disparities

Social research shows that innovation flowers from diversity. Since high tech thrives on innovation, it is puzzling that Hispanics[494] and blacks comprised a smaller share of Silicon Valley's computer workers in 2008 than they did in 2000, even as their share grew nationally. Black workers dropped by 16 percent, and Hispanic workers by 11 percent.[495]

Asians were the exception, comprising the majority of Silicon Valley workers in computer- related occupations. Vivek Wadhwa, who has studied the work-force dynamics of tech centers across the U.S.[496], attributes the disparity to the premium that high tech firms place on education. This "inherently gives Asians an advantage, because they tend to be stronger in math and science."[497] Achievement test scores for black and Latino students in Santa Clara County, where Silicon Valley is located, were even lower than for California overall.[498]

Clearly globalization is making its way deeper and deeper into local communities throughout America. Its presence is palpable, visible, and auditory—a life-changing phenomenon that is here to stay.

MIGRATION

Until mid-twentieth century, immigrants to the U.S. came, for the most part, from southern and eastern Europe. Since then Congress has opened up U.S. immigration policy, welcoming people from other parts of the world. These newer immigrants have been mostly Southeast Asians and Latinos from Mexico, Central America and South America. The Southeast Asian influx may have been a harbinger of the power shift from West to East.

Population Diversity

Multiculturalism

The millennial age is experiencing an erosion of ethnic, cultural and national boundaries to an extent never before seen, making this time of history an age of "hybridity."[499] A prime example is the U.S. 2000 census, which expanded the number of racial categories from five to sixty-three.[500]

President Barack Obama exemplifies much of the shift to multi-culturalism. He is African- American, having an African father (direct roots to Ardi's land) and an American mother. In addition, he lived in Indonesia (a predominantly Muslim country) as a child and had an Indonesian stepfather.[501]

In former years this would have caused anxiety in Whites (and, of course, still does in some people). Today, rather than fearing people of color, many Americans are beginning to reach out and embrace their differences, including Latino Muslims, black Buddhists and "Mien teenagers spouting Ebonics."[502]

"Arabs are becoming a prominent voting bloc in Dearborn Michigan; Cambodians an emerging group in Lowell, Massachusetts; Vietnamese a powerhouse in Houston; Cubans a central part of Florida's politics; and the gay capital may still be in San Francisco, but gay marriage is now legal in New Jersey and Massachusetts."[503] As of 2020, 37 U.S. states and the District of Columbia have legalized gay marriage. We are becoming global citizens in an increasingly global world.

Future ethnic status

The Census Bureau foresees majority ethnic status becoming obsolete well before mid-century, with the U.S. population growing both younger and older. Latinos, Asians and other minority groups are expected to become a majority of the nation's working-age population soon after 2035, with the white population starting to shrink as it dies at a rate faster than children are born. [504] Both greater diversity and immigration are causing the anticipated population growth of 44 percent between 2008 and 2050.[505]

Illegal immigrants

Illegal immigrants are part of the contributing factor. Nearly nine million people are living in "mixed-status" families, where one or both parents are undocumented while their children are citizens. The huge growth in children born to illegal immigrants has intensified calls to change the Constitution to remove the rights to citizenship by birth. Others counter that bringing unauthorized immigrants into the mainstream would stimulate the economy.[506]

Majority minority

The Asian and Latino population in California continued to surge even during the economic downturn.[507] In 2008 Whites comprised 38 percent of the population, Asians 31 percent and Hispanics 26 percent. [508] Although Whites, Asians and Hispanics are more evenly balanced in California than anywhere else in America, ten percent of the counties nationwide have become "majority minority," in which Whites are less than half the population.

Even before California's balancing figures were released, in 2006 shifting demographics had prompted the U.S. Senate to declare English the national language of the United States. Democrats denounced the action as racist, saying it could undercut civil rights law, but Republicans asserted the legislation would unify the nation's increasingly diverse population. [509]

Immigrants Rising

An argument against increased immigration, raised by both sides of the issue, has been that the surge has overwhelmed the U.S. with low-wage foreign laborers. However, data show about two-thirds of all immigrants in the country nearly evenly distributed across the job and income spectrum. In the largest metropolitan areas like San Francisco, Boston, and New York, more immigrants are employed in white-collar occupations than in lower-wage work like construction, manufacturing or cleaning. Moreover, cities with thriving immigrant populations have prospered the most over the past two decades.[510]

Nipping at the heels of arguments against increased immigration is a more recent scenario that suggests a new wave of illegal immigrants will be arriving from China. Until now, Mexico has supplied the U.S. with immigrant workers to fill low-wage jobs. However, "Mexican immigration—legal and undocumented—now stands at an all-time low and may have even stopped."

At the same time, it is predicted that an influx of Chinese immigrant workers will begin arriving in the U.S. when the U.S. job market grows stronger. China's new economy requires urban manpower to fill low-level construction, manufacturing and household services jobs. Low-wage urban labor markets have become so competitive that 20 million people have been left without work. This has precipitated "the largest peacetime migration in recorded human history," numbering 220 million people, almost half of China's entire urban population. It is estimated that several million of them will find their way to the U.S., many illegally.[511]

Year of the immigration movement

2006 could be called "Year of the Immigration Movement." In that year illegal immigrants— mostly Latinos— began to exercise political power by bringing together masses of people. Nationwide rallies drew both illegal immigrants and their supporters, seeking justice for all immigrants.[512] As they gathered, the movement itself gained momentum, inaugurating what some hopefully called "a new civil rights movement." Their cries for justice marked the emergence of a new voice in American politics.

Leaders of the rallies planned another national gathering for later in the year,[513] but gradually immigrant voices petered out, as their cries fell on deaf ears in Congress.

Immigrants and political life

Immigrants have blended into political life faster than many had expected, shattering the stereotypical picture of their reluctance to embrace political power. In 2006, the first Muslim member of Congress was sworn in, placing his hand on an English translation of the Koran once owned by Thomas Jefferson. That same year five Asian-American mayors were elected to office in a California county where one out of every four residents is Asian.[514] Asian-American mayors have emerged in numerous other U.S. cities as well.

Talented immigrants

Success stories such as these are hardly surprising when one considers the high achievement level of some immigrant students. In the Intel Science Talent Search, a prestigious competition funded by the Intel Foundation, four winners[515] in 2010 were of Chinese or Indian background. Their winning entries included: a more efficient way to produce hydrogen by growing a type of algae without oxygen; creating an algorithm that recognizes concepts, a project which led to the student helping researchers at NASA/Ames Research Center search for breaks in oil pipelines in Alaska; analyzing the chemical composition of stars of Andromeda, which could aid in the search for extraterrestrial life; and adding to knowledge of graph theory and game theory, with applications in neural networks, the Internet and other developing technology. The student[516] who submitted the latter entry also won a gold medal at the U.S.- China math Olympiad, placed in a short-story contest, won an art honorable mention and won the novice division of a debate contest.[517]

Immigration legislation and control

When Latinos were speaking out on streets across the United States, the Bush administration was focused in a different direction—the Mexican border. Enforcements at the border near Yuma, Arizona, included "a 20-foot-tall corrugated metal structure, an 8-foot-tall chain-link fence topped by razor-sharp concertina wire, powerful lights, watchtowers and video cameras."[518]

In a visit to the border site, then-president Bush announced 6,000 National Guard soldiers would be deployed there, too, because "the need to enforce the border is urgent." This was in response to a 13 percent spike in attempts to cross the border illegally near Yuma, after the border in eastern Arizona had been reinforced.[519]

While President Bush was struggling to enforce the Mexican border, many U.S. police departments were failing to report "suspected" illegal immigrants to federal authorities. They argued they would be violating the trust of immigrant communities that they needed to do their jobs.[520]

Although immigration legislation lost the immediate attention of the federal government during the economic crisis of 2008, President Obama later announced executive actions he would take to fix what he could.

SHIFTING WINDS: CHINA

U.S. Invades China Market

Though reluctant to admit it, the United States is being seriously challenged in its world standing. India, Brazil, and arguably others countries are making inroads in the world market. But America's chief competitor for #1 global status is China.

As early as 2006, China had become chipmaker Intel's second-largest consumer market after the United States, warranting a separate sales and marketing region from the rest of the Asia-Pacific area.[521]

That same year BlackBerry challenged its Chinese competitor, Redberry, by launching its mobile e-mail service in China.[522] This was riskier than it may have seemed at the time, given the fact that a year later the government of France banned the use of BlackBerrys by certain officials for fear the United States could spy on their wireless transmissions. Alain Juillet, head of French economic intelligence, said, "The risks of interception are real. It is economic war."[523]

Dell, too, faced with slackening sales and stiff competition here at home, began aggressively pursuing foreign markets. It targeted low income, first-time computer users in China with a new desktop computer available only in China, where business was strong, growing, and profitable. Jacqui Zhou, spokeswoman for Dell, said, "Today [2007] there are 1 billion people online worldwide, and many of the world's second billion users are right here in China."[524] Although the U.S. has 2½ times the number of Internet users that China has, Chinese users grew an astounding 44 percent between 2000 and 2006. If China were to undergo a 74.9 percent market penetration (as in Sweden), it would have 979 million total users, a 696 percent increase.[525]

By 2009 China had become the world's most populous mobile phone market. Thousands of unlocked iPhones had been brought into China from other markets and were in use there. Apple joined those already in the Chinese market by negotiating with China Unicorn about becoming their Chinese partner.[526]

Trimble Navigation followed other American companies that set up business in China. By 2009 it was expecting a double-digit percentage sales growth due to the country's economic stimulus spending, which was significantly larger than the U.S. stimulus for infrastructure. Trimble's global positioning technology helps guide farm tractors and bulldozers, enabling more efficient fertilization of fields and precise excavations for construction.[527]

Rise of China

Reaching out

During the past 20 years, China has undergone a makeover. Though crowds of people are still overwhelming, and air pollution chokes the visitor, other things have changed for the better.

The Beijing Olympics Bird's Nest with its cutting edge architecture is a symbol of a new China, willing to reach out to the rest of the world. Twenty years ago it would have been unthinkable for an American television network to broadcast even-handed coverage of anything from Beijing; yet it did so at the 2008 Olympics.[528] In addition, Chinese people are polite to visitors and many of them speak English.

These changes suggest that the government has made an effort to reshape China and buy into international give and take. A more recent sign was China's willingness to join the United States and other countries in endorsing sanctions against Iran, a clear shift in China's foreign policy.

Reaching in

In addition to "reaching out" to foreigners, China is also "reaching in" to people in its rural areas. Beijing launched a campaign in 2009, "Send Automobiles to the Countryside," an effort to hasten rural development and boost domestic consumption at a time when demand for Chinese exports was on a downturn. While new car sales were plunging in the U.S., sales jumped more than nine percent in China, giving China the status of overtaking the U.S. in car sales in 2009. [529]

A car, a house, a computer and a mobile phone. These remain the desires of the rising Chinese middle class, but mere production of these goods is no longer enough. People now want creative design, too.

To meet the demand, around 500 schools across the land have introduced design courses. An exciting entrepreneurial design culture is emerging, with interests ranging from architecture to research and development. In Beijing, architecture as daring as the Bird's Nest is emerging, embodying China's economic transformation and global ambitions. The Chinese government believes that the future of their economy depends on its becoming innovation-driven. That belief is becoming a reality.[530]

China and Clean Energy

Foremost in China's booming economy is a Green Revolution, stemming from awareness that energy technology is both a necessity and an opportunity. Thomas L. Friedman, columnist for *The New York Times*, goes so far as to name China's Green Revolution the most important thing to happen in the first decade of the 21st century. Just the volume of wind, solar, mass transit, nuclear and more efficient coal-burning projects launched in 2009 is in itself stunning. With China undergoing the biggest migration of people from rural to urban centers "in the history of mankind," the demand for energy is huge, and China has chosen to respond with clean services from within their own country. If the U.S. is to compete with China, it must establish a carbon price that comparably stimulates and rewards clean power innovation.[531]

An important part of China's Green Revolution is the hydropower generated by the Three Gorges Dam, which provides one-ninth of China's energy needs. The dam is designed to produce energy equivalent to the output of 18 coal or nuclear power plants and to increase China's shipping volume 400 percent.

Cost of the dam is great—both for the people and the environment. The dam project has displaced well over a million people and has shown disregard for its impact on wildlife in the river's ecosystem.[532]

China strives to be dominant in the emerging global clean-tech industry. Its central government has committed more than $100 billion a year to green technology research and has set up incentives to create markets for their green products. China is now the world's largest producer and exporter of solar cells. It is also the largest hydropower generator in the world and the largest manufacturer of wind turbines.

A group of Silicon Valley tech executives, concerned about China's rising status, sent a letter to U.S. Energy Secretary Steven Chu, saying: "Unless we move quickly and commit substantial resources on a sustained basis, we risk becoming an energy also-ran." They urged the government to provide financial assistance to clean energy industries.

The Obama administration responded by making a "robust" cleantech industry a top priority, awarding $80 billion from the stimulus bill to promote renewable energy. The president also proposed spending $150 billion in clean energy research over 10 years.[533]

Chinese Satisfaction

Out of 24 countries surveyed in 2008 by Pew Research Center, the nation that emerged as clear winner in terms of satisfaction of its people was China. No other nation came even close.

"Eighty-six percent of Chinese people surveyed said they were content with the country's direction, up from 48 percent in 2002… And 82 percent of Chinese were satisfied with their national economy, up from 52 percent," according to *The New York Times*.[534]

Yes, China punishes dissent, restricts freedom and persecutes all faiths that worship a God higher than the state. Yet two-thirds of all Chinese say the government is doing a good job in dealing with the issues of greatest concern to them.[535]

U.S. WORLD STATURE

Innovation

Leaders in information technology (IT) have had to work hard to persuade government officials to invest more heavily in research and support innovation. The government was slow to see the "IT revolution," even though it has been a major boost to U.S. economic growth, adding $2 trillion a year to the economy. IT has given new tools to businesses and improved productivity while controlling costs, according to IT leaders. Their goal has been to push an "innovation agenda" in Washington.[536]

Microsoft

Microsoft founder Bill Gates pushed the federal government in a different way, saying we need to double the number of science, technology and math graduates before 2015 and increase funding for basic research. He also urged Congress to make visas more readily available to foreign workers for high-tech industries, as they are vital to U.S. competitiveness. [537]

Stanford University

Universities, too, have chimed in. They need the federal government to loosen up on restrictions. Former Stanford University president, John Hennessy told Congress that current regulations are hampering research collaboration and innovation, which has become increasingly more team-based and international because of the Internet. "The conduct of science and technology has changed over the past two decades due to the end of the Cold War and the globalization of science and technology… regulation can lead to a loss of scientific leadership," he said.[538]

Patents

With pressure from many sectors of the American economy and recognizing the need to shore up U.S. stature in the eyes of the world, the federal government has taken measures to foster innovation.

One important step is the Patent Reform Act of 2007, which helps U.S. companies become more competitive and creative. Innovation has become increasingly abstract, tilting away from mechanical inventions and toward invisible properties. Patent protection is crucial, since American intellectual property is valued at $5.5 trillion, more than the gross domestic product of any other single country.

A downside of the Reform Act is the drain on the U.S. economy from legal expenses for patent disputes. Infringement awards reached $3.6 billion in 2006, dollars that could have been spent on research and development.[539]

Yet patent disputes were exacerbated when smartphone litigation began flooding courtrooms in the wake of the 2007 iPhone debut. Silicon Valley companies spent more than $5 billion on patents in 2011 alone—months before the year even ended! Determined to protect their patent rights, companies competed heavily for top patent lawyers and added new legal positions such as vice president of patents, manager of patent acquisitions, and head of intellectual-property litigation. "The world of intellectual property, and more specifically patent transactions, is really heating up," said Steve John, managing director at Lindsey & Africa in San Francisco.[540]

Despite the smartphone litigation craze, many believe that the Patent Reform Act is our best chance at promoting innovation and curbing litigation, as it provides a way for patent examiners to make informed decisions, and for inventors to dispute the validity of a patent without going to court.

Silicon Valley

The federal government may have been slow to shake off memories of the dot-com bust, but Silicon Valley has remained one of the globe's high-tech capitals. Though total employment in the Valley dipped to one of the lowest in the country during the recession, largely due to the loss of middle-wage jobs, wages have been up and innovation is sizzling. This is largely because technology dominates the work force in Silicon Valley more than in any other place in the country. After the dot-com bust, the region transformed itself, shedding jobs in old-line industries while creating new, high-wage positions in brand-new fields.

"The creativity in Silicon Valley has never been stronger," said Carl Guardino, head of Silicon Valley Leadership Group. "Whether that's clean and green tech or numerous other technology clusters, the innovation sector is strong." A consultant who has held a series of high-paying tech jobs was not surprised to hear this. "The innovation is done here by a few highly paid people, while all the work to keep it going is overseas."[541]

Biotechnology

In 2006 biotech firms in Northern California had 300 medical products on the market and nearly 400 more in late-stage tests. They were on the cusp of a commercial explosion.

Yet biotech experts saw writing on the wall. "We are starting to see part of a brain drain" of biotech talent heading to China, India, and other nations where it is cheaper to operate with fewer government regulations. "That is what's alarming," warned Dr. Daniel Perez, a venture partner with a San Francisco investment firm.[542]

U.S. Competition

With the developing trend of regional markets, Hong Kong became a world center for floating new stock listings. In 2006 it surged past New York to become number two in the world for launching IPO's, with London maintaining its #1 position and New York falling to number three. [543]

China was poised to overtake Germany to become the world's third-largest economy, behind those of the United States and Japan. In the first quarter of 2007 it grew 11.1 percent, following four consecutive years of double-digit economic growth. With exports jumping 28 percent, the Shanghai Stock Exchange also surged ahead, up more than 200 percent between January 2006 and April 2007.[544]

In 2009 five companies were named the most innovative ones in the world. All were U.S. companies—Google, Apple, Facebook, GE, and IDEO.[545] Yet Jet Airways was running a full- page ad at the time that subtly, or not so subtly, suggested the encroachment of Asian countries on the global status of the U.S.

The ad featured a black page with a single white caption in the top half that read: "India is about to get closer."[546]

India and China were already the two fastest-growing of the G-20 countries.[547] By 2010 China had secured the #2 position in a list of the world's largest economies, with the U.S. still #1 and Japan taking the #3 spot. Germany had slipped to #4.

Currently the United States holds a 20 percent share of the world GDP. Economists predict, however, that by 2030 China will account for 19 percent of world GDP, leaving the United States behind at 16 percent.[548]

In 2009, eight in 10 Americans were saying the U.S. would lose its innovation advantage in the global economy over the next decade, while close to half believed that Japan or China had already surpassed the U.S. in innovation. "Forty-three percent said remaining the world's innovation leader was the most important factor for future U.S. successes, ranking higher than economic size or military supremacy."[549]

WORLD LEADER: WASHINGTON OR BEIJING?

"The world is witnessing the passing of the United States as the greatest industrial power and the most self-sufficient republic the world had ever seen... An end to the Second American Century, as the Asian Century begins."
—Patrick Buchanan, syndicated columnist

While the U.S. was losing its popularity and influence internationally, China was gaining both. It became the first real alternative since the Cold War to the U.S. model of free markets and democracy, demonstrating that a regime can suppress organized opposition and need not establish its legitimacy through elections. This has been attractive to authoritarian leaders throughout the world, who are seeking to maintain their grip on power. Equally important to them, China shows that a ruling party can maintain considerable control over information and the Internet without slowing economic growth.[550]

At the World Economic Forum in 2010, questions were raised about the political stability of the United States, and whether or not a Beijing Consensus would replace the Washington Consensus.[551]

In contrast to the Washington Consensus, the Beijing Consensus has lots of "government guidance, strictly controlled capital markets and an authoritarian decision-making process... without having to heed daily public polls." Developing countries are seeking "a recipe for faster growth and greater stability" than the Washington Consensus now offers.[552]

The U.S. was still world innovation leader and accounted for nearly a third of the trillion dollars spent globally on research and development. More science and engineering doctorates were being awarded in the U.S. than in other places in the world, and American patents outnumbered those of any other country.

Yet China's annual growth in spending on research and development averaged 20 percent compared to America's five to six percent.

"The United States led the world's economies in the 20th century because we led the world in innovation. Today, the competition is keener; the challenge is tougher; and that is why innovation is more important than ever."
—President Barack Obama

The Obama administration took steps to address the lag by initiating the Educate to Innovate campaign to improve math and science education, making commitments to support green technologies, and investing in ubiquitous broadband.[553]

Despite these efforts, the CEO of Joint Venture Silicon Valley was concerned about the Valley's ability to recoup its worldwide reputation as "the epicenter of innovation." Eleven percent unemployment compared to the 10 percent national average, with a shrinking middle-income population in the Valley, portended a growing "hour-glass economy." In addition, venture capital, which used to be Silicon Valley's "secret sauce, hasn't made money in about ten years," due to the trend toward multi-million dollar buy-outs.[554] That was early 2010.

By summer 2011 the picture had changed. Silicon Valley saw a surge in hiring and new construction for expansion. Many of the new jobs were in information, computer design and scientific services, all crucial areas for innovation. By July, Silicon Valley employers had added 30,800 jobs and it was not expected to slow down during the rest of 2011 and into 2012.

"That's a good indicator of a pending recovery," said a labor market specialist.[555] Already Silicon Valley is seeing a rippling out of their gains in non-tech sectors.[556]

The demand for system administrators "is growing as fast as we've seen it, faster than the dot-com bubble."
—Jeff Freeland, Astreya Partners

BOUNDARY BREAKING

National Boundaries

Today's world of globalization is like clusters—or an aggregate of galaxies. With mass migration and instant communication, it is no simple matter to indicate the boundaries of one country. A map showing the world's true boundaries would need to be fluid, intangible, high tech, and multidimensional, with many crosscuts. Borders are not only on the ground, but also in cyberspace, multilateral agencies and the virtual world of international finance.[557] A fence to define a national boundary is a thing of the past.

"Where is the real U.S. border, for example, when U.S. customs agents check containers in the port of Amsterdam? Where should national borders be marked when drug traffickers launder money through illegal financial transactions that crisscross the globe electronically, violating multiple jurisdictions?. And when U.S. health officials fan out across Asia seeking to contain a disease outbreak, where do national lines truly lie?"[558]

Dual citizenship

National boundaries are but one of countless areas in which globalization has changed the playing field. A growing number of nations are now allowing dual citizenship, and more people are taking advantage of it.[559]

Accounting standards

The Securities and Exchange Commission voted to eliminate a requirement that foreign companies with U.S.-traded shares use U.S. accounting standards. Such companies may now choose between international and U.S. accounting standards, which could lead to the acceptance of a single, global accounting standard for public companies. [560]

Outer Space

Boundary breaking has extended even further. In 2008 a group of nine nations, including the U.S., agreed to explore the lunar surface together. The participating nations envisioned a multinational fleet of robot spacecraft returning to the moon, leading to the eventual return of astronauts, "sort of like the beginning of a 'beautiful friendship'[561]."[562]

After that, President Obama withdrew the U.S. from the agreement. He envisioned U.S. exploration of deep-space, rather than a return to the moon. "Space exploration is not a luxury, not an afterthought in America's brighter future. It is an essential part of that quest," he said. [563] That quest must now take a back seat to the economy's needs.

For the time being, we have the International Space Station, which is alive and healthy, and has become a hub for cross-cultural collaboration. Even though the U.S. is no longer part of that collaborative effort, it marks our long-range footprint in outer space—not as independent nations, but as Planet Earth.

For Reflection:

1. ....

....

....

2. ....

....

....

3. ....

....

....

CHAPTER 13
ENERGY

WORK

The 20th century swept through history in fulfillment of its era. Industries, transportation and communication flourished, ushering in a level of prosperity barely dreamed of in days following the Civil War.

A manufacturing boom supplied all corners of the United States with needed goods, as well as luxury items. Working men (most women were homemakers) banded together and formed unions, which protected rights for workers and balanced their interests against those of employers.

While unions were tempering corporate power, Congress reinforced their actions with anti- monopoly legislation to prevent companies from becoming "too big to fail." Power became relatively balanced between employers and employees, and companies were both stable and distinct from one another. Because of this, workers were generally loyal to their company, often working for the same employer in one location for their entire career.

World War II brought about a seismic shift in this work pattern. Perhaps the change began when women were called to become "Rosie the Riveter" in factories that churned out materials and equipment for the war effort. Many of them enjoyed this new experience of going to work each day and contributing to America's defense.

By the time the war ended, women had established their place on the workforce, and many of them continued to work outside the home. The rising Feminist Movement brought even more women into the workplace, increasing their numbers as the century marched on. Gradually women were accepted into jobs with more responsibility, but they have never been on a par with men in terms of pay and holding the highest positions.

Despite their lesser status in the workplace, women affected work in new ways. Men had generally observed a clear boundary between work and family life, but women could not leave family at home so easily. They had no wife at home to take care of a sick child, to pick up a child from day care when work went overtime, or to handle other emergencies.

As the situation began to encroach on the workplace, employers had to pay attention. This resulted in their paying for maternity leave (and increasingly even paternity leave) and employer- supported childcare; and some employers offered flex-time work scheduling, shared jobs, telecommuting and other benefits tailored to the needs of women, depending on their particular constituency.

Along with these boundary-breaking changes, companies also reached out to their communities by participating in civic affairs and community events, contributing to local causes, and sponsoring local sports teams. Larger companies engaged in this type of outreach at the national level, too.

With time, the environment of the workplace became more relaxed and open. Receptionists greeted visitors by their first name; women arrived at work in pants and pant suits; cubicles dotted large open spaces, supplanting private offices and encouraging rapport among employees; Friday became a "dress-down" day; doughnuts showed up during the morning coffee break; and Christmas office parties became "holiday" parties.

Toward the latter part of the century, the character of companies began to shift. The substance- oriented culture of manufacturing suddenly found itself competing with service technologies, scientific processes, and other abstract-oriented enterprises. Large corporations acted like Pac- Man, gobbling up smaller companies and becoming "too big to fail." Mergers and spin-offs became everyday newspaper headlines.

Loyalty to one's company petered out and became a thing of the past. Employees started looking out for their own welfare and hardly thought twice about leaving their company if a better deal came along.

No longer were workers settled in one location for most of their career. Instead, jetting around the country on business became commonplace, as was uprooted family life. Some married couples—even as parents—worked on opposite coasts of the U.S., flying one direction or the other on weekends, holidays and vacations to be together.

Some people chose to work independently, hiring themselves out as consultants and doing piecework for various companies, while others hired on for longer stints in various parts of the world. With computers that could go anywhere, some workers became adventurous and tried out free-lancing or signed computer-based contracts, working wherever they chose.

The "security card" of working for firmly rooted companies was traded in for a "freedom card." Wherever people landed, they kept an eye on the NASDAQ and watched their holdings rise. By the end of the century, life had reached a booming crescendo in the form of the dot.com boom.

Then—9/11. . .

JOBLESSNESS

The deep economic recession that occurred in the last half of the first decade of the new millennium brought widespread unemployment. With lost jobs totaling as many as 651,000 per month, the unemployment rate kept rising to double-digit figures, reaching more than 12 percent in Silicon Valley.[564]

Though the technology industry fared better than the private sector as a whole, it lost 250,000 jobs in 2009 after four straight years of job growth. The biggest losers were in high-tech manufacturing, including makers of electronic components and semiconductors.[565] Stores and factories closed, and many people predicted that lost jobs would not return.

Instead, the government would need to emphasize re-training workers for other careers.[566]

People complained when the stimulus bill passed by Congress, hefty as it was, failed to halt unemployment. "In terms of creating jobs, it doesn't seem like it's created very many," commented Emory University economist Thomas Smith. "It may well be employing lots of people but those two things are very different."[567]

Effect on the World

In our globalized world, joblessness could not be contained. Unemployment in the sixteen euro nations reached 10 percent in late 2009, indicating the stress the recession had caused in Europe. Spain registered the highest unemployment rate in the European Union (E.U.) at 19.4 percent. [568]

And joblessness did not stop there. Baltic countries were badly hit, too, with unemployment more than doubling in Latvia (22.3 percent), Estonia (15.2 percent) and Lithuania (14.6. percent).[569]

Responses to Job Loss

In a survey made in early 2010, the Conference Board found that 55 percent of Americans were dissatisfied with their work,[570] the highest level ever recorded by the research group. Part of the blame can be attributed to the recession—the worst since the 1930's—but worker dissatisfaction had been on the rise for more than two decades. "It says something troubling about work in America," said Linda Barrington of the Conference Board. Economists said if the job satisfaction trend is not reversed, it could stifle innovation and hurt America's competitiveness and productivity.[571]

Some fear that "patent reform," pushed by corporate lobbyists, would also hurt innovation. Corporations want Congress to reduce the use fee they currently pay for patented technology. Opponents of such legislation say it would reduce incentives for inventors and for venture capitalists. They call it "a crisis of arrogance and greed."[572]

WOMEN AND WORK

Since the 1960's, women have been fighting work discrimination in myriad forms. Airline stewardesses were one of the first to complain publicly.

Stewardesses Speak Out

At a Congressional meeting in 1964, airline executives testified that it was "imperative for businessmen that attractive women light their cigars and fix drinks." Representative Martha Griffiths retorted: "What are you running, an airline or a whorehouse?"[573] Things began to change.

The job of "stewardess" was changed to gender-neutral "flight attendant," men joined the ranks, and married women—even grandmothers—were welcomed. No more airline "ban on marriage, the age discrimination and the endless measurements to check for weight gain.[574]"[575]

Those were times when women "were not meant to compete with men, to act independently of men, to earn their own bread, or to have adventures on their own. . .They could not go into business without their husbands' permission or get credit without male co-signers.[576]"[577]

Women Take on Careers

Gradually the U.S. got used to the idea of women working outside the home, ostensibly to contribute to the family income, which was becoming inadequate for the mode of living Americans had adopted. By the 1980's, the idea of women making money had morphed into the idea of women having serious careers. More women than men attended college and the gender gap in pay began to narrow. However, even as of 2009, women were earning only 77 cents for every male dollar.[578]

Half of the law students and medical students today are female, and women now hold the majority of jobs.[579] Women have run for president, "fought for their country, argued before the Supreme Court, performed heart surgery," involvements in society that would have boggled the mind 50 years ago.[580]

Yet the Fortune 500 companies have only 15 female CEOs.[581]

Balancing work and home

As big as their accomplishments have been to the present time, women have not satisfactorily mastered the balancing act of holding down a good and demanding job while raising children. [582] As Amy Bloom put it, "Feminism did not resolve the conflicting desires for passion and domesticity... but it did not fail."[583]

Women Worldwide

Seen in relation to the rest of the world, women still have a long road ahead. The U.S. places number 12 among industrialized countries in terms of the share of women in the workforce. In fact, the U.S. female employment rate has fallen from its high of 67.8 percent of the workforce in 2000 to 65.9 percent as of 2007.[584] According to federal data, women in computer-related occupations saw declines around the country in 2008, having already fallen from 37 percent in 1999 to 33 percent in 2005 within the combined work force of ten of Silicon Valley's largest companies.[585] Men and women in technical careers are equally likely to hold mid-level jobs, "but men are 2.7 times more likely than women to be promoted to a high-ranking tech job."[586]

In Iceland, the world's leader in share of women in the labor force, over 81 percent of all women work, followed by Norway at over 74 percent. Turkey ranks lowest, with only 23 percent of its women working. According to Goldman Sachs, "if women in Italy and Spain were to reach the same employment rate as men, their countries' GDPs could grow by around 20 percent—well over double what the United States, Germany or Britain could expect."[587]

BREAKING THE GENDER BARRIER

"Female occupations"

The top three occupations with the highest percentage of female workers in 2005 were dental hygienists (98.6 percent), preschool and kindergarten teachers (97.7 percent), and secretaries and administrative assistants (96.9 percent).[588] Secretaries and administrative assistants ranked highest in total number of female workers, at 3.46 million, with registered nurses ranking second. However RNs ranked only 14th in percentage of female workers.[589] The top 15 occupations held by women constitute 12.8 million workers, compared with only 3.81 million workers in the top 15 occupations held by men.[590] In 12 of the top 15 "most female occupations," relationship with other people is central to the work. All 15 of the top "most male occupations" are focused on physical labor with "things" (such as cranes, logs, pipes, etc.).[591]

Women in "men's work"

Media give considerable attention to women if their work is outside the "most female occupations," especially when they are employed in occupations traditionally considered "men's work."

Politician

In January 2007 Nancy Pelosi became the first U.S. Speaker of the House and second in line to the presidency, a symbol of the rise of women in politics. As she commented during her acceptance speech, "We have broken the marble ceiling."[592] Though not making it as far as the White House, Hillary Clinton broke through new turf when she ran a close race for the U.S. presidency.

Nobel laureate, Rigoberta Menchu, sought to become president of her country, Guatemala, in 2007. Her bid was unsuccessful, but the fact that she even sought the presidency as a Mayan peasant woman is indicative of the political strides that women and Indians have made across Latin America.[593]

Lawyer

Justice Elena Kagan, while not the first woman on the U.S. Supreme Court, has had her share of "firsts." She was the first woman to be dean of Harvard Law School and the first woman to be solicitor general. In addition, her appointment to the Supreme Court probably marks a permanent shift away from a court with a "lone female justice, probably not going back to a court with only two women."[594] Whereas a few years ago, women cheered for a lone woman sitting at a boardroom conference table with a group of men, today we expect not one, but a reasonable number of women, to be present.[595]

Nearly 50 women are currently serving on federal appeals courts, the majority of whom have been married and have children. In claims of sex discrimination, "not only do males and females bring distinct approaches to these cases, but the presence of a female on a panel actual causes male judges to vote in a way they otherwise would not—in favor of plaintiffs. [596]"[597]

However, women lawyers have not fared as well as those in political life. Even though the gender gap has narrowed in terms of law firms luring female lawyers, women are facing intractable challenges in becoming partners.

As a result, women are leaving the legal profession at a much higher rate than men. According to a Boston study[598] of 1,000 Massachusetts lawyers, 31 percent of female associates had left private practice entirely, compared with 18 percent of male associates. "This shows that we are reaching a crisis point when it comes to the retention and advancement of women in the legal profession," said Lauren Stiller Rikleen[599], a senior law partner Bowditch & Dewey.[600]

The gender gap widens among legal associates with children, reflecting the cultural reality that women remain the primary caregivers of children and are therefore more likely to leave their firms for family reasons. Other factors contributing to the dropout rate among female lawyers are "demanding hours, inflexible schedule, lack of viable part-time options, emphasis on billable hours and failure by law firms to recognize that female lawyers' career trajectories may alternate between work and family."[601]

Sommelier

A growing number of females are taking on the traditionally male role of sommelier. "It's a proven fact that women have better palates than men," said Andrew Green, wine director for the Bacchus Management Group. "They can be more sensitive to aromas and flavors." Though still in the minority when it comes to Master Sommeliers, the number of female applicants for the Advanced Sommelier exam has quadrupled in the past five years.[602]

> **"Women have smashed every glass ceiling
> in the wine world, from managing vineyards
> to crafting cult wines."**
> —*Jessica Zadegaran, sommelier*

Other countries

Women in other parts of the Americas are also moving up the political ladder. The same year Nancy Pelosi became Speaker of the House, a raft of leftist females assumed Cabinet posts across South America.

Chile

Chile's first female president, Michelle Bachelet, named 10 women to her cabinet of 20 persons and promised equal numbers of men and women in 300 other decision-making posts.[603]

Among her Cabinet appointments was Vivianne Blanlot, named as Defense Minister. When Blanlot went as the government's envoy to the funeral of Augusto Pinochet, ex-dictator of Chile, she was booed loudly. President Bachelet, a socialist and former torture victim, had faced similar challenges when she was Defense Minister. Despite this, she garnered enough public respect to become Chile's president.[604]

Ecuador

In the same month that Bachelet became president, Ecuadorean president Rafael Correa filled seven of his 17 Cabinet posts with women. Among them was Guadalupe Larriva, Ecuador's first female defense minister, who reportedly held the full support of the military. When she was killed in a helicopter crash a month later, President Correa said he would appoint another woman as defense minister.[605]

Argentina

Nilda Garre became Argentina's first female minister of defense in 2005, 30 years after a dictatorship had been installed. Two years later she announced that former military officers could no longer use secrecy laws as an excuse not to testify about abductions, torture and disappearances under junta rule.[606]

Uruguay

Uruguay also chose a female defense chief, Azucena Berruti, who is a socialist and lawyer who defended political prisoners during the 1973-1985 military rule. She "did not hesitate to sack her army chief last year [2006] for unauthorized meetings with political foes of the president."[607]

Women now comprise one-third of the defense chief posts in South America.[608]

Challenges Facing Women Today

"The Shriver Report: A Woman's Nation" on the social condition and challenges facing women in 2009 was the first of its kind since Eleanor Roosevelt headed John F. Kennedy's President's Commission on the Status of Women in 1961. Today women comprise half of the U.S. workforce. Forty percent of those women are primary breadwinners.

When men moved away from farms and into the cities in the 1920s and '30s, industries adjusted to accommodate them with whatever was needed to make the work possible: parking lots, vacations, secretaries, telephone, etc. Now that women have moved into the workplace, they have needs for on-site day care services, flex time, and before- and after-school activities for older children, plus concerns about latchkey kids, the length of the school days and school schedules. Clearly these are not women's issues, as many businesses argue. They are national, social issues. "For want of Day Care facilities in the richest country in the world, the industries that deny it will soon themselves suffer from the loss of the worker pool it needs to be competitive," wrote Benedictine Sr. Joan Chittester[609]. With women now earning 60 percent of the college degrees and 50 percent of the PhDs and professional degrees in this country, women will undoubtedly remain a determining factor in the American work force for the foreseeable future. [610]

MONEY

Until the advent of money, not only was life simpler but also somewhat safer for peasant farmers. Nature could send a drought or other natural disaster, but going into debt was not even a blip on the average person's radar screen. Credit did not exist, so there was no way to borrow from the future. Life could be lived only *now*.

Patterns and Pitfalls in a Money-Based Economy

Ancient Palestine was typical of a money-less economy. Land was distributed equally among the twelve tribes and was to remain their tribal-family territory in perpetuity.

Their economy was a bartering-based system, which required payment of taxes in wheat, or barley, or whatever crops were available to them. In times of drought, peasants simply could not pay their taxes. No crops, no money, no payments. Period.

When money entered their lives, life changed drastically. Droughts still happened, but people could borrow money to pay their taxes. This began the spiraling downfall of many, many peasants.

If everything went well, they would repay the lender the following year—or years. At some point, however, their subsistence farming would not produce a sufficient amount to pay both their loan for previous year(s) and their current taxes. When this happened, they had to default on their loan, and the creditor took possession of their land, planting profitable vineyards in place of the subsistence crops. Sometimes the new, wealthy landowner would allow the peasant to continue living there and work the land as a tenant farmer[611], but that usually didn't last long. Soon the peasant would be unable to raise enough crops to feed his family, pay rent to the new owner, and meet his tax obligations, so he would be evicted, homeless with no job. A few were lucky enough to get hired in a temp job for the day, sometimes on what they still considered their own land. But this was rubbing salt in the wound.

Debt follows this same, recognizable pattern in virtually every agricultural society and can often be seen even in economies such as ours, though clothed differently. Wealth and greed of a few individuals lead to overwhelming debt of the majority; wealth and greed of corporations and governments lead to backbreaking debt of nations.

Wealth and Collapse

From history as ancient as Egypt's Great Pyramid of Giza to Malaysia's twin Petronas Towers, completed in 1998, skyscrapers have symbolized shifting trends in global wealth and power. The most recent structure to claim status as the world's tallest building is the Burj Dubai in United Arab Emirates (UAE).[612]

Rising 160 stories high at a cost of $4.1 billion, the Burj made its debut in 2010. This was good news/bad news for Dubai. Just one month earlier, its main government-backed development group announced it needed six months free from creditors to whom it owed nearly $60 billion. The amazing new architectural landmark became a farewell toast to an age of excess in Dubai. "This tower was conceived as a monument to Dubai's place on the international stage. It's now like a last hurrah to the boom years," said Christopher Davidson[613], who has written extensively about the UAE.[614]

This symbol speaks to the course of events in America's recent financial meltdown. Wall Street reached an excessive monetary height, followed by homes going underwater, unemployment reaching new highs, and foreclosures propelling the country into near-collapse. Only a bailout of those responsible for the downfall could save the country. This was another case of rubbing salt in the wound.

Downfall of America's Economy

Between 1951 and 1963, Americans with income over $400,000 paid taxes at a rate of more than 90 percent. Then, in the 1960's and 70's, income above $200,000 was taxed at a rate of 70 percent.[615]

Higher taxation on the wealthy proved to be beneficial for all. Infrastructure, public universities, scientific research, and entrepreneurial businesses all thrived without the necessity of the government borrowing money. Businesses and communities depended on each other to do well, so the health of the greater community was important for nurturing enterprises.[616]

When the top tax rate was lowered in the 1980's, some people could accumulate a vast fortune in one fast deal. Executives got rich quick and left their companies. Long-term business plans went out the window, employees were cut, and companies took advantage of customers. When businesses lost their interdependence with the community, it became more profitable to outsource or sell off manufacturing. Loyalty was out; greed was in.[617]

In recent years it has become even easier for the wealthy to become even richer. In 2006, the Senate passed a $69 billion package of tax cuts to ease the burden on investors and above- average earners.[618] Government felt the pinch of fewer tax dollars, which led to cuts in spending on schools and infrastructure. But even those cuts were not enough. The federal government had to borrow money, largely from China, to make up for a shortfall. We know the scenario: a massive debt that has cost us hundreds of billions of dollars in interest each year[619] and continues to grow. As a result, the U.S. is suffering not only the embarrassment of Congress being unable to agree on how to rectify the situation, but also the angst of leaving such a huge and far-reaching problem in the hands of just a small committee.

Thomas Friedman spelled out his vision of the vicious cycle that led to such massive debt:

> "We have created a system for growth that depended on our building more and more stores to sell more and more stuff made in more and more factories in China, powered by more and more coal that would cause more and more climate change but earn China more and more dollars to buy more and more U.S. T-bills so America would have more and more money to build more and more stores to sell more and more…

> "What if the crisis of 2008 represents something much more fundamental than a deep recession? What if it's telling us that the whole growth model… is unsustainable?"[620]

It is ironic that our economy cannot tolerate movement away from this buying pattern of more, more, more, which we know is unsustainable. A news item in 2010 read:

"Americans borrowed less for a 10th consecutive month in November with total credit and borrowing on credit cards falling by the largest amounts on records going back nearly seven decades.

"The dramatic declines raised new worries about whether consumers will cut back further on spending, making it harder for the economy to mount a sustained rebound."[621]

We know the answer to those worries: consumers *have* cut back.

Two Economies Meet

In 2006, Alvin Toffler[622] spoke to the World Affairs Council about his concept of "Revolutionary Wealth," the title of a book he had written. He said the changes we are seeing are more than economic: they are also social, political and cultural. A historical revolution is taking place.[623]

The revolution centers in a complex concept of wealth. "Wealth," in Toffler's eyes, now includes the social, political and cultural sectors of society, which are interrelated with the monetary system.

Our wealth system embraces two economies: a money economy and a non-monetary economy. "Non-monetary" refers to non-paid work, such as household tasks and volunteer work. Though they are not part of the money economy, they are essential to our country's wealth.

These two economies meet at the point where the money economy produces technology used for non-paid purposes. One example is the Linux operating system.

"Here's a guy, in Finland, sitting there... and sort of as a hobby, not being paid for it, and not officially asked to do it, writes... "Linux," puts it on the web, and pretty soon thousands of programmers are tweaking it... China and Brazil have made it official policy that their government agencies must use Linux."[624]

The New York Stock Exchange (NYSE) also uses Linux as their main operating system.

Toffler thinks "we're going to arm individuals with all kinds of tools and technologies that permit them to do things that previously they had to pay for." Photography is an early example. We no longer have to take a roll of film to the drug store, have it sent to Rochester for Kodak to process it and send it back, go to the drug store and pay for it, and finally get our photographs. We now do all that ourselves—plus change the color, transmit it, and anything else we choose to do with it.[625]

This is the direction we are watching unfold.

Money as God

We do not have to look far to see the deep roots of money in today's psyche: it is our god. Drug smugglers will risk going to jail in order to get money. In just one seizure, Mexican soldiers found 5 ½ tons of cocaine on a commercial plane arriving from Venezuela.[626]

Even our children have been smitten by the money-bug. In a program developed by Stanford University to increase learning in elementary school children, program administrators used cash as an incentive. The children received $20 for each test they completed up to $100.

Gift giving, too, has turned toward money. Gift cards[627] have become the third most popular item during the Christmas shopping season, behind only clothing, CD's and DVD's. Safeway, CVS pharmacies and Kroger supermarkets have introduced "gift card malls," where brand names and corporate logos provide a vast array of choices both of stores and dollar amounts. With the price tag still attached, it is no longer "the thought that counts." When it comes to gift cards, the dollar amount *is* the thought.[628]

On a larger scale, the mere mention of Goldman Sachs, AIG, banks or Wall Street brings dollarign racing through our minds, as anger courses through our bodies. Money is the bottom line in our society.

Financial Crisis

Stocks

October 2006 was a red-letter month on Wall Street. First, the Dow Jones Industrial Average reached a new high of 11,727 on October 3rd, breaking the previous record of the boom year 2000.[629]

Two days later, the New York Stock Exchange (NYSE) introduced the Hybrid Market trading system, which processes transactions by computers. This enabled the Exchange to handle many more transactions in a fraction of the time it took when floor bidders were used. "For traders, the leap into the digital age drastically curtails the need for human interaction and puts all of their jobs on the line," wrote Joe Bel Bruno.[630] But life on Wall Street looked rosy to most people.

Downward spiral

A poll conducted by the [San Francisco] Bay Area Council[631] early in 2007 showed that "economic issues did not top [Bay Area] residents' lists of worries."[632] People were saying, "I still have my job—and I'm not worried about losing it. I see opportunity out there."[633] Optimism continued to reign.

An eight percent tumble in the Shanghai stock market the following March sent the Dow to its biggest drop in nearly four years, underscoring the close linkage between the U.S. economy and those abroad. A few years earlier, such news from China might have been seen as a good thing, but people had come to recognize "global interconnectivity as part of the new economic way of life."[634] The Dow proved that reality.

By 2009 the mood of Americans had hit rock bottom. September 2008 had seen the beginning of the worst phase of the financial crisis.[635] With the housing bubble beginning to burst, stock prices plummeted—first in the home-building industry, and then spread like wildfire to most sectors of the economy. Banks were badly burned by fallen mortgage values, sending Citigroup's stock plunging to $2.60 from its early 2007 value of $55.66. A gallon of regular gas cost more than a share of General Motors, which had dropped to $2.22.[636]

Even the hardiest of bull market investors could no longer stomach the Market by 2010. Millions of small-time investors not only stopped buying, but had started selling, too.

Institutional investments

Professional institutional investors were almost solely responsible for the market making a comeback.[637] Their investments were sufficiently heavy to enable the stock market to rise, touching 11,000 for the first time in two years. However, this came with a decline in volume of stock sales, a worry to those in the know.[638]

Addressing the crisis

In September 2008 when the U.S. economy was at the breaking point, then-president Bush proposed to Congress the largest financial bailout in U.S. history. His proposal gave the Treasury authority to buy up to $700 billion in mortgage-related assets from financial institutions in the U.S., raising the national debt ceiling to $11.3 trillion. It placed no restrictions on the Administration except to submit semiannual reports to Congress, giving the Treasury virtually unfettered authority to buy and resell mortgage debt as it saw fit. The plan transferred bad debts of Wall Street into obligations of American taxpayers, amounting to more than $2,000 for every man, woman and child in the United States, roughly equal to the amount the country had spent in direct costs on the Iraq war.[639]

Though emergency funds kept the U.S. from going over the cliff, the economy still needed to be pumped back to life. In February 2009, newly-elected President Obama signed a federal stimulus bill, providing funds to shore up aging infrastructure and to create jobs.[640] However, the need was so great that the stimulus funds appeared to be just a drop in the bucket. Unemployment continued to soar and foreclosures kept happening, even as short sales[641] were on the rise. [642] The recession was bent on following its own course in its own time.

Late in 2009 President Obama met with bank executives to rewrite the rules governing the financial industry. Though banks gave the appearance of agreement, they were unanimously opposed to the creation of a new agency to protect consumers from bank abuses, a key part of the President's proposal.[643]

Senate investigation

Meanwhile the U.S. Senate was gearing up for its investigation to determine the basis for the recession. Their final report focused on four basic issues: how high risk mortgage lending contributed to the financial crisis; the Office of Thrift Supervision's failure to "stop the unsafe and unsound practices" that led to the downfall of the nation's largest banks; how inflated credit ratings of Moody and Standard & Poor masked the true risk of many mortgage related securities; and how investment banks contributed to the crisis.

Goldman Sachs was first to be investigated for profiting from the housing meltdown and reaping billions of dollars at the expense of clients. [644] Many other financial institutions underwent similar investigations.

Innovation

Craig Barrett, former chairman of Intel, saw an opportunity in the economic crisis and shared his thoughts with Thomas Friedman[645] during an interview.

Historically, new companies get born during times of recession, Microsoft being a prime example. When times are hard, people need to be inventive, searching for new ways to do things with less money. Barrett said, "The country that uses this crisis to make its population smarter and more innovative—and endows its people with more tools and basic research to invent new goods and services—will thrive down the road."[646]

> **"We might be able to stimulate our way back to stability, but we can only invent our way back to prosperity."**
> —Thomas Friedman, *New York Times* columnist

Barrett offered specifics: end H-1B visa restrictions on knowledge workers, as they would invent many more jobs than they would supplant; benchmark education standards against the best in the world, rather than against other states; double the budgets for basic scientific research; and extend health care to every American in a cost-efficient way.[647]

Governmental thinking outside the box

Innovative ideas have sprung up at various levels of government.

Outsourcing city services to private contractors is one idea. Among the most popular services for outsourcing are park maintenance, paving streets, trimming trees and garbage collection. Some cities, such as New York, have been doing this for several years, but now it has become mainstream. Privatization and competition provide incentives for companies to be innovative and efficient, resulting in cost savings for the cities.[648]

At the county level, banking and telecommunication contracts are being consolidated; Web site advertising and special event sponsorship packages are offered; and naming rights are allowed. [649]

Some counties are expanding on the idea of marketing rights.

"Huntington Beach's lifeguards drive Nissan Frontier pickup trucks, the 'official' beach vehicles for the Surf City, whose vending machines offer only beverages from Coca-Cola, the 'official' drink. Up in Washington, park visitors to King County can consult a kiosk, brought to them by Starbucks."[650]

Other counties are considering contracting with a single bank to allow its ATMs on all county- owned buildings and contracting with only one vendor for beverages and snacks, in return for an exclusivity fee.[651]

In addition to saving money and raising revenue for cities and counties, these ideas help draw companies back into community life, re-establishing a connection that was cut when taxes on the wealthy were lowered, and more recently exacerbated by outsourcing overseas.[652]

Trade Deficit

As early as Spring 2006 experts were predicting that the U.S. trade gap, which had been growing since 2001, would widen. The deficit with China briefly took a dip, but it was called merely "a positive blip in an overall deteriorating trend in the U.S. trade picture[653]."[654]

By September the U.S. trade deficit[655] had reached its second-highest level ever.[656] This raised questions in people's minds: What would happen if foreigners decided to hold fewer dollars in assets? Could this send U.S. stock prices and the value of the dollar plummeting and American interest rates sharply higher?[657]

The U.S. does lend to other countries, but the amount is paltry compared to the $2.67 trillion U.S. foreign debt.[658] The total amount owed to the U.S. government for all loans made during the period 1946 to 2006 is around $108 billion—$66 billion for economic assistance and $42 billion for military assistance.[659]

The "What if" question people had been asking began to play out by December 2006. Foreign investors sold stocks and Americans accelerated their purchases of foreign bonds. Emerging- market debt had its best three months in a year.[660] By the following year, both Republicans and Democrats saw the rising national debt[661] as one of the greatest threats to the country's economic future.

When the recession hit, tax collections tanked and federal spending increased, as the administration scrambled to avert an economic collapse. The Congressional Budget Office estimated the U.S. public debt would rise from 40 to 60 percent of the economy by the end of 2010, and would hit 90 percent by 2020. By June 2011 it had reached 65 percent of the economy.

A presidential commission was convened to address the problem, charged with the task of devising a plan to stop the federal borrowing binge. "After stopping a terrorist with a weapon of mass destruction, this is the single most important issue we confront as a nation," said Senator Judd Gregg, member of the deficit reduction commission.[662]

Capitalism's Future and the World

The rest of the world is hurting, too, from the deep recession and heavy U.S. debt load. Accordingly, the 2009 World Economic Forum chose as its theme: "Shaping the Post-Crisis World." When the Forum met, an air of uncertainty filled the meeting rooms as people tried to figure out what had gone wrong and exchanged ideas about how to emerge from the incredible downturn in the world economy. They were asking each other, "Are we going over the edge?" and "Is it even worse than we think?"

But the one question that rang most clearly throughout the conference was: Is capitalism as we know it in retreat, and will it be replaced by a system with more state intervention?[663]

This question may haunt us for years to come.

NATURAL ENERGY RESOURCES

Energy is one of many sectors of the world economy that must be seen internationally, given the interdependency of nation states relative to energy resources.

Coal, Oil, and Gas

Iran and oil

Iran has been a key player. In 2004, Iran's oil profits were 65% of the government's revenues. Yet experts were predicting that Iran's oil exports could totally dry up by 2015, given its existing rate of decline at 10 to 12% annually. "At the time, Iran was producing 300,000 barrels below the quota set by the Organization of Petroleum Exporting Countries (OPEC). This, plus failure to rectify leaks in its refineries, amounted to an annual loss of $10 billion to $11 billion, a huge chunk out of Iran's $50 billion a year enterprise." "That is a picture of an industry in collapse," said Roger Stern, an economic geographer at Johns Hopkins University. [664]

Stern was connecting Iran's economic situation to the hostile relationship between Iran and the United States. Iran's declining oil exports could destabilize the country, strengthening the appeal of nuclear power (financed by Russia) for production of more electricity. If the United States could "hold its breath" for a few years and not take on Iran militarily, Iran might become much more conciliatory. "What they are doing to themselves is much worse than anything we could do," he said. "The one thing that would unite the country right now is to bomb them."[665]

U.S. and oil

Oil prices soared in the U.S. in 2006, raising the trade deficit to an all-time high and forcing the U.S. to borrow more than $2 billion a day from foreigners to finance it.[666] By 2008, oil prices in the U.S. had hit new record highs. Americans balked.

The spigot was turned off. As the demand for oil plummeted worldwide, oil companies had to stash vast amounts of crude, waiting for demand to return. Iran found itself storing millions of barrels of their own crude into idle tankers, hoping to halt declining prices that were devastating their economy.

Oil trading has always been an uneven game at the production and consumption ends of the oil line: traders store and sell, bringing oil to the market when it can get the best prices. But this time it came as a shock. "Nobody expected this. The majority of people out there thought the market would keep rising to $200, even $250, a barrel," said Antoine Halff, an analyst with Newedge. [667]

Drilling in the U.S.

For years, the U.S. has known that its oil binge needs to be curbed. Yet popular demand for oil is so great, the U.S. has become hostage to its fluctuating availability and prices on the world market. Drilling here at home has become an increasingly attractive alternative.

Yet drilling in the U.S. has triggered a public relations cost from environmental groups, some local governments and concerned citizens, who have never ceased protesting. For example, the California attorney general and three environmental groups filed appeals seeking to halt oil and gas drilling in Los Padres National Forest.[668]

As for offshore drilling, the Exxon Valdez spill of 1990 was a wake-up call, leaving its reminder in the form of oil just under the surface on the beaches of Prince William Sound. Environmentalists have not forgotten the 250,000 seabirds and 3,000 sea otters that lost their lives there. It took years to unravel that disaster as wind, current and tide spread oil across the water. Even 10,000 workers, 1,000 boats and 100 aircraft were unable to bring about major success in mopping up the spill, which absorbed $2 billion in clean-up funds.

Twenty years later, BP's *Deepwater Horizon* oil spill in the Gulf of Mexico was much more disastrous than Exxon's in Alaska. Despite

Congress vowing that a catastrophic oil spill like Valdez would never happen again, and passing the Oil Pollution Act of 1990 mandating better ways to clean up oil spills, the clean-up tools remained unchanged at the time of the Gulf explosion[669]. Only after the oil started gushing from the ocean's floor were new devices tried. The gushing wellhead was finally capped and a relief well process successfully completed. This time the President stepped in and ordered a halt to planned oil drillings until assessments could be made. In December 2010 the Administration announced they would not allow offshore oil drilling in the eastern Gulf of Mexico or off the Atlantic and Pacific coasts as part of the next five-year drilling plan.[670]

Clean Technology

Ideas for clean technology are pouring out from various sectors of the U.S. economy, engendering a green revolution.

Private industry and environmentalists

One fresh idea came from the Environmental Defense and the Natural Resources Defense Council (NRDC), who built a national constituency through the Internet to prevent TXU[671] from building 11 coal-fired power plants. Two big buy-out firms[672] wanted to buy TXU at $45 billion, but they did not want to become embroiled in a war with environmentalists. They told Fred Krupp, president of Environmental Defense: "We only want to go forward if you and NRDC will praise what we are trying to do here."

After negotiations with the environmentalists, the private equity group finally agreed to reduce the number of coal plants from 11 to three; to support a U.S. cap on greenhouse gas emissions and invest $400 million in energy-efficiency programs at TXU; and double its wind power.

The environmental groups' going online shifted the local debate to a national one. Taking advantage of the transparency of the Internet age, they rendered public relations firms useless in managing TXU's reputation. As Krupp insightfully remarked: "What is the message when the largest buyout in history is made contingent (by the buyers) on winning praise for its greenhouse gas plan? The markets are ahead of the politicians. The world has changed, and these guys see it."[673]

Federal and state legislation

Legislation, too, is seeking to address the problem of greenhouse gases. Not waiting for federal legislation, California passed the California Global Warming Solutions Act in 2009, mandating the state's reduction of greenhouse-gas emissions to 1990 levels by 2020. The legislation fundamentally changed the consumption of energy, lessened dependency on foreign oil and reduced greenhouse gas emissions. In addition, the technology needed to enact the legislation provided an economic stimulus for Silicon Valley.[674] Since then, the federal government has also funded technology in the American Recovery and Reinvestment Act, giving tax credits for advanced energy manufacturing.[675]

Individual ideas: "Green Tea Party"

Individuals are also bringing forth new ideas in the media. The *New York Times* columnist, Thomas L. Friedman, posited the idea for a "Green Tea Party," a radical centrist movement, that would enlist the same passion for cutting emissions as the Tea Party has had for cutting deficits. By putting a "patriot fee" on imported oil, we would lower the global price of oil (which would hurt Iran and help the poor in Africa) and could reduce the U.S. trade deficit. In addition, it would be a strong security measure that would stretch across the energy, deficit, and environmental sectors of U.S. society[676].

Investments in clean tech

In early 2010 global investment in clean technology started gaining momentum. Venture-capital investments in international clean tech[677] surged to nearly $2 billion in the first quarter of the year, a new quarterly record. Transportation and solar power were leaders in amount of money raised, but energy efficiency showed more activity than any other sector.

In earlier days, clean- tech investment focused primarily on solar power and biofuels, but in recent years the field has broadened to become more diverse. Given that the clean-tech market now extends across the planet, investment in it is a huge opportunity. Though China and Europe dominate the solar and wind markets, and Brazil the alternative fuels, vast opportunities still exist for more players. In fact, a major company that does not have a green component today is an exception to the rule[678] and may find itself left behind in the dust.

Intermediary Energy Alternatives

Biofuels

Biofuels increased dramatically in 2009, as a federal mandate required that producers supply 36 billion gallons of them annually by 2022[679] and research funding became more available. The use of biofuels goes back to the days of Henry Ford, who designed the Model T to run on ethanol or gas. Prohibition ruined his plan because of the basic crop's alcoholic content, but his idea is now resurging.

Corn ethanol, the most common biofuel[680], is just one possibility. Today researchers are experimenting with everything from plant waste or dedicated "biofuel crops"[681] to pond algae, pecan shells and sugar cane.

The key for most ethanol production is a cheap source of sugar, which usually requires breaking down tough cell walls in plants to get at the sugar. The University of California at Berkeley has been analyzing rumen from cow stomachs, hoping to reverse the process by which bacteria break down plant cell walls, to turn grass into energy[682].

Algae are an exception to the centrality of sugar in designing an approach to energy production. Though they require the addition of sugar, algae produce more energy than other biofuels.

With the array of possibilities for biofuel production, the most likely scenario for the future is a smorgasbord of fuels. "We're going to end up with a number of different processes, creating a number of different transportation fuels," said Mike Leary, director of the National BioEnergy Center[683].[684]

Biodiesel fuel

Biodiesel fuel is also coming onstage. The number of diesel manufacturing plants in the United States more than tripled between 2004 and 2006. Some people are even using cooking oil or used frying grease from restaurants to run their cars. All that is needed is a biodiesel conversion kit, costing about $700 installed.[685]

Cows have shown their value for today's energy crisis beyond having their rumen analyzed by scientists. Since early 2008, Pacific Gas and Electric Company (PG&E) has been using natural gas from the manure of 5,000 cows to create electricity for 50,000 homes. Dairy farms in Texas and Wisconsin are engaged in similar projects.[686]

Cars and trucks

Powering vehicles is a focal point for much of the greening effort. Cars have seen significant advances in this area.

Electric vehicles

Battery technology has improved to the point where plug-in hybrid electric vehicles may well supplant gasoline-guzzling cars. They are dramatically cheaper to operate, consuming about two cents' worth of electricity to travel one mile, compared with the current cost of 20 to 25 cents for gasoline. Electric vehicles will most likely be adopted both domestically and worldwide simply because they are cheaper.[687]

In the summer of 2009, McDonald's started featuring free electric car-charging stations at one of its North Carolina restaurants. Management planned to add charging stations at some of its other restaurants across the country if the venture in Raleigh proved successful. Nova Charge, distributor of the ChargePoint stations, has distributed hundreds of units in the United States at a manufacturing cost of $5,000 apiece.[688] Now charging stations have become relatively commonplace across the country.

By 2020, we were seeing advertisements such as the following one from Toyota: "More hybrids than any other brand. With 11 hybrid models to choose from, we've got a vehicle for everyone."

Car-sharing

Another idea for reduction of hydrocarbons is car-sharing, which reduces the need for individual cars. Zipcar, a car-sharing company, enlists many college campuses nationwide—as well as the public at large—into their green-friendly program. Zipcars are available 24/7 for faculty, staff, and students to drive on and off campus by paying an annual $35 fee, plus $8 or $9 an hour.[689] Zipcars have become even more visible than charging stations, showing up on streets and shopping centers across the country.

Mileage and pollution limits

Following up on the first federal regulations (in 2009) of fuel efficiency and greenhouse gas emissions in cars and light trucks, President Obama announced mileage and pollution limits for commercial trucks and buses as well. His announcement came after the catastrophic oil spill in the Gulf of Mexico in 2010.[690]

Energy-efficient lighting

One greening strategy for the average household is switching to energy-efficient lighting. A coalition of private companies and government agencies[691] launched a marketing campaign, 18Seconds, getting Americans to replace incandescent bulbs with compact fluorescent ones, which are more energy efficient and last longer. "If every American swapped just one bulb, advocates say, the country could save $8 billion in energy costs and eliminate 2 million cars' worth of greenhouse gas emissions[692]."[693]

End-Stage: Clean Energy

Biofuels are useful for an intermediary stage when seeking to curtail greenhouse gases, but ultimately humanity needs to work within the parameters of natural law, which includes a clean environment. This will happen not because of government regulations, but because of free markets and economics.

Wind turbines and photovoltaics

While the price of traditional fuels—coal, oil, and gas—have risen dramatically off and on, technology has made a stunning reduction in the cost of wind turbines and photovoltaics, which converts sunlight into electricity. Since 2003, Texas has built more than five gigawatts of wind turbine capacity, representing almost 10 percent of the State's electrical supply. Given the fact that wind energy costs seven cents per kilowatt-hour, compared with 12 cents per kilowatt-hour to build a gas-fired power plant, Texas' action is not surprising.

The cost of photovoltaics has fallen to an almost marketable level, while retail electricity prices have been increasing by as much as 30 percent. At 30 cents per kilowatt-hour, the price it has reached in New York, a photovoltaic installation on the rooftop of a house will pay for itself in fewer than 10 years, with a greater than 10 percent return on one's capital investment. However, the biggest bang for the buck lies in the fact that solar energy (and wind) generate absolutely no greenhouse gases.[694]

Solar thermal

Some companies are advocating large-scale "solar thermal facilities," though environmentalists denounce them. California already has the largest operating collection of solar thermal facilities in the world, with 80 more on the drawing board. As the world's eighth-largest economy, California has a daunting challenge to provide renewables that will transform its electricity system. This is a system some people think will work.

A solar thermal plant consists of rows of gigantic mirrors covering an area bigger than two football fields. They are, in fact, giant boilers made of glass and steel, which use the sun's heat to create steam to power turbines that generate electricity. Though currently costing about 18 cents a kilowatt-hour, improved technology should lower the cost to about five cents a kilowatt-hour by 2025. Executives at Ausra, a solar thermal company, say that "a square patch of desert about 92 miles long on each side blanketed with Ausra's technology could generate enough electricity to meet the entire nation's demand."[695]

Geothermal and space solar

Geothermal technology, which taps into earth energy, is an alternative to home heating and cooling systems, saving as much as 70 percent on energy bills.[696] PG&E is pursuing yet another alternative: "space solar." Space solar installations would generate electricity from solar- powered satellites in space. The satellites would use solar cells to convert the sun's energy to electricity, then transmit that power to Earth as radio-frequency energy, which would convert the energy to electricity. The project was expected to deliver 200 megawatts of power[697] to California by 2016. In 2020, geothermal energy in California produced 11,345 gigawatt hours (GWh) of electricity.

Energy Alternatives Internationally

Even oil-producing giant United Arab Emirates (UAE) is exploring energy alternatives. The UAE has special reason to do so, with its high demand for energy to maintain its luxurious lifestyle of air conditioning, chilled swimming pools, and even an indoor ski slope.

To meet the demand, the UAE launched the Masdar Initiative[698] in 2006, which seeks to reduce demand on fossil fuels internationally by making the UAE a center for the development and implementation of clean-energy technology. This is a giant step for the fourth largest OPEC oil producer, with about 10 percent of the known resources. Up until now, the UAE has been singled out as one of the world's highest per capita emitters of greenhouse gases.

Energy needs—including the energy-intensive process of desalinating gulf waters—have led many of the Persian Gulf states to experiment in a limited way with alternative sources of energy. The Bahrain World Trade Center, for instance, has erected wind turbines that will meet up to 35 percent of its project's power needs.

Also, with a growing population in the region, domestic consumption is leaving a smaller share of oil for export. In 2006, Saudi Arabia and other Gulf states began looking into nuclear power as a possible source of energy. Iran insists that its nuclear program is intended to serve its mounting domestic energy demands.[699]

Other Technologies

The National Ignition Facility, the world's largest fusion facility, is hoping to harness fusion energy, the same force that powers our sun and the stars. It has the potential of creating fusion power plants for generating power without releasing greenhouse gases.[700]

Lee Felsenstein, a technology pioneer, is hoping to create electrical power from static magnetic fields to power computers and other electronics. His idea goes against rules of conservation of energy, which says the flow of electricity from static magnetic fields decreases the magnetism. However, "If engineers can create a phenomenon that hasn't been seen before, the physicists' job is to explain it," Felsenstein said. His idea would function as a battery that never runs out, making possible the powering of a whole society. Devices would be built with their power generator inside.[701]

Psychological Viewpoint

Energy is the "battery" of life on Earth and of transformation of matter. All of us desire it, both as psychic energy (inspiration, love, knowledge, etc.) and as material energy (money, oil, electricity, etc.). Our problem is not the use itself of energy, but the consequences of using energy that is not renewable.

The centrality of energy in ecology and psychology requires that inner and outer nature be considered equally, as both support the mobilization and transformation of energy. By listening to the symbolic content of a particular problem—inner or outer—we can determine what it is that life needs from humans.[702]

Humanity has passed through stages of using coal, oil and gas for its primary energy needs. Of course, we will continue to use these forms of energy, though in a much more limited way. We are now learning to tame our material energy use and be more proficient in our use of solar, wind, nuclear and other energies whose ideas have not yet surfaced. Meanwhile, humanity will experiment with a variety of technologies, searching for a silver bullet.

For Reflection:

1. ....

....

....

2. ....

....

....

3. ....

....

....

CHAPTER 14

VIOLENCE AND CRIME

"A black hole's power to devour stars, like a 'destruction derby,' is an example of creativity and destructivity both being part of reality."
—*Smithsonian*, April 2008.

Blessing or Curse?

A poor old woodcutter lived with his only son in a tiny village. Although he was very poor, he owned a beautiful white horse that was the envy of all the village folk. People offered to buy the horse at exorbitant sums, but he refused. "My horse is a friend, not a possession," he would answer.

One morning the woodcutter discovered that his horse was not in the stable. Villagers mocked him, saying he should have known that he couldn't protect such a valuable animal. He should have sold it. "Now your horse is gone, and you've been cursed with misfortune."

The old man said, "Wait. All we know is that the horse is not in the stable. How do you know if I've been cursed or not? All we can see is a fragment. Who can say what will come next?"

Two weeks later the horse returned—and brought with him a dozen wild horses. He hadn't been stolen; he had run away. Villagers admitted that the old man had been right and they were wrong. "What we thought was a curse was a blessing," they said.

"You can't make that judgment," said the man. "How do you know if it's a blessing or not? No one knows. All you know is the horse is back with a dozen others." The villagers retreated and said little, but down deep they knew it was a blessing.

The man's son started breaking the wild horses, but he fell from one of them and broke both legs. "You were right," the villagers said. "The dozen horses were a curse. Now you have no one to help you."

The woodcutter responded: "My son broke his legs. Who knows if it is a blessing or a curse? No one knows. We see only a fragment. Life comes in fragments."

A few weeks later the country went to war, and all the young men of the village were required to join the army—except for the woodcutter's son, because he was injured. Villagers wept for their sons. They told the woodcutter: "You were right. Your son's accident was a blessing, His legs may be broken, but at least you have him with you. Our sons area gone forever."

The old man replied, "It's impossible to talk with you. You always draw conclusions when all you have is a fragment. Your sons had to go to war, and mine did not. No one knows if it's a blessing or a curse. No one is wise enough to know." [703]

VIOLENCE

History of Violence

Violence in the universe

"Violence and destruction are dimensions of the universe. They are present at every level of existence: the elemental, the geological, the organic, the human."[704] No development can take place at any level of existence without a cost, "an inescapable cost," which is threefold: resistance in the universe (which insists on preserving the past), the cost of creating order (which points to the finite nature of the present), and the tendency in all things toward (future) fulfillment of their inner nature.[705]

"The more closely we look at any place in the fifteen billion years of the universe's story, the more we realize that the universe is both violent and creative, both destructive and cooperative."[706]

Brian Swimme and Thomas Berry ask: "When a female spider consumes her mate, is this a destruction on the part of the female or cooperation on the part of the male."[707]

We might ask similar questions: Was Jesus' death on the cross a destruction on the part of the Romans (or temple authorities) or cooperation on the part of Jesus? When the Internet consumes the materiality of books, newspapers and CDs, is this destruction on the part of technology or cooperation on the part of the media?

Unacceptable" aspects of the universe

Humanity has found some aspects of the universe unacceptable and has dealt with them by trying to dominate the universe. Swimme and Berry wrote:

> "The determination to dominate the universe so that all insecurity, limitation, destruction, and threat of destruction could be eliminated eventuated in racism, militarism, sexism, anthropocentrism, dysfunctional maneuvers of the human species in the quest to deal with what it regarded as the unacceptable aspects of the universe."[708]

Psychological Roots of Violence and Killing

For the first 35,000 years of humanity's development, in what we call the Paleolithic era, cave dwellers identified with the animal world around them, as an infant sees herself as part of her mother. Because humanity had not yet started to develop ego, there were no wars that we know of at that time.[709]

Only within the past 10,000 years has humanity developed another value, that of the female as the source of life, which is obvious in depictions that exaggerate the life-giving parts of the human body: breasts, a bulging stomach and defined labia. Mother was revered as the center of life because of her life-giving qualities, but society was not matriarchal, as there was no hierarchy; the world was one. "These two values—the world being one and the feminine at the center—lasted for many thousands of years, and during this time there were no wars."[710]

Gradually ego began to develop in humanity, such as we see in a two-year-old, differentiating itself from the rest of the world. People started to dominate and use other things. It began with violence against nature through agriculture and tools that penetrated the earth. Then humans started differentiating between men and women. As part of further ego development, the masculine came into its own, superseding and dominating the feminine. This initiated the age of patriarchy.[711]

Preservation of purity

"Violence between humans began, not because of overpopulation and territorial needs, nor because of shortage of resources, but to preserve purity.[712]"[713] It was important to keep from being tainted by those apart from one's own kind, so it became acceptable to do away with them. They could make you—and those like you—impure.

This way of thinking has persisted up to the present. Extremists use suicide bombs and other terrorist acts to preserve the purity of Islam, and the rest of the world seeks to eradicate their violence through "war on terrorists." As the world complexifies with greater and greater differentiation, there will continue to be more desperate attempts at keeping the world pure.[714]

Working with violence and evil

When we talk about violence or evil, we are talking about the structure of the universe. "One of the great mistakes is to suppose that we can eliminate violence or evil... The greatest evil of history has been committed by people trying to eliminate evil.[715]"[716]

If we are truly concerned about the trajectory of violence in the course of human history, and we know that violence lies in the very structure of the universe, what is humanity to do?

"We have to be able to think killing, on the one hand, and 'leaving the Virgin Goddess untouched' on the other, as identical."[717] Until we are able to let the "other" become dissolved within ourselves, as a sugar cube becomes dissolved in a cup of coffee, we are stuck with a future of repeating the past, and we cannot reach the "naked truth," which is embedded in the dissolution.[718]

Now what does *that* mean? Real engagement involves the ultimate form of penetrating the "other," which requires "killing" it—not literally, but obliterating it in our mind. By totally erasing it as even an idea, we enable it to become an integral part of ourselves. When we have fully digested it, and it has become one with us, we are able to encounter Truth within us in its ultimate form.[719]

Because humanity has not brought "killing" and the untouched "Virgin Goddess" together as a merged "one," we have had centuries of literalized killing. In literalizing the act, we have truncated a possible epiphany of Truth. It takes the non-literal kill to break through from one to the other and merge the opposites.

Violence in Christianity

Humanity's pattern of literal killing can be attributed, in part, to the way Christianity developed. In her book, *Saving Paradise*, Rita Nakashima Brock described the decisive turning point toward violence in Christianity.

Crusades

It occurred in 1095, when Pope Urban II launched the first crusade to quell the feudal violence plaguing Europe. Urban declared that war was not only just, but holy. Crusaders who killed Jesus and Muslims earned forgiveness for all their sins and were assured a place in paradise after death. Paradise *after death* had become a reward for killing *in this life*. This led to medieval atonement theology, which stated that Jesus' death as a martyr saved the world. Life-affirming forms of Christianity, which preceded the Crusades, had succumbed to the focus on redemptive violence that marks the second millennium of the Christian West.[720]

Religious art

Margaret Miles[721] has traced the development of violence through religious art. Scores of late medieval and Renaissance paintings and sculptures depict the Virgin Mary as a lactating mother with one breast exposed. This image was an important symbol of God's loving provision of life. With the development of public interest in medicine, however, male and female bodies became objects for study, not as subjects of religious experience. By 1750 the public meaning of naked breasts had become largely medical or erotic, making it impossible to symbolize God's love by depicting a nursing Virgin. Miles wrote, "I have not been able to find a single religious image of the breast painted after 1750."[722]

Meanwhile crucifixion scenes increased both in number and in their graphic depiction of violence and suffering. Miles asks: "Are crucifixion scenes the unconscious origin, deeply embedded in Western Christian societies, of the sacrificial rhetoric that surrounds war? Does the proliferation of crucifixion scenes habituate us to violence?"[723]

Deeply embedded acceptance of literal violence and projection of hope to an afterlife still persist in some communities of Christian faith. In 2006 five children ranging in age from six to 13 were victims of a deadly school shooting in an Amish community in Pennsylvania. Instead of lashing out in grief, the village members urged forgiveness of the killer and quietly accepted whatever came their way as God's will. "They know their children are going to heaven. They know their children are innocent... and they know that they will join them in death.[724]"[725]

Violence in Today's World

Since the end of the Cold War (1989) "Organized conflicts of all kinds—civil wars, genocides, repression by autocratic governments, and terrorist attacks—have declined throughout the world."
—Steven Pinker, *The Better Angels of Our Nature*

Violence in American Society

Virginia Tech massacre

After the Virginia Tech massacre in 2007, in which a student committed mass murder on the University campus and ended the rampage by shooting himself, citizens around the world saw reflected an America that fosters violence at home and abroad. "America has terrorism and they are exporting it to us," said a police officer in Iraq. "We did not have this violence in the Saddam era because the law was so tough on guns."[726] In spite of foreign reaction that centered on the proliferation of guns in the United States, many of the most recent efforts to change weapons laws in the U.S. have been about easing them.[727]

Census workers

Even census workers have found themselves targets of hostility by Americans who consider them the embodiment of intrusive government. During the 2010 census, census leaders were shot at with pellet guns, hit by baseball bats, and confronted with pickaxes and hammers. One crew leader was fatally shot seven times. The Census Bureau recorded more than double the number of incidents involving assaults or threats than they had tallied during the 2000 census.[728]

False alarm

A former member of the Air Force went in the opposite direction, claiming to be armed with potential means of committing violence, but having none. On a trans-Atlantic flight, he said he had explosives in his luggage and a fake passport, but neither claim turned out to be true. The man had lived a "squeaky-clean" life, according to his father, and had never been in trouble before.[729]

Violence Elsewhere

Pirates

Another scene conjures up antiquated images from *Treasure Island* or "The Pirates of Penzance." The waters off the Somalia coast have become roaming ground for pirates, who engage in battles with ships moving through the Persian Gulf. In one incident, the United States Navy captured at least 21 suspected pirates in just a few minutes' time. Some were prosecuted, but many nations are reluctant to become a center for prosecutions.[730]

Greece

The recent financial crisis sparked violence among protesters in Greece, killing three bank employees. Tens of thousands of demonstrators were objecting to cuts in government wages and pensions, necessitated by a deal Greece struck with the European Union and the International Monetary Fund for $141 billion in loans. Police resorted to barricades and tear gas to control the rioters. [731]

Thailand

Anti-government protesters in Thailand also struck out in violence, but they were met with rubber bullets, live ammunition and sharp shooters from Thai soldiers. Thirty civilians were left dead after four days of chaos in the streets of Bangkok. Demonstrators demanded that the United Nations intercede, but Thai leaders flatly rejected the demands. A government spokesman said intervention was not necessary, as troops were "not using weapons to crack down on civilians."[732]

Libya

Violence in Libya was one of the bloodiest in recent history. Anti-Gadafi protesters were met with sustained, overkill violence from Gadafi supporters for months before persistence paid off. In Summer 2011, protesters successfully overran Tripoli, completing the downfall of the Gadafi regime. Gadafi managed to escape but was finally captured and killed in October.

China

Self-inflicted violence has also taken its toll. A rash of copycat suicides erupted at the Foxconn factory in China, where high-tech products are made for Apple, Dell and Hewlett-Packard, among other industry giants. At least 13 suicides were committed at the factory during the first half of 2010. The company tried several different approaches to prevent more deaths.[733]

Contributing Factors to Violence

Movies

Someone gets "hit, stomped, blown away or otherwise seriously maimed" much more frequently in movies today than in the days of Errol Flynn.[734]

Violent games

Studies show that violent games tend to make students who play them more hostile and less forgiving than those who play non-violent games. Players of violent games are also more apt to believe "violence to be normal," according to a series of studies conducted by the American Psychological Association.[735]

Availability of guns

Having guns readily available may exacerbate violence. In a month-long series of mass killings, "nearly every gunman… was legally entitled to fire his weapons."[736]

Loosened restrictions

Yet recent efforts to change weapons laws have been about loosening restrictions. For instance, it is now legal for someone in Texas to carry a gun into a bar that does not have signs saying guns are not allowed inside. Tennessee is well on the way toward allowing guns to be carried in state and local parks. At the federal level, 65 House Democrats said they would block any attempt to restore an expired ban against assault weapons. "I think you're seeing a continuing change of culture," said Scott Vogel of the Freedom States Alliance, a gun control activist group. Studies conflict on whether stricter gun laws lessen gun violence.[737]

War on Terrorism

U.S. Policy

As early as 2005 then-president Bush, members of Congress and most experts agreed that ending terrorism would come only by addressing its underlying causes. We must "change the conditions that give rise to extremism and terror by spreading the universal principle of human liberty," said Bush.

The Pentagon continued to receive a much larger share of the counterterrorism budget for combat operations and Special Forces missions than for "indirect action" programs, such as diplomacy.[738] The U.S. view of counterterrorism was that "enemies simply need to be killed or imprisoned so that global terrorism or the Iraqi insurgency will end," said Bruce Hoffman, a senior fellow at the Combating Terrorism Center at West Point. He told a House Armed Services subcommittee that "al-Qaida's ability to continue this struggle is… predicated on its capacity to attract new recruits" by publicizing U.S. military actions.[739]

Middle East

In 2006, a series of incidents throughout the Middle East upped the ante on conflict in the region, as militant groups sought a rise in radicalism through violence. Israel imposed a naval blockade on Lebanon, bombed the suburbs of Beirut, and knocked out its airport. Hezbollah retaliated with militants firing missiles back at Israel. At least 57 people were killed in the fray and more than 100 wounded. When the United Nations Security Council devised a resolution accusing Israel of "disproportionate use of force," the United States used its veto power to block it.

Oil prices then surged to a record high of more than $78 a barrel on the world market. The region's agenda, as often in the past, was largely being set by militant elements, leaving less room for moderate voices, disarmament or an end to violence.[740]

Mumbai

Violence spread to India a year and a half later, erupting in terrorist attacks in Mumbai, a global financial capital. The attackers' ability to spread terror was largely increased by the use of advanced technology, which linked them in real time with Pakistan-based handlers. Among other locations, they attacked a luxury hotel and a Jewish travelers' center run by an ultra-Orthodox sect, leaving 166 people dead and 300 injured.[741]

Following the attack, India made numerous changes to increase their security. They deployed rapid-strike law enforcement officers in four cities; purchased night-scope equipment; increased the numbers of weapons and vehicles at police stations; created specially-trained early-response units; started checking identity cards of fishermen and boaters in the port; and strengthened intelligence links with the United States.

Despite these precautions, "many observers say the changes fall far short of providing protection from terrorists… and some assert that new safety measures have done nothing to protect Mumbai."[742] Even the Home Minister said that India is just as vulnerable as before.[743] To be sure, in July 2011 Mumbai was once again terrorized by three bomb blasts across the city, leaving at least 20 dead and 100 injured. This time, however, respondents to the attack were better prepared.

Terrorists or Terrorism?

In a column written for *The New York Times*, Thomas L. Friedman framed the violence of the first decade of the 21st century as a subtle distinction between "terrorists" and "terrorism." The war is not about a good war here or a bad war there. It is basically a war within Islam between Muslim mainstream and a violent jihadist minority, who train recruits to kill without any orders from al-Qaida. They are fighting to decide how and whether Islam should embrace modernity.

After 9/11 the United States' operation in Afghanistan was about the war on "terrorists," about getting bin-Laden. Iraq, on the other hand, was a war on "terrorism," trying to build a "decent, pluralistic, consensual" government in the heart of the Arab-Muslim world. In deciding to send more troops to Afghanistan, President Obama shifted the focus from a "war on terrorists" to a "war on terrorism," including nation building.[744]

Differing strategies: U.S. and France

The United States has tended to rely on technology (watch lists and sophisticated screening equipment) in its counterterrorism strategy, while Europe has emphasized domestic human intelligence. In recent years France alone has foiled 15 or more planned terrorist attacks by jihadist cells through information received from human sources, recruited among a Muslim population of about five million. "You have got to be proactive," said a former investigating magistrate.[745] "It is not a question of defense."

France's anti-terrorism policing—it is not a "war," specialists emphasize—has more latitude dealing with terrorism suspects than American counterparts. Under French law, "criminal association with intent to commit terrorism" is a crime. As a result, police carry out frequent raids, can demand a show of identity and can hold suspects for days without intervention by defense lawyers.[746]

New Characteristics of Violence Today

Role of the Internet

The problem of counterterrorism is confounded by many factors, of which the central role of the Internet is one. As early as 2007 the Internet was being used in insurgencies and conspiracies to broadcast propaganda and images to spread radical Islamist views supporting al-Qaida and other terrorist organizations.[747] Today the Web also enables threats to move at increasing speeds, with real time contact around the world, as in the first Mumbai attack. "The time needed to develop a terrorist plot, communicate it around the globe and put it into motion has been drastically reduced," said retired Vice Admiral John McConnell[748].[749]

> **"The timeline is no longer a calendar—it is a watch."**
> —Retired Vice Admiral John McConnell

Use of masks

Another tool that is characteristic of violence in today's world is the use of masks. Both the fighters of Hamas and Fatah used them in the Palestinian civil war in Gaza.

"These masks are the uniforms of the new armies of the 21st century and the new kind of violence, [which] no longer distinguishes between war against the stranger and war against members of your own society. Just as this new violence doesn't have a front, it doesn't have a face. It doesn't have boundaries.

"These young men do not report to anyone above them. They have no ranks. No leader can ever be sure of their allegiance… In today's environment, where the big divide is between the world of order and the world of disorder, you can expect to see a lot more confrontations between armies in uniforms and helmets and armies in blue jeans and masks.[750]"[751]

Other Factors

Though not new, two other factors need to be mentioned as part of the violence scene.

Second Amendment

The NRA has been fighting for terrorists' right to buy firearms. At the same time the Government Accountability Office has found that people on terrorist watch lists bought guns from U.S. dealers 1,119 times since 2004. This happened mostly because the federal government does not have the power to stop them. The Second Amendment's provision of the right to bear firearms has engendered an ongoing argument. [752]

Drug cartels

The second factor is the connection of drugs and violence, especially in high-level corruption.

In Mexico, drug cartels have been crippling the political process with brutal tactics, including beheading rivals. One mayor was arrested on suspicion of protecting two violent drug gangs, and gunmen killed a mayoral candidate. Other candidates have received threats, and some political parties could not find anyone to even run for mayor.[753]

Other parts of the Americas are experiencing violence and corruption, too:

Jamaica

In Jamaica supporters of a major drug trafficker with ties to the ruling party are fighting security forces to prevent his extradition to the United States.

Guatemala

Guatemala has to deal with a national anti-drug czar and police chief, who are under arrest in a case involving cocaine and slain police.

Colombia

Colombia's drug trafficking and its human toll has become so commonplace, it seldom attracts the news media these days.[754]

CRIME

In 2005 a surge in violent crime erupted, reversing a historic drop in the U.S. crime rate. The 2.5 percent increase in violent crimes was the largest jump in 15 years. During the first half of 2006 the pace accelerated, with homicides, assaults and other violent offenses up by nearly four percent. [755] Then, for three years in a row, crime dropped dramatically. This was surprising, as economic woes like the near-collapse of our economy usually mean rising crime rates.[756]

PERPETRATORS OF CRIME

Role of Culture

Richard Cohen of *The Washington Post* said culture, and not economics, is the root cause of crime. For the most part, people do not switch to a life of crime because they have been laid off or their home has gone "under water." When people accept this as truth, criminals will lose whatever status they now have as victims. "The latest crime statistics strongly suggest that bad times do not necessarily make bad people. Bad character does." [757]

CRIME ON THE STREETS

A former Air Force officer, Jerome Ersland, started a furious debate in Oklahoma City over vigilante justice and self-defense. While at work in a drugstore as a pharmacist, he was confronted by two holdup men. Ersland pulled a gun, shot one man in the head and chased the other away. Then he got another gun from behind the counter and fired five more bullets into the wounded one—a teenager—as he lay on the floor.[758]

Ersland "received an outpouring of cards, letters and checks from supporters, and became the darling of conservative talk radio."[759] Although Ersland faced a murder charge because the five additional shots were not in self-protection, many people concluded the teenager got what he deserved.[760]

Handgun ordinance

Chicago approved what city officials claim is the "strictest handgun ordinance in the nation" to combat offenses such as Ersland's. The law bans gun shops in Chicago and prohibits gun owners from carrying guns outside the confines of their own home, even onto their porches or in their garages.

The ordinance came just days after the Supreme Court ruled that Americans have the right to have handguns anywhere for self-defense.[761]

Role of combat exposure

The Army is exploring a possible link between violent crime and previous combat exposure. Soldiers in a single unit in Iraq killed eleven people after returning home, including a couple gunned down while posting a garage-sale sign. During two long tours in Iraq, the unit suffered 113 combat deaths.[762]

The unit has since moved to Afghanistan, where it suffered two combat deaths in its first two months in the country. Nationally at least 121 Iraq and Afghanistan veterans have killed, or been charged with killing, someone in the United States as of 2009.[763]

IMMIGRANTS AND CRIME

Statistics show that cities near the U.S.-Mexico border are among the safest in America, even as politicians were calling for more federal troops to stem rising violence there. Violent crimes in southwest border counties have dropped more than 30 percent. In fact, the top four big cities in America with the lowest violent crime rates are San Diego, Phoenix, El Paso and Austin—all in border states. Among America's 25 largest cities, San Diego has the lowest number of violent crimes per capita. One out of four residents there is an immigrant, and the city is right across the border from Tijuana, Mexico. Border patrol agents face far less danger than street police in most U.S. cities. Three per cent were assaulted in 2009, mostly by rocks being thrown, compared with 11 percent of police officers, who are usually attacked with guns or knives.[764]

Immigrants are very unlikely to be institutionalized in the United States, supporting data that show there is no relationship between the U.S. crime rate and immigration. The crime rate of immigrants is one-fifth that of native-born Americans, despite Arizona's tough law to make Arizonans safer by curbing the flow of immigrants.[765]

WHITE COLLAR CRIME

White-collar crime was so widespread in the first few years of the new century that in 2004 the FBI gave warning of an "epidemic of mortgage fraud" that could send the country into financial collapse. Attorney General Eric Holder re-directed his resources and made fighting white-collar crime a top priority.[766]

In 2005, a former CEO[767] of Brocade Communications was sentenced to serve 18 months in prison and pay a $15 million fine for his part in a stock-options backdating scandal, a scheme that was occurring in numerous companies at the time.[768] The federal judge trying the case said millions of people depend on the integrity of the financial markets and on honest disclosures of CEOs and CFOs, so his action was untenable.[769]

However, the Supreme Court made it more difficult to prosecute CEOs for corruption when it narrowed the 1988 law making it a crime to scheme to deprive the public of their "right of honest services." In June 2010 all nine justices agreed that secret deals or conflicts of interest are not a crime unless they involve taking a bribe or a kickback.

"The court has clearly raised the bar... What about the guy who secretly goes on a vacation paid for by the contractor and then several years later, awards him a big contract? This is a gray area now if you can't show a direct connection," said Patrick Collins, a former corruption prosecutor in Chicago. The ruling is expected to eliminate a large number of cases involving white-collar officials from coming to trial.[770]

INCARCERATIONS

WOMEN

Over the past 30 years, the number of women who are incarcerated has greatly increased. Those serving sentences of more than a year grew by 757 percent from 1977 to 2004, nearly twice the percentage increase for men. Regions differ sharply in the handling of female offenders, with Oklahoma, Mississippi and the Mountain States setting the pace in their imprisonment.[771]

YOUTH

Another marginalized group, youth, has revealed startling news about their time in detention centers. Ten percent of youths at correctional centers nationwide reported sexual abuse by (mostly) female staffers, who made up less than half of the workers. Although the level of abuse was not surprising, "the prevalence of sexual abuse by staff, particularly female workers, was shocking," said an executive[772] of Just Detention International[773].[774]

REHABILITATION

An innovative way to correct behavior issues in inmates is having them rehabilitate dogs. An eight-week training program at San Mateo County jail in California assigns inmates to unadoptable dogs from the Humane Society to correct behavior issues. The inmate handlers receive weekly instruction on training techniques in working with dogs and then practice those techniques throughout the week. The dogs stay at the women's jail, which is located next door to the men's facility, and sleep inside kennels in the women's rooms.[775]

CAPITAL PUNISHMENT

At the other end of the spectrum, people on death row have sparked an ongoing debate over the death penalty. Among problems with the death penalty, as it plays out, are the inconsistent and often unfair way in which it is imposed and the exorbitant expense it incurs. Even more important is the injustice that has sometimes been served through its imposition. DNA testing and other forensic advances through technology have raised public awareness that innocent people are being convicted and are furthering just response to crime. Over 100 innocent people

have been freed from death row in the past 35 years. Consequently, support for the death penalty has dropped from 79 percent to 66 percent. [776]

> **"California taxpayers pay an extra $90,000**
> **for every inmate on death row, a total of $60 million**
> **per year more than they spend on inmates serving life**
> **without parole."**
> —*San Jose Mercury News*

For Reflection:

1. ....

   ....

   ....

2. ....

   ....

   ....

3. ....

   ....

   ....

CHAPTER 15

WAR

"War is not an event; it's a process."
—"Pray the Devil Back to Hell" (DVD)

STRATEGIES OF WAR IN HUMAN HISTORY

The world has seen successive developments in processes and techniques of warfare throughout human history, leading to technological advances like Ground Positioning System (GPS) in our time. From the dawn of the gunpowder age around 1500 C.E. until the past few decades, gravity and sheer luck were basically what guided the projectiles of war. Even in World War II, pilots were lucky to land a bomb within half a mile of the target. This "hit or miss" approach spanned the Industrial Revolution of two world wars, with all their major military changes.[777] (See Appendix E)

Advances in microchip technology since the 1960s have led to the Information Revolution, which dramatically altered the conduct of warfare. The Gulf War introduced technologies such as GPS, surveillance aircraft including AWACs and Stealth Fighters, and precision-guided munitions, none of which had been available in previous wars. By 1991, one airplane, one pilot and one bomb could accomplish what it had taken a thousand airplanes to achieve in World War II.[778]

Technology has now reached the point where adaptation to the Information Age determines the emergent leaders in the world. Future leaders must make better use of technology than others, though not necessarily be the ones to develop the best technology. The bottom line for winning a war is having an effective organization for harnessing military power and utilizing the information technology of the day. This poses a huge challenge for the United States, as its military structure was designed for a different era and is overly rigid and bureaucratic.[779]

> "In many ways, the U.S. government is kind of the GM or Ford of governments, this old- style industrial bureaucracy that used to work extremely well, and no longer works so well, whereas the enemies that we face are very decentralized, very networked. They're sort of the eBay of terrorism."[780]

COMPLEXITY AND CHALLENGES OF WAR TODAY

With decentralized enemies, rapid advances in military technology and a shrinking world that puts us face to face with inscrutable cultures, war has become much more complex, raising new questions and problems.

War in Afghanistan

Taliban and al-Qaida

The complexity of the Taliban and al-Qaida networks in Afghanistan and Pakistan drove home the ineffectiveness of waging war in ways of the past. The Administration responded to the difficulty by targeting the terrorists more narrowly, but which was the greater priority—an intensified counterinsurgency campaign against the Taliban in Afghanistan, or more drone strikes against al-Qaida along the Pakistan border? It was hard to know. Dissecting the structure of these militant organizations and understanding the murky and evolving ties between the two was a tough challenge.[781]

Kandahari viewpoint

As the United States was preparing to mount an offensive in Kandahar province in 2010, residents were expressing sympathy to the Taliban and feared continuing conflict. This countered the US. military's hopes of bringing the Taliban to the negotiating table, which would undoubtedly have required more fighting and deaths. Most Kandaharis favored negotiations with the Taliban, and four of five Kandaharis said most members of the Taliban would stop fighting if given jobs. A tribal elder of Kandahar expressed the opinion of many Kandahar elders: "The only way out of this conflict is to talk with the opposition, to bring them into the system and give them an equal portion.[782]"[783]

Cultural Differences

Adding to the complexity of war have been cultural differences. One example is an argument that arose in Kabul between an American service member and an Afghan policeman because the American was drinking water in front of police during the Ramadan fast. This prompted the police officer to shoot the American, raising the ire of other American troops, who then seriously wounded the Afghan.[784]

Obesity and Filling the Ranks

Though all branches of the military met or exceeded recruitment goals needed for the offensive surge in Afghanistan, U.S. military expressed concern that 27 percent of all Americans ages 17 to 24 are too fat to join the military.[785] Weight problems have become the leading medical reason that recruits are rejected today, and the government spends tens of millions of dollars every year to train replacements for service members discharged because of weight problems. National security in the year 2030 is "absolutely dependent" on reversing child obesity rates, according to a report of Mission: Readiness, a retired officers group.

The United States' challenges in recent warfare have raised new questions about how to conduct warfare today in a way that is militarily effective, legal and moral.

NEW STRATEGIES AND TECHNOLOGIES OF WAR

Suicide Bombs

Suicide bombings have taken place since the early 1980s. By 2007 they were occurring so frequently—more than double the number in any war of the past—they surprised and worried U.S. intelligence and military analysts. Six hundred fifty-eight attacks took place around the world in 2007, including 542 in Afghanistan and Iraq. "Increasingly, we are seeing the globalization of suicide bombs, no longer confined to conflict zones but happening anywhere... [Suicide bombers are] martyrs without borders."[786]

Robots

The use of robots in war, traditionally considered science fiction, is already happening. Best known is the Predator drone, a pilot-less aerial vehicle used frequently in western Pakistan to collect intelligence, though drones have also been used to operate air-to-ground missile strikes. The Obama administration provided Pakistan with a dozen unarmed spy drones to encourage their cooperation in fighting Islamists on the Afghanistan border. Though these drones significantly upgraded the Pakistanis' reconnaissance and surveillance ability, Pakistani military leaders rebuffed U.S. pressure, saying they would not begin any assault for at least six months. [787]

Robots also enter combat zones to operate machine guns and explode Improvised Explosive Devices (IEDs). Their remote control is handled in a secluded area in western United States, making it seem more like a video game than a real war.

Ethical and safety questions around the use of robots are holding back any rush to use them extensively in fighting future wars. Because they are so effective, such as plugging themselves in when they need a charge, there is danger they could become run-away intelligence and take over their own decision-making.

Snipers

Advanced technology in the forms of new optical hardware and ballistic innovations has made the sniper the "go-to guy" for military operations in today's world. Navy SEALS are applauded for their skill in bringing down a target over a mile away, such as they did in a piracy incident in the Indian Ocean in 2009, and more recently for their secretive and successful mission to get Osama bin Laden. The public regards the sniper today as one who restores order by bringing cool logic to what is normally "hot, messy and exhausting combat."[788]

Invisibility

Scientists have demonstrated that they can cloak three-dimensional objects using artificially engineered materials that redirect light around the objects. Their research moves the world closer to hiding people and objects from visible light, a technology that could have strategic military applications.[789]

Space Warfare

In 2007 China destroyed one of its aging satellites in space, leaving a large "debris cloud" that could endanger other satellites. This act was considered "inconsistent with the spirit of cooperation… in the civil space area," said a spokesperson[790] for the National Security Council. The U.S. military, which depends heavily on satellites for navigation, communications and missile guidance, was especially concerned. They worried that anti-satellite technology could lead to a possible arms race in space.[791]

CYBER WARFARE

SCADA Systems

Near the end of the 20th century, media began reporting more frequently about cyber warfare. Industrial technology was advancing in increasingly complex ways, including remote-control technologies known as Supervisory Control and Data Acquisition (SCADA) systems. These systems allow remote monitoring and control of operations, such as production lines in manufacturing and civil-works projects like dams. The danger of SCADA systems in warfare is of concern: terrorists could sit with a keyboard, remotely shutting down factory assembly lines or devastating cities by opening a dam's floodgates.[792]

Chinese Countermeasures

The U.S. Defense Department learned early on that China was investing heavily in electronic countermeasures and defenses against such attacks. The Chinese army sees computer network operations "as critical to achieving 'electromagnetic dominance'" early in a conflict. Theoretically this could include China's intelligence agencies embedding a malicious code in Chinese-made computer chips, enabling them to take command of U.S. computers by remote control over the Internet.[793]

Cyber Attacks

With this in mind, the U.S. Air Force Cyberspace Command set out to learn how to disable an opponent's computer networks and to crash its databases. Now that many nations have a finger on the digital button, the specter of a cyber-conflict caused by a misidentified attacker or a simple glitch looms large.[794]

Extrapolating from attacks already tried, possible scenarios might be an attack on Wall Street or on the Federal Aviation Administration's air traffic control system.[795] Already thousands of daily attacks from organized criminals and hackers for nations (including Russia and China) are being launched on federal and private computer systems in the United States. Clearly a new international race is underway to develop cyber weapons and systems to protect against such attacks.[796]

Although cyber warfare would not be as deadly as atomic war, cyber-attacks with "the ability to threaten the U. S. money supply is the equivalent of today's nuclear weapon," said Mike McConnell, former director of U.S. national intelligence.[797]

International hackers

A case in point: a group of international hackers infiltrated the computer network of a major financial services company[798] in November 2008, when our country's attention was focused on the presidential election and a collapsing economy. In the span of 12 hours, the hackers hit 2,100 ATM terminals in 280 cities spanning the world and withdrew $9 million. The haul rivaled 1,000 typical bank robberies in the United States. This cyber scheme, one of the most sophisticated ever devised, exemplified the international scope and increasing precision of cyber-attacks. "What made this case different was the scope, the timing and the coordination," said Doris Gardner, an FBI special agent who worked on the case. "It was very sophisticated."[799]

Pentagon capability

In 2003 the Pentagon and U.S. intelligence agencies made plans for a cyber-attack to freeze billions of dollars in the bank accounts of Saddam Hussein to cripple his country's financial system before invading Iraq. This would have meant no money for Iraq's war supplies or money to pay troops. "We knew we could pull it off—we had the tools," said a Pentagon official at the time. But the attack was never approved and received little notice, appearing only on Newsmax.com. The Bush administration feared it might not be limited to Iraq but instead create worldwide financial havoc, perhaps spreading as far as the United States.[800]

Defense against cyber attacks

The larger question that needs to be answered is whether the best defense against cyber-attack is the development of a "robust capability" to wage cyber war. The Pentagon and intelligence agencies have already determined that higher firewalls and better virus detectors are not sufficient. "The fortress model simply will not work for cyber. Someone will always get in," said a senior military officer who has been deeply engaged in the debate for several years.[801]

Attracting computer geeks

The Pentagon has attracted thousands of "hacker soldiers," young computer geeks who know about new capabilities of technology and can blend them into U.S. war planning. President Barack Obama called this new face of war "one of the most serious economic and national security challenges we face as a nation."[802]

With the exotic nature of cyber defense and the deep recession, defense contractors Northrop Grumman, General Dynamics, Lockheed Martin and Raytheon have been able to attract top young talent that formerly would have gone to Silicon Valley.

> **"At a Raytheon facility… rock music blares and empty cans of Mountain Dew pile up as engineers create tools to protect the Pentagon's computers and crack into the networks of countries that could become adversaries."**
> —Christopher Drew and John Markoff, *The New York Times*

Cyber Weapons: Disruptive or Destructive?

In addressing the challenge, the Administration had to face questions like: How will cyber war affect civilians? Fears of collateral damage, along with laws of war, made the Obama administration cautious about pursuing cyber warfare. Laws of war require that attacks be proportional to the threat, and the chances are very high of hitting civilian targets like a hospital. Nevertheless, some hold fast to the belief that "cyber weapons are disruptive and not destructive."[803]

JUDEO-CHRISTIAN WEST VS. ARAB-MUSLIM EAST

Israeli-Palestinian Conflict

Perhaps the most entrenched conflict of modern times is that of the Israelis and Palestinians. Despite repeated attempts to bring them back to the negotiating table, they are still at odds with each other. Palestinians said they would not engage in negotiations unless Israel promised not to start new housing projects in East Jerusalem, and Netanyahu said he would not freeze construction in the city. For more than 40 years Palestinians have sought to end Israeli occupation and gain statehood.

Official U.S. position

While the official U.S. position has been to treat Israel and the Palestinians as equal partners, critics say this approach does not take into account the imbalance of power between the two sides.[804]

Violence or peaceful protest?

A change of Palestinian strategy, roughly modeled on the anti-apartheid struggle in South Africa, has given new hope to Palestinians. The seeming success in boycotting Israeli products is seen as evidence that peaceful protest, rather than violent struggle, may be the weak link they have been seeking.[805]

However, members of the Islamist Hamas movement, another faction of the Palestinian political spectrum, continue to advocate violence. Also, some Western diplomats fear that the nonviolent resistance campaign could backfire, causing the Israeli government to be more reluctant to negotiate.[806]

The Larger Struggle

The Palestinian-Israeli conflict is part of a much larger struggle in that area, spanning the Arabian Peninsula, northern Africa and the entire Mideast region.

Arabs and the Arab Spring

Arabs see themselves first and foremost as Arabs, and only secondarily as members of individual nation states. Other nations must recognize this or foreign policy will not mesh with reality.

Their connectedness began to unfold overtly in the Arab Spring, in which we saw the commonality of problems they face, their determination to break loose from tyrannical dictators and their support of one another.

Gaza flotilla

Israel has had particular issues with Turkey, a country that has historically played a pivotal role in keeping balance and stability between the East and West. Thomas Friedman[807] was concerned that the prime minister of Turkey[808] lashed out so vehemently at Israel over its attack on the Gaza flotilla taking humanitarian aid to Palestinians in the Gaza strip. While Friedman acknowledged justification for criticizing Israel, he thought Turkey's outrage was way out of balance when considering a number of horrific actions taken by several Arab states. He cited Syria's involvement in the murder of the prime minister of Lebanon; the Iranian regime's killing of its own citizens demonstrating for the right to have their votes counted; Muslim suicide bombers murdering nearly 100 Ahmadi Muslims in mosques in Pakistan; and pro-Hamas gunmen destroying a United Nations-sponsored summer camp in Gaza because it "wouldn't force Islamic fundamentalism down the throats of children." If Turkey moves too far to the East, he said, it will lose "its historic role as a country that can be Muslim, modern, democratic—with good relations with both Israel and the Arabs."[809]

Nicholas Kristof, also of the *New York Times*, saw the deadly attack on the Gaza flotilla differently. He was shocked that Israel would undermine its own interests by using lethal force on peace activists in international waters in front of scores of reporters. Continuing on such a path of self-destruction could eventually be catastrophic.[810]

Israel's storming of the peace vessel undermined efforts to win sanctions on Iran and antagonized its support base in the United States. General David Petraeus had noted a few months before the incident that the perception that America favors Israel breeds anti- Americanism and bolsters al-Qaida. As the chief of Israel's national intelligence agency[811] put it: "Israel is gradually turning from an asset to the United States to a burden."[812]

ADDRESSING PROBLEMS OF WARFARE

Cyber Conflicts

To deliberate momentous questions raised by cyber warfare, President Barack Obama created a new White House cyber command post, run by a "cyber czar." The U.S. cyber defense strategy, he said, would restrict access to government computers, protect the systems that run the stock exchanges, clear global banking transactions and manage the air traffic control system.[813]

The President's announcement of the new command post coincided with an announcement by the Pentagon of a comparable military command, preparing for both offensive and defensive computer warfare. Officials said they now view cyberspace as comparable to more traditional battlefields. "We are not comfortable discussing the question of offensive cyber operations, but we consider cyberspace a war-fighting domain," said Bryan Whitman, a Pentagon spokesman. [814]

Immediately the Pentagon's plan raised significant privacy and diplomatic concerns. Although President Obama said the cyber defense strategy "will not—I repeat—will not include monitoring private sector networks or Internet traffic," officials said there is simply no way to "effectively conduct computer operations without entering networks inside the United States… or traveling electronic paths that are not themselves American targets."[815] Foreign adversaries frequently attack through computer network hubs inside the U.S., so military officials may need to intercept e-mail messages sent from other countries to guard against computer viruses or potential terrorist action. Advocates suggested the process could be regarded as the digital equivalent of customs inspections. "The government is in a quandary," said Maren Leed, a bipartisan defense expert and former Pentagon special assistant on cyber operations.[816]

Land Mines

Land mines are one weapon of war that is being toned down—or perhaps eliminated. In 1997, 150 countries signed a treaty banning land mines, with the United States notably excluding itself from the accord, along with China and Russia. The treaty prohibits the manufacture, trade and stockpiling of land mines, which are responsible for killing or maiming about 5,000 people a year across 70 countries. Though the United States has not used anti-personnel mines since the Persian Gulf War in 1991, and stopped producing them in 1997, the military keeps about 10 million of them in reserve. The Obama administration actively sought ways to come into compliance with the treaty, which already has bipartisan support in Congress, without endangering national security needs. A primary concern was capability of responding to threats such as North Korea.[817]

Nuclear Weapons

The Non-Proliferation Treaty (NPT) of 1970 was designed to check the spread of nuclear arms worldwide. It declared that nations without nuclear weapons are committed not to acquire them; those with them are committed to move toward their elimination; and everyone has the right to develop peaceful nuclear energy. Treaty members—all nations except India, Pakistan, Israel and North Korea—meet every five years to discuss how it is working. Of greatest concern to the treaty members today were Iran's nuclear programs, Israel's secret bombs, North Korea (a treaty outsider), and the huge U.S. and Russian nuclear arsenals. President Obama emphasized his commitment to nuclear non-proliferation and reached an agreement with Russia in 2010 to reduce their thousands of long-range nuclear arms.[818]

National Security Strategy

In an annual strategic statement presented to Congress in 2010, President Barack Obama introduced a new national security strategy, which recognized the limitations of military superiority for maintaining U.S. strength and influence in the world today. His strategy called for building global institutions and expanding international partnerships beyond the traditional allies of the United States. Maintaining global leadership, he said, will also depend on a strong domestic economy, commitment to "education, clean energy, science and technology, and a reduced federal deficit." The report reiterated international engagement and collaboration as a first resort against national security threats, and it recognized "American innovation… as a leading source of American power" at home.[819]

COSTS AND EFFECTS OF WAR

War is costly, both monetarily and in human welfare. Most types of warfare also have a significant environmental impact, though this is seldom given equal attention. Following are three effects that make the greatest direct impact on human life today.

Erosion of International Relationships

The Iraq Study Group, mandated by the U.S. Congress Partto assess the war in Iraq, urged Congress to press the President to change course in Iraq. Despite their pleas for Congress not to nit-pick their report, but rather treat it as a whole, officials picked it apart.[820]

Congress' nit-picking added to the resentment already fomenting in other parts of the world over U.S. policy in Iraq. Critics said Americans squandered the goodwill of the world following the 9/11 attacks and made the world less safe. Rather than cure the world's ills, the war on terror had weakened civil liberties and other democratic rights.[821]

Monetary Costs

Throughout recent U.S. wars the monetary cost per service member per year has increased dramatically[822], though the total cost of wars has steadily decreased[823] —in dollars, in percentage of GDP, in number of troops involved and in number of deaths. Two other big changes are the shift from using draftees to volunteer enlistments, and no more full-scale mobilization of armed forces, as in World War II.[824]

Recent U.S. Wars			
World War II		**Vietnam War**	**Afghanistan**	**Iraq**
*Cost per U.S. service member per year	$67, 000 (peak of the war)	$132,000 (1968 peak of war)	**$1.2 million (to 2010)	$685,000 (to 2010)
Number of American troops involved	12 million (in 1945)	790,000	100,000 (after the surge)	100,000 (average)
Number of American military deaths	405, 399	58,209	1,135 (as of 2010)	4,404 (as of 2010)
Cost in the percentage of GDP	36% (in 1945)	2.3% (in 1968)	0.7% (2001 – 2010)	1.0% (in the peak year of the war, 2003-2010)
Total dollar cost	$810 billion (in 1945)	$104 billion	$321 billion (inflation-adjusted) 2001-2010	$784 billion (inflation-adjusted) 2003-2010
Draft or Volunteer	Draft	Draft	Volunteer	Volunteer

Sources: *Congressional Research Service* | Center for Strategic and Budgetary Assessments (Wikipedia) The Globalist Quiz, August 1, 2010.

* Adjusted for inflation to today's dollars

** Operating in Afghanistan has been extraordinarily expensive for the U.S. military due to the country's lack of infrastructure and its geographical position as a landlocked nation.

When an $83.4 billion war supplemental spending bill was presented to Congress in May 2009, critics arose on every front, reflecting "a discomfort that this is a one-way ticket to a quagmire."[825] Some worried that with no benchmarks to measure progress in Afghanistan and no exit strategy, the conflict was left open-ended. Others called for a much greater proportion of the funding directed to humanitarian aid and reconstruction.

The U.S. Iraq war cost was "$5,000 a second,
$434 million every day. Seven days a week,
no weekends off, no vacations. $12 billion every month."
—*Senate Majority Leader Harry Reid*

Some liberal democrats who opposed the bill were also strong supporters of Obama and were reluctant to vote against this early test of his national security strategy. Hoping to appease the opposition, both the Administration and Speaker Nancy Pelosi pledged that future war expenditures would be part of the regular budget. "My message to my members is: 'This is it,'" Pelosi said. "There won't be any more war supplementals."[826]

Even the Pentagon became worried about rising costs of the war. Military pay, which constitutes about one-quarter of defense spending, had steadily risen 42 percent since 2002. Rising personnel costs could "dramatically affect the readiness of the department," said the Undersecretary of Defense for personnel[827]. Yet military officials noted that the generous compensation packages enabled them to meet all their annual recruiting goals in 2009 for the first time since the all-volunteer force was established in 1973.[828]

Congress was left with a dilemma, voiced by a member of the House Armed Services Committee: "We end up with a false choice—are we going to fund weapons or are we going to fund people? The reality is, we need both.[829]"[830]

Human Costs

"Hidden wounds"

As recently as 2010, thirty-seven percent (250,000) of Gulf War veterans were still suffering fatigue, joint pain, insomnia and other "persistent unexplained medical symptoms" following their wartime service in the Gulf. In an investigation of Gulf War medical disorders, the National Academy of Sciences Institute of Medicine found that only post-traumatic stress disorder (PTSD), present in 2-15 percent of Gulf War vets, was clearly caused by the Gulf War. However, the medical experts did find "evidence of an association" between Gulf War service and anxiety disorder, alcohol abuse, dyspepsia, irritable bowel syndrome and "multi-symptom illness" (the Institute's name for Gulf War syndrome).[831]

> **"The Iraq conflict is not a war of death for U.S. troops nearly so much as it is a war of disabilities."**
> —*P. Steven Macedo, neurologist*

> **"We can save you. But you might not be what you were."**
> —*Neurosurgeon, Iraq*

> **"These are the war's injured who once would have been the war's dead."**
> —*Ronald Glasser, nephrologist*

These "hidden wounds," suffered by at least 30 percent of the troops fighting in a combat zone for four months or longer, are the signature symptom of the Iraq and Afghanistan wars. In previous wars, American fatalities were much higher than in Iraq and Afghanistan. These current wars were the first ones in which troops were very unlikely to die if they were still alive when a medic arrived.[832] In Iraq and Afghanistan the ratio of wounded service members to fatalities is 16-1[833], but that kind of "survival" is a gruesome measure of success. Those within close range of Improvised Explosive Devices (IEDs)—or even at some distance—have little chance of avoiding traumatic brain injury (TBI), which the medical world is poorly equipped to handle. The majority of TBI victims never fully recover. Though neurological surgeons are very skilled at treating open wounds, these brain injuries occur at a microscopic, sub-cellular level, forming small gas bubbles that litter the brain with tiny holes. The medical world has a long way to go to catch up with this devastating form of war injury.[834]

Hidden wounds are part of the hidden costs of war. (See Appendix E.) More than one-third of the $22 billion spent on disability payments to veterans of recent wars was accounted for by mental illnesses, a 76 percent surge since 2003. This is not surprising, considering that vets' psychological wounds are four to five times costlier than the average disability. And these hidden costs are often neither immediate nor visible. [835]

Suicide

Some military personnel have dealt with the trauma of war and despair through suicide. Since 2004, suicide rates in the Army have been rising, surpassing the rate for civilians and reaching the highest level since the Vietnam War. In 2007, 115 soldiers killed themselves, compared with 106 in 2006. About a third of these suicides took place during deployment, another third after deployment, and the remaining third had never been deployed.[836]

Iraqi method of coping

Iraqis adopted a way of dealing with the trauma of war by numbing themselves to its horrific effects. Senseless killings became such an everyday occurrence in Iraq that Iraqis failed to react emotionally. The Abu Ghurayb prison scandal convinced many Iraqis that under the U.S. military justice system, top leaders could get away with orchestrating crimes. A Baghdad sandwich vendor[837] summed up the way many Iraqis viewed the situation:

"Americans are terrorists and killers. And this is the way of life now. I don't care if they punish the American soldiers because they cannot bring back the lives of the dead."[838]

Between the U.S.-led invasion in 2003 and 2009, at minimum 110,600 Iraqis died in violence. More than 87,000 of those killed since 2005 were civilians.[839]

ENDING THE WAR IN AFGHANISTAN

After the war front shifted from Iraq to Afghanistan, where al-Qaida plotted the 9/11 attacks, fighting accelerated and Afghani casualties mounted. The campaign to win over the hostile population in the Taliban's southern heartland proved to be an extremely difficult maneuver, made even more difficult by the Afghan government's ineffectiveness, which was a drag on any momentum gained. That coupled with the uncertainty of Pakistan's loyalties and deadly clashing at the Pakistan/Afghanistan border left the outcome of the war undetermined.

Special Operations

With criticism being leveled at the Administration from all sides of the political spectrum for too much or too little aggression, President Obama made Special Operations an integral part of his global security strategy.[840] The strategy allowed the President to expand a largely secret U.S. war against al-Qaida without public notice, since "secret" forces rarely discuss their operations in public. Commanders have plans for pre-emptive or retaliatory strikes wherever and whenever a plot has been identified, or after an attack linked to a specific group.[841]

Special Operations forces have been especially relevant for the war in Afghanistan. Their units are trained in specialized warfare skills, like capturing fugitives and conducting sabotage, skills desperately needed for the war in Afghanistan, where U.S. officials were hoping to wipe out Taliban strongholds without destructive weapons. Since the Obama administration relied heavily on these covert operations, the Army planned to spend as much as $100 million to expand its Special Operations headquarters in northern Afghanistan.[842]

Bringing the Troops Home

President Obama planned to bring home U.S. soldiers from Afghanistan on an accelerated timetable, starting with 10,000 by the end of 2011 and an additional 23,000 by the end of Summer 2012. The remaining 68,000 were scheduled to return to the U.S. by 2014. The final withdrawal of the U.S. from Afghanistan occurred in August, 2021.

For Reflection:

1. ....

....

....

2. ....

....

....

3. ....

....

....

CHAPTER 16

BUSINESS AND GOVERNMENT

BUSINESS

Business since World War II

A postwar boom and rise in living standards marked the period from the end of World War II until 1973. During that time, family income doubled for everyone in all classes.

From then until 2005, national life became a mixed bag, as a widening gap in standard of living developed. Overall, middle income rose modestly, but male wages fell.[843] Technological advances brought cell phones, videos and the Internet to the general public. Yet traffic was becoming worse, commutes were longer, and economic risk was increasing. It is uncertain if there was any rise in the typical worker's pay, even though the U.S. economy became far richer and productive during that time than a generation earlier. It is clear only for the lucky few at the top, who made stunning economic gains between 1973 and 2005.[844]

By 2008 every American citizen was paying dearly for a schismatic division of wealth. Unlike other scary events in our recent history—the attack on Pearl Harbor, the Cuban missile crisis, the 9/11 attacks—*we* brought on the near-meltdown of our economy through sheer neglect of our financial system. This made it even more difficult to bear.

The crisis affected everyone because we are inescapably connected. "You can't save Main Street and punish Wall Street any more than you can be in a row boat with someone you hate and think that the leak in the bottom of the boat at his end is not going to sink you, too," wrote Thomas L. Friedman, *New York Times* columnist. The whole system needed to be saved, even if it meant bailing out people who didn't deserve it.[845]

Two years later the economy looked hopeful. Construction spending, which had been one of the hardest hit industries, climbed more than it had in nearly a decade, and manufacturing expanded for ten straight months. Export orders rose in America despite economic troubles in Europe. Even the employment index reached its highest level since 2004.[846]

Yet within a month or two, economists were discussing the real possibility of a "double dip" recession. Then the situation improved again, so talk of a "double-dip" subsided.

And so it went. The roller coaster ride has continued...

Mergers, Buyouts and Partnerships

For years companies have bought out other companies to become more competitive. Increasingly, though, companies have opted to sell themselves to the point where 25 Silicon Valley companies had vanished by 2007 through acquisitions. This left 280 publicly traded companies in the Valley, down from a bubble-induced high of 417 in 2000.[847]

The silicon chip industry took the lion's share of buyouts. LSI Logic purchased Agere Systems, a major merger of LSI's strength in the enterprise market with Agere's in the consumer and personal computer businesses.[848] Yahoo joined forces with Microsoft[849] and Time Warner spun off AOL into a separate publicly traded company.[850] By 2010 AOL had found another marriage partner in Facebook, which was struggling to pass its greatest rival, Google.[851]

More and more frequently acquisitions involved major companies buying out smaller ones. Toys R Us acquired FAO Schwarz, a high-end specialty toy store.[852] CVS Caremark and Walgreen bid against each other for the acquisition of a regional drugstore chain, Longs Drugs Stores, until Walgreen finally pulled out of the bidding, leaving the prey in the hands of CVS. "It never, ever stops being a shark tank. The smaller players have gotten squeezed, their profits have gotten squeezed and at some time they decide to throw in the towel.[853]"

Blurring of store categories added more competitive pressure to both chains and independent stores. "You can buy all the things that you can get in a drugstore in another kind of store," said Laura Miller, senior economist at the National Association of Chain Drug Stores. "And increasingly you can buy all the things you can get at a supermarket or a mass merchant at a drugstore."[854]

Some companies looked around the world to hook up. British Broadcasting Corp. (BBC) became the first international broadcaster to sign a major deal with Google-owned YouTube, showing excerpts from its news and entertainment programs on YouTube's web site.[855] Citigroup acquired Japanese brokerage, Nikko Cordial, to boost its presence in Japan for selling mutual funds and other services.[856] India's TataMotors bought Jaguar and Land Rover from Ford Motor, flexing its muscles as a fledgling international economic player. "They have developed the technology and ability to become world-class car manufacturers," said Seshan Rammohan, executive director of TiE Silicon Valley.[857]

Cisco Systems made a splash in South Korea, where it showcased a complete "city in a box." In conjunction with South Korea, it built New Songdo City, designed for a million people beside the Yellow Sea. In the midst of this technologically-sophisticated city is 100-acre Songdo Park, modeled after Central Park in Manhattan. New Songdo City provides a model for world governments as they seek to handle rural-to-urban migration of tens of millions of people across the developing world.[858]

Outsourcing

Another way American companies sought to improve the bottom line was by outsourcing to Asian countries or offshoring to Latin America, which saved even more production costs and provided call center workers without heavy foreign accents.

Saving the Auto Industry

U.S. auto manufacturers had found it necessary in early 2007 to close down plants to stay competitive in their own home market. They laid off thousands of American workers and started building their cars outside the U.S.[859]

The recession that followed brought down the three largest auto manufacturers in the United States, requiring a costly bailout for survival. The federal government found individual solutions to save all three manufacturers.[860] One of them, General Motors, expected to have a profitable year in 2011, its first since 2004. By 2021, GM was reporting $10 billion in profit, its highest ever.

Infosys

India's outsourcing giant, Infosys, developed a new model for global businesses that it claimed is the wave of the future. It hired young

Americans, flew them to India for an intensive, six-month training program, and then redeployed them in the United States. An Infosys vice president[861] called it a "rewrite of the Industrial Revolution for the digital economy." Infosys said it believed that any knowledge-based work could and would be outsourced.

"Much of the tech world has, in fact, embraced this new model that deploys an army of low-cost engineers who use the ubiquity of high-speed fiber-optic cables and the Internet to provide services for customers around the world… IBM, Accenture, Oracle—they all have come to India, hiring engineers as fast as they can."[862]

Green Products

In 2007 the marketing of green products to other countries— especially China, where coal-fired power plants have been built at the rate of one a week—became a new field of opportunity. Companies that formerly looked to China to manufacture PCs and iPods found profit in China's environmental meltdown. Reduction of energy through use of green products meant fewer tons of coal burned to produce electricity.[863]

High Tech Trade Deficit

While China and India were growing their economies, U.S technology started importing more computers, high-tech components and consumer electronics than they exported, jacking up the U.S. trade deficit in their industry to $102 billion. Some of these imports were from American companies that were designing chips in the United States, manufacturing them in their overseas plants, and then importing them. Though this was a drag on the U.S. trade deficit, high-tech exports accounted for 21 percent of all U.S. exports in 2006, up nine percent from the prior year. [864]

Finding new consumer markets in foreign lands was a lifesaver for some companies in the midst of the economic recession, but it was not enough for many workers. Jobs—even tech jobs— disappeared. Some were outsourced or offshored, and some just evaporated.[865]

Products for Other Cultures

By 2009, the globalized world was making an about-face with regard to innovation and marketing. The mindset of U.S. technology companies to seek out low-cost talent abroad to carry out their innovative ideas was shifting (in some companies) toward designing products for other cultures, primarily targeting Asia, the Middle East and Latin America—but not the United States.

Commenting on foreign markets, William Miller of Stanford University's Graduate School of Business said, "At one time, they were just producer markets. Now they have become consumer markets." Although most companies still view the U.S. as the center of their business plans, startups are rapidly shifting focus toward creating technology for marketing in other countries. [866]

Innovative Practices Within the U.S.

Advertising

While foreign countries were exhibiting credentials as major players in global markets, consumers here at home were ignoring traditional advertising. U.S. companies had to buckle down to become more innovative in reaching the public.

One idea was the use of artificial reality games, which blur reality and fantasy. The Internet marketing agency, 42Entertainment, came up with the idea of using artificial reality games as a form of viral marketing. The basic idea was to give consumers entertainment value before pitching their product or asking for money.

Vanishing Point, the game devised to advertise Microsoft's Windows Vista operating system, presented giant puzzles to be solved by teams of strangers on the Internet, whose only connection with one another was a love for online treasure hunts. The person who solved the overall puzzle first [867] would win a trip into space on a private rocket.

Clues for Vanishing Point included messages hidden in a "Bill Gates speech, a light show that used the fountains outside the Bellagio Hotel in Las Vegas as a canvas for clues, skywritten messages above four cities, coded images projected onto the walls of various monuments [868] and a fireworks extravaganza with a secret message in the skies above Seattle.[869]"

The game drew 70,000 participants to the puzzles and more than 20 million page views at the Vanishing Point website.

"This is where marketing is going in the future: games that are really more like promotions, and campaigns with high-production values where the participants don't realize or care if they're the targets of marketing messages."[870]

Luring business travelers

Americans may be shifting away from the Puritan work ethic. Not only are advertisers reaching them through games, but also hotels are luring business travelers by welcoming the whole family and making their visit convenient and fun. The workplace has become more flexible about letting employees juggle work duties with family life, resulting in 62 percent of business travelers adding a leisure component to at least one business trip a year. Some companies even encourage bringing family on business trips as a way to keep employees happy and productive.

Many conventions court business by offering babysitting services and family outings. Some hotels provide a crib, baby swing and a CD of lullabies for families with an infant, thanks to hotel partnerships with companies such as Fisher Price. They also serve baby food at their restaurant and arrange excursions for the whole family.[871]

Design of business space

Back at the office life is changing, too. Until the latter half of the 20th century, offices were discreet units with doors, providing absolute privacy. Then the norm gradually shifted to a large, common space broken up with individual cubicles. Now that form has morphed into open areas with armchairs, extra conference rooms and tables that workers can use with laptops. Cisco and Intel, among other companies, have made this shift in response to a trend that stresses the bottom line and as a move toward greater efficiency. Employers are finding that more work gets done with this space arrangement, and workers interact better as a team, which is becoming more of a requirement in our complexifying world. Also, the design saves space and money, and encourages collaboration.[872]

Repairing Damage from the Recession

Re-inventing companies

One way in which companies have tightened the belt and addressed fallout from the economic crisis was to innovate and reinvent themselves. Behnam Tabrizi, author of *Rapid Transformation, a 90-Day Plan for Fast and Effective Change*, says that such change is good. It also should be rapid, as the environment and the market can change quickly, and organizations become resistant to change when it occurs too slowly.

> **"As organizations grow, they are like organisms.**
> **They develop strong antibodies,**
> **which are resistant to change."**
> —*Behnam Tabrizi, Stanford School of Engineering*

Companies that have succeeded at transforming themselves[873] have moved very fast. An important ingredient for their success was bringing key people together in multi-disciplinary teams and asking for their help in defining and reinventing the company. Suddenly key people realize they are key and are part of the solution. "While your competitors are just cutting and cutting, you are rethinking all your assumptions.[874]"[875]

Automation

Hewlett Packard cut costs in the sluggish economy by automating corporate data centers, which eliminated 9,000 jobs. The company said this is the next big trend following on the heels of cutting costs by moving jobs overseas. Consolidation, not innovation, is the new HP way.[876]

Cloud Computing

Another way of consolidating corporate data is "cloud computing," storing data in a common cyberspace location, which enables people to post something in one place that can be read in many places. A primary advantage to cloud computing is that all data is available to the user wherever there is an Internet connection.

Back in the '80s, several companies offered e-mail, but members of one service could not exchange messages with someone using another service. Then e-mail providers started using the Internet to connect to other providers. Since that time applications have been developed that allow some integration between websites, such as displaying Twitter feed on Facebook, but for the most part, moving data between sites like Facebook and Yahoo requires business relationships between the two companies (unlike Internet e-mail).

In 2009, Yahoo added "applications" to its front page, allowing users to see data from Yahoo and non-Yahoo accounts, including G-mail, eBay and Facebook. The day is rapidly coming when Web-wide standards for data exchange will allow posts on any service provider to be viewed or updated from another.[877]

Entrepreneurs and Other Individuals

Shareholder activists

In early 2007, companies[878] began to change their policy with regard to shareholder activists. They started listening, trying to avoid public fights with investor groups. This new approach became almost a necessity as investor demands became more difficult for companies to ignore. Not only did shareholders step up their proxy fights, but also they had a 59 percent success rate. Commenting on the success of a shareholder resolution at Applebee's that triggered a nine percent jump in its shares, a Bear Stearns analyst[879] said, "Our immediate reaction is one of surprise that the long-term course of this company could be altered by pressure from a relatively small activist shareholder."[880] Yet by 2015, activists were even going so far as to demand the splitting up of a corporate entity, or the spinning off of part of a company to another owner.

Reaching the "unbanked"

Wizzit, a South African company, developed an innovative approach in offering banking services to the world's 5.5 billion "unbanked," using messaging functions of cell phones for basic banking transactions. This helps the world's poorest take the first step out of poverty. With the use of a cell phone, a farm laborer can get her wages deposited directly into an account, pay her rent, buy groceries and send money home to her parents.[881]

> **"Industry estimates say there are more than
> 3 billion [cell phone] handsets worldwide,
> three times the number of people with bank accounts."**
> —*Craig Timberg, **The Washington Post***

Low-cost baby incubator

Students, too, are using technology to promote the public good. Three students at Stanford's Graduate School of Business filmed a video and posted it to YouTube promoting Embrace, a nonprofit organization that created an innovative low-cost baby incubator. The video was noticed on YouTube by the CEO of India's first interactive digital billboard company, who posted it on digital billboards all across India.[882]

Innovative tools to raise living standards can now find pathways to people who will benefit from them, no matter where they live in the world.

GOVERNMENT

Polarization of American Politics

At the core of America's two-party political system is an inherent split: freedom and equality. Both parties value both of these, but people tend to lean more toward one than the other. In today's world conservatives tend to favor freedom, while liberals are more concerned with equality—primarily equality of opportunity in social justice issues.[883]

Equality of opportunity may now be morphing into equality of progressive politics. For example, an active group of progressive Washington, D.C. Council members is making a subtle shift from traditional social justice issues—such as expanding jobs and opportunities for the poor—to those that stress quality of life, focusing on popular environmental and social issues. The changes embrace a vast array of concerns: legal marriages for gay and lesbian couples; health insurance for every resident, regardless of immigration status or income; same-day voter registration; bicycle lanes; bag tax; access to marijuana from approved dispensaries; and more organic and less fatty foods at school. Some people say Council policies are now more "top down" because unions and churches have lost their influence, and policies are geared toward the affluent instead of benefiting everyone.[884]

If current research proves to be right, political leanings toward progressivism or conservatism are part of our DNA[885]—perhaps to preserve the balance and momentum that opposites provide. Findings show that issues such as gun control, pacifism and capital punishment are strongly associated with innate physiological traits, in which differing levels of fear are key. Researchers found that conservatives are more vigilant to environmental threats, which leads them to support policies that protest the social order. It follows that such persons would be more aggressive in arming themselves and more wary of foreigners and different religious beliefs.[886]

Such was the case when the first Muslim, Keith Ellison[887], was elected to Congress in 2006. Representative Virgil Goode, Jr. a Virginia Republican, warned that Ellison's election posed a serious threat to the nation's traditional values, and some Virginia voters were outraged by his plan to use the Koran during his swearing-in ceremony. Goode chimed in, saying Americans needed to "wake up" or else there would "likely be many more Muslims elected to office and demanding the use of the Koran."[888]

In a book called *Authoritarianism and Polarization in American Politics*, the authors[889] presented related material. They explored data that show a remarkably strong correlation between state attitudes toward spanking children and voting patterns. States that condone spanking go Republican, whereas those that encourage timeouts go Democratic. They contended that the differences stem from "profound differences in cognitive styles." Spankers tend to see the world in black-and-white terms, perceive the social order as vulnerable or under attack, make strong distinctions between "us" and "them," and emphasize order and physical responses to threats.

Some middle-of-the-roaders are moved toward that worldview by shocks like 9/11 or the severe economic recession, with its job losses and housing foreclosures. Their attitudinal shift is often reflected in the voting pattern of ensuing elections.[890]

With strong polarization in the government today, middle-of-the-roaders have become isolated, leaving unrepresented the very area in the political spectrum where most things get done. Today both Republicans and Democrats are alienating independent voters, driving them further away from center by their ideologues. Partly (or mostly) because of this, moderate political candidates of both parties find it necessary to leave their parties and run as independents, if they have any hope of being elected. "We have a deadlocked democracy," said Patrick J. Buchanan[891]. "Both parties, held hostage by their extremes, are incapable of tackling the issues that threaten this country."[892]

In recent years extreme American leaders have shown a strong reluctance to change. They have become more set in their stance on increasingly complex issues, whether it is the January 6th hearings, global warming, school choice or virtually any bill before Congress. People become entrenched in a position and refuse to change their minds, regardless of new evidence that is brought to light. They even attack those who show a realistic, intellectually honest willingness to face the facts of a situation and change their minds in accord with their values. [893]

> **"People root for their team and cheer when it scores points, without asking whether they chose the right side."**
> —*Francis Fukuyama, professor of international studies*

Presidential Election of 2008

Use of the Web

The presidential election of 2008 demonstrated deeper inroads of the Web into political life.

Undermining candidates

One use was to undermine candidates. Damaging video clips of presidential-hopeful Sen. John McCain reversing his position on an issue were replayed in a series of two-minute Web videos to turn McCain's own words against him.[894]

Fundraising

The Web was also used to magnify the impact of small donors in campaign fundraising. Bundled contributions from the average American transformed Internet fundraising into an around-the- clock supplier of major dollars.[895] The Internet became the online version of neighborhood fundraising, outperforming direct mail and other sources to become the single largest source of revenue for most presidential campaigns.[896]

Caucusing

At the other end of the technological spectrum, Iowa reverted to a folksy, laid-back approach in their caucuses that would "make a cattle call look organized[897]."

In one precinct, the precinct chair gave a loud whistle to get the attention of about 400 people, who then started horse-trading votes for presidential candidates, hoping to make the 15 percent threshold. "This is 18th century democracy in action," declared the man[898] who signed people in.[899]

Absentee voting

Absentee voting became a growing trend during the 2008 elections. While it makes voting less communal, people who choose that method are more likely to actually vote than others, and it saves taxpayer dollars. Polling places draw a 20 to 30 percent turnout, while 75 percent of permanent absentee voters return their ballots.[900]

A New Electorate

When the American people finally made their choice of Barack Obama as President, traditional politics found itself on shaky ground. Not only did his election smash the racial barrier and bury baby boomer presidency, but it also paved the way for emergence of a new 21st century American electorate.

This new group of voters was young, increasingly nonwhite[901] and embraced a different kind of politics. They "value action over partisanship, favor consensus over ideology and believe government can be a partner, not the enemy[902]." The generational change has brought us to a turning point in our history where people have lost faith in the old order and are looking for something new.[903]

> **"The Me Generation is ceding to the We Generation."**
> —*Mary Anne Ostrom,* **San Jose Mercury News**

Millenial generation

The emergent "Millennial" generation[904] has slipped into that space where people are seeking the new, and by 2016 they will comprise one-third of the electorate. Their strong desire to get things done was helped greatly during the 2008 presidential election by the confluence of technology and politics, which allowed them to bypass mainstream media and build online communities to push their agendas. Bundled contributions were one important result, as well as ongoing networking.[905] In future elections, more formalized, widespread and established social networks like Facebook and YouTube will undoubtedly make Internet use even more effective.

As the mid-term elections of 2010 drew closer, the Millennial Generation's impatience with partisan politics and desire to get things done spread widely. A general impatience with politics as usual swept the country, eliciting an anti-incumbent mood that appeared to be more than a temporary trend. This attitude forged a disconnect between traditional politicians and the voters who actually make the choices. The country had moved past the days of "clearing the field" for a preferred candidate. A new generation of politicians, raised with more consumer choice and less loyalty to institutions, had come on the scene. With their diminished affinity for political parties, they endangered incumbent politicians, who needed strong party backing. The situation enabled just a few committed activists to upset the apple cart. A politics of personal conviction had largely displaced the politics of issues.[906]

Public vs. Private Sector

Invasion of privacy

Inevitably governmental bodies wrangle their constituencies, but one recent Administration sparked negative emotions even more deeply than most. In 2006, when it leaked out that the federal government was secretly collecting phone-call records on millions of Americans, a political firestorm erupted. Ever since 9/11 some telephone companies had been turning over records to the National Security Agency, which hoped to build a database of every call made within the United States.

Many individuals and companies were infuriated that the government was violating their privacy.[907] In addition, some were adamant that this governmental policy transgressed the Fourth Amendment to the Constitution, which guarantees no "unreasonable search and seizure."[908]

Foreign tax credit reform

In August 2010 Congress legislated foreign tax credit reform, upending a long-standing law that allowed American companies to defer payment of taxes on foreign earnings as long as the funds were kept overseas. Under this legislation, some corporations have to pay billions of dollars in U.S. taxes on their foreign earnings. For some companies, foreign earnings amount to half or more of their sales. Industry representatives claimed that lower foreign tax rates provided a level playing field on which they could compete overseas against foreign companies[909].[910]

While money was the *overt* basis for outrage over taxation of foreign profits, the allure of money was *covertly* undermining the whole monetary system. This resulted in Goldman Sachs executives being summoned to the Senate floor to testify to criminal charges brought by the Securities and Exchange Commission (SEC) that they had defrauded investors.[911]

Public-private partnerships

Sometimes, however, public and private realms strike a beneficial partnership. Many cities have been experimenting with the private operation of public places.[912]

One of the first was New York City. In late 2006, Bryant Park began operating entirely by the support of commercial sponsors and fees, drawing the attention of urban planners worldwide. Since then Central Park has been put under the auspices of a private conservancy with a staff of 300, aided by 1,300 volunteers.[913]

Similar public-private experiments are now taking place throughout the country. Non-profit foundations are managing parks in Atlanta, St. Louis and Boston. A private conservancy is refurbishing San Diego's Balboa Park, and non-profit groups are helping manage restoration of the Los Angeles River. Even the federal government enlisted private donations to fix up the nation's 390 federal parks and monuments. The ability of urban parkland to survive is largely due to the generosity of the private sector. This is in keeping with Generation Y values, which reflect humanity's moving into adulthood.

Foreign Relations

Colombia

In a landslide victory in 2006, Colombia re-elected president Alvaro Uribe, the first incumbent to be re-elected in his country in a century. Critics said he has shown disinterest in social programs in the midst of rampant poverty, and they feared he would become more autocratic in his new term as president.[914]

Cuba

Uribe's re-election bucked an emerging trend to the left in the Latin American region, which included Colombia's northern neighbor, Cuba. As its interim leader, Raul Castro[915], hinted at a collaborative leadership style, encouraging debate between leaders and granting power to civilian authorities. "They all give opinions. They all discuss and, in the end, if I see that there is not a true majority consensus, we don't reach any conclusions as long as there isn't any pressing emergencies," said Raul Castro at an annual conference of the University Student Federation. He appeared to be laying the groundwork for moving the nation forward, while remaining loyal to Cuba's communist system.[916]

In April 2011 when Fidel Castro resigned from leadership of the Cuba Communist Party, his brother, Raul, became President, urging a "rejuvenation" of the Communist Party. This included limiting top political positions to two five-year terms.

Within a few months President Obama lifted the ban on Americans traveling to Cuba.

France

A voter turnout of 84 percent of eligible voters in the 2007 presidential election in France reflected urgency in an election that centered on the country's fear of economic decline at home and diminishing influence abroad. The massive voter turnout showed enthusiasm for the "more modern, personality-driven, American-style campaigns[917]" in which both candidates represented the baby boomer generation, a first for France. Although the right-wing former interior minister, Nicolas Sarkozy, won the election, the female Socialist candidate, Segolene Royal, drew 24 percent of the vote in the first-round balloting, compared with Sarkozy's 30 percent.[918]

During Sarkozy's visit to the White House in 2010, he commented, "Seldom in the history of our two countries have the shared values between the United States of America and France been so aligned."

Iran

Nuclear energy in Iran has been the focus of international attention since 2003, when Tehran agreed to suspend nuclear enrichment work, and then reactivated its program two years later. By 2006 Iran had managed to enrich small amounts of uranium to 3.5 percent, the level needed to generate electric power but far below the 80 percent level needed for weapons.[919]

United Nations inspectors reported in September 2011 that Iran seems to be accelerating key components of its nuclear program and are possibly engaged in ongoing research on nuclear warhead design, despite their repeated insistence that Iran's nuclear program is peaceful.[920]

South Korea

A proposed free-trade agreement between South Korea and the United States set off a demonstration of thousands in Seoul in 2006, with labor, agriculture and social groups resisting most fiercely. The proposal slashed tariffs on many goods and services from the two nations, [921] engendering numerous points for discussion since then between the two nations. Although the U.S. agreement was signed in 2007, it was never ratified by the two countries' legislatures.

During a visit to Seoul in April 2011, then-Secretary of State Hillary Clinton said the free-trade agreement, which removes 95 percent of tariffs between the two economies, would be one of her top priorities in the coming months. The U.S. has a strong commitment to ratify the pact before the end of the year, she said.

For Reflection:

1. ....

....

....

2. ....

....

....

3. ....

....

....

CHAPTER 17

INFORMATION AND COMMUNICATION

For astrology aficionados, today's massive changes in the ways we communicate come as no surprise. After all, this is the Age of Aquarius, the age of communication that officially began in 2000.

A visible sign of the dramatic shift in communication is the change in composition of the Dow Jones industrial average. In June of 2009, the Dow replaced General Motors with Cisco Systems on their stock index, upping the number of technology firms to five.[922] Smokestack industries were clearly being edged out by high tech—and not so slowly.

The Dow said their action reflected a sea change for corporate America:

"Just as automobiles were essential to America in the 20th century, communications and computer networking products are vital to an economy and culture still adapting to the Information Age."[923]

PRINT MEDIA

Newspapers

Advertisers move to the Web

After the burst of the dot.com bubble in 2001, and a precursor to the recession set in, print advertisers began searching for the "biggest bang for the buck."

Corporate America stepped into the picture, happy to fill the need. Intel started delivering editorial content directly to the public through the Internet, which began a quasi-boom in pairing company-created information with interested readers. The printed word through newspapers and magazines was gradually being eased out.[924]

As advertisers discovered that online advertising cost them a small fraction of what they had been paying to newspapers for prime ad space, they sent classified ads into a sharp decline. This served a serious blow to print media, not only in lost advertising income, but also in lost readers. [925]

Survival through local news

By the middle of 2007, experts were trying to placate the public—or themselves—with the conviction that newspapers would survive, even in the tough times they faced. However, they added, most newspapers that survive will focus on local news.

> **"We're hardly the first industry or medium to go through a sea change. Magazines had to significantly revamp their model after radio came on the scene, and radio had to change after television arrived. Newspapers will adapt, survive and thrive in the coming years."**
> —*Mac Tully, Vice president of the Bay Area News group*[926]

International coverage

In early 2007, the digital world had begun to deal a death blow to media coverage of international affairs. At the very time when the world was becoming interdependent, and knowledge of other nations was increasingly needed, media sources were not financially able to maintain foreign bureaus. At the same time, Web sites and blogs were edging out traditional coverage with their instant information.

Foreign correspondents shrank from 188 to 141; foreign bureaus were replaced with individual roving correspondents, free lancers and news wire agencies; and newspapers dropped a broad worldview for more narrowly focused reporting. Newspapers banded together to send only one correspondent to cover a particular issue, forcing not only the closure of foreign bureaus and investigative teaming up, but also lay-offs of reporters and editors.

Journalist awards

As a tribute to those whose journalism careers had been cut short because of hard times in the newspaper industry, the Society of Professional Journalists awarded its highest honor in northern California in 2008 to the "Vanishing Journalist."[927]

At about the same time, a rule change began, allowing online-only news organizations to compete for Pulitzer Prizes for the first time, though none of the entries won any prizes.[928]

Low point for newspaper industry

Increasing numbers and percentages of lay-offs took their toll, even at high-ranking papers like the *Chicago Tribune*, the *Christian Science Monitor* and the *Philadelphia Inquirer*. 2008 was one of the most depressing years ever for the newspaper industry.[929] Only *USA Today* and the *Wall Street Journal* were able to eke out a gain—less than one percent each.[930]

Experimentation to meet the challenge

Newspapers experimented with different ways to address their situation, ranging from raising prices and reducing the number of pages to laying off more journalists. However, these did not work well for readers who continued to subscribe, as they were now paying more for less.

Electronic and print editions

One by one, newspapers started publishing both electronic and print editions, giving people breaking news online and depth news in print.[931]

Charging for online content

Rupert Murdoch, head of NewsCorp, began charging for content for all his online newspapers. By 2013 the News Corp media company had split into 21st Century Fox and News Corp.[932] *The Wall Street Journal* may end up being the only newspaper to be successful in charging for online access. [933]

Nonprofit wire service

Science news was hit hard. With fewer science reporters, and the number of newspapers that carry a science section reduced from 150 in 1990 to fewer than 20 in 2009, universities were concerned that journalism's economic problems were reducing Americans' understanding of science and medicine. To remedy the situation, 35 top universities in the nation formed their own nonprofit wire service, Futurity. It fed top news sites on the Internet with accounts of their discoveries and provided an independent, objective look at what they were doing. Though journalists admitted the reliability and high quality of their research in news releases, some were concerned that there was no skepticism or investigative side to their report.[934]

Advertising revenue

By 2010, advertising revenue was seeing its smallest drop—ten percent—since the recession began in late 2007. However, that was little consolation for a hurting industry, as it brought the newspaper industry to a subsistence level of 46 percent less ad revenue than in 2006.[935]

Newspapers digitized

The British Library announced in mid-2010 that it was digitizing up to 40 million pages of newspapers, dating back three and a half centuries, and would make the results fully searchable and accessible online.[936] This could be considered a closing tribute to a slowly-dying newspaper industry.

New model needed

A new model must be found if printed newspapers are to survive. Print ad revenues have edged down to a point where gains in online revenue are not enough to compensate.

Great Britain is trying "a model that finances the BBC's TV, radio and online programming with a $237 tax on whatever device you use to watch TV, be it a computer, personal video recorder, mobile phone or TV set.[937]"[938] The U.S. may need to take equally drastic steps to adapt to the shift in media news dissemination, which is inexorable.

Magazines

Though newspapers may have taken the hardest hit when traditional advertising began to move online, magazines were also affected. They, too, have had to experiment with new ways to keep their heads above water.

Time Inc.

Time Inc. was one of the first major magazine publishers to tighten the belt, eliminating 300 jobs in an effort to adapt to the massive exodus to the Internet by readers and advertisers.[939] Time has also experimented with personalized magazines that allow readers to mix and match sections from eight different titles.

Esquire and Entertainment Weekly

In 2008 *Esquire* animated the front of its 75th anniversary edition with digital "e-ink[940]". The following year they experimented with what they called "augmented reality," an issue that included several pages—and cover—in 3-D. Though it is too expensive to use every month, they hoped to use it as often as possible.

That same year *Entertainment Weekly* ran a video screen in its fall TV preview issue.[941]

Comic books

A new magazine format for an adult audience that was originally designed for youngsters is the comic book. In recent years it has shown increasing popularity among adults. Even movie producers have catered to that new interest by producing animated adult films, a close cousin to the comic strip. Reality/fantasy presented in comic book/animated form is clearly a growing part of our sound bite culture today.[942]

Matchbook magazine

An unemployed writer[943] decided to print his quarterly literary magazine on matchbooks for a dime a copy, charging nothing to his customers. He solicited submissions from his readers, selecting and editing one 300-word submission for each issue, then distributed the matchbooks to bookstores, information desks and bars.[944]

Books

In 2006, when people were replacing their CDs with iPods and downloading TV shows from iTunes, the book industry stood firmly grounded in actual printed text. Both publishers and readers strongly resisted the Internet revolution. While recognizing the practicality and economy of digitized media, they felt a deep emotion tugging against it. As one publisher[945] stated it: "I consider myself as multimedia-friendly as anybody, and if the Internet enables us to reach more readers, that's a good thing. But there's a part of me that's still bothered when they refer to a book as 'content.'"[946]

> **"It ends up coming back to a very simple emotion.**
> **I still get that profound pleasure the first time**
> **I get a copy of a book we're publishing and hold it**
> **in my hands. And the force of that feeling is matched**
> **by what the consumer feels."**
> —*Jonathan Burnham, publisher of HarperCollins*

Books have fared no better than newspapers and magazines. In fact, more members of the public have felt emotion around the slow petering out of books than of other media forms. Despite their emotion, e-books may represent the beginning of the end for books and bookstores, in much the same way as iTunes initiated the demise of CDs and music stores.

> **"Textbooks, as we have known them,**
> **are dinosaurs stumbling toward extinction."**
> —*Scott Duke Harris,* **San Jose Mercury News**

Richard Cohen of *The Washington Post* captured the feelings of many book lovers when he wrote in a column:

"I understand it's bulky and expensive to ship and that it entails the consumption of paper, which is probably not green, but then what is? The book has been around for a very long time and I love it so… I loathe Amazon even though I know it is the future and it will prevail...

"My friends, book lovers all, have bought Kindles. At first, I was shocked: *You? A Kindle?* It's like discovering some sort of secret perversion."[947]

Innovations in the book world

Just as magazines have experimented with innovative ways to draw the public's attention, so has the book world.

Personalized romance novels

One entrepreneur[948] publishes personalized romance novels in which the reader is the star. [949] After the customer provides details about herself and her beloved, the company weaves that information into the chosen pre-formatted novel.[950]

Texting librarians and e-books

Some libraries across the country have experimented with allowing people to text-message city librarians for answers.[951]

Libraries are also allowing people to use their local library card to borrow digital copies of books. This makes overdue charges a thing of the past, as the book simply expires from your device after the due date.[952]

Bookless library

As online information accumulates, libraries at research universities are shifting their sense of identity. Before, shelving and checking out books was a basic concern. Focus now is on research and discovery, the basic tools of scholarship.

An example of how this plays out is a "bookless library" at Stanford University. The university emptied books from both the Physics and Engineering libraries, paving the way for a smaller but more efficient one. It is largely an electronic library that can accommodate "the vast, expanding and interrelated literature of physics, computer science and engineering.[953]"[954]

Libraries struggle with identity

All libraries have struggled with the question: Do we see ourselves as a rigid book warehouse or a flexible library? Needless to say, the suggestion of leveling off or cutting back on library book collections has met with resistance from book lovers, many of whom have given time, energy and money through the years to support their local libraries. Yet moving into the new era is what many library officials recommend, predicting that the digital era will only grow. They have increasingly observed that readership habits of the younger generation change as fast as new technology emerges. This cannot be ignored in planning for the future.[955]

Company break-ups

By 2011 some book companies, among others, were spinning off acquisitions they had made in more prosperous times, in an effort to raise their share price in the sluggish economy. McGraw- Hill spun off its education division to focus on its business information unit, primarily the operations of Standard & Poor's.[956]

A New Era

Experts out; self-publishing in

The decline in circulation and advertising has been accompanied by even more changes in the word world. Writing is no longer left only to professionals. Bloggers and other self-publishers have leveled the playing field, with experts no longer the only ones to inform the public. Alissa Quart wrote in the Columbia Journalism Review (CJR): "The attitude toward our craft tends not to be one of mourning for the ashram gone. Rather, it is of not needing a guru at all."[957]

Ongoing news dispatches

Another change in journalism shatters the model of discrete articles. Rather than having a beginning and an end, articles have morphed into an ongoing series of news dispatches.[958]

The business of news? Information

These profound changes have forced the newspaper industry to take an honest look at their purpose: The news business is not about print. It is about information. The information formerly conveyed through print media is as important as it always has been; only the form of transmission has changed. Why should it matter how the public receives the information? What matters is that we continue to have "a cadre of talented, honest and enterprising journalists to dig up facts, dispel myths and keep powerful people in check."[959] A newsroom of reporters and editors has the experience and resources to do this. A single blogger does not.[960]

As publishers try to straddle the printed word and the Internet, they may find that perseverance pays off. The question now is: exactly what will the results look like—and for how long?[961]

DIGITAL COMMUNICATION

Digital communication has overrun the print news media, spreading from Generation Y to the Baby Boomers.[962] President Obama created his weekly addresses to the nation for YouTube viewers. A Pulitzer Prize was awarded for the first time to an online, nonprofit news organization, ProPublica, in 2010. Forms of digital communication have been complexifying rapidly, from e-mail to iPads and beyond. Yet the United States has continued to lag behind the rest of the world in terms of broadband speed.[963]

Adults flocked to e-mail in 2006, at the very time it was turning off the younger generation. It was not fast enough for them. "E-mail is more like snail mail. You don't know when they're going to get it," said teenager Alex Stikeleather.

Instant messaging was then in vogue, followed by posting messages on MySpace, and later on Facebook. Whatever the medium, teenagers were determined to stay connected with their friends, and providers were ready to supply them with more alternative ways to communicate. "The more friends you have, the more cool you are."[964] Technology really helps your social life, they say.[965]

Although stalwarts like The Wall Street Journal and research firms say e-mail is on its way out, many of those who use it cannot buy that. E-mail in-boxes are as full as ever. Many people say they almost dread going on vacation or taking sick days from work because of the hundreds of e-mail messages facing them when they return. E-mail isn't over until it's over.[966]

TV/Cable

Sharing similar revenue problems with newspapers and magazines, TV news coverage was becoming increasingly selective and superficial by early 2007. Twenty-seven states had no reporters on Capitol Hill, and in-depth news providers vanished. Although 80 percent of the public was getting most of its news from TV, foreign coverage had to concentrate on just a few big areas because foreign bureaus had closed down.

TV news anchor Walter Cronkite said:

"The need for high-quality reporting is greater than ever... It's not just the journalist's job at risk here. It's American democracy.

"More than ever, Americans need to know what's going on around the globe. But foreign correspondents for mainstream media are vanishing."[967]

TV Programming

While some folks were spending evenings with e-mail, others were tuning in to "The O'Reilly Factor," a top-rated cable news program. Started as an antidote to left-wing media, its "right or wrong" attitude garnered wide appeal from the public, and it quickly rose to the top of the charts. [968] By 2009 many people were trading up to High Definition flat-screen to make their viewing even more appealing.

Then came Internet-ready TVs that allowed viewers to stream thousands of TV shows and movies through Amazon or Netflix, while simultaneously looking online to get news or view photos.[969]

Upgrades: 3-D, apps and video calling

But that was just the beginning. In 2010 Toshiba offered a TV that allowed viewers to transform ordinary video into 3-D. Samsung went in a different direction, providing software tools that let developers create shopping or travel apps for its televisions. And LG and Panasonic came out with TVs that allow consumers to place video calls.[970]

By late spring of 2010 Google had gone a step further, promising the public an interactive system that completely dissolves the wall between television and the Internet. Google TV lets users search TV the way they already search the Web, via a search box that seeks out a specific piece of content, whether it was scheduled for a TV broadcast or a video available on a website. This was a considerable breakthrough, as it took years of advances in microprocessors, Web design and open-source software to "marry a 50-year-old technology with a much newer technology.[971]"[972]

Cell Phones

In just two short decades cell phones became an inescapable part of life, connecting us to, and distancing us from, the world. They hold our web of connections—family, friends, restaurants and more—becoming a repository of what defines us. At the same time they close us off from the person standing next to us, as we engage in intimate conversations within our own private bubble.[973]

Smart Phones

Cell phones have also become smarter through the years. They have shifted from being merely a one-on-one conversation to more of a companion. Applications (Apps) now available for iPhones or other mobile devices number well over 27,000. In fact, most buyers of smartphones use them to navigate a car, find a restaurant, read a book, play a game or search the Internet, and only occasionally to make a phone call. Talking on cell phones is now less than half of the traffic on mobile networks.[974] "I can't live without it," said a college freshman[975] cradling his iPhone. "It's like water or food."[976]

Voice Mail

As cell phones absorb more users' time, voice mail is falling by the wayside. With the cascade of text messages, e-mail, and Facebook postings, something's got to give—and its voice mail. It takes seven to 10 steps to check a voice-mail message versus zero to three for e-mail. Some people advise callers on their outgoing voice message to call their cell phone or send an e-mail if they need to reach them right away. Research shows that people take longer to reply to voice messages than other types of communication. Twenty to 30 percent of voice messages go unheard for several days, whereas 91 percent of people under 30 respond to text messages within an hour. Even adults 30 and over are twice as likely to respond within minutes to a text than to a voice message. Because of this trend, wireless providers are now offering some form of Visual Voicemail, which displays messages in a visual in-box, just like e-mail.[977]

Between 2008 and 2010 voice minutes plunged for the Millennial Generation, while texting more than doubled. Puzzling to older generations, Millennials consider phone calls rude and intrusive. Before phoning someone, they often text the person to make an appointment to talk. Experts say that texting and e-mail condition youth to be cautious about how they communicate when they are not face-to-face.[978]

> **"A generation of e-mailing, followed by an explosion
> in texting, has pushed the telephone conversation
> into serious decline, creating new tensions
> between baby boomers and millennials."**
> —*Ian Shapira,* **The Washington Post**

Texting

Millennials may be happy with texting, but it causes problems at school. Two-thirds of middle- and high-schoolers have accidentally used instant-messaging style in their academic work, according to a Pew survey[979]. Amanda Lenhart, senior research specialist at the Pew project, is not worried about what she calls "a new slang." She said, "This is different only in that the language comes out of text instead of spoken language, which is how most of our slang has emerged in the past." The trend toward more casual writing does not surprise teachers or students. They say instant messaging has become the primary form of communication for today's students.

Yet teachers are determined to teach students the differences between formal and informal writing and what is appropriate for each of them. B4, LOL and other texting language simply do not make the cut in acceptable classroom writing.[980]

An extraordinarily clever editorial regarding texting language, quoted here in its entirety, appeared in the *Boston Globe*:

"the revenge of e.e. cummings"

We had to LOL when we read how txt-msg lingo is replacing stndrd english in student academic pprs. 1 casualty of da trend is uz of capital letter to start a sentence. kids feel free to lowercase everything. pnktu8n is also dissed. tchaz try to help but it's often 2 l8.

new paragraphs r not used in txting either. kids prolly think all dis iz ok cuz even Richard Sterling, emeritus xecutiv director of the ntl riting prjct, gives it the nod. natl riting prjct is sposd 2 improve riting instruxn in america's schoolz.

"I think in the future, capitalization will disappear," he sed in the nytimes. 4 lazy students dis is 2G2BT!

a big natl study by the College Board and Pew Project on the Internet and American Life finds teenagers riting more b/c of txting but in a hybrid language with conventions of its own: call it Textlish. they don't consider it frml english but 64 percent admit it seeps into their writing at school.

we get da need for shorthand when thumbs fly on tiny keypads. but we thot technology wd enhance communication, not blur every boundary b/w frml language and slang. and don't even get us started on emoticons!

1 yng friend of rs recently sent us a hand-ritten thank-u note. we were thrilled at 1st but her spelling wuz awful b/c deres no spellcheck for pen and ppr. same ish w/ txting. ppl get uzd 2 slang and 4get the real words. btw, all of us w/ email addresses r guilty 2, since email usernames r all lowercase and include many weird squiggles. somehow, tho, gnr8ns of secys managed to transl8 Gregg or Pitman shorthand squiggles n2 grammatically correct correspondence 4 their bosses.

well, tempora quid faciunt. Dis not lingo but latin: times change. early america's founders wud uppercase almost every noun; maybe Sterling really is a visionary. Still, on the 25th anniversary of "A Nation at Risk," the seminal report on America's educational challenges, who wudda thot the big threat to riting wd b the cellfone?"

—Editorial in the *Boston Globe*, April 2008.

Landlines have nearly left the scene, as 97% of Americans now use cellphones, 85% of which are smartphones. [981]

E-Reading

Development of e-books

Although the e-book has been around for the past few decades or more, it was not until 2002 when Sony introduced the Sony Reader that sales began to rise. In 2008 the concept dug deeper roots, largely due to the growing popularity of Amazon's wireless Kindle. Sony's Reader stepped up the competition, followed by nearly two-dozen device makers wanting a share of the pie. Yet e- books still comprised only a small percentage of the publishing business.[982]

E-books were given a huge boost later that year by Apple's iPhone, as several e-book-reading programs were created for it. Every major publisher like Simon & Schuster, Random House and Penguin got in on the act, tailoring their software for various kinds of smartphones.[983] By 2009 e-books were the fastest growing segment of the book publishing industry, with an estimated 5 million e-readers sold in 2010 alone.

Google's Book Search project

In 2004 Google embarked on a huge project of scanning all the estimated 50 million to 100 million books in the world to provide digital versions of them to the public at large. The company's intent was to preserve material indefinitely and to enable broad access to it. Book Search, as it is called, will make it possible to track down a book on any subject, read a small portion and, if it is not protected by copyright, download the whole thing. It will also provide information on copies to buy or borrow.

Despite its lofty goals and having the support of many publishers, authors and librarians, some of them have sued Google. They claim Google is infringing on copyrighted material. Google, on the other hand, points to a legal principle that allows limited copying of protected works.

Book Search, they say, allows Web surfers to retrieve only snippets of copyrighted material.[984]

Other sources of freebies

Many library resources are already online round-the-clock for free. In addition to books, libraries offer thousands of e-books for reading on a computer screen, or CD and MP3 audiobooks, as well as handheld devices. Over 200,000 e-books, audiobooks, videos and music recordings are available to the public.[985]

Authors and e-books

Though many authors have embraced the e-book concept, some notable persons have been wary of its future. One of the longest hold-outs—six years—was the estate of J.R.R. Tolkien, author of *The Lord of the Rings* trilogy. "We were finally able to convince the Tolkien estate that the e-book is a legitimate, widespread format," said David Brawn, publishing operations director at HarperCollins UK.[986]

INNOVATIVE PUBLISHING

Some individual publishers have been experimenting with innovative approaches to publishing for today's market.

Publication snippets

In addition to full-length books, they have found a niche for snippets of books. Short stories were the first of this kind, sold for $2.99 each.[987] Then the craving for shorter works spread to poetry and to buying books by the chapter or page. This accomplished for the literary world what iTunes Music Store did for music; that is, it managed to "free the content from its physical packaging."[988]

Pubic edits and rewrites

Classic, staid *Encyclopedia Britannica*, trying to keep up with the world's most popular encyclopedia, Wikipedia, started inviting public edits and rewrites on its Britannica Online.[989]

Self-publishing e-books

Others publishers were looking out for authors' needs. Mark Coker[990] tried to democratize publishing by developing Smashwords, a free platform for publishing e-books that would never go out of print and always be available to browse on the Web. He said self-published authors "simply upload their finished manuscript as a Microsoft Word file into our system and then we automatically convert that file into about 10 different e-book formats" so they can be read on various e-book reading devices. Authors own the copyright, set their own price for the book and choose what percent of the book is offered as a free sample. The author receives 85 percent of the sales, contrasted with the usual e-book royalty rate of 25 percent. Unlike Lulu, Wordclay or Createspace, Smashwords is focused entirely on electronic books.[991]

COMMUNICATIONS INTERNATIONALLY

"One Laptop Per Child"

By 2007, new technology was making headway in various parts of the world besides the United States. "One Laptop Per Child" project had been launched two years earlier with the placement of low-cost portable PCs in the hands of school children in Nigeria and Thailand, hoping eventually to reach all developing countries. In 2007 they extended their project into Uruguay, loading the laptops with children's books in local languages, along with encyclopedias.[992]

MySpace and YouTube

Early in the same year, MySpace set up communities in more than ten countries, including the United Kingdom (UK) and Japan. YouTube followed suit a few months later when it created local versions of its site in France, the UK and seven other countries. The sites were fully translated in their respective countries' languages. "Video is universal and allows people around the world to communicate and exchange ideas," said Chad Hurley, co-founder and CEO of YouTube.[993]

Global dialog through YouTube

YouTube also appeared on the international scene that year in Davos, Switzerland, at the meeting of the World Economic Forum. A "global dialogue" was set up through YouTube, asking: "What key action do you think countries, companies or individuals should take to make the world a better place in 2008?" The query engendered one million hits and hundreds of video replies. [994]

India

As traditional media was petering out and new technology was pricking interest worldwide, India was a throwback. Newspapers were thriving there, even growing at an astonishing rate. India's middle class and booming economy were fueling an explosion in consumer spending and advertising, and reading a newspaper became a sign of upward mobility. In fact, advertising in India's print media shot up nearly a quarter.

Despite India's reputation as an information technology powerhouse, only a sliver of the population could afford home computers and high-speed Internet access. Projections said widespread Internet access would not be arriving there for a decade.[995]

Cell phone as leveler

India is an interesting mix, straddling several centuries at the same time, with the cell phone as the great leveler.[996] In remote areas of

Tibet, too, cell phones appear as an anachronism. Homes often have no outhouse (much less a toilet)—not even a designated hole in the ground. But they have a cell phone.

As of 2008, there was one cell phone for every two humans on Earth, that is, over 3.3 billion cell phones on a planet of 6.6 billion humans in the course of 26 years. "This is the fastest global diffusion of any technology in human history.[997]"[998]

Status of Languages

ICANN

In 1998 the Internet Corporation for Assigned Names and Numbers (ICANN) was established to oversee the assignment of Internet domain names, and control of it was given to the United States. As the Internet became more firmly rooted throughout the world, other countries wanted to manage their own domain names, such as .uk and .eu[999].[1000] ICANN granted the request.

The organization took a further step in 2009 in assignment of domain names. It approved the use of scripts not based on Latin characters, making the Web dramatically more inclusive. Arabic and Chinese had been among the highest in demand for approval. Rod Beckstrom, I CANN's CEO said: "This represents one small step for I CANN, but one big step for half of mankind who use non-Latin scripts."[1001]

Mother tongues

As part of its goal to raise awareness of the importance of mother tongues, the United Nations Educational, Scientific and Cultural Organization (UNESCO) announced in 2009 that 2,500 languages out of a total of 6,000 world languages are in danger of becoming extinct or have recently disappeared. In the United States alone, more than a fourth of the 192 languages once spoken here have vanished, and 71 more are severely endangered. The world has lost 200 in just the past three generations.

Updating new world atlas

When the third edition of a new world atlas of endangered languages was published, it appeared in both digital and paper versions. The digital version invites users to contribute with updates and allows them to search according to country, degree of endangerment, language name or number of speakers.[1002]

Translation service

Amazon.com contributed to the honoring of worldwide languages by introducing an English translation service for foreign-language books. This gives status to lesser-known works written in languages unknown to most Americans.[1003]

Censorship and Control of the Internet

Internet censorship around the world had become sophisticated by 2007, with governments filtering content in at least 25 countries. Their primary targets were political, social and cultural content, along with apps such as Google Maps and Skype[1004]. Filtering of political content was especially pervasive in Burma, China, Iran, Syria, Tunisia and Vietnam.

Communicating and organizing through the Internet

At the same time, groups and individuals were beginning to use modern technology to communicate and organize for political demonstrations. Governments saw this as a threat and were tempted to censor even more heavily.[1005]

Predictably, clashing erupted.

China

One of the first signs of modern technology reaching beyond censorship occurred in China in 2007. A local government was promoting the construction of a giant chemical factory in the suburban area of Xiamen, setting off hundreds of thousands of urgent text messages warning of the coming catastrophe. People were sure the plant would cause leukemia and deformed babies.

The explosion of public anger forced a halt in construction and produced two days of large demonstrations, a rarity in China. Citizen journalists sent text messages about the protest to bloggers, who posted real-time reports for the country to see. Sites carrying the live reports recorded thousands of hits. One blogger[1006] wrote later: "The Chinese government controls the traditional press, so the news circulated on the Internet and cell phones. This showed that the Chinese people can send out their own news, and the authorities have no way to stop it entirely."[1007]

By June of 2009 Internet users in China had become the world's largest online population, swelling to more than 250 million people. This did not go unnoticed by the Chinese government. As the 20th anniversary of the bloody crackdown on Tiananmen Square approached, the government began blocking social networking sites that might foster discussion of those 1989 events.

YouTube was the first to be shut down, followed a few months later by Twitter and Flickr. Clearly the Chinese government understood the potential of such technology to spread the word about student protests and any event that could cause problems for them.

To counteract such possibilities, the Chinese government went right to the source. They began requiring PC makers to include filtering software on personal computers sold in China. Ostensibly this would provide the government with censorship control over pornography, though it could also be used to block Web sites based on keywords rather than specific Web addresses. In addition, said John Palfrey, an Internet censorship expert at Harvard University, it raises concern that a future update could give China surveillance capabilities.[1008]

Within a few days of China's announcement, a lobbying group for the computer industry in the United States urged President Obama to challenge China on its new requirement. Hackles were raised even more when researchers at the University of Michigan discovered that the required software blocked not only pornography but also some political content.[1009]

Iran

Just a few weeks after China's crack-down on its people, the Iranian government silenced blogs and news outlets in Iran. This prompted one of the largest anti-government demonstrations in Iran since the 1979 revolution, luring hundreds of thousands of people to a silent march through the streets of Tehran, protesting the disputed presidential election. This was considered an extraordinary show of defiance of an official ban from a broad cross section of society.

The government was able to quell their demonstrations but, as in China, the protests merely shifted to online, where tech-savvy Iranians supported the marching protesters by tweeting pictures and messages to the world in real-time as events unfolded.[1010] At the same time, Web hackers targeted Web pages of Iran's leadership, demanding Internet freedom. This was part of a widening front of attempts at cyberattacks by activists. The fighting continued in cyberspace.

To protect the activists, a site called NedaNet[1011] was launched. Its goal was to provide a system of proxy sites that would cloak the location of users in Iran from the Iranian government. [1012]

A San Francisco man[1013] in turn, assisted the Iranian techies by launching Haystack, a program to help them wiggle past government filters. "It's an arms race. There is no precedence for this," said Rebecca MacKinnon, an expert on Chinese censorship.[1014]

Expansion of government censorship

As Web censoring has become more severe and widespread, it has drawn much criticism and concern throughout the world. A transparency tool used by Google showed that government censorship expanded from four countries in 2002 to 40 in 2010. Google's tool tracked the biggest Web censors by country, providing a global view of efforts to remove content or obtain data about its users. One would expect that Iran, North Korea or China would top the list, but that was not always the case. Instead, governments making the most requests for information about users or requests to remove content in the last part of 2009 included Brazil, the United States and India.[1015]

For Reflection:

1. ....

....

....

2. ....

....

....

3. ....

....

....

CHAPTER 18

TECHNOLOGY

"Antiques Roadshow" may have been the most popular show on public television in America, but life is moving in a different direction. "Innovation" is the keyword of today, surpassing any of the pat standards of the past: solid, tried-and-true, traditional, American, rooted, classic, etc.

Some people denounce technology's concern with innovation, yet innovative technology is neither bad nor good. It just "is." To be sure, there is no stopping its development, but humanity can set limits to guide how, and for what purposes, it is used.

Classical Greek mythology tells a story of the Greek god, Zeus, and his son, Prometheus. In one version of the myth, when Zeus discovers that Prometheus has stolen his fire (Zeus' technology), Zeus says to him, "I am giving you two gifts that will keep you from getting into trouble with the fire you have stolen from me. Always keep them close to the fire."

The two gifts were justice and reverence. They may be wise guardians to keep "close to the fire" today.

NANOTECHNOLOGY

A new science has taken hold and is in process of revolutionizing production of goods in many fields for the next 50 to 100 years, according to David Rejeski, director of the Project on Emerging Nanotechnologies at the (nonprofit) Woodrow Wilson International Center for Scholars. In fact, scientists predict it will dwarf the computer revolution in its scope.

Called nano-technology, it is the science of working with nanometers, a billionth of a meter in size. To provide some sense of its scale, the period at the end of this sentence is almost 500,000 nanometers in diameter.

Technically speaking, nanotech is more a tool than a field, as it is the practice of using small quantities[1016], which is not in itself a scientific field. Rather, it is something used in many different fields of science, including biology, chemistry, and physics. For the past 20 years nanotech has been used for sunblock to make its zinc oxide invisible, and it has been giving added strength to tennis rackets and bicycles.

"For the first time we're actually building active circuitry on the smallest scale that life itself uses."
—*Phil Kueke, Hewlett Packard research lab*

Applied Nanotech

Nanotech in schools

Schools are increasing educational focus on nanotech to enrich core scientific training. Educators agree that students must have a solid education in their field of choice and then apply their field to specific nano-projects that mirror real world industry.

Handheld laboratory

Two graduate students[1017] combined their knowledge in different fields—electrical engineering and medical and bioengineering—to win the first Change the World Competition[1018] in 2009 with their handheld laboratory to diagnose illness in remote areas of the world. Their NanoLab detects proteins where laboratory equipment and technicians are not available. It is very simple, easy to use, and can be taken and used anywhere.[1019]

"Bucky paper"

Bucky paper is one of nanotech's vast potential uses. Made from nanotubes, bucky paper looks like ordinary carbon paper but is ten times lighter, and it is 500 times stronger than steel. It is being eyed for light, energy-efficient aircraft and cars. "This very well could be a very, very game-changing or revolutionary technology to the aerospace business," said Les Kramer, chief technologist for Lockheed Martin Missiles and Fire Control.[1020]

Batteries

A Stanford scientist, Yi Cui, is hoping to "reinvent the battery and cause a transportation revolution akin to reinventing the wheel" through his work with silicon nanowires, which last ten times as long as standard batteries. Because silicon is the second most abundant element, and the semiconductor industry is mature enough to handle it, the cost is low.

Injected nanotubes

Nanotubes could be filled with drugs and then injected into a cancer patient to target tumors. The greatest advantage over traditional means of administering drugs is its size. The nanotubes are so small the body will not recognize them as foreign objects and try to reject them.

Invisibility cloak

Nanotech could create computers with nearly unlimited memory. Some scientists are even experimenting with bending light through use of nanotech, which could lead to creating an "invisibility cloak." Its possibilities seem endless.

National Nanotechnology Initiative

The federal government has seen nanotechnology as such a game-changer that in 2001 it launched a National Nanotechnology Initiative to further the technology, investing $12 billion as of 2009. In addition, the private sector has invested billions more.

> **"Nanotechnology is not the wave of the future. It has arrived."**
> —*Arden Pennell, Palo Alto **Weekly***

Need for international Regulations

As promising as nanotechnology is, we need to exercise caution in using it. It could cause an economic breakdown or a vicious arms race. If it spread to use in households across the country, it would seriously disrupt manufacturing and traditional commerce.[1021] Scientists warn that international regulations for nanotech must be established soon before weapons grow more complex. Regulations need to include oversight of military applications, and possibly intellectual property patents.[1022]

ROBOTIC TECHNOLOGY

Driverless Cars

Pentagon-sponsored robot race

Perhaps the widest use of robotic technology is for transportation purposes. As early as 2005, engineers were competing with driverless cars for a $2 million prize in a Pentagon-sponsored robot race in the southern California desert.[1023] By 2007, competing cars were averaging 214 miles per hour, guided by cameras, lasers and an on-board computer. Cars had to navigate traffic circles, follow all the speed laws and stop at intersections.[1024]

Google's robotic competition

Google also sponsors a robotic competition, the Lemor X prize, which will award $20 million to the first team to land an automated rover on the moon that can send back high-definition images and video.[1025]

This is part of Google's more general interest in extending the frontiers of the Internet. Hoping to regain ground it had lost to Microsoft's VirtualEarth, Google quietly licensed the sensing technology developed by a team of Stanford University students who won the 2005 DARPA race. That technology enabled Google to map out photo-realistic 3-D versions of cities around the world. Although Google already had 3-D cities, it was first to use buildings modeled solely by computers, not by people.[1026]

Researching safer driving

When driving long distances and navigating city streets without a driver had been successfully accomplished, researchers set to work on autonomous race cars that can drive at high speeds under extreme conditions. This could lead to safer driving and one day allow ordinary vehicles to drive on their own. Volkswagen has set a goal of creating fully autonomous vehicles by 2028.

"Shelley" in Pike's Peak competition

Stanford University researchers have equipped an Audi TTS with GPS receivers that can be programmed to follow any route using a digital map. In the fall of 2010 they tested "Shelley" in the world-famous International Hill Climb at Pike's Peak, which has been a challenge for professional drivers since 1916. It drove the entire 12.42 miles, including 156 precarious turns, without a driver at the wheel.[1027]

Airport pod cars

Also in 2010, Santa Clara Valley Transportation Authority financed a $1.8 million feasibility study to develop driverless shuttles the size of a Smart car at San Jose Airport. A pod-car system costs a fraction of heavy rail or automated people movers, provides flexibility and has no emissions.[1028]

These so-called "pod cars" will be computer-driven electric vehicles that run on elevated rail lines on a loop, with stops at nearby hotels, convention center and train station. They accommodate one to six passengers, who will pay $1.50 or less for transport at 40 miles per hour. Riders will get in, punch in their destination and be taken there nonstop. Pod cars are already operating at London's Heathrow Airport, and three other locations[1029] are developing similar systems.

Other Robotic Uses

Helper

Japan has addressed the need to serve their aging population, which is 80 percent of the nation, since the weakening of family ties in recent years has left the elderly without the care traditionally provided by children and grandchildren. To meet this need, the country is using cutting-edge technology to care for a rapidly aging population. At the cost of $3500 each, robots help the elderly with a spoon- and fork-fitted swiveling arm to help them eat. When they try to lift a heavy object, a "muscle suit" detects it and signals air pumps to provide support. An intelligent wheelchair operates similarly to pod cars, using a positioning system to take the person automatically to a preset destination. Other wheelchairs respond to oral commands like "forward" and "back," "right" and "left." "It's all about empowering people to help themselves," said Shigehisa Kobayashi of Tokyo-based Secom Company, which develops the robots.[1030]

Teacher

In addition to assisting with physical tasks, scientists are developing machines to interact with humans. Highly programmed robots engage people and teach them simple skills, including household tasks and vocabulary. They also teach children to play through elementary imitation and taking turns. The most advanced models are fully autonomous, guided by artificial intelligence software. While still "works in progress," they should begin to learn as they teach, being most effective in subjects like foreign language or in repetitive therapies used to treat developmental problems.

For instance, a robot designed for affective learning can help an autistic child learn to play through mimicking physical movements and taking turns. The machine is able to elicit gaze- following, an essential first step of social exchange. This is how learning begins.

A robot named RUBI has taught Finnish to preschool children in a San Diego classroom. Researchers found that the robot enables preschoolers to score significantly better on tests, compared with less interactive learning, as from tapes. Another robot taught grade-school students how to set a table in one 20-minute session, improving their accuracy by about 25 percent.[1031]

Worker

Security robots

Employing communication technologies similar to Skype, and robotic technologies like those in robots used to explore Mars, a robot from Anybots allows you to work remotely while sending an avatar to the office in your place. It has cameras to see, microphones and a speaker to communicate, and it can roll where you direct it.

While Anybots' CEO, Trevor Blackwell, vacationed in Hawaii, Anybots' fire alarm sounded, bringing the fire department's captain and crew to check out the problem. When they arrived at the office building, Anybot was waiting at the front door as if to greet them. Then it followed them as they inspected the building. After they shut off the alarm, it spoke to them in the voice of Blackwell, who was controlling the robot over the Internet.

"It was just like, 'you're kidding!'" the fire captain Vern Chestnut said. "It was definitely different being met by a robot."[1032]

BP oilrig explosion

After a BP oil rig exploded off the coast of Louisiana in 2010, and non-stop oil gushed into the Gulf of Mexico from a ruptured pipeline, officials turned to the quickest and "best option" to stop the leaking oil: remote-controlled robots.

Nine submersible robots, operating 5,000 feet beneath the ocean's surface, carried out various tasks from turning valves to transmitting videos, trying to activate the blowout preventer, a task that requires "the expertise of a rocket scientist and the precision of a surgeon." Although in the end it was necessary to take a longer, slower method to achieve the goal, it is clear that the promise of robots to perform heroic tasks is a hope for future emergencies.[1033]

BIOTECHNOLOGY

In 2007, Stanford University announced its formation of an innovative Bio-X program promoting collaborations between wide-ranging fields of scientists. Carla Shatz, who was chosen to lead the program, said: "This is where the future of biomedical research is going—working at the interface of quantitative science, physics, engineering and biology."[1034]

Her prescience is evident in both the pure and applied research that has taken place since then.

Pure Research

Stem cells

In November 2004 California voters approved a ballot initiative that awarded $3 billion in funding for stem cell research. Although the measure immediately faced legal challenges, the court supported the initiative in a strongly worded ruling.[1035]

By February 2007 the granting institution, California Institute for Regenerative Medicine, had awarded millions of dollars to colleges, universities and other research institutions. Grants and gifts from private sources began rolling in to virtually every major university in California. Many prominent stem cell researchers flocked to California, and 232 grant applications poured in. The agency decided to award $300 million dollars annually for ten years, at which time the stem cell experiment would be ready for a full evaluation.[1036]

A fly in the ointment from the beginning had been political and ethical concerns surrounding the use of embryonic stem cells. So it was welcome news when scientists reported in the fall of 2008 that they had found a promising alternative to embryonic stem cells. They had been able to coax adult cells to regress into an embryonic state, opening up a much wider path for stem-cell research.

By July 2010 federal regulators had finally given the green light to a biotech firm[1037] to proceed with the world's first human test of a treatment made from embryonic stem cells, and a few months later the test was underway. Scientists designed the stem-cell treatment to be injected into patients with spinal injuries to restore their motor function.[1038]

"The treatment is to help patients regrow a spinal insulating material called myelin, that often gets stripped away during injuries, disrupting the body's ability to transmit sensory signals and resulting in paralysis. [1039]"[1040]

DNA/Genome

Human genome

Craig Ventner is a gene pioneer. He was the first person to sequence the genome of a living organism and the first to publish the genome of a specific human being—himself.

While it took thirteen years and cost about 1 billion to complete that first sequence of the human genome in 2000, bioengineers are raced to sequence an entire human genome, that is, three billion base pairs, in less than 30 minutes for a $1,000 reward. Today it costs about $3,000 to $5,000 and takes just one to two days to complete.

Predictions say that this will transform medicine similarly to PC's becoming a game-changer to the world of main-frame computing, and that over time, sequencing will move into diagnostic settings like community hospitals.

Synthetic genome

Another series of experiments led to a milestone in 2010. For years scientists had moved single genes and large chunks of DNA from one species to another, but just a few years ago researchers transplanted an entire natural genome, turning a goat germ into a cattle germ. Next, they built from scratch another smaller genome, using DNA fragments made from laboratory chemicals. This culminated in May 2010 when scientists announced they had produced the world's first synthetic cell, a living cell powered by human-made DNA.

The announcement of this milestone brought an immediate response from the White House. President Obama directed his Presidential Commission for the Study of Bioethical Issues to make a study of this achievement as its first order of business. He wanted the Commission to make recommendations about any actions the federal government should take to ensure that America reaps the benefits and minimizes the risks involved.[1041]

Although the ability to synthesize life could lead to developing a sustainable energy supply of biofuels, it could also lead to constructing bioweapons, such as smallpox. However, "it shouldn't be discarded because of the pitfalls," said David C. Magnus, director of Stanford University's Center for Biomedical Ethics. "We just need to make sure we stay on top of the pitfalls."[1042] [1043]

Two companies

Two startups in DNA research have developed contrasting but complementary technologies, one focused specifically on human DNA, and the other including concern with health care, agriculture, food products and the development of biofuels.

Complete Genomics sees itself as an "assembly line" geared for sequencing genomes in large volume. By building up a database of the DNA architecture, they are taking the first step toward enabling researchers to decode the relationship of DNA to potential illnesses.[1044]

Pacific Biosciences (PacBio) has developed a far-reaching technology called SMRT Biology, which refers to its "single molecule, real-time" analysis platform. SMRT functions as a microscope that combines chemistry, nanotechnology, robotics, lasers and optics to explore the processes of DNA, RNA and protein synthesis. Ultimately it promises to enrich understanding of all forms of life and influence the diagnosis and treatment of disease, as well as improve the production of food and biofuels.

SMRT is part of an expanding market for DNA sequencing, driven by both research and commercial users, which was expected to grow from $1.2 billion in 2009 to more than $3.6 billion in 2014.[1045] [1046]

One feat of PacBio's machines is enabling scientists to observe the molecular processes of DNA replication when cells divide. This carries significant implications for *in vitro* fertilization. Experiments have led to greater certainty of viable cells, making it possible to forego the need for more than one implanted egg for a successful pregnancy.

> **"PacBio executives say their technology
> 'eaves-drops' on the natural creation of DNA
> when cells split."**
> —*Scott Duke Harris,* ***San Jose Mercury News***

Applied Research

Proof of the pudding of biotechnology comes, of course, at the level of applied research. What do scientists have to show for the millions of dollars of research money and years of research time that have been invested in biotechnology?

Below are listed some of the most immediate and practical applications. Long-range possibilities, with even greater consequences in the long run, are often not obvious and emerge only with time.

Engineered fuel

An American biotech firm, Amyris, has linked up with a large Brazilian ethanol maker to develop clean fuel from Brazil's plentiful sugarcane. Using Amyris' synthetic biology technology, they are creating renewable diesel for cars, trucks, jets and generators.[1047]

Engineered food

People for the Ethical Treatment of Animals were so captured by the idea of fake meat that they offered a million dollars to the first person to develop "commercially viable quantities of in vitro meat at competitive prices by 2012." According to New Harvest, a non-profit organization founded to promote the field, these meat substitutes "can be safer, more nutritious, less polluting and more humane than conventional meat."[1048]

The cultured meat market was valued at $1.64 million in 2021, and is estimated to reach $2788.1 million by 2030

In 2018 the U.S. Food and Drug Administration (FDA) granted permission for genetically-modified salmon to be sold in the United States. This is the first genetically-engineered animal for human consumption. Next in line for possible approval is the enviropig.[1049]

Crime

Since 2006, DNA databases have contained enough information to be useful in identifying criminals whose DNA has not been cataloged through their kinship to people already listed. (A similar method was used to identify victims of the World Trade Center attacks.) Although the databases record DNA at only 13 sites along a person's genome, a minute fraction of the genomic information, it is sufficient to indicate the degree of kinship between two donors. Because of this, genetic surveillance is shifting from the individual to the family.[1050]

Immigrant testing

Federal officials have used genetic testing in a pilot program to verify the biological bonds between new citizens and overseas relatives they hoped to bring to the United States. This has led to joyful reunions, as well as to the unearthing of buried secrets that reveal heartbreaking news. Frequently DNA testing divulges an unfaithful wife or one who was raped—but too ashamed to tell her husband.[1051]

Discovering that up to 87 percent of familial claims are fraudulent— mostly applicants in Africa[1052]— the pilot program was halted in 2008. However, the Obama administration considered reopening the program with revised procedures.[1053]

Telemedicine

Several companies, including Cisco Systems, Hewlett-Packard, Polycom and Teleris, sell videoconferencing systems designed specifically for health care.

Cisco, best situated to drive the technology forward, uses their system for an internist in San Jose to see a patient at Cisco's North Carolina campus. Along with its Health Presence video system, a nurse in North Carolina uses electronic devices to send data, including heart rate and temperature, to the internist in real time.

"Telemedicine" programs are especially useful in cities and remote areas of the globe, as well as filling the growing shortfall of medical students choosing to become primary care physicians.

However, a study conducted in 2021 showed that, when given a choice, "the vast majority of patients prefer in-person care; and the total addressable market for Telehealth is less than 1% of the health economy.

Climate change

Google is playing a leading role in climate change assessments. First, it launched a new feature on its Google Earth Web site called Cal-Adapt. Google partnered with the state of California on this project to show Californians how warming temperatures, rising sea levels, precipitation shifts and more frequent, intense wildfires impact their environment. [1054]

Soon afterwards, Google announced it had partnered with NASA in launching a new program called Earth Engine, designed to monitor carbon dioxide pollution and levels of forest destruction that contribute to global warming. Earth Engine is essentially a massive storehouse for satellite and other data that forest countries can access for free, as of late 2010. Since deforestation is the biggest climate change culprit in much of the developing world, Google's system could help everyone keep track of which forests are saved. Moreover, it could solve one of the largest questions looming over any climate change accord that may develop among nations: How will the world know if nations are living up to their pledges? NASA and Google's combined efforts provide an answer: outer space and cyberspace.[1055]

Evolution

Perhaps the most basic of new findings in biotechnology is also the most elusive in terms of practical application. With more sophisticated genetic testing, researchers are now able to probe the molecular differences between species, uncovering surprises in the process. For three centuries, scientists have classified species by how they look. Now scientists have discovered that common traits sometimes defy such analysis.

For example, in 2010 two identical-looking elephants, formerly considered of a singular species of African elephant, were found to be actually two cryptic species[1056]: the African bush elephant and the African forest elephant. Since estimates indicate that 10-30 percent of animal species are cryptic, studying them can help scientists understand the evolutionary pressures they face. This knowledge is valuable because cryptic species must compete for common territory. [1057]

For Reflection:

1. ....

   ....

   ....

2. ....

   ....

   ....

3. ....

   ....

   ....

CHAPTER 19

ELECTRONICS TECHNOLOGY

COMPUTER TECHNOLOGY: HISTORY

Computer technology that touches the life of the average person came into being in the late 1970's when Apple introduced a personal computer. At the time only huge mainframe computers existed. In fact, something the size of Apple's computer was unthinkable in most people's minds. Since that time, Apple has continued to forge ahead in creating innovative designs, with other companies following their lead and reaping benefits from Apple's innovations.

It was not until 1981 that IBM started making PC's and overtook Apple's sales. A bit later Hewlett Packard joined in, and by 2010 it had become the leading PC maker.

In 1984 Apple introduced the Macintosh, which had immediate public appeal and spurred Microsoft to develop its own "Windows"[1058].[1059] By 1990 its first popular version, Windows 3.0, grabbed public attention and enabled Microsoft to continue dominating the PC market after that time.

Microsoft, along with the Blackberry, has also led the smartphone market, continuing to outsell Apple's iPhones. Meanwhile Apple has continually swamped the tablet market, having sold three million iPads within three months of their release.[1060]

MICROPROCESSOR CHIPS

By 2010, the chip industry as a whole was enjoying a record-setting boom, indicating its health, even as the rest of the economy struggled to rebound from the Great Recession. This is partly because microprocessor chips[1061] are the "brain" of most electronic devices, such as computers, cell phones and components of modern automobiles. Global chip sales in 2010 were the biggest in the industry's history, topping $300 billion, 28 percent more than in 2009.[1062]

COMPUTERS AND THE HUMAN BRAIN

Chess Champion Outwitted

In 1997 we began to see the power of a computer's "brain" when Deep Blue, an IBM computer programmed to play chess, beat the world chess champion. Such an outcome seemed so impossible in those days that Garry Kasparov, the champion-but-loser, implied that the computer had received human coaching during the match. Yet computers kept on winning chess matches. The era of human dominance was over.[1063]

Cosmic Game

William Saletan of *Slate* magazine reflected on the comparative intelligence as a cosmic game:

"When the cosmic game between humans and computers is complete, here's how the sequence of moves will read. In the opening, we evolved through engagement with nature. In the middle game, we projected our intelligence onto computers and co-evolved through engagement with them. In the endgame, we merged computers with our minds and bodies, bringing that projected intelligence back into ourselves. The distinction between human and artificial intelligence will turn out to have been artificial."[1064]

Singularity

While Saletan envisions a cosmic endgame, others speak of humanity's relationship to computers in terms of a "singularity[1065]," a point where machines become smarter than their makers.

In 2007 hundreds of Silicon Valley technologists and scientists came together at "The Singularity Summit: AI and the Future of Humanity." Together they imagined a future of self- programming computers and brain implants that would allow humans to think at speeds nearing today's microprocessors. Future technological developments in artificial intelligence (AI) would explode traditional assumptions about the limitations of the human mind. In fact, Ray Kurzweil[1066], author of *The Singularity is Near*, said that smarter-than-human intelligence is the future's only logical outcome. He even went so far as to set a date for it: 2029.

Kurzweil is not alone in his thinking. The number of transistors on a chip double about every two years, while the entire evolution of modern humans from primates has resulted in only a threefold increase in brain capacity. Given the rapid advances in biotechnology and information technology, there is no scientific reason why human thinking could not be pushed to speeds up to a million times faster.

Taking in the ramifications of such a development, researchers at the conference warned that now is the time to develop ethical guidelines. Concerns ranged from amending the Geneva Convention with standards for the use of robots in the conduct of war, to figuring out how to keep the future's super-intelligent machines from deciding to arm themselves, to a possible self- improving, but amoral, artificial intelligence that turns hostile.

Cognitive Computing

The federal government has shown considerable interest in these new possibilities and has funded studies of so-called "cognitive computing." As part of the government's effort, IBM and Lawrence Berkeley National

Laboratory have joined together to perform a computer simulation that matches the scale and complexity of a cat's brain, surpassing earlier studies that simulated the much simpler brain structure of a creature the size of a mouse. IBM also joined with Stanford University to develop an algorithm for mapping the human brain at new levels of detail. These two projects may lead to a computer that mimics a human brain.

Currently computers are designed on a model that differentiates between processing and storing data. The human brain, however, can integrate and react to a constant stream of sensory information. IBM project manager Dharmendra Modha sees the need for a new kind of intelligence:

"As our digital and physical worlds collide, there is a tsunami of information. There is a need for a new kind of intelligence that can sort through, prioritize and extract the most important information, much like how the brain deals with sight, sounds, tastes, touch and smell."[1067]

Though some critics mock so-called "singularists" for doomsday-type predictions, advocates argue it would be irresponsible to ignore the possibility of dire outcomes.[1068]

Recent Advances

Thoughts and prosthetics

Already we are seeing initial signs of a movement toward what prognosticators have been predicting, but with a happier outcome. Patients in research tests can now control prosthetic arms using only their thoughts. By rerouting nerves from an amputated arm to the chest muscles, arms move almost as fast and accurately as healthy arms. These motions operate electrically, as contrasted with existing prosthetic arms, which are biomechanical. There are drawbacks to the new technique, however. Its costs are high, and it requires extensive surgery and recuperation. [1069]

Deciphering brain patterns

The quest to enable people to operate electronic devices solely with their thought is ubiquitous. Intel is working with scientists at Carnegie Mellon University to decipher brain patterns. "By analyzing the brain's electrical activity and blood flow when people ponder certain words and actions, scientists have identified patterns that computers can be programmed to read.[1070]"

Practical applications

This has led to numerous applications. Paralytics have been fitted with brain-reading gadgets that let them change TV stations, turn on lights and write on a computer merely by thinking about doing those activities. There's even a game called "Force Trainer" in which players move real objects by wearing a headset that reads their brainwaves. Researchers hope eventually to produce a chip-controlled brain device to help boost the memories of Alzheimer patients.

Thought helmet

In 2008 the U.S. Army awarded $4 million to three universities to study how to harness brain waves to send nonverbal messages on the battlefield. Their idea is to develop a "thought helmet," which would record the brain's electrical impulses for silent communication. As improbable as it sounds, synthetic telepathy, as the technology is called, is getting closer to battlefield reality.

Microchip implants

Some experts believe that placing sensors inside the skull will produce faster and clearer readings of thoughts. Dr, Jerry Shih[1071] has shown that this method can enable people to write letters on a computer by thinking. Someday brains may be implanted with microchips similar to those made for personal computers.

Downside

As usual, there is a downside to developing such technology. It could expose people's brains to malicious hackers, who might cause a fatal heart rhythm by compromising an implanted cardiac defibrillator. Some ethicists have raised concerns about brain-wave readings being admitted into court trials as evidence of a person's truthfulness. This, of course, "raises all kinds of issue around privacy," said Anita Silvers, chair of the philosophy department at San Francisco State University. While recognizing the usefulness of controlling machines with one's mind, she reminded us "every piece of technology can be used for good or for evil."[1072]

> **"If we could access the global information network simply by using the power of our thoughts, it would open up incredible new opportunities for computing technology."**
> —*Dean Pomerleau, Intel researcher*

OTHER APPLICATIONS OF COMPUTER TECHNOLOGY

A significant feature of technological advancement is its growing complexity. Today new electronic devices have multiple functions, making them more and more complex. Cellphones play videos, cars are Internet-connected and remote controls operate not only the television, but also a DVD player and TiVo digital video recorder[1073].

And that was 2007! Much water flows over the dam in the course of just a few months in the computer world.

Video Games

Early in this century, software sales for video games were high but became mired in slow growth for the next several years.

Then new hardware hit the market. In November 2005 Microsoft released its Xbox360, and a year later Sony produced three winners: PlayStation3, Nintendo and the Wii. These releases of new hardware were largely responsible for 2006 being a strong year for the game industry.

Yet 2007 was even stronger. Despite the economic woes, consumers splurged on video games, sending sales across the board—hardware, software and accessories—up 43 percent from the previous year to a record high of almost $18 billion.[1074]

Nintendo's Wii proved to be the biggest winner, topping the charts in video game sales. In May 2008 alone, five of the top 10 games sold were for the Wii.[1075]

By the end of the year, sales had again broken previous records in the video game industry. This occurred despite consumer spending taking an overall downturn, while the stock market plummeted and thousands of people lost their jobs. Robert Thompson, a professor of popular culture at Syracuse University offered an explanation: "The whole gaming industry is not only recession-proof, it can thrive in times of recession" in the same way that Hollywood thrived during the Great Depression, offering Americans a cheap, communal escape from the gloomy realities of the day.[1076]

Uses at Athletic Events

The 2009 season of the San Francisco Giants baseball team saw signs of new technology forming a complex web at AT&T Park. The park became the first professional sports venue to provide Wi-Fi[1077] to fans, and for a while was the only baseball stadium that offered instant video replays via smartphones. Instantly updated player statistics accompanied the clicking of smartphones, texting to friends in other parts of the stadium and sending photo tweets to friends at home.[1078]

Scoring with smartphones

Yankee group analyst Vince Vittore commented on the ubiquitous use of smartphones at the games: "When I was growing up, I remember scoring games with a pencil and a program. This is the digital version of that."[1079]

Other features

A $5 million video system analyzes every movement on the field, giving the Giants a wealth of new statistical information.[1080] The Wi-Fi system enables closed captioning of PA announcements for the hearing-impaired, and a "food finder" app provides information on nearby food booths.[1081]

Modern Conveniences

The 2010 World Expo in Shanghai displayed modern conveniences most of us never dreamed of. Among them were: noting groceries you wish to buy on a handheld device and picking them up as you leave the store; a toilet that analyzes urine via a digital screen; a refrigerator that orders your groceries; a house that builds itself; a single global currency; a "seastead" (a homestead on the ocean); and a city orbiting in outer space.[1082]

Automated Services

Less glitzy, but practical, are software and automated systems that lower the cost of operating data centers by tracking payroll and inventory, processing sales and providing customer service.

Although such services may not replace offshoring jobs, standardized platforms for such services are the wave of the future. "We think the next five to 10 years is all going to be about who can best use technology to automate the delivery of services.[1083]"[1084]

Uses in Courtrooms

Courtrooms are also incorporating advanced technology into their operations. Innovations include a document camera that can display pictures and evidence to flat-screen TV's around the room; an annotation panel that allows attorneys or witnesses to make marks on exhibits with the touch of a finger; flat screen TVs that offer everyone in the room a clear view of witnesses' expressions; a WiFi connection that enables attorneys to do research, check e-mails, and use their phones without having to step outside; and a closed-circuit TV in an adjacent courtroom where overflow crowds can watch trials.[1085]

BROADBAND

With the advent of the Internet and broadband, the tele-communications industry moved into the realm of information services, despite the Federal Communications Commission's (FCC) struggle to cling to the old name. Broadband high-speed Internet connectivity has been called the most transformational technological advance since the printing press, and it is certainly the most important industry in the world today.

Broadband is still in its growing stage, even here in the United States. Its importance for connectivity is comparable to the linkage in transportation in the 20th century when a web of railroads, highways, roads and bridges connected people across the United States. That, of course, was a tangible connection; broadband is intangible.

As more people continue to shift to the Internet for news and other information, the computer industry's dependence on broadband increases dramatically. In 2007 YouTube consumed as much bandwidth as the entire Internet consumed in 2000. People downloaded 100 million files daily, a 1,000 percent increase over the course of just one year. This mushrooming of data is pushing the Internet to its limits. With its thousands of networks stitched together, maintenance must continually innovate and upgrade the network to meet the phenomenal growth—or "exaflood"—in data to avoid a traffic jam.[1086]

> **"It took two centuries to fill the shelves of the Library of Congress with more than 57 million manuscripts, 29 million books and periodicals, 12 million photographs, and more. Now, the world generates an equivalent amount of digital information nearly 100 times each day."**
> —*Bruce Mehlman and Larry Irving, in an article written for*
> ***The Washington Post***

As for broadband users, in mid-2009 the nationwide average was 63 percent, up from 55 percent the prior year. This increased demand, even through the recession, suggests the significance of broadband for the general public.

Yet there is a growing gap in quality of information, access to it and the ability to participate in the digital world. Some call this a crisis that is threatening our democracy. "Every advance in communications technology expands the possibilities for American democracy, but every information system also creates potential winners and losers.[1087]" Though more information is available, there is a decrease of it on a geographic basis, including a dwindling amount of high- quality information for local communities.[1088]

However, the elderly, the poor and rural residents, who have lagged behind in the broadband surge, have started to gain on those who got a head start. Help has come largely from the U.S. government, which designated $7.2 billion in stimulus money for expanding the availability of broadband.[1089]

Applications for the money varied greatly from place to place: an Indian tribe in Idaho wanted to connect homes on the reservation; a handful of poor Detroit neighborhoods had been denied access by telecom providers; people in Appalachia were having to make a long distance phone call to get online; and the city of Philadelphia wanted to connect city services and organizations. [1090]

MOBILE COMPUTING

In November 2006 a family driving through Oregon in inclement weather became lost and stranded for a week in a deep canyon area. They traveled with three mobile phones and two laptops but no Global Positioning System (GPS) devices. Yet when they needed them most, none of them worked.

A public health administrator[1091] in an adjacent county commented that she travels with a pager, two cell phones (different carriers), a Pocket PC, a laptop with wireless access, a satellite telephone, a CB radio and OnStar, but sometimes none of them work. "Dumb things like weather and terrain beat out satellites in space.[1092]"[1093]

Technological devices have their limits—and their promises.

Invasion of the TV Market

For several years the Consumer Electronics Show in Las Vegas has been center stage for technology events, but only in 2007 did the computer industry show up. They needed to defend themselves in the battle consumer electronics companies were waging against them for invading the TV market. Now, thanks to their common bonding in the Internet, everyone from cell phone makers to TV companies are searching for ways to enable consumers to watch YouTube videos, or movies or TV shows on any gadget.[1094]

Smartphones and Applications (APPS)

The market is bursting with innovative electronic devices, beginning with Apple's iPhones, which paved the way for a smorgasbord of choices in the smartphone[1095] industry. Now other companies have developed their own smartphones and keep upgrading them with new applications (apps). These apps include Android's virtual on-screen keyboard, video recording and support for stereo Bluetooth headsets, Microsoft's Windows Mobile 7, and AT&T's doubling the potential speed for surfing the Web.[1096]

A newer generation of smartphones has added "location-based services" (LBS) to pinpoint a user's location. This innovation could significantly change the way we live on this planet, integrating the virtual into our everyday lives. When it comes to virtual reality and reality, it is no longer either/or, but both/and. The line between them has become blurred. We live in a real world that is wrapped in virtual data.

For instance, an app called "Where" finds the nearest movie theater, restaurant or events around you. Another app tells you the name of mountains you can see from where you are. SkyMap identifies stars and constellations you see overhead, and "Sit and Squat" locates the nearest public bathroom.[1097]

More parents are using cellphone apps to entertain and "watch" their children. They download a rattle to soothe a fussy baby, provide trivia questions for their young children while waiting for a dental appointment, play the "Who Wants to Be a Millionaire?" game with their older kids and entertain them by flipping through pictures of the kids and their dog. They even leave a cellphone by their sleeping baby when they are out of range for their regular baby monitor to alert them if the baby makes a noise.[1098]

End of an Era

Innovative devices and uses indicate the end of the PC era and the beginning of a new one, but it may have been Microsoft that cinched it. In 2010 they launched Windows Phone Series 7, which was not just a miniature version of their Windows operating system for smartphones. Loss of market share had forced them to scrap the Windows-based version and risk thinking mobile first. The result was their building a new operating system from scratch, a first for smartphones. Put simply by Joe Belfiore, a Microsoft VP: "The phone is not a PC."

Clearly a new era had arrived. We now stand squarely in the age of mobile computing.[1099]

SENSOR TECHNOLOGY

Cameras

Cameras, which are now widely found on cellphones, merit a closer look, as they move beyond personal usefulness for greater social benefits. Tessera foresees its miniature camera technology being used to prevent underage teenagers from buying vending-machine cigarettes[1100], to warn motorists when they are too sleepy to drive[1101], and to enable toys to respond appropriately when a child smiles or frowns.[1102]

3-D Takes Off

In 2010 3-D capabilities were introduced to monitors and games as well as to other products. Kick-off to the wider public came with the movie "Avatar," when theaters provided special viewing glasses for patrons to see stereoscopic images.[1103]

Image Sensors

This ushered in a new generation of image sensors[1104] in cameras, enabling touch-free controls for all sorts of gadgets. The sensors are 3-D, recording not only the image, but also its distance from the camera.

This technology allows people to play video games by moving their hands or kicking their feet. It could replace remote controls for televisions with the waving of hands by TV viewers. In smartphones, you could move from touch-screen interfaces to no-touch ones by merely replacing the camera.

A new development may cause the popularity of sensor technology to surge. A startup, Canesta, has developed a sensor that is built on just one microchip, making mass production of them relatively low cost. This will most likely encourage a wide range of uses for miniature cameras beyond counting prescription pills, which is already in effect. They could be used as weight detectors to determine if a child is in a car seat, whether an airbag should deploy, and even detect a thief in the car or a baby accidentally left behind.

These are not futuristic dreams. Such products were expected to be available before 2014 Under Hopes, Realities, and Possibilities.[1105]

CONSUMER ELECTRONICS INTERNATIONALLY

Where does that leave the United States internationally in terms of consumer electronics? According to an Accenture global survey, Americans spend less money on consumer electronics and use fewer mobile phone apps than other countries in their study.[1106] Though the U.S. ranked second to Singapore in the percentage who own personal computers[1107] and mobile phones[1108], Americans are not leaders in any other category surveyed. Even in the use of social networking sites, several countries posted similar growth to the U.S.[1109]

ELECTRONIC EXPOSURE: PROS AND CONS

Survey Results

People often worry that technology isolates and pulls people apart, but a survey in 2008[1110] found "that couples use their phones to connect and coordinate their lives, especially if they have children at home."[1111]

At the same time, families with multiple communication devices were "somewhat less likely to eat dinner with other household members and somewhat less likely to report high levels of satisfaction." However, 25 percent of respondents in the survey said they felt "that their family today is closer than their family when they were growing up thanks to the use of the Internet and cell phones." [1112]

Another finding of the survey showed the Internet has decreased the amount of time people spend watching TV, though not on social time spent with friends, family or attending social events. In fact, we may find that electronic devices are actually helping today's children, teens and young adults to "maintain longer and stronger relationships with their friends than was the case with previous generations.[1113]"[1114]

Social Interaction

When teens check out their Facebook page, it is a type of media consumption, but it is really social interaction. They are producing media in the form of posts, photos and videos, which is unlike the passive media consumption of previous generations. Teens of past generations would spend time in malls, cafes, and talking on landlines, while today's teens hang out online.[1115]

Video Games

Researchers have found that video games can be powerful learning tools, helping younger children develop planning and problem-solving skills and giving adolescents practice in staying in the here and now. Another finding showed that laparoscopic surgeons who played video games were 27 percent faster at advanced surgical procedures and made 37 percent fewer errors than those who didn't play.[1116]

Kaiser Study

A report from a Kaiser Family Foundation study[1117] of the use of media by children and teens showed that they are involved with media almost every minute they are awake and not in school. Between 2004 and 2009 their "entertainment media" use rose dramatically, with most youths saying they have no rules regarding media use at home. As a result, they average 7 hours, 38 minutes a day using entertainment media. Many of them are also multi-tasking, which sends their total time up to 11 hours a day.

A few particular findings of the study are:

- Heavy media users get lower grades.
- Black and Hispanic youth spend 4 ½ more hours daily with media than white youth and watch TV nearly six hours every day.
- TV watching has declined since 2004, but TV consumption online and on cell phones has gone up.
- Engagement with social networking takes up about one hour daily.
- Over 66 percent of 8- to 18-year-olds have cell phones and 76 percent have iPods and other media players.
- Elementary age children use cell phones 33 minutes daily, while teens text 118 messages a day.[1118]

Overuse of Digital Media

Two studies conducted in 2010 showed the harmful effects of the overuse of digital media.

Australian study

An Australian study[1119] quantified the effect of TV viewing on risk of death. It found a strong correlation between the number of hours spent watching TV and death from cardiovascular disease, even among people who had a healthy weight and exercised. This suggests that being sedentary may have general deleterious effects. "The message here is that in addition to promoting regular exercise, we also need to promote avoiding long periods of sitting, such as spending long hours in front of the computer screen.[1120]"[1121]

"People who watched TV more than four hours a day showed an 80 percent greater risk of death from cardiovascular disease."
—*Jeannine Stein,* **Los Angeles Times**

University of California – San Francisco (UCSF) Study

A study at UCSF showed that people who give nonstop digital input to their brains forfeit beneficial downtime. For instance, it is not unusual today for a person working out at a gym to be listening to an audiobook on an iPhone while watching TV as she exercises. "Downtime lets the brain go over experiences it's had, solidify them and turn them into permanent long-term memories.[1122]"[1123]

PRIVACY ISSUES

Cultural Rules

Technology is advancing so fast that our cultural rules for using it cannot keep up. Just as families argue about when it is appropriate to watch television at home or read a newspaper at the breakfast table, people complain about others' use of electronic gadgets.[1124] Ninety percent of a group of people surveyed[1125] was unhappy with the bad etiquette of other users of electronic gadgets, while failing to admit their own lapses. The worst offense, according to respondents, was typing on a cellphone or some other mobile device while driving. Over half of those surveyed complained about people talking about private matters on a device in public, but only 28 percent admitted engaging in the same behavior.[1126]

Trend Toward Openness

These complaints are part of a much larger issue around privacy in general. Our notion of privacy has changed dramatically over time. Just before the turn of the century, caller ID service and newspaper Web sites asking readers to register their e-mail address raised hackles over privacy.

Since then the growing popularity of Facebook has magnified the concern, arousing ambivalent feelings by users of social websites. Whatever users feel, the trend is toward more sharing of personal information.

Satellite imaging

Another aspect of privacy concerns government officials' use of satellite imaging and sophisticated aerial photography. Of course, it is being used in many other ways that most people would applaud: to prevent drowning, to solve Greece's financial crisis, to update property assessment rolls and to hunt crime suspects. At the same time as technology advances, distinguishing between public and private information becomes an increasingly murky area. [1127]

TECHNOLOGY'S EFFECTS ON SOCIAL PROBLEMS

JOBS

An immediate and key problem raised by technological advances is its effect on jobs. Thomas L. Friedman[1128] addressed the issue:

"Technology is destroying older, less skilled jobs that paid a decent wage at a faster pace than ever while spinning off more new skilled jobs that pay a decent wage *but require more education than ever.*

"There is only one way to deal with this challenge: more innovation to stimulate new industries and jobs that can pay workers $40 an hour, coupled with a huge initiative to train more Americans to win these jobs over their global competitors."[1129]

Legal Issues

Issues raised by advances in electronic devices frequently cause legal disputes among companies and create openings for crime.

Patents

One long contested issue is that of patenting business methods, a matter that has become crucial as companies conduct business in more abstract ways. Traditionally, patents have been reserved for inventors of tangible things, but in 2010 the Supreme Court made the final decision on the matter, affirming the legality of business method patents.

Old industries vs. new

A dispute between radio broadcasts and the recording industry turned toward the government's mandating that all new cell phones include a built-in FM radio chip. Manufacturers and wireless providers were alarmed by the prospect that the government could mandate a design for such a ubiquitous consumer device. "This is two old-media industries attacking the new wireless broadband industry," said the head of the Consumers Electronics Association, Gary Shapiro. [1130]

Spread of online con artists

Most of us are familiar with online crime at an individual level in cases of identity theft, scamming by e-mail and defrauding through phony goods or services online. However, much other crime stemming from electronic devices has moved into the public realm.

Uniqueness of crimes

When con artists started moving online in the early 90's, they stole trade secrets, counterfeited software and organized identity theft. A unique problem in solving such crimes is the fact that each crime is different. Officials rarely see the same thing twice.

Effect of cloud computing

Cloud computing may also be contributing to crime, as criminals use overseas factories to make counterfeit software on discs. Though these cases may decline as more software is sold online, cloud computing adds to the complexity of solving crimes by creating more openings for crooks to steal intellectual property. Many cases involve organized rings of hackers based in Eastern Europe or Asia.[1131]

TECHNOLOGY and GOVERNMENT

National Data Exchange
Perhaps the most pervasive technology incorporated by the federal government is housed in the National Data Exchange, a domestic intelligence system that connects thousands of law enforcement agencies. Google beat out rivals for providing the necessary cloud-computing services for government agencies all across the nation, handling almost everything except classified data.[1132]

Digitation
Digitation is useful in handling crimes as well as in rooting out terror plots. It helps pinpoint suspects by searching scraps of information and mapping links among people, places and events. "It's going from the horse-and-buggy days to the space age, that's what it's like.[1133]"[1134]

Cyber Command

Chief technology officer (CTO)
In 2009 President Obama established the federal position of chief technology officer to head up overall technology in the United States. Technologists regarded this shift in leadership on technology issues to the White House as an important symbol that would have an effect on policy-making.[1135]

Cyber security
Within days of the President's action, the White House initiated a study of the nation's cyber security, looking at protection of everything

from the nation's electrical grid and stock markets to tax data, airline flight systems and nuclear launch codes. At the time, millions of dollars were being spent each year responding to, and repairing damage from, cyber-attacks on the United States.[1136]

Pentagon cyber-command

A year later, the Pentagon announced formation of a new cyber-command that was charged with protection of its computer networks, and is capable of launching attacks against enemy computer networks.[1137]

Daily attacks on the U.S. cyber system have raised a basic question about the meaning of "cyberwar" in today's world: When a cyber-attack on the United States occurs, at what point does this mean war?

Security breaches

The Pentagon's networks and computing devices are being probed thousands of times daily, but the most significant breach took place in 2008 when a flash drive was inserted into a U.S. military laptop at a post in the Middle East. This was classified information until 2010, when Deputy Defense Secretary William Lynn declassified it to raise congressional and public concern about the threats facing U.S. computer systems. Lynn wrote in an article for *Foreign Affairs*:

> "It was a network administrator's worst fear: a rogue program operating silently, poised to deliver operational plans into the hands of an unknown adversary."[1138]

Wikileaks

Not all security breaches come from enemies of the United States. Both the Pentagon and CIA have declared Wikileaks, an amorphous network run by volunteers in more than a dozen countries, a security threat. Its small non-profit website airs classified documents to fight what it considers excessive secrecy.

"We believe that the way to justice is transparency, and we are clear that the end goal is to expose injustices in the world and try to rectify them.[1139]"[1140]

HOPES, REALITIES AND POSSIBILITIES

Tech Industry Defied Recession

Along with problems around technology, hopeful signs in the industry suggest that the horizon is brighter than it may seem. Even in 2008, when the economy was slumping badly and tech companies like Google, IBM and Microsoft were laying off employees, labor statistics[1141] showed that the tech industry as a whole added 77,000 new jobs, while the private sector as a whole lost about 800,000 jobs. Gains in the software industry alone more than made up for job losses in manufacturing and communications. [1142]

Improved Chip Design

This hopeful sign derives primarily from a major shift in chip design. For decades, semiconductor manufacturers kept shrinking the size of their chips and crammed them full of more and more transistors[1143]. Now, more than a billion transistors crowd into some microprocessors no bigger than a fingernail[1144]. This new technology is being used for everything from weather forecasting to processing medical images.

Virtual Models

Using the 3-D camera technique, a computer already can create a virtual model of a person's body, which can try on clothes. A similar model could simulate effects of treating tumors "using chemotherapy, radiation, surgery, a combination of approaches or no intervention at all. [1145]"[1146]

> **"Consumers will be able to fix their automobiles
> while the car gives step-by-step advice,
> attack their ailments by making computer models of
> various treatments to find the best one, and duck
> into virtual fitting rooms to try on a store's
> clothes without leaving home."**
> —*Steve Johnson,* ***San Jose Mercury News***

Spintronics

In the wings may be an even greater breakthrough in chip design. Physicists at Stanford University found that electrons in bismuth telluride (a chemical compound) can travel without resistance, losing no energy. This may provide a way to carry more information than silicon- based chips can handle. Instead of optical computing or nanochemistry, the new discovery uses electronic spin to carry information, which has spawned a new field called "Spintronics." This could pave the way for a paradigm shift in microchip development.[1147]

Financial Records for Collective Clout

Red Ink, a Web site developed by a Massachusetts Institute of Technology (MIT) graduate student, Ryan O'Toole, invites the public to share parts of their bank accounts, tax forms and mortgage records to make them smarter consumers with greater economic clout. This "would level the playing field between individuals and banks and businesses who already make use of their access to your financial information.[1148]" People could wield their influence by collectively spending—or not spending—at certain businesses.

Other possibilities being explored through pilot projects include increasing charitable giving through releasing information about income and one's own charitable giving; reducing national gas usage by posting one's gas bill online; and sharing medical and educational data.[1149]

For Reflection:

1. ....

....

....

2. ....

....

....

3. ....

....

....

CHAPTER 20
THE INTERNET

For some years it was a maxim that new communication technologies isolate us from each other. However, a Pew Internet and American Life Project study shows the opposite: that people who use the Web or cell phones have larger and more diverse networks of confidantes than those who do not.

Technology actually encourages more communication with more people. "Like-minded people can connect quickly through e-mail, then build relationships that deepen once they're face to face out in the community," said one entrepreneur, Randy Hlavin. Because Internet use is often associated with engagement in public places like parks and cafes, exposure to a more diverse group of people and points of view is increased. Technology is a social adhesive rather than something driving us apart. [1150]

DEMISE OF BRICK-AND-MORTAR BUSINESSES

Since the turn of the century, traditional brick-and-mortar businesses have gradually been inched out of American society, while the Internet floods our everyday world.

Music stores were one of the first to experience their demise. As Web sites started offering sheet music and recorded music for the downloading, music stores began to close. Bookstores, too, became challenged by Web sites like Amazon, and newspapers began experiencing serious competition from Web sites and blogs.

As a last gasp, "old-time" businesses tried pointing out their value in knowing their customers and what their customers needed and wanted, but Internet retailers one-upped them by saying they had that information, too—plus knowing customers' credit card numbers and e-mail addresses. [1151]

DIGITAL FORM REPLACES PHYSICAL FORM

As more and more music stores closed, MP3s were replacing music CDs, and digitally distributed videos were supplementing, and sometimes supplanting, DVDs. Internet games that previously required consoles were now streaming to consumers over the Internet.[1152] The distribution of content digitally over the Internet, rather than in physical form, had become the wave of the future.

Music

As recently as 2006, music albums were still on the market, though they had declined five percent from the previous year. At the same time, total music sales were up, due to a huge increase in digital downloads. As Brian Garritz, senior correspondent for *Billboard* Magazine, rhetorically asked: "At the end of the day, pop music is a singles-driven business, so why would I want to buy a whole album?"[1153]

Printed Resumes

With the convenience of online communication, more companies moved to online job assessments, leaving printed resumes to go extinct. They began using customized online forms and online tests for applicants to fill out. Applicants say this shift in the application process has created a wedge between the applicant and potential employer, making it more difficult to snag an interview. Yet, if some predictions are correct, it makes no difference. Interviews, too, may be on their way out, as some employers think that computer-based filters do a better job at paring down candidates. [1154]

Real Estate

Many realtors changed their approach to young customers by jacking up their Web sites, hiring younger sales agents and switching 50 percent of their advertising dollars to non-traditional venues. They discovered that 80 percent of all homebuyers start their search on the Web, so development of sophisticated Web sites with statistics, data and information became a necessity. Hoarding market information no longer served the industry. Bob Peltier, president of Edina Realty, said succinctly that information "is free and plentiful."[1155]

Free and plentiful information did not end there. Real estate agents began to create "single- listing" Web sites for their customers, making it possible to include more information than within the restricted space of "multiple-listing" sites. Each single-listing site is devoted to one for-sale home, which includes many pictures, lots of text, virtual tours and possibly documents such as property inspection reports.[1156]

Online Retailing

It took several years to accomplish, but in 2006 the sale of online clothing overtook computer hardware and software, paving the way for online retailing to go mainstream. Some online retailers offered free overnight shipping and free returns, trying to lure customers. With high-speed Internet reaching 50 percent of American households, consumers felt a new level of comfort buying merchandise online.[1157]

Online Advertising

Many parts of the economy began shifting advertising dollars to the Internet. During 2006 U.S. online ad revenue climbed 34 percent, setting a new record for the third consecutive year.[1158] The Internet as a whole accounted for 5.9 percent of all U.S. ad spending.[1159] Online advertising was rapidly establishing a strong foothold in the future.

Phone Booths and Phone Books

Phone booths and phone books began disappearing, as many people could find white pages through their cell phones. By the fall of 2009, decline of traditional land lines and an increase in Internet use led some phone companies to stop automatic delivery of residential white pages.

AT&T had already introduced an "opt-in" program, giving customers a choice about receiving a print copy.[1160]

Post Offices

The number of mailboxes began to shrink, too, as post offices coped with a multibillion-dollar deficit. E-mail and electronic bill-paying were eating into the mail stream, resulting in a decline of mail volume and revenues. A crowning blow was the recession, which added a sharp pullback in advertising mail.

To meet this reality, the United States Postal Service (USPS) has closed post offices and shrunk its postal operations. Every year hundreds of postal operations close down. The fall of 2009 may have been the biggest consolidation in USPS history, when 3,200 (mostly metropolitan) post offices out of 34,000 were reviewed for possible closure or consolidation. People cry out when their own beloved post office is at stake, yet more Americans prefer having the Postal Service curtail operations than seek a bailout or raise stamp prices.[1161]

MEDIA AND INTERNET CONTENT

Centrality of Content

The exploding number of electronic delivery systems has decreased the importance of any one way of conveying content. The future is in content, not in delivery systems. Servers like Comcast recognized that over time cable TV would matter less, as people watched more video on PCs and cell phones, so they set out to deliver more programming to their subscribers. Time Warner and NBC Universal were already less tied to one format over another and were serving consumers in multiple ways.[1162]

User-Generated Content

Former vice president Al Gore anticipated in 2002 the convergence of conventional media and the Internet. He incorporated Current Media, a cable TV company that relied heavily on viewer- generated video for its news and other productions. The company launched in 2005, inviting viewers to submit videos and vote for favorites that were aired. YouTube now exemplifies this "vanguard journalism," as Gore termed it.[1163]

Other forms of innovation had a messier, less-clear kind of development. Blogging, WiFi and even the Internet itself had to find their own way, as water finds its own way in a stream. Each took a meandering, uncertain path, "charted by no one and navigated by many,[1164]" while giant telecommunications and technology firms were focused on investing in dead-ends like interactive TV.[1165]

> **"The efforts to identify a 'first blog' are comical, and ultimately, futile, because blogging was not invented; it evolved."**
> *—Scott Rosenberg, author*

The Pentagon and Social Media

One of the big users of online postings is the Pentagon. It monitors social-media reactions to high-profile events like the Air Force One flyover of New York City in 2009, as well as tracking YouTube, Twitter and various online blogs. Social media sites are very useful to the military for recruiting and communicating with other federal agencies, but postings are vulnerable to being lost or stolen by the enemy.[1166]

Achieving Success

Making ends meet

In 2008 most media companies believed that offering free content on the Internet was the formula for success. A year later they were contemplating making the consumer pay.

The *Christian Science Monitor* stopped publishing printed editions and moved whole-hog into online-only versions. The *New York Times* and *Los Angeles Times* published both print and online versions. They tried charging for access to some online content, and then dropped the idea because it cost them audience and advertising revenue.[1167] Media companies looked at micro- payments, subscription, membership, licensing—some way, any way to draw payment for their offerings from consumers. "People reading news for free on the Web, that's got to change," said Rupert Murdock. But the question remained: How do you get consumers to pay for something they have grown used to getting free?[1168]

Google's model

In *What Would Google Do?*[1169] Jeff Jarvis[1170] explores the successful model used by Google, lifting up its key tenets.

According to Jarvis, Google's counterintuitive vision includes:

* "The idea that today's economy is based on abundance, not scarcity.
* That companies now reach maximum success by charging not as much but as little as possible, so the number of people served can reach enormous proportions.
* That middlemen who used to maximize profits by building a wall between creators and users of products or services, and charging for access, have lost their foothold.
* That enterprises achieve greater success by yielding considerable control over their products and practices to their customers.
* That 'virtuous circles[1171]' make for today's success stories."[1172]

Paradigm shift

Jarvis said, "The Internet is a three-dimensional space of reciprocal links whose value multiplies with use and time... Seek and ye shall find anything you want in fractions of a second. Each time that happens... another connection is made between a person and information or another person."

Jarvis believed this model was an early stage in a planet-wide paradigm shift that could be as significant as the discovery that the Earth was round, not flat. It was an unstoppable movement that would force even nay-sayers to embrace Google's tenets.[1173]

Importance of speed

With the number of Internet searches through Google increasing to several billion in 2009, the company has had to be concerned about speed.[1174] White space loads instantaneously, so Google developed a simplistic home page. In addition, Google rendered its blue shopping cart in painstaking HTML, which was worth the effort because it loads faster. Through experimentation Google found that customer searches dropped off when they injected a 400-millisecond delay— just the blink of an eye—into its delivery of search results. That small time delay represents several hundred million dollars a year in potential ad revenue.

Google is eager to share its secrets about Internet speed. "We really think that if the Web gets better and the Web gets faster it is good for everyone," said Marissa Mayer, a vice president of search products at Google.[1175]

SOCIAL WEB SITES

It was big news in 2006 when projections said that Americans would average more than 9½ hours a day with media.[1176] Now, they occupy our time closer to 24/7.

Social Web sites have been perhaps the biggest contributors, making it possible to live in our own little world around the clock within American society.

Superfluous Speech

Andy Wood[1177] flew from San Jose to New York, rented a car and drove back 3,000 miles to San Jose uttering only five words—"Andy Wood," "Andy Wood," and "sauce." During the five- day trip he went through airports, motels, restaurants and gas stations, confirming what he already suspected: that speaking with people has become superfluous in most public situations. He calls this "omnitopia," a place and state driven by the sameness of experiences in modern public places and enabled by personal technology.[1178]

MySpace

In early 2009 MySpace, which had peaked in the fall of 2008, found itself struggling to keep up with Facebook. As fast as Facebook was adding users, MySpace was losing them. Although it was drawing 130 million users globally every month, its owner, News Corp., had been slow to innovate, and Facebook had overtaken it as the biggest social network in the world.[1179]

An analyst[1180] at RBC Capital Markets noted a difference between the two social websites: "MySpace is where you go to express yourself, while Facebook[1181] has been a place where you go for two-directional conversation."[1182]

Facebook

Mark Zuckerberg, founder of Facebook, said the idea behind Facebook is that "people want to share and stay connected with their friends and the people around them." In fact, he has "an almost missionary zeal when it comes to getting people to share information.[1183]"

However, Zuckerberg's zeal backfired with a number of Facebook users, who questioned the company's commitment to users' easy control of personal information. When they complained loud enough, Facebook made changes to its privacy policy, switching the default position of maximum exposure to new, simplified privacy settings. Yet Facebook continues to believe that radical transparency makes a society that is more tolerant of people's actions, recognizing that "everybody sometimes does bad or embarrassing things.[1184]"

Whatever one feels about Facebook and privacy, the company has attracted 750 million active users as of September 2011, which has led toward its becoming the world's second-most visited Web site after Google and perhaps "the fastest-growing company of any type in history,"[1185] according to David Kirkpatrick, author of *The Facebook Effect*. He said 20 per cent of the people on the global Internet use Facebook regularly, including 35 percent of the U.S. population. Users of Facebook continue to grow at a rate of five percent per month, and the average user spends almost an hour there each day.[1186]

FACEBOOK BY THE NUMBERS

- **More than 400 million people use Facebook, about 30 percent within the U.S.**
- **Average user has 130 "friends" on Facebook.**
- **About 50 percent of users' log on in any given day.**
- **More than 50 percent of users have customized their privacy settings.**
- **More than 25 billion pieces of content (web links, news stories, blog posts, notes, photo albums, etc.) are shared each month.**
- **More than 70 translations are available on the site.**

—*San Jose Mercury News*, June 27, 2010

Blogging

Blogging had its hey-day in 2005 with those under age 30, but as tweeting and texting developed, younger folks found these shorter forms more to their liking. They switched over, and older adults took their place in the blogging realm. As a result, the overall number of bloggers has remained fairly consistent since 2005, numbering around 30 million people, or one in ten online adults.

Twitter

> **"If you think of Google as the Internet's memory—
> the process that can access every image,
> sound and bit of knowledge that our collective
> online existence has generated and stored—then
> Twitter is its stream of consciousness."**
> **—David Sarno, *Los Angeles Times***

Twitter is a form of social network sharing (in 140 characters or less) of what is on people's minds—right now. It standardizes the word "streaming," which today is used in a larger context. As with stream of consciousness, not all thoughts are useful, but whatever they are, they come from someone you have chosen to "follow": friends, celebrities, academics, etc. In this way it reverses the usual notion of a group. "Instead of creating the group you want, you send it and the group self-assembles.[1187]" By the spring of 2010, Twitter had users worldwide that represented growth of 1,500 percent a year since 2007. More than 60 percent of its 106 million new users came from outside the United States.[1188]

JobShouts

An example of its usefulness in broadcasting messages widely is JobShouts, which posts jobs that are instantly tweeted to all the company's followers. Many of its followers re-tweet the notices to their own mini-audiences. People also have found it especially useful for building up a job-search network in just a couple of hours, creating a whole self-presentation in the Twittersphere. It is easier to form common interest groups on JobShouts than on Facebook or LinkedIn and, unlike Monster.com and Craigslist, it is free. Company managers like Twitter because they can easily target recruitment ads and "follow" potential candidates online.[1189]

Use by the military

Even the military uses Twitter—as well as Facebook and YouTube—tweeting news before making a formal announcement to the media. This gives officers the chance to get out their side of the story, such as they did with news of Afghanistan. They also encouraged troops in Afghanistan to post stories and photos on Web sites that may not have made the news. [1190]

Archive of tweets

An ambitious project preserving Twitter's entire archive of public tweets (an estimated 50 million a day) is underway at the Library of Congress. Many people have scoffed at their project, citing the fact that historians have always preserved the tangible: letters, journals and official documents. Twitter involves just random thoughts, many of them half-baked, people say. And Twitter's scope is only momentary.

View of historians

Historians see it otherwise. Michael Beschloss[1191] retorts: "What historian today wouldn't give his right arm to have the adult Madison's contemporaneous Twitters about the secret debates inside the Constitutional Convention in Philadelphia?"

**"If you believe that God is in the details—
and all biographers do, then Twitter will be a godsend!"**
—*Kitty Kelley, biographer of Oprah Winfrey*

Lives of non-celebrities

Martha Anderson of the Library of Congress would agree with Beschloss. She said: "We're trying to figure out the best way to leave evidence for future generations of scholarship." For centuries, history has been biased toward the powerful: presidents, kings, and starlets. Only recently has public interest turned toward the lives of non-celebrities. Yet it is very difficult to write about ordinary people during ordinary times. Their lives have been considered too humdrum to write about, so their stories have been left unwritten.

Twitter is useful because it is informal, so people drop their guard and are spontaneous. This provides a deeply personal insight into the daily lives of ordinary people on an unprecedented scale. Its value includes not only lives of average individuals but human expression on a massive scale.[1192]

Insights into public sentiment

Taken collectively, tweets are useful for providing insights into public sentiment. They allow companies to see what customers are thinking as they use their products, and to adjust them accordingly. Tweets can also keep outsiders informed in situations like mass protests or natural disasters. Stunning examples are the Arab Spring uprisings and the 2011 earthquake and tsunami in Japan.

Problem solving

One of Twitter's most practical uses is for problem solving. When Twitter is paired with vibration sensors, machines can send alerts. Along with frontline news reports, it can send home security alerts, tell doctors when a patient's blood sugar or heart rate climbs too high or enable physicians to ask for help and share information about procedures. It might even help prevent a nuclear reactor from meltdown.[1193]

Social Epidemics

Social communicators

In best-selling *The Tipping Point: How Little Things Can Make a Big Difference*, Malcolm Gladwell says: "In a social epidemic, Mavens are data banks. They provide the message. Connectors are social glue: they spread it… salesmen. . . persuade us when we are unconvinced of what we are hearing.[1194]"

"Mavens" refers to "information brokers," people who want to help but do not twist your arm. Because their opinions are personal and disinterested, they are more compelling than an expert's. "Connectors" know lots of people and speak to everybody. They probably know more than a maven but are not as persuasive. Gladwell uses "salesmen" in a traditional way.

With social websites going viral and reaching epidemic proportions, perhaps social communicators, as referred to by Gladwell, have re-located as facets of the Web.

Brains and larger social groups

British anthropologist, Robin Dunbar, says brains evolve and get bigger in order to handle the complexities of larger social groups. Humans socialize in the largest groups of all primates because our brains are large enough to handle the complexities required. Dunbar says 150 is the upper limit to the number of individuals with whom we can have a genuinely social relationship. Therefore, if groups are to serve as incubators for contagious messages, they must be fewer than 150 people[1195]. Creating a contagious movement usually requires the creation of many small movements first.

Fundraising and Branding

Social network sites raised big sums for Obama's campaign for the presidency, but most charitable groups have been less successful, partly because of the sheer deluge of information online. However, "it's really a great branding tool," said Sue Citro, digital membership director for The Nature Conservancy. "It's helping spread the word, educating people about our organization and its mission."[1196]

Connecting Seniors

Many older people who have become isolated are using social-networking sites to stay connected. (One of the greatest challenges of aging is not about health, but about deterioration of one's social network.)

Joseph Coughlin, director of the AgeLab at the Massachusetts Institute of Technology (MIT), said: "The new future of old age is about staying… very connected. And technology is going to be a very big part of that, because the new reality is, increasingly, a virtual reality." Researchers who focus on aging are studying the phenomenon to see to what extent social networks can provide some of the benefits of a group of friends. Their studies could help determine whether online social connections can help delay dementia, which some research suggests is hastened by loneliness.[1197]

Teaching

High school

Creative teachers are trying to figure out how to make effective use of social Web sites and cell phones, which are often banned at school, in a classroom setting. Rather than fight the idea of students using the Web to communicate with each other, they encourage it. They believe that the use of interactive technology prepares students for our "collaborative culture," which will likely be with us for a long time. "Whether it's a Wiki[1198] or Twitter, the notion of a participatory culture—upstream and downstream—is not going away," said Chris Lehman, principal of Science Leadership Academy in Philadelphia.[1199]

Another high school principal[1200] in Woodside, California is on the same wavelength. He asked his teachers to build Websites to communicate with students. He also initiated classes on using digital tools to record music, and got funding for iPads to teach Mandarin. As recipient of a $3 million grant for a multimedia center, he is well aware that unchecked use of digital devices can create a culture in which students become addicted to the virtual world and lost in it.[1201]

Adult

From the point of view of religious education, Facebook is enormously important professionally and in teaching. It allows for a "communitarian approach to teaching," said Associate Professor Darleen Pryds at the Franciscan School of Theology[1202]. "With Facebook, we can communicate with an international community of students and scholars." In regard to those who criticize Facebook, she suggests viewing it as "a digital version of shooting the breeze around the company water cooler. Sometimes those water cooler conversations lead to innovations and important insights… the same is true with Facebook."[1203]

When Elizabeth Drescher was assistant professor at the Church Divinity School of the Pacific[1204], she pointed out that in the past, online learning involved automation of face-to- face learning. Today's social media, in contrast, involves high levels of collaborative effort over broad geographical areas.

Our understanding of knowledge has changed, too. It is no longer located in specific persons, but in places like a Facebook page, where people create their unique understandings and learn to understand others. The Internet has so dramatically changed our perception of fixed relationships and bodies of knowledge that Drescher suggests we might call our new situation the "Digital Reformation."[1205]

> **"We can be with people all over the world**
> **at any time, and this is changing consciousness."**
> —*Elizabeth Drescher*

Privacy and Openness

Not long ago people were leery of using their real names on the Web and afraid to buy things online, but times have changed. Startups that capitalize on online openness have become the rage among venture capitalists.

A host of Web sites encourage users to expose themselves in ways that would have been unthinkable as recently as ten years ago. Blippy displays to your friends every transaction you make with your credit card, which you register with their Web site. Foursquare lets you announce your precise location to the world. Skimble, an iPhone app, reveals how many push-ups you are doing and how long you spend in yoga class. A London-based site, DailyBooth, asks people to publish a picture of themselves every day, which they claim is "the richest and quickest way to share how you are doing and what you are feeling.[1206]" Swipely helps people find great restaurants or movies through their friends. Angus David, who was a tester for Swipely, commented: "I really believe that the lens of your friends is fast becoming the most powerful way to discover things on the Internet."[1207]

Too much information? (TMI)

TMI? Perhaps, but social networking companies thrive on personal data, and a youthful generation raised on the Internet are bucking cultural norms in order to pull the 21st century toward more transparency.

Hazards of TMI, say opponents, range from embarrassment to job dismissals to fraud. We do not even know possible consequences of advancing technologies. For instance, improvements in facial recognition could lead to identification of individuals from photos and videos on the Web.

Young adults and privacy

A popular view has been that young adults, having grown up with the Internet, are less worried about personal privacy than their elders, but surveys[1208] found a keen interest regardless of age. Younger adults are more likely to actively "manage" their online data than submit to Facebook's default settings. Though people who are surveyed say they care deeply about privacy, the actions they take do not protect it.

Concern in Washington

Concern about privacy includes Washington, where the desire to protect personal information is shared by Republicans and Democrats alike. Two House bills have been drafted and circulated, making it more difficult for advertisers and media firms to create profiles on users for behavioral advertising.[1209]

The White House, too, has drafted a plan for a voluntary identification system, in which people could get a smart identity card or a digital certificate to prove who they are as they make online transactions. The challenge is to balance efforts to maintain privacy while finding out enough about someone to ensure identity. Cyber security experts say technologies for creating such identifiers already exist and are being used by banks and other businesses. But many companies are not buying in to more expensive or complex identification systems.[1210]

MOBILE APPLICATIONS (APPS)

A new wave has washed over the computer world, following the PC and the Web: the disorganized but exploding world of mobile applications (apps).[1211] About a quarter of American adults—mostly male, well-educated, affluent and younger than 50—were using apps on smart phones in 2010. By 2022 Americans across the board were spending 88% of their mobile time on APPS. 21% of Millennials open an APP 50+ times per day. 49% of people in general open an APP 11+ times each day. The Apple App Store has 1.96 million Apps to choose from, available for download. At the rate apps are developing[1212], and the number of places where people can download them is growing, there could be as many as 5 million apps available in the foreseeable future.[1213]

Blurring of Online/Offline

Apps may be revolutionizing the shopping experience by blurring the online/offline wall and enabling people to carry the virtual world with them into actual stores. "People who walk into your store now are no longer comparing you to the next brick-and-mortar site but to everything else offline and on. Shoppers are shopping and comparing prices on a global level," said Manish Rathi of the consumer electronics-shopping site Retrevo.

Shopping Apps

Mobile purchasing empowers consumers and aids them even in the parking lot. One mapping app finds a particular product in a mall and virtually escorts you to it. Another app locates your car in the parking lot after you've taken a photo of it and the GPS has locked its location into your phone.[1214]

"The future of online is offline."
—*Cyriac Roeding, CEO of ShopKick*

SOCIAL EFFECTS OF WEBSITES AND GADGETS

For some years prior to the presidential race of 2008, a sound-bite culture held sway. By the time the campaigns reached the final year, however, the American public was pushing back against spotty information and turning to the Internet for a more complete picture.[1215]

Today a prediction from the fall of 2008 sounds quaint: "The next generation of the Internet will be all about collaboration… consumers, computers and cell phones could work together to do everything from arrange *ad hoc* carpools to find reservations at a Las Vegas steak house... services will link up with partners and connect consumers to each other."[1216] This statement from just a few short years ago offers perspective on the speed of change in today's world.

Business

Hiring and Drawing Customers

Winemaking

A winemaker in California was looking to hire a "lifestyle correspondent at $10,000 a month to tweet and use other social media skills" to hype up interest in its wines. Applications were submitted via videos no longer than 60 seconds.[1217]

Tourism

Tourism officials in Queensland, Australia, also invited people to submit videos for "The Best Job in the World." It involved spending six months as "caretaker of a palm-fringed, azure-seas island and using blogs, video updates, photo diaries and other online media to promote tourism." The $105,000 job drew more than 34,000 applicants[1218].[1219]

Restaurants

In New York a burger shop, "4food," opened in the fall of 2010. Customers are encouraged to develop their own creations and add them to the menu, as well as share them with friends on Facebook and Twitter. If someone orders your dish, you get a 25-cent credit. You can develop your creation in the store, guided by a staffer, or work it out on one of the bolted-down iPads. There is also free WiFi for browsing the Web while eating, or you can watch Foursquare check- ins and tweets about the experience on a huge LED monitor.[1220]

Collaboration

Google Documents

One of the most promising results of new forms of communication is collaboration. In the spring of 2010 Google upgraded Google Documents to enable as many as 50 people to work simultaneously on analyzing a sales problem with a spreadsheet, drafting a contract, or working together on some other piece of writing—in real time.[1221] The upgrade included a built-in instant messenger, which enables an ongoing conversation about the project being worked on. [1222]

Research-Gate

Scientists, too, are becoming connected worldwide through the Internet. In 2008, a startup called Research-Gate began connecting scientists, free of charge, to do collaborative research and learn from one another. As of the fall of 2010, 500,000 of the 5 to 10 million scientists and researchers worldwide were registered users. The three largest fields of science that have formed groups on Research-Gate are biology, medicine and computer science. Neuroscience has the busiest discussion, followed by genetics and immunology. The service accelerates research by minimizing redundant experiments and providing for active collaboration. It produces faster, better, and cheaper results.[1223]

MathOverflow

In the fall of 2010, UC Berkeley and Stanford announced the creation of a free Web site, MathOverflow, which is transforming math research. By linking questions and answers from the smartest minds on Earth around the most difficult problems, "each small solution builds toward a larger understanding, accelerating research.[1224]" Having a repository of global knowledge demonstrates that mass collaboration can dramatically expand and speed up problem-solving abilities.[1225]

Government

Reaching youth

When the swine flu outbreak of 2009 was imminent, health officials turned to Facebook and Twitter to get youth and children onboard their campaign to fight it. They wanted to be sure the younger generation had correct information and health updates to share with their friends.

The health officials were following the path the federal government had already tested earlier in the spring, when they produced podcasts on hand washing, Twitter feeds with the latest infection numbers, and eCards on managing swine flu symptoms. In July the U.S. Department of Health and Human Services followed up by soliciting youth videos (for a $2500 prize) that would educate and entertain their peers, making hand washing seem "as appealing as 'Gossip Girl'."[1226]

Parents, Children and Youth

Children and youth

Many parents are concerned about the effect social Web sites—and electronics technology in general—are having on their children. However, a national study[1227] says children and teens on the Internet "are picking up basic social and technological skills they need to fully participate in contemporary society." They are learning to be competent citizens in the digital age. And— good news to parents—the study showed no evidence that kids are engaging in behavior online that is riskier than what they do offline.[1228] In fact, they use online networks to learn from each other, explore interests and develop expertise, in addition to staying connected with their friends.

Multitasking

However, the news is not all good if your child is a multitasker. A study[1229] showed that HMM (heavy media multitaskers, in research parlance) people "do not pay attention, cannot control their memory or cannot switch easily from one job to another as adeptly as low-tech people who concentrated on one job at a time.[1230]"[1231]

Other researchers have corroborated this finding. Though students have always faced distractions, the constant stream of stimuli offered by computers and cell phones pose a profound new challenge to focusing and learning. The risk, they say, is that developing brains can become habituated to constantly switching tasks, making it more difficult in sustaining attention. Executive director[1232] of the Center on Media and Child Health in Boston worries that we may be raising a generation of children "whose brains are going to be wired differently."[1233]

> **"Their brains are rewarded not for staying**
> **on task but for jumping to the next thing."**
> —*Michael Rich, Center on Media and Child Health*

Sleep deprivation

Sleep deprivation is pervasive among teenagers, many of whom sleep with their cell phones and are texting 24/7. Though teens have always been sleep-deprived to some extent, technology today is making it worse. Teen texting rates took a jump of 566 percent between 2007 and 2009, averaging 97 texts a day, 3,000 a month. Most troublesome is the nighttime texting, when children and teens should be sleeping.

Even 12-year-olds engage in occasional texting all-nighters, usually during sleepovers when others are at home, texting. Psychologists say they want to avoid being left out. If they are on top of everything that is going on, they belong.

Norman Constantine, director of University of California-Berkeley's Center for Research on Adolescent Health and Development, says stakes are higher than many parents realize. Sleep deprivation is linked to memory and concentration problems, anxiety and depression, moodiness and hyperactivity.[1234]

> **"The phenomenon of 24/7 texting has been called**
> **"the CNN syndrome of teenhood— round-the-clock**
> **reports on breaking news about everything from**
> **homework to wardrobe choices to frappuccino cravings."**
> —*Margie Ryerson, therapist*

Nagging parents

Many parents have tried, with varying degrees of success, to enter into this strange world of their children by using text messages to stay in touch. It is not unusual for a mother to text each of her children a few times every day, adding to the texting deluge that has hit school classrooms. One high school principal[1235] said so many parents text students during school hours that she discouraged it at a freshman orientation.

Parents text kids to remind them about laundry, being on time to baseball practice, mowing the lawn—whatever comes to mind in the moment that they feel must be communicated to their children. An innovative dad texted his daughter: "Take a picture of your room clean and send it to me." Some say this newfangled form of nagging has made their nagging less annoying because it does not carry the emotional charge of face-to-face confrontation.[1236]

> **"Hey, Kid. Don't make me text you twice."**
> —*Headline from **The Washington Post***

Hopeful Kaiser study

With all the downsides, studies by the Kaiser Family Foundation found that plugged-in teens appear to be well adjusted and healthy. Yes, 86 percent of children use social media sites, and they use electronic gadgets for more than 7.5 hours a day, but this may not be as disastrous as parents' fear. Electronics appear to be the path by which children today develop emotional bonds and their own identities. Moreover, those who spend the most time on social media sites are the healthiest psychologically.

The digital world may simply be a new, multidimensional place to form identities separate from those of parents, which has always been the work of adolescence. [1237]

Young Adults

A Pew survey in 2009 showed that 83 percent of adults from 18 to 24 had a social networking profile, and two-thirds of them participated in political activity on Facebook or similar sites. These younger Internet users chose to visit Web sites that expressed their own point of view, a reflection of the polarization in our culture at large.

Perhaps most significant of the findings was that younger users have adopted an activist model, sharing information with others and asking, "What can I do?" This is unlike the traditional League of Women Voters model, in which the average person looks to those deemed "experts" for information. Instead, they look to each other.[1238] Experts are like middlemen: they can keep you from direct access to information.

Distracted college students

Sustaining attention has become a serious problem even in college classrooms. Several universities have placed a ban on cell phones in class because texting during class has become so rampant. At Wilkes University texting has surpassed doodling, daydreaming and note-passing to become the top classroom distraction. Nine out of ten Wilkes students admit to sending text messages during class. An anonymous survey[1239] showed that a clear majority of 62 percent of the students at Wilkes said they should be allowed to text in class as long as they do not disturb other members of the class. "Students these days are so used to multitasking... they believe they are able to process information just as effectively when they are texting as when they are not," said Deborah Tindell, an author of the study.[1240]

Romantic break-ups

Listening to stories of romances breaking up in the Facebook age drives home the inextricable entanglements social networking has introduced—problems never before imagined.

One problem derives from sharing online passwords to e-mail accounts, bank accounts and photo-sharing sites, which is the way intimacy is expressed in today's relationships.[1241] This can lead to deep hurtfulness when a break-up occurs. Bonding does not end with the two persons directly involved because each has a large network of social Web site friends. In former days a spurned lover could cut an ex out of a photo. Today digital images of the smiling couple get dispersed so quickly through a large network of social Web site friends, it is nearly impossible to delete them. In addition, status dates and tweets on exes also continue to haunt an already wounded lover.

"When you make a decision to be with a person in cyberspace you are making a commitment to their network of friends and acquaintances. People have so many online strings that bind them that cutting one does not sever the relationship. There are always more.[1242]"

Users, of course, can control their own postings, but often their photos, videos and comments get forwarded, retweeted or reposted to friends' accounts or even on public Web sites. Once they are integrated into other people's pages, you have no control.

A medical student[1243] struck the core of the hurt that can result when she said, "The thing is you never really get out of the relationship."[1244]

Adults

Vacations

In this new Communication Age, living has changed across the board. Vacation, in the traditional understanding of getting away from it all, has become blurred. As early as 2007, 80 percent of American adults took a cell phone with them on vacation, 20 percent checked work messages or voice mail, and 19 percent took laptops with them.[1245]

Workplace

Just as people on vacation can work in their pajamas, so can some professionals—on an everyday basis. A case in point is Virtual Law Partners, a law firm with about 40 attorneys, yet has no location—it is everywhere.

RingCentral

A cloud computing software company, RingCentral, created a communications system that holds everything together for the lawyers, while giving the impression of a traditional practice with a central location and phone number. With little overhead, lawyers are available at cheaper rates. Virtual Law Partners is but one of RingCentral's nearly 100,000 small business clients across the globe.[1246]

Seniors

Scientists have conducted a study showing that Internet searching for as little as two weeks can improve seniors' cognitive fitness and short-term memory. Gary Small, neuroscientist at UCLA who was part of the study, believes that "society's growing reliance on technology is likely helping to 'rewire' our brains in ways that are not fully understood.[1247]"[1248]

Social Relationships

Birth announcements

Miss Manners now says that e-mail is preferable to a handwritten letter or formal announcement for announcing births.[1249]

Matchmaking

Web sites have become so sophisticated that Dating4Disabled.com, based in Tel Aviv, Israel, specializes in matchmaking for persons with disabilities.[1250]

Presidential debates

The presidential debates in 2008 showed the potential of interactive TV, which engaged the public more deeply through videos (in addition to tweets and blogs) and made them more critical of what they saw and heard.[1251]

Emergency alerts

Some areas, like Santa Clara County, California, are using social-networking sites to encourage those without land lines to sign up for emergency disaster alerts. City alert systems often fail to reach cell phone-only users. A new emergency alert system would replace the existing disparate system with a single system.[1252]

For Reflection:

1. ....

   ....

   ....

2. ....

   ....

   ....

3. ....

   ....

   ....

CHAPTER 21
VIRTUAL REALITY

Virtuality is an abstracting process at the heart of many developments in the world today. We often think of it in connection with social Web sites, but the process extends to other areas of life, too, blurring the line between virtuality and reality.

INTERSECTION OF TWO WORLDS

In the early part of this century, virtual reality moved beyond the fantasia-like concept that had formed in the mind of the average person. Stanford University's Virtual Human Interaction Lab was studying ways in which the virtual world affects the real one, recognizing that "kids spend more time on Facebook than they do talking to physical people."[1253]

George Bush/John Kerry Study

Disciplines ranging from the U.S. government to political science to philosophy and psychology found the Lab's work useful. For instance, in a study conducted a week before the 2004 presidential election, photos of George Bush and John Kerry were subtly altered so that one candidate's picture contained a morphed image of the actual subjects. Researchers discovered that strongly partisan voters were not swayed by the alteration, but voters who were on the fence showed a "strong preference" for the candidate who looked vaguely like themselves.

Swimming with Fish

A concern stemming from the findings of this study was that powerful imagery could blur the line between a manufactured reality and the real thing. To test this, a group of five- to seven-year olds, who had never swum with fish, were shown images of their own faces on virtual bodies swimming with a pair of fish. Many of them said it had actually happened.

Swapping Bodies

Neuroscientists in Sweden[1254] conducted a similar experiment to explore how people can be tricked into the false perception of owning another body in order to answer the age-old question: "why we feel that the self is in our bodies.[1255]"

To study this scientifically, they attached electrodes and virtual reality goggles on the subjects. The goggles were hooked up to cameras fitted to the head of a male mannequin. Then the experimenter brushed markers against the subject's belly and that of the mannequin simultaneously. Seventy to eighty percent of the subjects experienced the illusion "very strongly" that they had swapped bodies with the mannequin.[1256]

> **"In the past you had to use your imagination to put yourself in somebody else's shoes. Using the VR equipment, you can actually become that person and view the world through his eyes."**
> —Sun Joo Ahn, doctoral candidate, Stanford University

Sci-Fi Movie: Fantasy or Reality?

A sci-fi TV movie[1257] carries blurred reality to an extreme. In the movie, a virtual reality program allows crew members on a ten-year intergalactic voyage to amuse themselves by simulating anything from fighting a Civil War battle to surfing in Hawaii.

The producers financed the voyage by turning it into a reality show. In order to keep up the ratings, the show's executive producer encourages phony psychodramas among crew members, which soon mutate into reality. At one point the crew members find themselves being raped and murdered in their own dream worlds, causing them to wonder if the virtual reality program has developed a virus, or if it is drawing the violence out of their own dark fantasies.

It is more than a rhetorical question when the starship commander demands of an officer: "I'm asking if you know fantasy from reality." The answer is never clear.[1258]

VIRTUALIZING REAL LIFE

Virtualizing real life situations and things has grown steadily in the past several years.

Anti-Fur Protest

Stella McCartney, like her late mother, Linda, has been a longtime supporter of animal rights. In 2007 she co-hosted a virtual anti-fur protest on a dedicated island in Second Life[1259].[1260]

Online Safe Deposit Boxes

A year later Wells Fargo Bank introduced a service that offers online safe-deposit boxes for storing vital records, called "v-Safe." It works well for storing and easily retrieving digital versions of birth certificates, wills, driver's licenses, passports, family photos and other important documents. Contents of the "boxes" can be retrieved from any computing device with an Internet connection.[1261]

Memorials for the Dead

Virtual reality is also used to create memorials for the dead on social networking Web sites. MyDeathSpace.com, which lists thousands of articles about young adults who have died, gets up to 15,000 visitors a day. This virtual cemetery is readily available to many more people than "real-life" tributes to the dead, such as flowers or photos on gravestones or candle-lit memorials. Looking at a deceased person's social networking Web site "is like looking at a snapshot of that person's life at the moment they passed away," said the creator of MyDeathSpace, Michael Patterson. Even those who never knew the deceased take part in online discussions about them.

Why would people be so interested in the lives and deaths of strangers? one might ask. A psychology professor[1262] said: "I'm not sure we're talking about deaths of strangers. They're part of the same online world. It opens up the definition of 'friend.'"

Why the interest in death itself, especially young people? A human development professor[1263] who has written a book about online tributes answers:

> "Even though we see death a lot in the movies, real death is kept separate from us, including real bereavement. With making death more hidden, it's become more interesting and also more taboo. Particularly in the case of teenagers—what are they going to do but go to a taboo site?"[1264]

Online Snail Mail

By 2009, virtuality had moved into many areas of life. A company called "Earth Class Mail" introduced a service that scans all snail mail—letters, bills, catalogs, etc.—and delivers it online for $11.95 a month. No more "change of addresses," no such thing as vacation mail. Packages can be sent to your home, and the company will shred, recycle or forward mail to you. In Switzerland, the national postal operator uses the technology developed by Earth Class Mail to deliver regular mail online in six European countries.[1265]

Job Fairs

Job fairs have moved online, too. As with real job fairs, job seekers can choose to visit different pavilions such as High Tech, Healthcare, Professional and Skilled, and submit resumes with just a few clicks.[1266]

Paperless Ticketing

Ticketmaster Entertainment developed a system to shut out brokers and scalpers from re-selling tickets. The company issues paperless ticketing, making customers prove their purchase by showing a credit card and ID when they arrive at an event. Without paper tickets, there is nothing for scalpers to re-sell.[1267] Many airlines and other companies have adopted similar systems.

Paperless Offices

Companies such as Cisco Systems have found ways to move toward a paperless office by providing convenient electronic access to documents from anywhere at any time, and then making paper use inconvenient.[1268]

Paper consumption peaked in 2001, and then slowly started to decline. This is significant in terms of environmental impact, as pulp and paper production is the second largest user of energy and water, and third largest contributor to pollution.[1269]

Scams

Virtual scams have wormed their way into real life, causing much distress.

Phony parking tickets

Some scammers place phony parking tickets on cars, directing the owners to an "official" Web site that claims to have photos of the alleged violation. When victims go there, they inadvertently download a nasty virus that compromises their computer. "This very clever ploy bridges the [real] world with the virtual world, and I fear we'll be seeing more of these types of attacks in the future," said Lenny Zeltser, a computer security expert.[1270]

Virtual kidnappings

Perhaps the cruelest of scams is "virtual kidnappings," which pose real risks in Latin America. This scheme is aimed at quickly extracting ransom without an actual abduction. Because actual kidnappings are so frequent there—especially in Mexico, Haiti and Colombia—their scheme is believable to the victims. With the use of a telephone and inside information about household details[1271] the "kidnappers" make the phone call demanding money when the family is separated.

In one Brazilian state[1272] police reported 3,000 virtual kidnapping complaints in a six-week period, and it is estimated that 36,295 kidnappings took place in the country in 2004[1273]. Yet approximately 90 percent of victims do not report the crime.[1274]

VIRTUAL WORLDS: SECOND LIFE

**"In the world of Second life, people create 'avatars,'
or virtual personas, after downloading a free program.
A few mouse clicks launch users into a 'real time'
community with an average population of 40,000
to 50,000. The visual environment is created by the users."**
—*Kara Andrade, San Jose Mercury News*

Differing Attitudes

When a journalist at a shopping center asked five people—male and female from three different age groups: "Are online communities like Second Life productive uses of time?" their responses represented the span of attitudes toward virtual communities across generations.

Predictably, students said they thought it was a productive use of their time, pointing out that it "keeps people from dealing dope and things like that[1275]," though they recognized that parents would not agree. Indeed, people in their parents' age group did not agree, pointing to the importance of experiencing life directly. An artist[1276] responded: "I don't think people do enough with their first life. If you have enough time to do something in the virtual world, you can do something more productive… in the real world." An older man, a professor[1277], was on the same page with those of parenting age.[1278]

Origin of Second Life

Back in 2003, Linden Lab created an Internet site, resembling a 3-D virtual world, called "Second Life" (SL). According to its literature, SL members design the site's "global community working together to build a new online space for creativity, collaboration, commerce, and entertainment." Its creators said it was the next evolutionary stage of the Internet, merging the Web with "online games, social networking, user-generated content, creativity, and telecommunications technologies[1279]." As early as 2008, the site had garnered more than 14 million residents, most being over the age of 30.[1280]

Residents log in to Second Life to "socialize, stroll beaches, visit islands and cities, shop, attend lectures and classes, visit libraries and night clubs and do business[1281]."[1282] People from other parts of the world speaking different languages can use a voice program to talk.[1283]

Businesses and universities use SL for teaching, global conferences, product testing and merchandise sales. Nonprofits, too, use the site for outreach, working collaboratively to address global problems such as starvation, health care and climate change.

Avatars

At the heart of SL are avatars, onscreen characters that may have nothing to do with their real selves. Men can be women; some users are animals, teddy bears, or Alice in Wonderland; you can even look like yourself, with the help of a professional at LindenLab.[1284]

"In online environments… the avatar is our entire self-representation," said Nick Yee, a researcher at Stanford's Department of Communications.

Avatars allow undeveloped parts of our real personality to bloom by helping people try on different lives never before experienced. This offers the potential for greater empathy. They let us become our best—or worst—selves.[1285]

Avatars waiting for a performance to begin

Merging of real and virtual

"People often become leaders here even though they've never had any ability to lead anything in their real life," said Maressa Orzack, a psychologist at Harvard Medical School who studies computer addiction. The virtual self is especially powerful because the human brain is not wired to differentiate between the real and the virtual[1286].[1287]

Skeptics wonder: Why bother using real time and brain space on electronic environments? Orzack explains: "People are living in the virtual world. To them, it's real."[1288]

Downside

Blurring of the line between real and virtual can take its toll in human relations. An SL user[1289] tells of reading a *Wall Street Journal* article about "a man who spent up to 14 hours daily in Second Life... with a beautiful avatar wife—while his real wife was watching television in the living room[1290]." Would a virtual relationship in Second Life be considered cheating?[1291]

For someone in England the answer is clearly "yes." A British woman filed for divorce when she discovered her husband cheating in Second Life. She said:

"I caught him cuddling a woman on a sofa in the game. It looked really affectionate. He confessed he'd been talking to this woman player in America for one or two weeks, and said our marriage was over and he didn't love me anymore."[1292]

Because gambling[1293], porn and other illicit activities became widespread in Second Life, Linden Lab banned gambling and moved adult-oriented content to a new, X-rated continent, where people[1294] can continue to frolic as their heart desires. At the same time, they implemented a three-tiered rating system: PG, Mature and Adult.

Social Activism

Eco-Topia

One of many focuses in SL is activism, which users hope will play out in the natural world. For instance, Eco-Topia is a virtual "new town," modeled on New Urbanism, that is walkable and not oil dependent.[1295]

Center for Water Studies

At its Center for Water Studies you can see an animated pond freeze in winter and breed tadpoles in spring, while an ocean environment allows you to click from clear to contaminated water to see the effects of pollution on an underwater ecosystem.

Environmental problems

Like real life, SL is not perfect, though it would be possible. Instead, people replicate environmental problems of real life. Landscape has become overdeveloped[1296] and littering is a problem. A rusting sports car was dumped in the grass and stray advertisements litter the boardwalk. Virtual trees have withered, as they were programmed to need water, but nobody came to water them.

A frustrated SL environmentalist, Profoky Neva, addressed the problem by starting the SL Public Land Preserve, a virtual, communally-owned land trust. "I've learned an awful lot being here about what goes into urban planning," wrote Neva's real life self, who lives in New York City. "I would never have thought about these issues if I hadn't become a virtual land baron."[1297]

Study of online social activism

A study made by the Center for the Digital Future at the University of Southern California's Annenberg School found that nearly two-thirds of online community members who are involved in social activism on the Internet were not familiar with their chosen cause before joining SL. Now 20 percent participate at least once a year in offline activity that mirrors their online endeavor. Their report said 44 percent of the study participants had become more politically active since joining an online social network. More stunning, 43 percent of online community members said they "feel as strongly about their virtual community as they do about their real- world communities."

TOWN SQUARE

Fun and games

When it's holiday time—anytime from Halloween to Valentine's Day—Second Lifers head for the Internet to open surprise, gift-wrapped packages strewn around Paragon City, have a snowball fight, or engage in holiday festivities in their own way—whatever way they choose. They decorate their homes with wreaths and trees and gather others to go caroling in the streets of their virtual town. Grant McDaniel, senior producer of "Star Wars Galaxies," sums it up: "People want to celebrate in the real world with their families, and they want to do that with their friends online, too."[1298]

Shops

Shops in SL—as well as in other virtual worlds—line the streets with virtual goods and services for sale. Even at the height of the recession, sales were not slowed.

Virtual goods

One youth-oriented virtual world, Gaia Online, has 7 million avatar inhabitants and sells more than $1 million a month of virtual goods. For fifty cents, teenagers can buy a pair of Elvis Presley's blue suede shoes for their avatar or a pair of Snoop Dogg Dobermans for $3. Ben & Jerry's Homemade gave away 500,000 virtual ice cream cones as part of a Free Cone Day promotion in stores. Customers spend about $1.5 billion a year on virtual goods worldwide, with China leading the pack.[1299]

Retailers in SL

1-800-FLOWERS, a real-world retailer, sells virtual bouquets in SL. The company dispatches simulated employees around the virtual community to hand out fliers inviting avatars to stop by their greenhouse to collect a virtual floral bouquet or to learn how to care for their tulips. Visitors can also shop there for actual flowers to send to people in real life. 1-800-FLOWERS spent an estimated $50,000 (real life dollars) to establish itself in SL, including salaries for 40 employees who rotate answering questions from Second Life residents. Their company is but one of dozens of real-life companies operating in SL, retailers as diverse as American Apparel, Circuit City and Sears.[1300]

Legal issues a deterrent

EBay, on the other hand, wanted nothing to do with virtual sales. Early in 2007 the company nixed auctions of virtual items like gold coins from the online game" World of Warcraft," items that are often difficult to come by in the games. EBay cited "complex legal issues" as their reason for stopping auctions of such items.[1301] By 2009, however, EBay had reversed its position. Online advertisements now offer virtual goods for sale.

Currency and credit

SL has its own economy and currency. People can buy and exchange Linden dollars (L$) to buy and sell virtual land, buildings, homes, furniture, cars and clothes, and take vacations.[1302] Despite the popularity of virtual currency, some experts, both here and abroad have spurned it.

Chinese virtual currency

In 2008, tens of millions of Chinese young people traded virtual goods and credits for real goods like clothes and cosmetics, as well as for cash. Overall, this amounted to $2 billion in virtual currency sales in China that year. Due to the large scale of such activity, the "QQ coins," as the Chinese virtual currency is called, have sometimes risen sharply in value against China's official currency, alarming officials at the nation's central bank. Chinese authorities were so afraid of the widespread buying and selling of virtual currencies that in 2009 they issued regulations to restrict the trade and use of it, banning the exchange of virtual currencies for goods.[1303]

Threat to world economies

A U.S. professor of telecommunications[1304] said he believes virtual currencies could pose a threat to world economies: "As virtual currencies take over more and more purchasing power, control over the effective money supply shifts from the central bank to the game developers."[1305]

Borrowing through Kwedit

Even as some authorities want virtual currencies restricted, others are making it easier for everyone to participate in online environments.

Kwedit is a startup that helps teenagers and others buy virtual goods online by issuing credit:

"You promise to pay later to get stuff now. If you keep your promise, your Kwedit score goes up and you can borrow larger amounts of money. But if you don't keep your promise… your Kwedit score would go down, [even though] your real-world credit score wouldn't.[1306]

Borrowers can pay off Kwedit through snail mail or at any 7-Eleven store.[1307]

Facebook apps without credit card

Facebook has entered the credit world, too. It partnered with a Malaysian company in the summer of 2010 to sell credits at 7-Eleven stores, Internet cafes and online banks in Asia[1308] for buying virtual goods and playing games on Facebook. This partnership marked the first time that consumers could buy credit for Facebook apps like "FarmVille" without credit cards.[1309]

The first brick-and-mortar retailer in the U.S. to sell Facebook's virtual currency was Target. It started offering Facebook Credits gift cards in the fall of 2010 in $15, $25 and $50 increments. [1310] Estimates predicted that the market for virtual goods could reach $1.6 billion by the end of 2010 for items bought in social networking games[1311].[1312]

MEETING PLACE

Another function of SL is that of meeting place for governments, universities, companies and businesses.

Politics

During campaigns for the presidency in 2008, several candidates visited Second Life. Hillary Clinton held town meetings there. Her campaign there focused on a stage with a large, spotlighted picture of her as backdrop. Kiosks sported Hillary golf shirts, and information on how to join her campaign dotted the surrounding area. Behind the stage a police HUMV watched over a helipad and a long line of stretch limos.[1313]

Testimony at congressional hearing

In the same year Philip Rosedale, founder of Second Life, testified at a congressional hearing on the expanding potential of Second Life and other virtual worlds. He said:

"Scientists and researchers are sharing information in virtual meetings, Cisco Systems and Intel are using it as a form of teleconferencing and IBM is experimenting with Second Life for simulations and training sessions. Politicians are holding virtual town halls, and more than 400 universities are using the technology for teaching. "This is changing the nature of communications itself."[1314]

Simultaneous version in SL

Congress held the hearing simultaneously with a version in Second Life that was complete with a 3-D model of the committee room. Socrates, Electric sheep, Pica Paperdoll and other avatars who were following the event in the virtual world, attended the SL version. TV monitors carried the congressional session as usual, but one screen showed the Second Life version streaming in real time, along with the avatars' text-chat, such as: "There's another softball question."

Fears of Congress

Many Members of Congress expressed fears about virtual worlds becoming addictive or helping sexual predators and terrorists. Rosedale responded that Linden Lab, the maker of Second Life, "has cooperated with law enforcement and seen no evidence of activity by terrorists. He also said he suspected that law enforcement had created its own avatars to check out virtual worlds[1315]."[1316]

Universities

A skyrocketing number of universities across the country—and world—have leapt into the virtual world of Second Life.

Stanford University

Stanford University Libraries operate an island in SL, where they have a teahouse, 18 collections libraries, an archive of recorded sound—and even a steam-powered train. Visitors from all over the world listen to jazz collections in the archive of recorded sound, look at 16th and 17th century books, see a first edition of the King James Bible and a letter by Mark Twain, written in his own hand.

Vassar College

Vassar College has a virtual, 3-D recreation of the Sistine Chapel for teaching art students.[1317]

San Jose State University

San Jose State University has created 3-D models of its campus in SL—its bell tower, classrooms, student union and faculty offices, including staff hours—as well as affirming the use of SL as a classroom.

Jeremy Kemp, a professor at the university's School of Library and Information Science, teaches from his laptop in an SL classroom. A student may be dressed as a monarch butterfly and others could be making a virtual flying carpet. Kemp says one's emotional experience in Second Life is key to the learning process, both as a motivating factor and as a connector to the content. Students enjoy being thrown into a situation where they have to learn from each other, as well as learning to present their ideas in a visual way, translating real-life objects into Second Life. For distant learners, SL offers a sense of being present.

The virtual campus "has changed the whole concept of place—there's no need to move here to become a librarian," said Linda Main, associate director of the School of Library and Information Science at San Jose State University.[1318]

Big Business

"We sell more furniture worldwide than Ikea."
—*Paul Thind, General Manager of virtual Habbo Hotel,*
where visitors decorate their rooms with furniture they buy

Second Life is not only a big business in itself; it is big business for big businesses. By 2007, major corporations[1319] were establishing a marketing foothold in Second Life and other virtual worlds. The leap into Second Life was easy for them, as numerous digital design companies do business there. The average cost of a project in Second Life for a large company runs in the low six-figure range, a relatively modest investment for major corporations.

Sun Microsystems

Sun Microsystems, Inc. holds client meetings there and has a public virtual sandbox, where people can learn about building 3-D objects that can be textured, animated and lit.[1320]

Toyota

When Toyota wanted to market their Scion for younger buyers, they turned to a major digital design company in Second Life. The company, Millions of Us, worked out a "futuristic urban island with a dealership that sells the cars and a racetrack where consumers' online personas can take them for virtual test drives[1321]."[1322]

No wonder teenagers and young adults are so attracted to Scion City and virtual worlds in general, reflected Amy Jo Kim, who directs creation of games and services for Shufflebrain. "They are playing around with identity,"[1323]

Guidelines for personal appearance

Companies diverge when it comes to personal appearance in Second Life. Sun Microsystems' only requirement is that employees show up looking like **humans**.[1324] IBM published guidelines that suggest being "especially sensitive to the appropriateness of your avatar or persona's appearance when you are meeting with IBM clients or conducting IBM business."[1325] Some companies let their employees appear as they wish.

At a lecture on software development that Intel sponsored in Second Life, the employer who opened the event was a "tuxedoed half-man, half-lynx." Following his introduction, he turned the meeting over to the speaker, Zombie Bob, who was dressed in a tight, white shirt. "In the audience, a woman with a ponytail and sunglasses slept in the front row and a blue-skinned man with spiky hair listened attentively."[1326]

Needless to say, creative self-expression is prized and expected in Second Life.

LEGAL ISSUES

With blurring of the line between "real" and "virtual," legal issues keep arising.

Property Rights and Taxes

Property rights in virtual worlds have become a thorny question. Courts have struggled to figure out how to apply laws from real life to the virtual world, as no precedent exists to clarify whether people own the electronic goods they make, buy or accumulate in virtual worlds.

Intellectual property rights

Early on, Linden Lab made the unusual decision to grant users intellectual property rights for what they create, but some legal experts believe there is more to online rights than intellectual property. Legal reasons lead them to think that property rights to objects can exist in a virtual realm.

Income tax

Congress took note of the issue, wondering how this might affect income taxes. Accordingly, they conducted a study of whether income in the virtual economy, such as from the sale of digital designer gowns, furniture, automobiles and other virtual wares, should be taxed by the Internal Revenue Service.[1327]

Drug Dealers and Terrorists

Dean Takahashi[1328] has reflected on

"what would happen if there were drug dealers or terrorists lurking in virtual worlds such as Second Life. If the FBI or National Security Agency wanted to place wiretaps on conversations in those worlds, would they be able to do it? And if they did record conversations in virtual worlds, could the people spied upon escape prosecution by saying that they were only pretending to be terrorists or drug dealers?"[1329]

If they say they are "just pretending," authorities would have to find evidence in the real world to corroborate the evidence from the virtual world because "what occurs in the virtual world is tantamount to free speech," says Sean Kane, a virtual world legal expert. "You have a right as an author to make statements without it being considered treason."[1330]

Sports

Fantasy sports present a different kind of controversial issue.

Royalties

In 2009, CBS Interactive sued the National Football League Players Association to prevent it from demanding royalties for using players' names and statistics in fantasy sport leagues, saying the material it used was publicly available. This prompted a counter suit, with a judge finally ruling the information is in the public domain and can be used for free in fantasy sports leagues. [1331]

Virtual sports for kids

Even with legal problems surrounding the use of national sports teams, developers of virtual worlds did whatever was necessary to launch a sport-based virtual world for kids. Six Degrees Games, the company behind the venture, managed to secure licenses with the National Basketball Association, Major League Baseball and the National Football League to use team logos and jerseys in their virtual world. They also "struck a deal with ESPN to include real-time sports news and scores as well as videos related to the Xgames, an extreme sports competition[1332]."[1333]

MASH-UPS

Second Life and Facebook originally developed two distinct neighborhoods in cyberspace, but the wave of technological openness spreading across the Internet made the blending of sites inevitable. The new openness elicited innovations in the form of apps that transformed social Web site pages into "much more living organisms[1334]" that combine features from different Web sites.

Facebook

Facebook was the first social networking site to cash in on the potential of "mash-ups," combinations that mix the features of two sites. When they began permitting companies and software makers to develop apps for Facebook, they unleashed thousands of innovative apps. These enabled more life-like gatherings, similar to online-game communities, where users from around the world meet and compete.

Game Developers

Game developers, too, have made a conscious turn toward creating better social experiences for gamers by combining games and social networks.

Overcoming isolation with a "social hearth"

Trip Hawkins, the CEO of cell phone gamemaker Digital Chocolate, says those who use mash-ups hope to represent a way to carry on a virtual life that improves upon the real world because people in modern society are suffering from the "lost village" syndrome. Instead of living in close-knit villages, "people reside among strangers in big cities far from families, work away from home, and don't know their neighbors[1335]." They are desperately turning to technology to overcome their sense of isolation. A solitary gamer staring into a screen may seem unappealing, but when technology connects gamers to like-minded people, it becomes a social experience. Hawkins believes that the "social center for humans has evolved over time from camp fires to fireplaces to TVs. He thinks the cell phone and its text messaging capabilities will replace the TV as the 'social hearth' for networks of friends[1336]."[1337]

Games: Farmville

**(Speaking of FarmVille) "It's like crack, I guess.
It just sucks you in a little bit at a time."**
—*Chris Lion of San Jose, California*

The Web has become a playground for millions of people. Zynga's "Farmville" and some other games are free but make millions of dollars by selling virtual add-ons such as seeds and farmland. Sometimes proceeds are used for charitable causes, such as when Zynga's players raised more than $1.5 million for Haiti earthquake victims in five days by purchasing virtual items.[1338] By late 2009, Zynga's "FarmVille" had become Facebook's most popular game[1339] with 69 million monthly users, "including 26.6 million who daily tend their virtual crops and maybe milk digital cows[1340]."

"The most successful games encourage social interaction, enable self-expression and help users feel that their investment of time is worthwhile," said Zynga's founder and CEO, Mark Pincus.

Feel-good games

Users say they like the casual aspect of games like Farmville, which contrasts sharply with the deeper involvement of role-playing destinations such as Second Life or Roll 20. They also find these "feel- good" games a welcome change to the mayhem of the military, mobster and vampire staples of the video-game industry. One FarmVille devotee[1341] calls it a "Pollyannish" place, where untended crops may die but animals never do—and where you can earn Good Samaritan points for adopting a "lonely pink cow" or fertilizing a friend's crops.[1342]

Others much prefer role-playing Web sites like Second Life, and feel they are more worthy of their time.

That may be the secret of social Web sites' success: there's something for everyone.

For Reflection:

1. ....

....

....

2. ....

....

....

3. ....

....

....

PART THREE
CRITIC'S REVIEW

CHAPTER 22

BEHIND THE SCENES

From the data gathered in Part II of this book, I have chosen the most energetic living ideas to comprise this final section, though energy, of course, moves in *all* thought.

> **"The core themes of our time [living ideas] can be seen as carrying the unconscious projection of core needs of the soul."**
> —*Brigitte Eggers, from April 2008 newsletter of The Jung Society of Washington.*

LIVING IDEAS

Ideas are at the very core of life itself. Jacques Monod, Nobel Prize-winning biologist, says an "abstract kingdom" of ideas rises above the biosphere, similar to the biosphere standing above the world of nonliving matter. Ideas spawn in the human brain and have the power to spread infectiously through human culture via language.[1343] I call these "living ideas."

The living ideas evidenced in this chapter are the few that are moving with the most energy and contagion within humanity today. By looking at them, we glimpse what is of greatest concern to the universe relative to human choices and actions as a species. This provides a course for humanity's cooperation in fulfilling its role as consciousness for the universe.

INTERDEPENDENCE OF THE UNIVERSE AND HUMANITY

Humanity is *driven* with bursts of energy in areas that need special attention at any given time, but humans *choose* how to address these concerns in the actualized world. The universe is pragmatic and goal-oriented; humanity is rational and moral. As consciousness for the universe, humanity needs to bring the functions of both the universe and humanity to any given situation, choosing a course that moves in the direction needed by the universe, like a driver guiding a team of energetic horses. Humanity and the universe are interdependent: the universe provides direction and energy; humanity provides consciousness and choice-making.

At this moment of history, primary concerns of the universe relative to humanity are: 1) preserving the universe as an organic whole that will continue to evolve and expand. For humanity this means keeping Planet Earth in proper relationship to, and in balance with, the rest of the created world; and 2) assuring that human consciousness continues to evolve quickly enough to keep abreast with rapidly-complexifying patterns of creation, including human cultural developments.

A word to remember: What follows is not about linear movement, progressing from one development to another, or events causing other events, though the temptation to see them that way is great. In the holistic world of the universe, all movements occur outside of time and are intertwined.

DEVELOPING CONSCIOUSNESS

ROLE OF THE UNIVERSE

Human Development

Human beings are uniquely designed to be intelligent creatures. Much smaller creatures than we are could not develop the complexity necessary for intelligence; much larger ones would be limited by the time it takes information to travel across their brains.

As the human brain evolves, it keeps growing in size. This enables it to absorb increasing amounts of information at a fast enough rate to handle the complexity.

Studies of the brain show that thinking is a network function. When a person performs more than one task at a time, a larger portion of the brain must be used. Therefore, today's multitasking teenagers—or "digital natives," as they are sometimes called—may, in fact, be increasing the size of the human brain. This could be a reflection of soulf's need for humanity to engage with more parts of life at one time, rather than segregating life into discreet units.

Throughout history the rate of human evolutionary change has been increasing, rising to more than 100 times historical levels, with the brain evolving at a faster rate than any other part of the human body. At the same time, humans have had increasingly better health and longer lives, offering nature more time to evolve the human brain. All of this is requisite in developing the higher consciousness needed by the universe today.

The human brain is not wired to differentiate between reality and fantasy, so virtual experiences are often as helpful as real ones. For years this knowledge has been utilized in the practice of hypnotherapy. Athletes can benefit almost as much by shooting hoops, practicing tennis serves or putting a golf ball in a hypnotic state as they do from actual practice.

The blurred line between reality and fantasy also makes human experiences in virtual worlds valuable in developing higher consciousness. Opportunities to experiment with real choice- making within a virtual world like Second Life can improve the quality of choice-making in the real world.

Population Growth

Researchers examining variants of DNA have found that genetic evolution and brain size are directly related to population growth. As the human population grows in number, its genes evolve faster; and the fastest-evolving genes are those related to development of the human brain.

The greater the population, the bigger the brain must be to handle the complexities of larger social groups. These complexities include relating to other constituents and cohering as a single group. Because human brains are large enough to handle these complexities, humans socialize in the largest groups of all primates.

The human population size is greater than that of any other animal species. Accordingly, the human brain—notably the human frontal lobe— is also larger than other animal brains.

The human brain would not have developed to its current size without high population growth. According to the United Nations, as of October 2011 the Earth's population exceeded 7 billion people, just twelve years after reaching 6 billion. It will grow to more than 8 billion in 2023, and by 2037, the number will exceed 9 billion.

Some concerned people believe that the rate of our population growth, which has recently been doubling every 50 years, is at the core of many problems confronting us today: global warming, race relations, poverty, crime, etc. Yet during five years of collecting data for this book, not one news item about population growth emerged—until the announcement of our reaching the 7 billion mark! Could this oversight be related to the need for genes in the human brain to evolve faster to meet increasing complexities in today's world? (Remember, the universe is pragmatic and a-moral, following the course of least resistance toward its goal, with no capacity for rational or moral thinking.) If so, faster evolution of the human brain may be related to the growing number of children who have autism and ADHD. The brains of these children may have genetically enlarged too rapidly for adaptation and have gone out of control.

Unconscious Assistance from Humanity

Although we have no control over the fast rate of human brain development, we are assisting with its furtherance. Today most young people are attracted to electronic games—in fact, some even become addicted to them. Speed is at the heart of those games, forcing the brain to work faster and faster. (Studies have shown that neuro-surgeons who play video games are faster and make fewer mistakes in surgery than those who do not play.) In fact, faster growth of the human brain and consciousness may be reflected in the increased speed humanity is experiencing in almost every aspect of its living—from computer games, to multitasking, to packed schedules, to texting 24/7, to jumping from hyperlink to hyperlink. All of these things are taking place— unconsciously, of course—as a means of helping develop the human brain for the complex, fast- changing tasks of today's world. Speed, speed, speed.

ROLE OF HUMANITY: ARTIFICIAL INTELLIGENCE

Humanity has also been addressing the need for sufficient intelligence to make wise choices in our complexifying world through development of artificial intelligence.

For several decades humanity has been experimenting with increasingly sophisticated and complex innovations that are leading toward a machine's brain outperforming the human brain. The point where artificial intelligence (AI) matches the intelligence of the human brain is known in AI circles as "singularity."

Singularity

That point was first reached in 1997 when a computer called "Deep Blue" won a chess match against the world's chess champion, Garry Kasparov. At first people thought it was a fluke—or rigged, but Deep Blue continued to win chess matches. In early 2011 a newer computer, Watson, accomplished the difficult feat of winning a Jeopardy tournament. This convinced many people that it is merely a question of time before singularity becomes a living reality. Some have even set a date for it: 2029.

William Saletan of *Slate* magazine reflected on this movement toward singularity as a cosmic game:

"When the cosmic game between humans and computers is complete, here's how the sequence of moves will read. In the opening, we evolved through engagement with nature. In the middle game, we projected our intelligence onto computers and co-evolved through engagement with them. In the endgame, we merged computers with our minds and bodies, bringing that projected intelligence back into ourselves. The distinction between human and artificial intelligence will turn out to have been artificial."[1344]

Microprocessor Chips

Many developments in microprocessor chips, the "brain" of most electronic devices, has taken place in recent years. A major shift in chip design has made it possible for a billion transistors to crowd onto a microprocessor the size of a fingernail. Another, possibly even greater, development in chip design uses electronic spin ("Spintronics") to carry information. With this method, electrons travel without resistance, losing no energy, and may provide a way to carry more information than even the most advanced silicon-based chips can handle. Nanotechnology ("building active circuitry on the smallest scale that life itself uses") is being used across the board to build computers with almost unlimited memory.

Some scientists are working toward developing a computer that mimics the human brain. A human brain can integrate and react to a constant stream of information, but computers differentiate between processing and storing data. To address the computer's shortcoming, researchers are developing an algorithm for detailed mapping of the human brain.

Other scientists are deciphering brain patterns by analyzing the brain's electrical activity and blood flow when people are pondering certain words and actions. Computers can then be programmed to read these brain patterns.

One of the most significant developments relative to consciousness and choice-making has been chips that enable patients to control prosthetic arms, change TV stations, turn on lights and write on a computer using only their thoughts. Similar technology is being used by the military to develop a "thought helmet" to send silent messages on the battlefield by inserting a microprocessor chip into the helmets of soldiers. Researchers are now moving toward placing a nanosize microchip inside the human skull for faster, clearer reading of thoughts and to provide ready-access to all information on the Internet without any other device.

Connections of the Psyche

Connection at the level of the psyche may be the next frontier. An individual could access the consciousness of another individual directly—from psyche to psyche—similar to the way we now communicate via cell phone and other digital devices with anyone anywhere in the world at any time.

Going a step further, if all the contents of individual human psyches were available from a "cloud" in cyberspace, consciousness would be dramatically advanced. Just as all the information of various cultures, which used to be held in outer containers, has now been put on the Internet, so could all the information stored within a human being be released from its container and stored in a "cloud," where there would be virtually unlimited storage capacity. Consciousness could even reach the point of total accord with the pace of evolution, enabling humanity to move on the forefront of soulf's wave instead of lagging behind. As consciousness for the universe, humanity as a whole would be fulfilling its role—in spades!

Dangers of Artificial Intelligence

The possibilities for AI are immense—and so are its dangers. "Every piece of technology can be used for good or evil."[1345] AI could outperform the human brain, raising the possibility of its choosing to make its own decisions and follow an undesirable course of action. It could also expose people's brains to malicious hackers, who might cause a fatal heart rhythm by compromising an implanted cardiac defibrillator. Scientists are well aware of these hazards and are already recommending that parameters be set before things get out of hand. The intelligence needed by the universe is available. It is now a question of humanity setting limits for its use.

Given the push from the universe in human brain development, and advancement from human scientists in brain research and artificial intelligence, the ability of consciousness to meet the complexities of today's world looks hopeful. The one big open question is whether or not humanity as a whole will open itself to sufficient consciousness to choose a course of action that supports the universe as a single organism. Or is humanity too ego-centered to think in such expansive terms? Humanity's choice in this matter is crucial.

CONNECTING HUMANITY AND CULTURE

As important as evolutionary changes in humanity are, the universe needs more. Its primary concern is with humanity *as a whole*, which requires that people be connected with each other, and with the world, at a much deeper level. In addition, all people must have equal opportunity to expand their consciousness. Otherwise, a few will continue to rise to the task, leaving the masses behind. This is not sufficient, as humanity's level of consciousness is determined by the masses, not by an elite few.

CONNECTING PEOPLE WITH INFORMATION

Abstracting Information

To this end, energy moved humanity toward abstracting a huge chunk of the material world to make information available to everyone for wise choice-making. At the same time, it energized humans to develop new ways of distributing this information to all people everywhere. By making information available across the board, the standard for consciousness is raised rather than settling for the lowest common denominator. Humanity as a whole is now able to reach a level where it can—if it chooses—make choices at a higher level of consciousness. That cannot happen through just a few enlightened individuals; it needs participation of the masses.

The Internet

Accordingly, humanity was energized to release contents of communication from their containers. iTunes was one of the first to buy in, offering single pieces of music as downloads. Overcoming this huge psychological hurdle resulted in a novel system that connected transmissions electronically in a worldwide web, the Internet. The Internet is pushing the edges of the world we live in, the way the universe is expanding its outer "edges," and we are expanding the edges of consciousness.

The British library began digitizing 3½ centuries of newspapers and made them available to everyone online; Google designed a plan to scan all the books in the world and stock the Internet with them; and the 2008 World Economic Forum even hosted a "Global dialog" through YouTube. Before long, people around the world were contributing information to this communication freeway, necessitating its continual enlargement as contents outgrew the size of the pathway.

This was a giant step in leveling humanity and making wise choice-making more possible for everyone. No longer was information available only to educated persons. People in all countries and from all walks of life could dip into the pool of wisdom gathered from every culture throughout the ages. Humanity had begun its long journey toward raising the consciousness level of humanity as a whole.

Broadband

As time went on, the plethora of information exceeded the Internet's capacity, and some people in remote areas were excluded from the information highway. To meet this challenge, Broadband came into existence. It dramatically expanded and extended the communication highway, like the lines of a roadmap reaching the smallest lane in a remote

WHERE IN THE WORLD IS GOD?—HUMANITY AS MIRROR

area. That made it possible for virtually everyone to be included in the information exchange. This high-speed Internet connectivity has been called the most transformational technological advance since the printing press, comparable to the linkage in transportation in the 20th century. The only drawback has been lack of funds. However, countries throughout the world have made development of Broadband a priority, so in time it will happen. As of early 2020, 93.7% of the American population had broadband access

CONNECTING PEOPLE WITH EACH OTHER

Person to Person

Along with dissemination of information through the Internet, humans themselves needed to be connected worldwide to become viscerally conscious of their oneness. Humanity was nudged to expand the existing worldwide connections to include human relationships. Finding a path of least resistance, driving energy gave birth to MySpace, Facebook and other social websites, immediately drawing people around the world into their domain. People began to sense that everyone is part of even the remotest areas of the world. In reflecting on the phenomenon, Elizabeth Drescher, assistant professor at the Graduate Theological Union, said "We can be with people all over the world at any time, and this is changing consciousness."[1346]

As wonderful as this was, a gnawing within humanity desired more: to be freed from a desktop computer, which limited them to its location.

New Containers

Among the multiple forms of containers that developed after contents were abstracted from books, newspapers, magazines, phone books, CD's, etc. were smartphones. They became an immediate hit because people could access friends and information regardless of where they happened to be at the moment. Within a few months, ten thousand applications (APPS) flooded the market, fleshing out countless possibilities. Among these innovations were location-based services (LBS), which provide information about one's immediate surroundings—where to find a restaurant, bank, or the nearest public bathroom—and override the feeling of being a stranger in a foreign land. A college freshman captured the feeling of many people toward smartphones in saying, "I can't live without it. It's like water or food."

The task of connecting individuals worldwide had happened.

COHERING HUMANITY: GLOBALIZING

With expansion and openness of communication, centuries of encrusted boundaries began to dissolve at every level of society—internationally, nationally and publicly, as well as socially and personally. Categories were starting to blur, and people were drawn even closer together. The time was right for globalization, as the human brain and population size were becoming large enough to handle the complexities of living globally.

Globalization at its most pervasive, but unseen, level occurs every spring. Ozone from Asia wafts into states west of the Rocky Mountains. At the same time, emissions from the United States drift across the Atlantic Ocean to Europe.

It also happens in visible ways, as countries across the globe reach out to one another in business transactions and collaboration, offering aid to one another and sharing cultural developments. For instance, telemedicine (which transfers medical information through interactive, audiovisual media for consulting, conducting examinations and directing medical procedures) is now available for cities and remote areas all over the globe. A South African company offers banking services via cell phone for the world's 5.5 billion "unbanked" poor people.

Outsourcing

People usually connect globalization with outsourcing but fail to see beyond the pluses (or minuses, depending on one's viewpoint) for the United States. Formerly manufacturing was done in one location. Now it is often split between two locations: one in the homeland for research and development, and another somewhere overseas to keep it going. For example, in Silicon Valley a few, highly-paid people do the innovating, and the work to keep it going is sent overseas, a process that is similar to the separation of content from container. In both cases, the connection between countries moves the world closer together.

Outsourcing works in a variety of ways. The Indian edition of Craigslist ran a listing for a newspaper journalist, based in India, to report on the city government of Pasadena, California, a feat that would have been impossible to accomplish without the current speed of electronic devices. In a reverse situation, India's outsourcing giant, Infosys, hires young Americans, trains them in India, and redeploys them to the United States. This model has been embraced by much of the tech world, and U.S. companies such as IBM, Accenture, and Oracle all go to India, hiring engineers as fast as they can.

Collaboration

People with a common interest such as science and technology have entered into collaborative research across the world. Collaboration has taken place before, but researchers did not have common access to the Internet and its applications to connect them globally in real time. With this advantage, collaborative research is progressing more quickly with less duplication of experiments. Each scientist can build on the findings of others.

Scientists are collaborating widely in terms of disciplines. Stanford University has formed an innovative Bio-X program promoting collaborations between wide-ranging fields of scientists working at the interface of quantitative science, physics, engineering and biology.

Public/private ventures

Some scientists are engaged in public/private ventures. NASA and Google have collaborated to monitor CO_2 pollution and forest destruction, contributors to global warming.

A widely-used form of collaboration between the public and private sectors is outsourcing city services to private contractors, especially paving roads, trimming trees and collecting garbage. Some cities, including New York, have hired private conservancies and non-profit groups or foundations to operate their parks.

Collaboration stretches across the continents. Cisco Systems collaborated with South Korea in building New Songdo City, designed for a million people. The city includes a 100-acre park modeled after Central Park in Manhattan and is fully equipped with sophisticated technology.

Some collaboration recognizes roots of the seen world in the unseen world, an indispensable understanding for higher consciousness. The International Space Station, for example, has become a hub for cross-cultural collaboration, and eight nations have agreed to explore the lunar surface together. Along with probing in outer space, discoveries in the sub-atomic world have opened a deeper level of understanding of evolution. These collaborative efforts at the edges of the known and the seen make it possible for humanity to cooperate more fully with the evolutionary thrusts of the universe.

DISSOLVING BOUNDARIES

Another way besides globalization in which cosmic energy has moved to draw humanity closer to each other and to the natural world is through dissolving boundaries. This is happening in many sectors of society, from office arrangements to news articles, from personal to social relationships, from relationship with animals to components of electronic devises. Boundary-breaking is happening all around us, often leading to the blurring of categories and the need to rethink meanings of words.

Work

Until the latter half of the 20th century, offices were usually discreet units with doors, offering maximum privacy. The norm gradually shifted to a large, common space broken up with individual cubicles. Now office configuration has morphed into open areas with armchairs, extra conference rooms, and tables that workers can use with laptops. Privacy is out. Collaboration is in.

Journalism has followed a similar course. Framing discrete articles is falling by the wayside, releasing them to become an ongoing series of news dispatches. This aligns journalism more closely with the mode of the universe, which energizes happenings without boundaries.

Electronics

Electronics exhibit the most obvious boundary breaking. A recent example is Google's interactive system that completely dissolves the wall between television and the Internet. Users can search TV the way they search the Web, seeking out a specific piece of content, whether it was scheduled for a TV broadcast or a website video.

One would be hard-pressed to find *any* electronic gadget today that does not incorporate at least two or three different functions. Given multiple functions, the "phone" part of smartphones has become almost irrelevant. People use them to tweet friends, check stock market fluctuations, read a book or find a restaurant, but seldom do they use them to call someone.

Pets and Humans

The human-made boundary between humanity and the natural world is also being dissolved. A striking example is the relationship between humans and animals, a path of least resistance.

Animals frequently appear as "human interest" stories in the media, as more American households have pets than children. Sometimes animals are mentioned first in headlines, such as "Pets, family escape bedroom blaze." Pets may even trump the family entirely and move to center stage, leaving the family as almost an afterthought: "Firefighters rescue dog from fire that ruins house." The news item went on to say, "The first crew went in with water hoses and found a 'very affectionate' but frightened dog in a bedroom. It appeared to be a terrier. . .Four people had escaped from the house before or during the fire."[1347]

Dogs have been upgraded from "Man's best friend" to "member of the family." (Two-thirds of pet owners consider their pets family members.) In keeping with their new status, legislation in some parts of the country now refers to those who have pets as "guardians" rather than "owners." Both dogs and cats are welcome in most hotels, and PetSmart intends to increase the number of PetsHotels to 435. The pet industry has become big business, expanding 36 percent to $45 billion in 2006.

Most dogs and cats now have "people" names, like Max (which rates #1), leaving the Fidos, Snoopys and Lassies to their ancestors. Many dogs and cats also have Facebook accounts and followers in Twitter.

The lifestyle of pets is starting to parallel the lifestyle of humans, a sign that pets have become a channel for humanity to draw closer to the natural world.

Personal and Social Boundaries

Breaking boundaries in personal and social relationships is occurring at an almost breathtaking rate. Informality has been easing its way into all aspects of our culture for several decades, with Fridays becoming dress-down days, receptionists greeting visitors by their first name, and women wearing pants to work. These have become so commonplace they no longer draw attention.

Gays and Lesbians

Taboos are constantly being shattered. Mary Cheney, daughter of the former Vice President, is a prime example. As a lesbian, she had a sperm donor, was pregnant out of wedlock, has a lesbian partner, and lives in Virginia where same-sex marriage and civil unions were banned. Yet this did not rock the boat in mainstream media. It was merely another day's news item.

Since then, acceptance of gays and lesbians has gained traction. The armed forces have broken down the barrier to those who are openly gay, same-sex marriage is now federally legal in all 50 states, and about half of Americans say that gay marriages should be legal. Gay story lines have become more prominent in movies, and bisexual, lesbian and transgender characters are almost commonplace on television. California has gone so far as to legislate that history textbooks include discussion of the contributions of gays, bisexuals and transgender people to the state and nation's history.

Sex

Explicit sex is no longer censored from the morning news, spoken of euphemistically or relegated to X-rated films. Media unabashedly speak of oral sex, orgasm, condoms and you- name-it. "Sex in the City" and "Tell Me That You Love Me," which has been dubbed "the most sexually explicit-show to ever air on mainstream TV," leave the bedroom door open without a blush. The National Health Service of Sheffield, England, sent a leaflet to schools likening the health benefits of eating fruits and vegetables, and exercising, to the benefits of masturbating twice a week. Their slogan was: "(A)n orgasm a day keeps the doctor away."

Marriage

Living with a partner outside of marriage has become ho-hum, and unwed mothers hardly raise an eyebrow. In the United States co-habitation continues to increase, while married households are now in the minority. As a senior fellow at the Brookings Institute said, "The culture is shifting, and marriage has almost become a luxury item, one that only the well-educated and well paid are interested in." In some European countries with declining birthrates, this is especially true. People are more concerned with a newborn's health than with the marriage status of the parents.

Birth

Birth options, too, have opened up, breaking boundaries that never disclosed their hidden possibilities. Ready-made embryos are available, and giving birth at an advanced age is possible, not to mention the proliferation of fertility clinics to guide people in choosing from an array of possibilities for giving birth.

All these changes have brought into question the true meaning of words such as "father" and "mother." Unconscious boundaries that have always encased their meaning have eroded, throwing into question not only what *they* mean, but all words that cling to assumptions about their meaning.

Children and Youth

The "modesty shield" between parents and offspring has been shattered. Children and teenagers have lost any sense of privacy, as parents can check on them 24/7 via webcams, surveillance cameras, cell phones, Facebook, and GPS. Whether or not this boundary-breaking results in closer relationships is in question.

Family Law

Family law and its terminology have been deeply affected by changes in relationships. Every state in the U.S. now allows no-fault divorce. "Alimony," which used to refer to a man's support of his wife after divorce, has been replaced by "maintenance" and" support," which are gender-neutral. "Parenting-time" is now used instead of "custody" and "visitation" to suggest equal importance of both parents. These are just a few of the countless changes that new forms of relationship have brought about.

Transparency

Growing concern with dissolving boundaries is not limited to personal relationships. Finances and other personal data, which have traditionally been considered taboo for public revelation, are also being exposed to public view.

A web site, Red Ink, invites the public to share parts of their bank accounts, tax forms and mortgage records to make them smarter consumers with greater economic clout. The site believes this "would level the playing field between individuals and banks and businesses who already make use of their access to your financial information." People could potentially wield influence by collectively spending—or not spending—at certain businesses.

Pilot projects are exploring ways to increase charitable giving through releasing information about income and one's own charitable giving; reducing national gas usage by posting one's gas bill online; and sharing medical and educational data.

The energy behind the desire for openness and transparency is most evident through Wikileaks, an amorphous network in more than a dozen countries that reveals classified documents. Their web site says, "Publishing improves transparency, and this transparency creates a better society for all people."

Blurring of Categories

One dissolving boundary is so pervasive that we are usually unconscious of the profound impact it is making on our lives over time: the boundary between reality and virtuality. It is often not clear where one stops and the other begins. Virtual reality has blurred that line.

Vanishing Point was an artificial reality game used as a form of viral marketing, in which teams of strangers collaborated on the Internet to solve giant puzzles, with clues in widely scattered locations. Clues included messages hidden in a "Bill Gates speech, a light show that used the fountains outside the Bellagio Hotel in Las Vegas as a canvas for clues, skywritten messages above four cities, coded images projected onto the walls of various monuments and a fireworks extravaganza with a secret message in the skies above Seattle." The game drew 70,000 participants to the puzzles and more than 20 million page views at the Vanishing Point website. [1348]

Second Life is a web site where a person (visually represented by their choice of an avatar) enters a virtual world to explore, shop, go to restaurants, play games, see movies—do the same things they would do in real life. According to its literature, members of Second Life design the site's "global community working together to build a new online space for creativity [and] collaboration," building a virtual world in which people have authority to enter in and experiment in any way they wish. An opportunity Second Life offers that real life does *not* is trying something out without backlash if the choice does not pan out. The chance to make mistakes without punishment can build confidence, broaden experiences and enable people to become more nearly the unique individuals they truly are.

Successful experiences online often transfer over to real life. For example, people who have never been especially interested in environmental concerns frequently become involved with them in Second Life. Many report that their experience in Second Life has carried over to real life, where they are now involved in some way with environmental concerns.

A reverse blurring is happening in the real world, where apps are revolutionizing the shopping experience by blurring the online/offline wall. While shopping in actual stores, shoppers can check their smart phone to compare prices and other information about products, store locations, and which stores carry the merchandise they want. Is this called shopping online? Or offline?

FULFILLMENT OF INDIVIDUALS

A third facet of cohering humanity worldwide is enabling people to fulfill their lives as individuals. This matters because the consciousness level of the masses determines the consciousness level of humanity. These are average people, not the powerful, highly educated and famous.

Leveling of the power and authority of the privileged few is required to open the eyes of the masses to the possibility of their personal fulfillment.

Emergence of the Individual

Social websites

When individuals are connected with their innate authority and power, the resulting self-esteem opens the door to personal fulfillment. The Internet provides a path of least resistance for this to happen through social websites like MySpace, Facebook and Twitter. Facebook shows one's picture(s), lots of biographical information, likes and dislikes, and anything else one wishes to share with others. Twitter acts like a stream of consciousness, recording whatever is on your mind—right now—and putting it out to whoever is interested in reading it. Blogs, too, add to the growing number of possibilities for self-publishing, raising the status of individuals by providing a space for self-expression, opinions and ideas that are put on the Internet for the entire world to see.

New status of YOU

Early on, *Time* magazine recognized the powerful significance of what was happening to individuals by naming "YOU" as Person of the Year in 2006, underscoring its pronouncement with a mirror on the front cover of its magazine. There was no mistaking that the editors, indeed, meant YOU, whoever you are, the individual, average person, and that YOU now have VIP status.

This new birthing sprouted in many forms and places, encouraged by various segments of society. Average people were invited to ask questions via YouTube videos for the political conventions of 2008 and to submit ideas for SuperBowl commercials for beer. They choose the new American Idol and update Wikipedia. Colleges are more interested in a prospective student's unique passion in life and show less enthusiasm for those who fit into a cookie cutter mold, despite acceptable GPA and College Board scores. Suddenly the average, unique person has gained prominence, while expert opinions and collective norms are fading into the background.

Individuals and institutions

For some time, individuals have been showing less loyalty to institutions. Lifetime marriage to one's work fell by the wayside when individuals started exercising their own inner authority and moved on to a different company when it benefited them personally. A new generation of politicians revealed less loyalty to their own political party, endangering incumbent politicians, who needed strong party backing. They demonstrated that just a few individual activists could upset the applecart. Shareholders in stock companies showed less loyalty to the recommendations of Boards of Directors and stepped up their proxy resolutions, netting them a 59 percent success rate. Commenting on the success of a shareholder resolution at Applebee's that triggered a nine percent jump in its shares, a Bear Stearns analyst said, "Our immediate reaction is one of surprise that the long-term course of this company could be altered by pressure from a relatively small activist shareholder." But it happened.

Exerting power and authority

Individuals popped up all over the globe, in positive and negative ways, exercising their newfound power and authority. Parents began to see the individual needs of children and summoned their own inner authority to develop charter schools. Summer camps started catering to individual interests, shifting from "generalist" to "specialized," and featuring tennis, art, computers or the like—but not all of the above. Children chose the area of their own particular interest. Gift card malls sprung up at Safeway, Walgreen's and Target to match one's personal choice of gifts. When a birthday, Christmas, graduation or other occasion comes along, no one knows better than the recipient what the perfect gift is. Gift-giving today has put a different slant on "It's the thought that counts."

Entrepreneurs exhibited a new mode, taking back former projections onto experts and using their own power and authority to address the world's problems. No longer did "entrepreneur" automatically refer to the Nelson Rockefellers, Jimmy Carters, or Zuke Zuckerbergs of the world. "Entrepreneur" could refer to anyone, even ordinary citizens.

One entrepreneur developed NanoLab, a handheld lab for areas where lab equipment is not available. A few graduate students promoted a low-cost baby incubator through a video on YouTube. A single college student developed Orphans Against AIDS, which pays for schooling for children affected by AIDS in poor countries. Another college student collected old reading glasses while in college and shipped them to poor countries, providing care for 200,000 people.

Collective use of individual authority

Perhaps the most visible sign of inner authority and power rising within the average person was seen in the streets of the Middle East and northern Africa. When hundreds of thousands of Iranians marched silently through the streets of Tehran, protesting the disputed presidential election, the government was able to quell their demonstrations. However, the protests merely shifted to online, where tech-savvy Iranians tweeted pictures and messages to the world in real- time as events unfolded. At the same time, hackers targeted Web pages of Iran's leadership, demanding Internet freedom. To protect the activists, a web site called NedaNet was launched, providing a system of proxy sites to cloak the location of users in Iran from the Iranian government. In turn, a San Franciscan assisted the Iranian techies by launching Haystack, a program to help them wiggle past government filters. Each step of the way, individuals saw the need and brought their own particular abilities to the protest, helping one another in whatever way they were able.

More recently an outbreak of demonstrations in the Arab world has become viral. Individuals across Egypt, Libya, Yemen, Bahrain and Syria took to the streets in peaceful protest of their repressive regimes, with resulting success in some of them—at least for now. Fred Hyatt of the

Washington Post commented on the phenomenon: "In just a few months, ordinary people across the region—ordinary in everything but their courage—have upended decades of expert assurances that Arabs would never rebel against their dreadful dictators.

All generations have demonstrated, but the demonstrations of these courageous individuals have a different formation. They are not "groups," but "individuals" linking their own inner authority with that of others to exert a common power. They are informed through the Internet and have chosen to express their own concerns. These are average, everyday citizens making a difference to society in ways that are in keeping with their personality, interests, gifts and capabilities. One measure of their effectiveness is governmental censorship, which expanded from four countries in 2002 to 40 in 2010.

Energy from within these individuals rose up in defense of their own rights, and they responded with inner authority and innate power. While their minds were on the task at hand, they were doing their part in raising consciousness to a higher level.

REGRESSIVE ENERGY

In any evolutionary thrust, negative and positive energy pull in opposite directions—balanced in favor of the positive—providing the grist needed to propel the movement forward. Accordingly, the energy engaged in drawing humanity together—through the Internet, developing robots, dissolving boundaries and releasing the inner authority and power of the individual—has also actualized negative forms.

Cyber Warfare

Balancing the many positive uses of the Internet to cohere humanity is its use to attack another country, thus separating people. The Pentagon considers cyberspace a war-fighting domain, and President Obama declared that cyber-attacks on the United States could be considered an act of war.

The Pentagon employed thousands of young computer geeks ("hacker soldiers") to blend new technologies into U.S. war planning. The scenario, as drawn by Christopher Drew and John Markoff of the *New York Times*, boggles the mind: "At a Pentagon facility… rock music blares and empty cans of Mountain Dew pile up as engineers create tools to protect the Pentagon's computers." Every day thousands of attacks from organized criminals and hackers for nations, including Russia and China, are launched on federal and private computer systems in the United States. [1349]

The danger of cyber warfare is of great concern. David Ignatius, espionage expert, wrote for the *Washington Post*: "[At the White House] the Situation Room's biggest nightmare is cyberwar— electronic malware that would penetrate to the inner lobes of the national security brain." Terrorists could sit with a keyboard, remotely shutting down factory assembly lines or devastating cities by opening a dam's floodgates. China's intelligence agencies could embed a malicious code in Chinese-made computer chips, enabling them to take command of U.S. computers by remote control over the Internet. Already international hackers have withdrawn $9 million from 2,100 ATM terminals in 280 cities across the globe in 12 hours. Although cyber warfare would not be as deadly as atomic war, cyber-attacks "with the ability to threaten the U.S. money supply is the equivalent of today's nuclear weapon," said Mike McConnell, former director of U.S. national intelligence.[1350]

Robots

While some boundaries are broken down through use of robots, others are erected through their use in war. Robots operate machine guns and explode Improvised Explosive Devices (IEDs) in combat zones. Predator drones, pilot-less aerial vehicles, collected intelligence and conducted bombing raids. The Pentagon set 2015 as the deadline for one-third of its ground combat vehicles to be unmanned, self-thinking machines to fight in war zones. However, ethical and safety questions around the use of robots are holding back any rush to use them extensively in fighting future wars.

They are so effective, such as plugging themselves in when they need a charge, there is danger they could take over their own decision-making.

Terrorists

As energy rises in most of humanity to break down boundaries that fulfill the individual and benefit the world, some individuals use their newfound authority and power for destructive purposes. Terrorists are the ones of greatest concern internationally.

Terrorists present a new and different kind of challenge for governments worldwide, whose armed forces were designed for warfare between two highly consolidated and structured armies. According to Max Boot, Council on Foreign Relations, the enemies of the United States today are "very decentralized, very networked. They're sort of the eBay of terrorism."[1351]

Mumbai

A prime example was the terrorist attack on the global financial capital of India. A group of terrorists attacked a luxury hotel in Mumbai and a Jewish travelers' center run by an ultra- orthodox sect, leaving 166 people dead and 300 injured. Their ability to spread terror was largely increased by the use of the Internet and other advanced technology, which linked them in real time with Pakistan-based handlers.

Masks

Another problem for traditional armies is the use of masks, which were used by both the fighters of Hamas and Fatah in the Palestinian civil war in Gaza. Political theorist Yaron Ezrahi, said:

"These masks are the uniforms of the new armies of the 21st century and the new kind of violence, [which] no longer distinguishes between war against the stranger and war against members of your own society… this new violence doesn't have a front, it doesn't have a face. It doesn't have boundaries."

"These young men do not report to anyone above them. They have no ranks. No leader can ever be sure of their allegiance… You can expect to see a lot more confrontations between armies in uniforms and helmets and armies in blue jeans and masks."[1352]

The fact that "no leader can ever be sure of their allegiance" caused a major problem for the United States in Afghanistan and Pakistan. Figuring out loyalties of the Taliban and al-Qaida was like a shell game, always shifting, never sure.

Suicide bombers

An even more direct form of individuals using their inner authority and power for destructive purposes is with suicide bombs. Suicide bombers are globalized, observing no national boundaries. Originally they were confined to combat zones, but they have spread virally throughout the world. They are "martyrs without borders."

HEALING IMBALANCES

With the world drawing closer together and boundaries between individuals and nations beginning to fade, a layer of imbalanced relationships surfaced. In order for humanity to become one people in one world, these relationships needed to transform.

Three particular forms of imbalance glared openly: imbalance between the East and West, humanity and the natural world, and the powerful few and the masses.

BALANCING EASTERN AND WESTERN WORLDS

With developing consciousness, Americans began to see their own country more realistically in relation to the rest of the world. They observed the balance scales tipping toward the East in terms of world prominence and power and saw that China had become a major player on the world scene. What the rest of the world had recognized for some time, Americans could no longer deny: As the United States struggles to stay #1 in the world,

China is rising in world stature, overshadowing the spotlight on the United States. At the rate it is changing and growing, China will overtake the United States as front-runner in the world by the middle of the 21st century.

A sure sign of this new consciousness is the demand for learning Chinese in the United States. As of 2010, Chinese became the third most-tested Advanced Placement language on the College Board exams. Although this interest probably derived from the business and trade world, it is nonetheless significant that the next generation sees China as a major world partner in their future.

China's business and trade are flourishing. China is Intel's second-largest consumer market after the U.S., and U.S. imports from China increased 101 percent between 2000 and 2005. China overtook the U.S. in car sales in 2009 and is the world's most populous mobile phone market. Even more worrisome to the United States is Hong Kong's becoming second in the world for launching IPO's, a fact that supports the belief of nearly half of Americans that China has already surpassed the United States in innovation.

Internally, China has also undergone significant change. It is experiencing the biggest migration of people from rural to urban centers "in the history of mankind," while its illiteracy rate has dropped significantly below the rate for developing countries as a whole.

One-ninth of China's energy needs are now being met by hydropower generated by the Three Gorges Dam. The dam was designed to produce energy equivalent to the output of 18 coal or nuclear power plants and to increase China's shipping volume 400 percent.

Perhaps the most significant choice of direction for China has been its Green Revolution, seen by Thomas Friedman of the *New York Times* as the most important thing to happen in the first decade of the 21st century. China became aware that energy technology is both a necessity and an opportunity. Just the volume of wind, solar, mass transit, nuclear and more efficient coal- burning projects launched in 2009 is itself stunning.

According to a survey in 2008, the people of China are more satisfied than people of any other nation. Eighty-six percent are content with their country's direction and 82 percent are satisfied with their national economy.

With confidence, a new China is now willing to reach out to the world, symbolized by the Beijing Olympics Bird's Nest and its cutting edge architecture. Internal development, trade and outreach to the rest of the world has made it one of the two fastest-growing of the G-20 countries, with the third largest economy in the world. Dollars that spell "higher debt" to Americans read "higher earnings" to the Chinese. In 2010 the World Economic Forum even questioned whether a Beijing Consensus would replace the Washington Consensus (the free- market, pro-trade and globalization policies promoted by the U.S.).

Patrick Buchanan wrote: "The world is witnessing the passing of the United States as the greatest industrial power and the most self-sufficient republic the world had ever seen... An end to the Second American Century, as the Asian Century begins." [1353]

BALANCING HUMANITY AND THE NATURAL WORLD

If the environment is sick, so are humans, as humanity is an intrinsic part of the natural world. There is no escape.

Dawning consciousness of this reality brought humanity to concerted action following the release of Al Gore's film, "An Inconvenient Truth." Scientists had noticed global warming for decades prior to the film, but a reluctant humanity kept denying it. The specter of scaled-down living was too great.

Greening the Environment

After release of Gore's film, greening the environment became a cool thing to endorse, as if floodgates had suddenly burst open. Even major oil companies felt the need to hop aboard the bandwagon, one of which took a stance with the environment and kept advertising "We agree!" A green movement coalesced and spread around the Earth, making it "politically correct" to heal humanity's relationship with the natural world. The universe had found a course of least resistance to restore the health of Planet Earth.

Alternative energy

This new attitude toward healing the environment erupted in a multitude of ways throughout the world. The core focus was on development of alternative energy. Everything from corn ethanol to pond algae to pecan shells was used to make biofuels. Pacific Gas and Electric Company started using natural gas from the manure of 5,000 cows to create electricity for 250,000 homes. Wind turbines sprung up on hilltops, while rows of gigantic mirrors placed in sunny, open spaces set to work as giant boilers to provide solar thermal energy. Experimentation with geothermal, space solar, photovoltaic and fusion energy began. No method of harnessing energy was off the table, though nuclear energy remained highly controversial.

Government involvement

All levels of government became involved, and venture capital investment in international clean tech surged. The United Nations' Montreal Protocol, which replaced chlorofluorocarbons with hydrofluorocarbons, was ratified by 195 nations, and 22 of the world's largest cities joined the "Clinton Climate Initiative" to limit global warming. The United Arab Emirates Masdar Initiative made the UAE (the fourth largest OPEC oil producer) a center for the development and implementation of clean energy technology. Before the Initiative, the UAE had been singled out as one of the world's highest per capita emitters of greenhouse gases.

Tired of waiting for federal action, California mandated its own Global Warming Solutions Act of 2009 to reduce greenhouse gas emissions to 1990 levels by 2020. At the city level, Washington, D.C. started requiring both government and private buildings to be certified as "green."

Involvement of businesses and environmentalists

Businesses, too, became involved. Plug-in hybrid vehicles were developed, and Zipcars for car- sharing showed up on streets throughout the U.S. Wal-Mart developed an "eco-rating" system for hundreds of thousands of its products and experimented with alternative building materials, lighting, power systems and designs in two new green stores. Silicon Valley venture firms invested $1 billion in clean technologies. And New Resources Bank started loaning to businesses developing environmentally friendly products, and looked for depositors who wanted their money used for projects that create jobs and profits by reducing global warming.

Environmental groups, of course, continue to prod and support efforts to heal the natural world, bringing ingenious ideas into play to reach their goal. Two environmental groups made the buy- out of TXU, which stood poised to build 11 coal-fired power plants, contingent (by the buyers) on winning praise for its greenhouse gas plan. Wangari Maathai, 2004 recipient of the Nobel Peace Prize, founded a movement that planted 30 million trees throughout Africa and inspired others to follow suit in different areas of the world.

BALANCING THE SEEN AND UNSEEN WORLDS

"Our main ecological problems, like climate change… are linked to our overuse of material energy," says Brigitte Eggers, Jungian analyst and ecologist. Both the material and psychic spheres impact everything, so any imbalance between the two upsets the careful balancing of the universe as a whole. If we have hopes of healing our rift with the universe, we must consider inner and outer nature equally, as both are needed for the transformation of energy.[1354]

Obesity

Human obesity

Obesity in humans, the form of obesity we know best, is an example of overuse of material energy, causing a serious health problem for our nation. Beginning early in the 1960s, Americans started down a dangerous road of developing an imbalance with their own human nature. The nation gradually gained weight until the 1980s when stomachs suddenly ballooned. Now the trend is pushing the United States toward becoming a nation of obese and overweight people.

The obesity rate in children and teens has tripled since 1980. Forty percent of young women and 25 percent of young men weigh too much to enlist in the United States military. Obesity has not spared even the newest family members, dogs. Veterinarians say it has reached epidemic proportions in them and appears to be increasing. Five percent of dogs in the U.S. are obese and another 20 to 30 percent overweight, making obesity one of their biggest health issues.

Newer editions of *The Joy of Cooking* have lowered the predicted number of servings for identical recipes from previous editions, as our voracious appetites have gone out of control. However, changes began to sprout up when First Lady Michelle Obama awakened Americans' consciousness by starting a vegetable garden at the White House, and later publishing a cookbook of recipes created in the White House kitchen. She highlighted healthy eating and the health hazard of obesity. This resulted in many restaurants posting nutritional information on their menus and lowering the number of calories in food preparation.

Galaxies and obesity

Left without restraint, galaxies would have suffered a similar fate to that of humans by consuming too many stars, planets and other bits of matter. However, the universe governed its growth with "dark energy," which "prevents the biggest clusters of galaxies from getting too fat … from essentially overeating." [1355] Since humanity was created from stardust, we could say humanity has "inherited" its propensity toward obesity from the natural world but has yet to discover its own form of "dark energy" to prevent the population from getting too fat. A recent study by the Institute of Medicine suggests that giving toddlers the amount of food they should eat may help curb obesity in the future, as 2- and 3–year-olds are sensitive to portion size. Humanity may be inadvertently training them to overeat by giving them larger portions than their bodies need.

Symbolic obesity

Looking at obesity symbolically, one discovers that it is running wild in the world, far beyond human stomachs. The world's population is doubling every fifty years, crowding out other species and seriously affecting biodiversity. Large corporations have added to their weight by gobbling up smaller companies, like Pac Man on a spree. Financial institutions grew "too big to fail," necessitating the huge bailout in 2008, when they encountered obesity's downside. Humanity has made almost suicidal use of material energy, including oil, forests and other material resources. Excessive consumerism and growth of personal debt got out of hand, leading to the massive debt crisis that is affecting not only the United States but the entire world. As Thomas Friedman wrote:

> "We have created a system for growth that depended on our building more and more stores to sell more and more stuff made in more and more factories in China, powered by more and more coal that would cause more and more climate change but earn China more and more dollars to buy more and more U.S. T-bills so America would have more and more money to build more and more stores to sell more and more…

> "What if the crisis of 2008 represents something much more fundamental than a deep recession? What if it's telling us that the whole growth model… is unsustainable?"[1356]

What is the "dark energy" that will rebalance the "dark matter" in humanity and stop it from growing fatter? What will release humanity from "too much-ness" and enable it to find deeper, healthier satisfaction in the unseen world?

Abstractualization (See Appendix F)

The broadest new way of rebalancing matter and energy is through a process of "abstractualization," *abstracting* creations from the *actualized* world and providing a new home for their contents in the unseen world. The life within creations is released from its material form and transformed into a non-material level of existence, leaving the material world less crowded with things.

Examples of this process have already been noted, without explanation, in the chapters about development of the Internet and electronic devices. Texting abstractualizes communications by abstracting formal language into texting language and digitizing the content. Information is abstractualized into cyberspace. Books, magazines, CDs, newspapers, mailboxes, post offices, music stores, book stores, telephone booths, voting booths, maps, heavy cameras, desktop computers—*all* have been increasingly left behind as the life within them, their real value to the universe, has been digitized.

Abstractualizing to the Web requires Internet users to work with abstracted material—something real from everyday life, but in abstracted form. That ability is also necessary for sublating Religion and Mythology within ourselves, as we must be able to accept those concepts as abstractions. The attractiveness of the Internet may be paving the way for this to happen more easily throughout humanity.

As we know, whenever consciousness moves to a higher level, it leaves nothing behind. Contents of former levels are always sublated into the new form. This is especially obvious in the case of Americans Elect, which is breathing new life into the political process of the Massachusetts "town meeting" of early America, and seemingly crafting "a more perfect union" in the process. This could be democracy at its finest.

While the most pervasive example of abstractualization is digitizing into cyberspace, other areas of living manifest a similar process, especially in work life.

Work

The recession of 2008 may have been more than it appears to be on the surface. It triggered the closing of stores and factories and the loss of millions of jobs. Joblessness was exacerbated by more people entering into a "do it yourself" mindset, doing everything from home projects to pumping their own gas to using ATM machines instead of tellers to ordering purchases online instead of shopping in real stores. Many of those who were lucky enough to be employed were not happy with their jobs.

More significant for the universe, a widespread abstractualization of work was taking place in the form of tasks becoming digitized (which requires fewer, but more highly educated, workers) and robots performing more tasks. A huge makeover was happening.

In the past, technological innovations and the kinds of jobs they led to were largely in the mechanical realm. Many—perhaps most—of those jobs that have disappeared are never going to return. Too much water has gone over the dam that separates the past from the present needs of the world. Work has shifted toward digitized jobs.

Today innovation itself is abstractualized, as new technology increasingly tilts toward invisible properties. Service technologies, scientific processes and other abstract-oriented enterprises have taken center stage, easing mechanical inventions to the wings.

Robots and other automated services are relieving humanity of manual tasks, freeing humanity for its primary work of developing higher consciousness. The universe needs individuals who engage life in ways that utilize their unique gifts and abilities to fulfill individual personalities. To the (pragmatic) universe, fulfillment of humanity's task trumps the job losses incurred and propels humanity into designing novel ways of meeting the new challenge.

When loyalty to the workplace dissolved, people began migrating toward freedom of time and space in their work life, opting for telecommuting, consulting and jobs that would accompany them and their laptop to wherever they chose to be. They continue to look for ways to abstractualize work and free themselves from the material world.

Corporations have chosen a similar path, releasing companies from the limitations of time and space. Some businesses automate their corporate data centers, a method Hewlett Packard used to cut costs in the sluggish economy. Customer service is increasingly handed over to automation. Companies outsource and offshore work to other countries, keep records in "clouds," and hold international conferences in real time via Skype or Second Life, while online sales continue to grow rapidly every year. Abstractualization is the name of the game. Not only business transactions, but also businesses themselves, are becoming increasingly abstractualized.

MILLENNIAL GENERATION (GEN Y)

The strongest energy of the universe, at any time in history, is invested in the newest generation. They carry the latest genes into the world, are fresh to the world scene and exhibit greater malleability than older generations. They are open to what is, instead of to what has been, are responsive to the energy rising within them, and eager to live the fullness of life.

The Millennials are no exception. But they have something more to offer. They are becoming adults at the same time that humanity itself is entering adulthood. This combination makes it possible for them to live more mature lives than has generally been the case in the past, and to carry humanity to a higher level of consciousness. They came into the world prepared for that task and are already living into a new consciousness.

In addition, they entered the scene at the turn of the millennium when life moved into the Aquarian Age, the age of communication. Amazing strides in communications technology were taking place, making their generation the first to be raised with an innate sense of cyberspace and with the Internet as an integral part of their life.

No other generation can fully understand what it is like to be in their shoes because their psyche has been shaped by an electronic world. Gary Small, neuroscientist at UCLA, may be right. He believes that "society's growing reliance on technology is likely helping to 'rewire' our brains in ways that are not fully understood." The brains of Gen Y, who have spent their entire lives with electronic technology, may already have become rewired. If so, their brains likely have greater plasticity than the brains of older generations.

This would feed into their predisposition to move in new directions of energy flow, making them the most important carriers of life's forward movement today, in terms of needs of the universe. Only their generation has the particular viewpoint, innate wisdom, life experience and aptitude to guide the world in the direction it needs to move in this time of history. Their living is testimony to the universal energy moving in the world today to connect and cohere humanity, and to heal imbalances in the world, areas explored earlier in this chapter.

Many imbalances in the world are a non-issue for Millennials in their everyday interactions, as Millennials accept gays and lesbians, racial differences (40 percent of Millennials are non-white) and cultural practices as a "no-brainer." Raised with ecological consciousness, they have respect for, and regard themselves as part of, the environment. It is just the way life is, and they cooperate with it.

Millennials take to the universe's need for bonding of humanity like a duck takes to water. Facebook, texting and other social media keep them connected to a wide community of people around the clock and provide venues for self-expression. These opportunities reinforce emergence of the "average person" and breaking boundaries between themselves and the world.

Millennials want immediate access to information along with the latest container for it. They are first to move ahead with newer and faster gadgets, leaving behind slower-paced innovations of the past. When adults were flocking to e-mail in 2006, the younger generation was turned off by it because it was not fast enough. They moved on to instant messaging and posting messages on MySpace, and then shifted to Facebook and on to texting, iPads and beyond. As newer, faster forms of digital communication come on the scene, Millennials are there to welcome them.

They feel no need to have information in material form, not even within themselves. With information so readily available on the Internet, why bother holding it in your head? they query. This viewpoint makes much schoolwork seem as archaic as a slide rule or spelling bees, when you have the reliability of calculations and spell check at your fingertips.

Millennials show a particular aptitude for responding to the increased pace of living and to speed in general. They were prepared for this early in life with busily scheduled days, going from soccer practice to music lessons to Boy Scouts, not to mention hours of homework sandwiched in between—or after hours.

They sense intuitively the importance of speed in handling today's complexities and practice it continually through multi-tasking. They routinely juggle an incoming text from a friend, munching on a handful of chips, keeping their eye on a video, checking their Facebook page— oh yes, and doing homework.

As exasperating as this may be for parents, it furthers the child's experience in dealing with complexities. Millennials have developed their own shorthand language for texting and thrive on the competitive speed of computer games. Their genetic makeup, the environment in which they were raised, and their brain structuring have programmed them to respond in these unfamiliar ways, which match the needs of the universe in today's technological developments.

The Millennial generation has been endowed with a sense of the individual's inner authority, and they are eager to exercise it. Some adults scoff at their audacity, seeing it as a sense of entitlement, but Millennials may be learning how to use authority and power in creative ways. It is a needed skill for our time, and trial and error may be the only way they can learn it. No longer do experts and officials hold sway over them, as they are living out the potential of becoming their own saviors. When Millennials need advice and support, they turn to each other, not to experts.

Their boldness in exercising authority has contributed greatly to the movement toward a more egalitarian network of power. A mere glance at the uprisings in the Arab Spring confirms this. It has followed the universal process of opposites becoming sublated within each other and jumping to a higher level of consciousness. In this case, *individuals* have chosen to join with *individuals* who have a common desire, and they have exerted their united power as a *group*. This is different from uprisings of the past, in which a *group*—or *groups*—have come together and exerted their common power. Humanity is beginning to act out the new, higher level of consciousness that is awaiting its full recognition into actuality.

Millennials are uniquely programmed to embrace all these changes in living and to move with them into the future. This challenges the rest of humanity to act counter-intuitively, bucking the age-old belief that the greatest wisdom necessarily resides in the oldest generation. To be sure, those who have experienced the most of life for the longest time make an important contribution in passing on the wisdom they have gleaned, and in connecting the world with its past. But the world also needs to recognize and respect the special wisdom that the newest generation is bringing to our world, take them seriously, and work cooperatively with them. As life continues to evolve in new directions, it will happen increasingly through the Millennial Generation.

For Reflection:

1. ....

....

....

2. ....

....

....

3. ....

....

....

APPENDIX A

LIVING IDEAS

"Living ideas" emerge at the interface of the seen and unseen worlds. They indicate new levels of consciousness breaking through old consciousness.

When the time is "right" in the created world for a new emergence—large or small, at any level of consciousness—the universe senses the readiness. A living idea often builds on a thought that has been growing through time, though sometimes it is a virginal idea. The thought may be at any level of reality and in any form or structure of reality. When a thought that is ripe for furtherance emerges newly in the world, it becomes a "living idea."

Through the universe's connection with humanity in psyche, humanity becomes fascinated by a living idea and often spreads it—and sometimes does not. It depends on the amount of energy vested in the idea, i.e. how much consolidated energy from various parts of humanity adds to its weight. This differs greatly from one living idea to another because of differing levels of consciousness. If consciousness falls on a bell curve, as I think it does, then the middle group— the "average person"—carries energy from the largest number of people, but not necessarily the most energy around a living idea.

Newer levels carry more weight with the universe than older ones, though energy is carried at all levels. The universe responds much more passionately to innovative ideas than to tried-and-true ideas, so novelty holds more energy from the universe.

At the same time, fewer persons are drawn to change and letting go of the past. Most people are reluctant to risk jumping into something brand new. This is why incumbents are usually re- elected.

When humanity becomes more conscious of "living ideas," it will be able to choose whether or not, and how, to actualize them in a particular form at a new level of consciousness. At that point of choice making, a particle-wave actualizes the human choice. Then the "living idea" can spread like a virus.

This book focuses only on those living ideas that are most energized at the newest level of consciousness because they are the ones that hold the most passion from the universe and humanity. They are ideas that have become unstoppable.

APPENDIX B

THE DEVELOPMENT OF CONSCIOUSNESS

In the beginning, before the Big Bang, there was no-thing, only Primal Energy. But a potential seed of consciousness was in that energy.

With the Big Bang, two dimensions came into being—space and time. They are closely associated with Self and Soul, respectively. Self-energy comprises potential forms; Soul-energy comprises potential substance. Together, as spirit-matter, they become actualized creation.

For eons, Self-Soul actualized galaxies. Within one galaxy a particular star was born at exactly the right place and time, with the right conditions, to allow something more to develop. There, at the intersection of time and space, Self and Soul gave birth to consciousness, a new dimension. Whenever Self and Soul actualize a form in this new dimension, they become "soulf." (See Appendix C for a simpler, yet fuller, expression of this structure.)

As time went on, and Self-Soul actualized ever-greater complex forms, animals came into being. At this point consciousness took a jump. From inanimate matter with quasi-consciousness, followed by the plant kingdom with a primitive consciousness, animals developed refined instincts. Each succeeding class of animals developed more highly formed instincts until they fulfilled the limits of their ability to carry consciousness in the evolutionary process.*

---

* A similar process continues simultaneously within former levels of consciousness in all living things. At the lower levels, however, it involves merely maintenance and continuation of the process of their level of consciousness, which is already fully developed within those phyla.

Then a new species of animals developed called anthropos, or the human being, with another leap in the development of consciousness. This new species had, in addition to instincts, a brain with a much larger frontal lobe relative to its size than prior species. This enabled it to carry consciousness to a higher level.

As consciousness grew within humanity, instinctual capacity faded—not completely, but it became much weaker. The fullness of the instinctual level of consciousness continued to be carried by lower forms of animals, and continues to this day. In fact, not only lower animals, nor all species of living things, but inanimate creations as well, still carry the highest form of consciousness, or quasi-consciousness, possible at the time of their creation. A whole series of infinitesimal steps in the development of consciousness has taken place since the time of the Big Bang, each one superseding the previous, highest one at the time of its development.

In the Western world, the formation of human consciousness was expressed in the myth of Adam and Eve, in which God breathes life into Adam. Within that myth, choice making is created to carry consciousness toward its highest level by that species. When anthropos has developed consciousness as far as possible, another species will evolve to carry consciousness in its next created form.

A fuller development of consciousness appears in the figure of Jesus. There the human being breaks away from mythological consciousness and begins development of the conscious ego. Jesus is portrayed as an individual who makes choices in relation to his God, but against his cultural and religious traditions.

How does consciousness develop within humanity? Self, the source of potential forms of energy, carries the seed for consciousness. Soul, catalyst for actualization of potential forms of energy, brings the seed to fruition within humanity. The fertilized seed has become soulf in the world of creation.

The development of human consciousness can most easily be understood by looking at the stages of human development in individuals, a process that is mimicked by humanity as a whole. The infancy stage, in which a child is totally identified with her mother, seeing herself as an extension of her, was mimicked by humanity in animism, in which humanity totally identified with its natural surroundings, "Mother Nature." Humanity's consciousness was one with the animals and nature as a whole.

As humans began to differentiate from their surroundings, they entered a magical stage, the way a young child does at age five or six. They no longer saw themselves as one with nature, but their consciousness saw in nature a magical quality that could aid or harm them. People believed that, if they could tap into this magic through specific actions or words, they could affect their fate.

This magical quality was later projected outside themselves onto gods and goddesses, whom they regarded as rulers of the world, needing to be appeased and venerated. Animist religions had evolved into mythological religions.

With the beginning of truer understandings of the universe, and particularly Earth's no longer being seen as the center of the universe, the heavenly abode of gods and goddesses began to crumble. Along with that, faith in divine figures that had been so powerful in people's lives began to diminish, and people felt a vacuum opening up inside themselves. If there are no gods and goddesses up there in the heavens, does that mean God has abandoned us? they wondered. People were faced with seeing themselves and their place in the universe more objectively, which made it possible for a new, adult consciousness to develop within them.

But humanity, like a horse refusing to cross a stream of water, would not stop clinging to its historical/mythological consciousness and proceed with soulf into a new consciousness. So soulf moved on with the few that were willing to risk something new, while most of humanity remained behind in a juvenile consciousness.

Attributes projected onto gods and goddesses have not been lost. They reside within humanity. If people were willing to see this, they would be less reluctant to move into the new consciousness. Instead of looking to human parents for safety and guidance and power, or to heavenly parents in the form of gods and goddesses, humanity would look within themselves for these qualities. We are now the ones in charge of our own lives and life on the planet in general.

Most humans are not yet willing to accept this responsibility. It seems too overwhelming to admit that such power and authority is within us. And yet, we have outgrown mythological and historical consciousness; it has lost its power. We now must recognize, and become one with, the psychological consciousness that already exists within us—and outside us.

This consciousness contains everything that was there before—all the previous levels of consciousness, all the powers and energies and autonomy. Everything that ever has been in any form of consciousness—and more— still resides within us. The "more" is the merging of soulf with humanity that occurred when the mythological and religious worlds became dissolved within us. That process of "sublation" (See Appendix D) carried with it awareness of our oneness, our total oneness with soulf, and all the power, authority and responsibility that goes with it. Everything we need to live this reality resides within us.

APPENDIX C
THE WORLD THAT JACK BUILT

(For those who have difficulty understanding
the structure of the universe as it has been described)

This is the world that Jack Built.

Here are events that shape the world that Jack built.

We are the folks who play the parts that make
events that shape the world that Jack built.

Soulf has ideas that pop like corn, guiding the folks who play the parts
that make events that shape the world that Jack built.

A crossing exists that hides the unseen, tended by soulf who stokes
ideas that pop like corn, guiding the folks who play the parts that
make events that shape the world that Jack built.

There is a land of Self and Soul behind the crossing that makes them
soulf, who stokes ideas that pop like corn, guiding the folks who
play the parts that make events that shape the world that Jack
built.

A pinprick of darkness before the Big Bang
suddenly burst with a terrible Whang!
opening space for Self and Soul behind the crossing that makes
them soulf, who stokes ideas that pop like corn,
guiding the folks who play the parts that make events
that shape the world that Jack built.

APPENDIX D

PROCESS OF SUBLATION

The developmental process of sublation is threefold:

1. Opposites (e.g. ego-Soul) are seen as undifferentiated. (They are experienced as one and the same.)
2. A gate of separation comes between the opposites, negating their undifferentiated oneness. (Only one opposite is experienced at any given moment.)
3. The negation (the gate of separation) is negated in *thought*, and the opposites collapse into each other. (The opposites are now held together in thought, each containing the other in a living relationship.

(Based on Wolfgang Giegerich, The Soul's Logical Life)

These three stages echo the basic stages of psychological development:

1. Infancy, a stage of undifferentiated oneness with Soul (undifferentiated ego-Soul)

2. Toddler stage, when development of an ego begins (emergence of the gate separating the ego from Soul), and continues throughout later stages of childhood until

3. Full maturity (arrived at by some, and not by others). At this stage, the ego and Soul merge within a new, higher level of consciousness (negation, in thought, of the gate of separation). The ego and Soul collapse into one another, each opposite being fully present in itself within consciousness.

The process at maturity is similar to that of the particle-wave in physics. A particle-wave pulsates back and forth until it actualizes itself in the world of space and time, at which point it folds in on itself and expresses itself as a particle. One could say that the particle-wave has become internally sublated and is now manifesting itself as one.

APPENDIX E

KILLING in WAR

An official study of soldiers in World War II showed that 75 percent of them never shot a bullet at enemy combatants because their conscience interfered when the time came to shoot. They could not bring themselves to pull the trigger when the moment arrived.

This led to the current training procedures for combat duty. By training soldiers to by-pass their conscience on the battlefield, a high percentage will now shoot another human being in a war zone. However, many of them—whether or not they have shot and killed someone in war—say that something remains in their psyche, something they never get rid of. It is as if their conscience is still being pricked, even if they rationally believe they did the right thing for the right cause by killing.

It is telling that the only way the military is able to get people to shoot another human being is to train them to respond without thinking. Instead of dwelling on the meaning of what they are doing, they are taught to ask themselves after every shot fired, "What's the next target?" Their training also includes learning to shout aloud, "Kill, kill, kill!" The human element must be removed from each soldier that is expected to kill on the battlefield. It appears to be a totally abhorrent task for human beings today to perform.

The upside is to know that for 75 percent of the people, killing another human being is so unnatural and distasteful that only the most drastic of measures can wipe that away—and never entirely. Its residue always remains in the human psyche, as witnessed by the overwhelming number of Post Traumatic Stress Disorder (PTSD) casualties in the wars in Iraq and Afghanistan.

The downside, and most perplexing, is that we do not stop to ask ourselves why it is so hard to get soldiers to shoot. If we have to use such drastic means to fight a war, why is nature not cooperating with us? If this is what humanity ought to be doing, there should be something built into people to carry it out, a natural capacity to kill another human being. But we know that is not the case.

So maybe we should ask, not why nature is not cooperating with us, but how we can cooperate with nature—human nature—and still accomplish what is needed.

If we are abstracting a major portion of our lives to virtual living, why not address the hostilities of the world in a virtual way rather than through war?

Inasmuch as "thought" is the heart of Soul and consciousness, training that bypasses "thinking" suggests that something must be going against the deepest thrust of soulf. Soulf has been working out the thought of "war" for centuries. Though we have only historical records to go by, an educated guess would say that soldiers in past times have not had as much difficulty in shooting to kill as they do today. But soulf's "thought" has now developed to a point where it has evolved beyond war to new possibilities.

APPENDIX F

ABSTRACTUALIZATION

"Abstractualization" (a combination of "abstract" and "actual") is perhaps the newest and most pervasive means of consciousness development. For years psychologists have known about projection as a psychological phenomenon in which people see outside themselves something that really exists within them. For instance, when we fall in love, we see attributes in our beloved that are, in fact, undeveloped attributes within ourselves. Or if we hate with a passion a politician whom we feel is responsible for everything that's going wrong in Washington, we are seeing within that person some ugly parts of ourselves that we'd rather not face directly. In both cases our own reality has been projected outside ourselves.

Another form of projection has been our material creations—paintings, dance, buildings, tools, etc.—all sorts of cultural works that are created forms of ideas from within us. In all forms of psychological projection, a "living idea" within the psyche is projected onto the external world, shaping the "living world" we see and live in, which is somewhat different for each one of us.

Consciousness has now reached the point where we "own" those material actualizations we have created. They have become a real part of ourselves, so we no longer need to project onto them in the outer world.

This is where "abstractualization" enters the picture. Those living ideas that were formerly actualized in material form outside us are now abstracted and given a virtual form—often a digitized one. We can literally observe the disappearance of many actualized forms: music stores, books, telephone booths, magazines, maps, newspapers, filing cabinets, mail boxes, handwritten letters, CD's and voting booths, to name a few. They are disappearing from our material world, but the living ideas they contained continue to exist—in new, virtual forms. The "actualized" material forms have been "abstracted" into non-material forms, a process I call "abstractualization."

Why is "abstractualization" taking place? A compelling reason is that human population growth and consumerism have gone out of control. This reckless spending of energy in the visible world needs to be balanced by energy in the unseen world. To balance the seen and unseen worlds is a major concern of soulf. Humanity must learn how to live with—and within—the unseen world, which is an abstraction, while engaging with the created world.

Another reason underlies the abstractualization taking place. Humanity's adulthood makes us capable of handling abstractions to a far greater degree than ever before. Abstract thinking is required for increasingly complicated problems, as the world rapidly continues to complexify.

Undoubtedly we will continue to see more abstractualizations in the coming years, affecting every aspect of our living, from finding jobs and work life, to teaching school and the consequent brain restructuring, to an altered sense of time and space in social relationships. It's not a question of whether or not we want this to happen—it is the reality we live with today.

BIBLIOGRAPHY

Achenbach, Joel, "At the Heart of All Matter: the hunt for the God particle," *National Geographic*, March 2008.

Ansary, Tamim, *Destiny Disrupted: A History of the World Through Islamic Eyes,* Public Affairs, 2009.

Arntz, William, Betsy Chasse and Mark Vicente, *What the Bleep Do We Know?* Health Communications, Inc., 2005.

Arntz, William, producer/director, "What the Bleep Do We Know?" docudrama, Captured Light Industries.

Barbour, Ian, *Religion and Science, Historical and Contemporary Issues*, HarperSanFrancisco, 1997.

Brock, Rita Nakashima and Rebecca Ann Parker, *Saving Paradise: How Christianity Traded Love of This World for Crucifixion and Empire*, Beacon Press, 2008.

Brooks, David, "The Neural Buddhists," *The New York Times*, May 13, 2008. Bruteau, Beatrice, "Prayer and Identity," *Contemplative Review*, Fall 1983.

Collins, Gail, *When Everything Changed: the Amazing Journey of American Women From 1960 to the Present*, Little, Brown & Company, 2009.

"Cyberspace and Its Limits: Hypermodern Detours in the Evolution of Consciousness," XXV Annual Gebser Conference, October 1999.

Davies, Paul, *The Fifth Miracle*, Simon and Schuster, 1999.

Dyson, Freeman J., *Infinite In All Directions,* Harper & Row, 1988. "Evolutionary Timeline", www.talkorigins.org.

Feynman, Richard P., *Six Easy Pieces, Essentials of Physics Explained By Its Most Brilliant Teacher,* Addison-Wesley, 1994.

Gebser, Jean, *The Ever-Present Origin,* (Noel Barstad and Algis Mickunas, translators), Ohio University Press, 1985.

Gibbs, W. Wayt, "Beyond Physics," *Scientific American,* August 1998.

Giegerich, Wolfgang, "The End of Meaning and the Birth of Man," *Journal of Jungian Theory and Practice* (6, no.1), 2004, pp. 1-65.

Giegerich, Wolfgang, *The Soul's Logical Life: Towards a Rigorous Notion of Psychology,* Peter Lang, 2007.

Giegerich, Wolfgang, "Technology and the Soul: From the nuclear bomb to the World Wide Web," Collected English Papers, Vol. II, *Spring* Journal, Inc., pp. 281-308 and 333-336, May 15, 2007.

Gladwell, Malcolm, *The Tipping Point: How Little Things Can Make a Big Difference,* Little, Brown and Company, 2000.

Goodenough, Ursula, *The Sacred Depths of Nature,* Oxford University Press, 1998.

Hawking, Stephen W., *A Brief History of Time, From the Big Bang to Black Holes,* Bantam, 1998.

Hitchcock, John L., *The Web of the Universe: Jung, the "New Physics," and Human Spirituality, 1991.*

Irion, Robert, "Black Holes", *Smithsonian,* April 2008.

Jaspers, Karl, *The Origin and Goal of History,* Yale University Press, 1953. King, Karen L., *The Gospel of Mary of Magdala,* Polebridge Press, 2003.

Koonz, Mark, "The Generosity of Thomas Forsyth Torrance: a memoir with letters," The Princeton Theological Review, Fall 2008.

Krauss, Lawrence M. and Glenn D. Starkman, "The Fate of Life in the Universe," *Scientific American,* November 1999.

Lerner, Michael, *The Left Hand of God*, HarperCollins, 2006.

Magee, Patrick, "The New Physics, Cosmology and Religion," Zephyr Point Presbyterian Conference Center, Lake Tahoe, California.

Masterpasqua, Frank, "Toward a Dynamical Developmental Understanding of Disorder," *The Psychological Meaning of Chaos: Translating Theory Into Practice*, American Psychological Association, 1997.

May, Herbert G. and Bruce M. Metzger, ed., *The New Oxford Annotated Bible With the Apocrypha*, Revised Standard Version, Oxford University Press, 1977.

McGrath, Alister E., *Science and Religion: An Introduction,* Blackwell, 1999. McTaggart, Lynne, *The Field*, Harper Perennial, 2002.

Peebles, P. James E., David N. Schramm, Edwin L. Turner, and Richard G. Kron, "The Evolution of the Universe," *Scientific American Online*, July, 1998.

Primack, Joel R. and Nancy Ellen Abrams, *The View from the Center of the Universe: Discovering Our Extraordinary Place in the Cosmos,* Riverhead Books, 2006.

Purser, Ronald E., "Global Cyber-Tech and Integral Consciousness," XXV Annual Gebser Conference, October 1999.

Russell, Robert John, "Bridging Science and Religion: Why It Must Be Done," The Center for Theology and the Natural Sciences, Berkeley, California.

Schilling, Harold K., *The New Consciousness in Science and Religion*, United Church Press, 1973.

Serrone, Sue, "Starburst" (interview with Brian Swimme), *Festivals,* Vol. 6, No. 2. Spong, John Shelby, *A New Christianity For a New World,* HarperSanFrancisco, 2001. Spong, John Shelby, *Why Christianity Must Change or Die*, HarperSan Francisco, 1998.

Swimme, Brian and Thomas Berry, The Universe Story: From the Primordial Flaring Forth to the Ecozoic Era, HarperCollins, 1994.

Tolle, Eckhart, *A New Earth: Awakening to Your Life's Purpose*, Plume, 2006.

"Wall Street and the Financial Crisis: Anatomy of a Financial Collapse," United States Senate Permanent Subcommittee on Investigations, April 13, 2011.

Weinberg, Steven, *The First Three Minutes, A Modern View of the Origin of the Universe*, Bantam, 1977.

Wells, Spencer, *The Journey of Man*, Random House, 2003.

Whitney, Donald S., "A Review of Eckhart Tolle's *A New Earth*," website of The Center for Biblical Spirituality, 2008.

Wilkens, Robert Louis, *The Myth of Christian Beginnings*, Wipf & Stock Publishers, 2009.

NOTES

—CHAPTER 2—

[1]   Comparison of changing paradigms:

Ancient view: A flat earth, with the heavens separating "waters above from waters below."

Greek (and medieval) view: Earth as a sphere, at the center of the universe, with the sun, planets and stars revolving around the Earth.

Newtonian view: Everything in one galaxy, with the sun at the center of the universe and planets in elliptical orbits around it.

20th century view: Universe started from a Big Bang, continually expanding. Millions of galaxies are clumped within large areas of space that have no galaxies. The world is comprised of chance, probabilities, paradox, and mystery.

[2]   Alister E. McGrath, *Science and Religion: An Introduction,* p. 125.

[3]   Paul Davies, *The Fifth Miracle*, p. 176.

[4]   Scientists today are scrambling to provide a Theory of Everything that would prove this scientifically.

[5]   William Arntz, Betsy Chasse and Mark Vicente, *What the Bleep Do We Know,* p. 207.

[6]   Joel R. Primack and Nancy Ellen Abrams, *The View from the Center of the Universe.*

[7]   Ibid.

[8]   "Leading edge research is suggesting that the so-called 'empty space' within and between atoms is not empty at all; it's so lively with energy that one cubic centimeter—about a thimbleful or an area the size of a pebble—contains more energy than all the solid matter in the entire known universe!" (*What the Bleep Do We Know?* p. 36.)

[9]   For some time, scientists had accepted without explanation the paradoxical nature of particle- wave; sometimes they spoke of matter and light as particles and at other times as waves.

[10]   Richard P. Feynman, *Six Easy Pieces*, pp. 118-138.

[11]   This particle-wave behavior could be seen, theologically, like the account of God creating the universe at the beginning of *Genesis* 1. God commands the waves of chaos saying: "'Let there be light!' And there was light." The word of God (which presumably included observation that there was no light) collapses the particle-wave into a *particle* of light.

[12]   *What the Bleep Do We Know?* p. 58.

[13]   Ibid., 55.

[14]   Ibid., 30.

[15]   Quoted by James Gleick, "Have Meme, Will Travel," *Smithsonian*, May 2011.

[16]   Patrick Magee, "The New Physics, Cosmology and Religion."

[17]   Steven W. Hawking wrote in *A Brief History of Time*: "If the rate of expansion [of the early universe] one second after the Big Bang had been smaller by even one part in a hundred thousand million million, the universe would have recollapsed before it ever reached its present size."

       Patrick Magee said if the expansion rate had been greater by one part in a million, it would have expanded too rapidly for stars and planets to form.

       In recent years Einstein's original mathematical finding (which he rejected as untrustworthy) of a gravitational force that pushes instead of pulls has been substantiated. This antigravity, called "dark energy," uniformly fills space, "much as steam fills a sauna, only invisibly." Dark energy is the force that is causing the expansion rate of the universe to be speeding up rather than slowing down. Before the discovery of dark energy, researchers had anticipated that the gravitational attraction of matter in the sky would slow the expansion, much as Earth's gravity slows the speed of a ball tossed upward. (Brian Greene, "Darkness on the Edge of the Universe," *The New York Times*, January 15, 2011.)

[18]   "It takes the solar system about 226 million years to orbit the Milky Way . . . The sun is one of about 100 billion stars in the Milky Way, one of the billions of ordinary galaxies in the universe . . . And every object in the universe is moving apart from the other objects as the universe expands at a constantly accelerating rate." (Associated Press report, June 2, 1999)

[19]   Albert Einstein was at the forefront of space-time research, which culminated with his theories of relativity.

       A new understanding of relativity, based on Einstein's theory, concurs with Einstein that space and time are relative. It adds that time tends to disappear as scientists probe closer to the Big Bang. Since measurements of time intervals are relative, one cannot accurately speak of past, present and future. Only "before" and "after" offer accurate communication.

[20]   While it is difficult for us to imagine a world without time—or space, for that matter—a journalist covering the aftermath of the devastating tsunami of 2004 discovered a native group who shed some light on this. The tribe had no word for anything involving a concept of time such as how old their children were, hello, goodbye, tomorrow, etc. In their consciousness, they were living in a world that was out of linear time.

[21]   "The average density in space declines as the universe expands . . . In an explosion the fastest particles move out into empty space, but in the big bang cosmology, particles uniformly fill all space. The expansion of the universe has had little influence on the size of galaxies or even clusters of galaxies that are bound by gravity; space is simply opening up between them . . . similar to a rising loaf of raisin bread. As the dough expands, the raisins move apart. Moreover, the speed with which any two raisins move apart is directly and positively related to the amount of dough separating them." (P. James E. Peebles, David N. Schramm, Edwin L. Turner and Richard G. Kron, "The Evolution of the Universe," *Scientific American*, March 1998.)

[22]   In subsequent chapters the time dimension will be closely identified with "Soul" and the space dimension with "Self." (See Appendix B.)

[23]   Joel Achenbach, "At the Heart of All Matter: the hunt for the God particle," *National Geographic*, March 2008.

[24]   Ibid.

[25]   "Physical reality has been evolving . . . from simple relationships and structures to increasingly complex ones." (Harold K. Schilling, *The New Consciousness in Science and Religion*, p. 29.)

[26]   "Physical reality not only builds but destroys, not only enriches but impoverishes." (Harold   K. Schilling, *The New Consciousness in Science and Religion*, p. 29.)

[27]   Frank Masterpasqua, "Toward a Dynamical Developmental Understanding of Disorder," *The Psychological Meaning of Chaos: Translating Theory Into Practice*, 1997.

[28]   Lawrence M. Krauss and Glenn D. Starkman, "The Fate of Life in the Universe," *Scientific American*, November 1999.

[29]   "We are made from remains of supernovas (recycled stardust)." (Patrick Magee)

[30]   Particles of matter only *attract* to one another—*not* repel—through gravitational force. Because of this, matter will at some point become so dense it will collapse into black holes.

[31] Lawrence M. Krauss and Glenn D. Starkman, "The Fate of Life in the Universe," *Scientific American*, November 1999.

[32] David N. Schramm, *The Big Bang and Other Explosions in Nuclear and Particle Astrophysics*, World Scientific Publishing Company, Inc. 1996.

[33] *What the Bleep Do We Know?* p. 207.

—CHAPTER 3—

[34] Author and former professor of theology at the National University of Ireland, Maynooth.

[35] *What the Bleep Do We Know?* Pp. 247- 248.

[36] Wolfgang Giegerich, "The End of Meaning and the Birth of Man," Section 7.

[37] Ibid.

[38] Based on the thinking of Wolfgang Giegerich.

[39] *What the Bleep Do We Know?* p. 78.

[40] Ibid., 73.

[41] Ibid., 79.

[42] *Ibid.,* 99.

[43] William Tiller (physicist, former professor at Stanford University), *What the Bleep Do We Know?* p. 82.

[44] Peter Russell (studied experimental psychology at Cambridge University, with a post- graduate degree in computer science), *What the Bleep Do We Know?* p. 81.

[45] *What the Bleep Do We Know?* p. 81.

[46] [46] *Ibid.,* 82-83.

[47] *Ibid.,* 210.

[48] Stuart Hameroff, M.D., (professor of anesthesiology and psychology, University of Arizona), *What the Bleep Do We Know?* p. 139.

[49] *What the Bleep Do We Know?* p. 175.

[50] Ibid., 165.

[51] Ibid.

[52] Joseph Dispenza (neurologist), *What the Bleep Do We Know?* p. 155.

[53] *What the Bleep Do We Know?* p. 221.

[54] Ibid., 222.

[55] Ibid., *225.*

[56]   Lynne McTaggart, *The Field*, p. 213.

[57]   Ibid.

[58]   Ibid., 213-214.

[59]   Wolfgang Giegerich, "Technology and the Soul," pp. 335-336.

[60]   Ibid., 309.

[61]   Wolfgang Giegerich, *The Soul's Logical Life*, p. 262.

[62]   Ibid., 48.

[63]   Ibid., 201.

—CHAPTER 4—

[64]   Kim Vo, "Immersion fonts and baptism," *San Jose Mercury News*, April 16, 2007.

[65]   Verena Dobnik, Associated Press, April 2009.

[66]   Roni Caryn Rabin, "Study links religion and terminal care," *The New York Times*, March 18, 2009.

[67]   Lindsey Tanner, Associated Press, August 2008.

[68]   *San Jose Mercury News*, April 15, 2007.

[69]   Rachel Zoll, Associated Press, April 13, 2008.

[70]   Ian Fisher, "Pope visits Spain, flash point for church-state tensions," *The New York Times*, July 9, 2006.

[71]   Barry Goldman-Hall, *San Jose Mercury News*, May 2009.

[72]   Michelle Boorstein and Jacqueline L. Salmon, *The Washington Post*.

[73]   Jack Chang, McClatchy Rio de Janeiro Bureau, May 2007.

[74]   Rev. Jay Scott Newman, *YahooNews,* November 14, 2008.

[75]   Kim Vo, "Defiant female priest says mass," *San Jose Mercury News*, May 28, 2006.

[76]   Suzette Laboy, Associated Press, May-June 2009.

[77]   Larry Rohter, "As Pope heads to Brazil, a rival theology persists," *The New York Times*, May 7, 2007.

[78]   Jack Chang, McClatchy Rio de Janeiro Bureau.

[79]   Tracy Wilkinson, "Pope leaves Brazil with fierce speech," *Los Angeles Times*, May 14, 2007.

[80]   Nicole Winfield, Associated Press, April 21, 2007.

[81]   Rachel Donadio, "Pope deplores 'Ideological Manipulation'," *The New York*

Times, May 10, 2009.

[82]   Elisabeth Rosenthal, "Pope calls for reconciliation of Chinese Catholics," *The New York Times*, July 1, 2007.

[83]   Paul Krugman, "Church narrows the gap on state," *The New York Times* columnist, April 13, 2007.

[84]   Tom Coyne, Associated Press, May 17, 2009.

[85]   Michael Brick, "Defeat and some success for Texas evolution foes," *The New York Times*, March 26, 2009.

[86]   Amy Forliti, Associated Press, June 2009.

[87]   Mary Anne Ostrom, "Candidates upholding faith connections in campaigns," *San Jose Mercury News*, December 6, 2007.

[88]   *San Jose Mercury News*, November 23, 2004.

[89]   Paul Watson, "Indonesians ignore religious edicts against smoking, yoga," *Los Angeles Times*, February 6, 2009.

[90]   Edward Wong, "China creates specter of dueling Dalai Lamas," *The New York Times*, June 7, 2009.

[91]   Scott Wilson, "Obama calls on Muslims for a 'New Beginning' with U.S.," *The Washington Post*, June 5, 2009.

[92]   Michelle Boorstein, *The Washington Post*, March 9, 2009.

[93]   Michelle Boorstein and Jacqueline L. Salmon, "In major poll, U.S. religious identity appears very slippery," *The Washington Post,* February 26, 2008.

[94]   Ibid.

[95]   Dylan T. Lovan, Associated Press, April 3, 2009.

[96]   *Spiegel Online.*

[97]   *San Jose Mercury News,* November 25, 2007.

[98]   Sabrina Tavernise, "Violence Leaves Young Iraqis Doubting Clerics," *The New York Times*, March 4, 2008.

[99]   Ellen Goodman, "A leap of faith for House atheist," *Boston Globe* columnist, March 23, 2007.

[100] Mary Jordan, "Christian groups answer atheists with own ads on British buses," *The Washington Post*, February 6, 2009.

[101] Susan Carpenter, *Los Angeles Times*, 2009.

[102] Ryan Huff, *MediaNews*, May 13, 2007.

[103] Susan Carpenter, *Los Angeles Times*, 2009.

[104] Bruce Reyes-Chow, *New Vision*, Noe Valley Ministry Presbyterian Church, September/October, 2008. (Reyes-Chow is a minister of the Presbyterian

Church (U.S.A.) and former Moderator of its General Assembly.)

[105] Russell Schoch, "Boyung Lee Finds a Home: Challenging meta-narratives and breaking barriers," *Bulletin*, Pacific School of Religion, Spring, 2008.

—CHAPTER 5—

[106] Glennda Chui, *San Jose Mercury News*, June 1, 2004.

[107] David Cline, Dark Matter Search Project, University of California-Los Angeles, quoted in *San Jose Mercury News*, June 1, 2004.

[108] Associated Press, December 17, 2008.

[109] Produced by Graham Booth, executive producer for Tigress Productions, and Dan Korn, executive producer for Science Channel, May 2008.

[110] Mike Hale, "Television Review," *San Jose Mercury News*, May 27, 2008.

[111] Jerry Adler, "Finding a Home in the Cosmos," *Smithsonian*, July 2006.

[112] Ibid.

[113] Ibid.

[114] Michael J. Crumb, Associated Press, June 12, 2009.

[115] Sandi Doughton, *Seattle Times*, December 9, 2006.

[116] Neil de Grasse Tyson, "Space: Where we're headed," USA Weekend, July 6-8, 2007.

[117] http://phoenix.lpl.arizona.edu August 2, 2009.

[118] Neil de Grasse Tyson, "Space: Where we're headed," USA Weekend, July 6-8, 2007.

[119] Marcia Dunn, Associated Press, May 14, 2009.

[120] John Johnson, Jr., *Los Angeles Times*, November 14, 2008.

[121] Miguel Helft, *The New York Times*, August 22, 2007.

[122] Mark de la Vina, *San Jose Mercury News*, October 17, 2008.

[123] Ian Hoffman and Betsy Mason, MediaNews, October 3, 2006.

[124] Thomas H. Maugh II, *Los Angeles Times*, October 8, 2008.

—CHAPTER 6—

[125] From an article written for the *San Jose Mercury News*, November 12, 2008.

[126] Robert John Russell, "Bridging Science and Religion". (Russell is founder of The Center for Theology and the Natural Sciences at the Graduate Theological Union)

[127]   Frank Davies, "Chu on climate threat: Earth is like the Titanic," *San Jose Mercury News*, April 8, 2009.

[128]   Mitchell Landsberg, "China may lead in greenhouse gases," *Los Angeles Times*, June 21, 2007.

[129]   Thomas L. Friedman, columnist, *The New York Times*, March 29, 2009, quoting a *Washington Post* report of February 1, 2009.

[130]   Ross Gelbspan, *San Jose Mercury News*, April 9, 2006. Gelbspan is a former journalist with the *Boston Globe* and author of *The Heat Is On* (1998) and *Boiling Point* (2004).

[131]   Dion Nissenbaum and Mark Gladstone, "Governor bucks Bush, will set own goals," *San Jose Mercury News*, May 29, 2005.

[132]   San Jose Mercury News, April 20, 2006.

[133]   Robert Lee Hotz, "Report warns of warming in West," *Los Angeles Times*, October 6, 2006.

[134]   Charmaine Noronhan, Associated Press, September 4, 2008.

[135]   Seth Borenstein, Associated Press, March 26, 2008.

[136]   *San Jose Mercury News*, April 20, 2005.

[137]   Adam Nossiter, "Drought sapping Southeast, farmers," *The New York Times*, July 4, 2007.

[138]   Alicia Chang, Associated Press, 2006.

[139]   Associated Press, "Snow shuts down federal government operations," *San Jose Mercury News*, February 10, 2010.

[140]   Associated Press, London, May 15, 2006.

[141]   Ibid.

[142]   Charles J. Hanley, Associated Press, December 25, 2006.

[143]   Juliet Eilperin, "Researchers fear southern fence will endanger species further," *The Washington Post*, April 20, 2008.

[144]   Jerry Harmer, Associated Press, March 4, 2007.

[145]   *San Jose Mercury News*, May 21, 2008.

[146]   Kenneth R. Weiss, "25% of wild mammal species are imperiled," *Los Angeles Times*, October 7, 2008.

[147]   Juliet Eilperin, "22 cities join Clinton anti-warming effort," *The Washington Post*, August 2, 2006.

[148]   Thomas L. Friedman, columnist, "The power of green," *The New York Times*, April 15, 2007.

[149]   Frank Davies, "Chu on climate threat: Earth is like the Titanic," *San Jose Mercury News*, April 8, 2009.

[150]   John Heilprin, Associated Press, April 30, 2009.

[151]   Symposium, "Globalization", Wellesley College, July 2006.

[152]   James A. Lima, San Jose, California.

[153]   Mary Anne Ostrom, *San Jose Mercury News*, July 23, 2006.

[154]   *San Jose Mercury News*, June 1, 2008.

[155]   Kelli Kennedy, Associated Press, February 18, 2007.

[156]   Michelle Locke, Associated Press, April 1, 2007.

[157]   *San Jose Mercury News*, May 1, 2006.

[158]   Matt Nauman, *San Jose Mercury News*, January 18, 2008.

[159]   Matt Nauman, *San Jose Mercury News*, November 29, 2007.

[160]   John Boudreau, *San Jose Mercury News*, March 7, 2009.

[161]   *San Jose Mercury News*, April 22, 2006.

[162]   Barbara E. Hernandez, MediaNews.

[163]   Katherine Conrad, "Builder finds green complex brings in green," *San Jose Mercury News*, September 4, 2007.

[164]   Paul Rogers, "Where it's easy being green," *San Jose Mercury News* November 14, 2006.

[165]   *Los Angeles Times*, July 19, 2009.

[166]   Thomas L. Friedman, columnist, "The power of green," *The New York Times*, April 15, 2007.

—CHAPTER 7—

[167]   Quoted by Jonathan Yardley, "Animal Lovers," *The Washington Post*, July 20-26, 2008.

[168]   Jonathan Yardley, "Animal Lovers," *The Washington Post*, July 20-26, 2008.

[169]   Ibid.

[170]   Kathryn Shevelow, *For the Love of Animals*, quoted by Jonathan Yardley, "Animal Lovers," *The Washington Post*, July 20-26, 2008.

[171]   Randal C. Archibold, "Poachers in West hunt big antlers to feed big egos," *The New York Times*, December 9, 2006.

[172]   Ibid.

[173]   Tracie Cone, Associated Press, May 2009.

[174]   Ibid.

[175]   Nedra Pickler, Associated Press.

[176]   Rob Stein, "Glowing green monkeys illustrate important but controversial advance," *The Washington Post*, May 28, 2009.

[177]   Erin Digitale, "Humane food practices to come before voters," *San Jose Mercury News*, April 29, 2008.

[178]   Ibid.

[179]   "Governor signs ban on killing horses for food," *San Jose Mercury News*, May 25, 2007.

[180]   Erin Digitale, "Humane food practices to come before voters," *San Jose Mercury News*, April 29, 2008.

[181]   Ibid.

[182]   Linda Goldston, "Mountain lion shooting criticized," *San Jose Mercury News*, March 26, 2008.

[183]   Rick Weiss, "FDA rules override warnings about drug," *The Washington Post*, March 4, 2007.

[184]   Mary Anne Ostrom, "Police: UCSC researchers targeted in firebombings," *San Jose Mercury News*, August 3, 2008.

[185]   Charlene Thornton, special agent for the FBI, quoted by Dana Hull, *San Jose Mercury News*, April 22, 2009.

[186]   Rick Weiss, "FDA rules override warnings about drug," *The Washington Post*, March 4, 2007.

[187]   Associated Press, "Tourists cheer rescue of baby tern," *San Jose Mercury News*.

[188]   *San Jose Mercury News*, May 1, 2006.

[189]   "John Kelly's Washington," *The Washington Post*, September 2, 2009.

[190]   Ibid.

[191]   "Tiny birds cover huge distances," *San Jose Mercury News*, February 13, 2009.

[192]   *San Jose Mercury News*, April 14, 2006.

[193]   *San Jose Mercury News*, April 13, 2006.

[194]   Ibid.

[195]   For example, Linda Goldston, "Animal Friends," *San Jose Mercury News*.

[196]   "Pets, family escape bedroom blaze," *San Jose Mercury News,* June 19, 2009.

[197]   "Firefighters rescue dog from fire that ruins house," *San Jose Mercury News,* August 31, 2009.

[198]   *San Jose Mercury News*, April 13, 2006.

[199]   Ibid.

[200] Steven W. Barnes, Hearst Newspapers, *San Jose Mercury News*, March 6, 2009.

[201] Melinda Sacks, "The Pet Effect," *Vital*: Bay Area Health Fitness and Beauty, *San Jose Mercury News*, August/September, 2007.

[202] Ibid.

[203] Malcolm Ritter, Associated Press, May 1, 2009.

[204] Adrian Higgins, *The Washington Post*, May 14, 2009.

[205] *San Jose Mercury News*, April 14, 2008.

[206] Steve Dale, "AnimalSmart," *USA Weekend*, November 2007.

[207] Santa Clara Superior Court Rules, Santa Clara County, California.

[208] Alan Fram, Associated Press, "Most pet owners can translate animals' barks and meows," *San Jose Mercury News*, December 2008.

[209] Mark Abramson, Bay Area News Group, April 19, 2008.

[210] *San Jose Mercury News*, April 17, 2006.

[211] Alan Fram, Associated Press, "Most pet owners can translate animals' barks and meows," *San Jose Mercury News*, December 2008.

[212] Linda Goldston, "Food for Pets of the Aged," *San Jose Mercury News*, August 14, 2007.

[213] Steven W. Barnes, Hearst Newspapers, *San Jose Mercury News*, March 6, 2009.

[214] Ibid.

[215] Mitch Stacy, Associated Press, September 16, 2009.

[216] Teresa G. Odle, Bay Area News Group, August 2, 2009.

[217] Douglas Brown, MediaNews, October 7, 2007.

[218] "Four Seasons for four-legged family," *San Jose Mercury News,* May 10, 2007.

[219] Ibid.

[220] Ibid.

[221] Michael Martinez, "The Pampered Guest," *San Jose Mercury News*, December 16, 2007.

[222] Ibid.

[223] Ibid.

[224] Ibid.

[225] Ibid.

[226] "N.Y. named friendliest city for traveling pets," Associated Press, 2008.

[227]   AARP *Bulletin*, September 2009.

[228]   Linda Goldston, "Society Dog brings pets and their humans together," *San Jose Mercury News*, August 30, 2008.

[229]   Cynthia Liu, "Dish," San Francisco *Chronicle*, December 23, 2005.

[230]   Ibid.

[231]   Lis Leff, Associated Press, July 30, 2007.

[232]   Carol Wolf, *Bloomberg News*, January 2, 2007.

[233]   Michael Felberbaum, Associated Press, August 7, 2008.

[234]   Ibid.

[235]   Linda Goldston, "Green revolution extends to pet world," *San Jose Mercury News*, March 8, 2008.

[236]   Stephanie Saul, "New diet drug is approved with pudgy dogs in mind," *The New York Times*, January 6, 2007.

[237]   Ibid.

[238]   "FDA OK's cancer drug for dogs," *Los Angeles Times*, June 2009.

[239]   Betsy Taylor, "Purina to offer pet insurance," Associated Press, June 15, 2008.

[240]   Cynthia Hubert, *McClatchy-Tribune*, November 25, 2006.

[241]   Ibid.

—CHAPTER 8—

[242]   *San Jose Mercury News*, April 17, 2006.

[243]   "Report warns cities of population surge," *San Jose Mercury News*, June 28, 2007.

[244]   *San Jose Mercury News*, November 27, 2006.

[245]   *San Jose Mercury News*, April 18, 2006.

[246]   Elizabeth Kolbert, "Why are we so fat?" *The New Yorker*, July 20, 2009.

[247]   Ibid.

[248]   Ibid.

[249]   Marilynn Marchione, Associated Press, August 27, 2009.

[250]   Tara Bahrampour, *The Washington Post*, September 10, 2009.

[251]   "Knowledge (of calories) is power (over obesity)," Op/Ed, *San Jose Mercury News*, May 10, 2007.

[252]   Elizabeth Kolbert, "Why are we so fat?" *The New Yorker*, July 20, 2009.

[253] Francis Delpeuch, Bernard Maire, Emmanuel Monnier, and Michelle Holdsworth, *Globesity*, quoted by Elizabeth Kolbert, "Why are we so fat?" *The New Yorker,* July 20, 2009.

[254] Elizabeth Kolbert, "Why are we so fat?" *The New Yorker*, July 20, 2009.

[255] *San Jose Mercury News*, May 1, 2006.

[256] Donna St. George, "Getting lost in the great indoors," *The Washington Post*, June 19, 2007.

[257] OP/ED, *San Jose Mercury News*, June 29, 2007.

[258] Tedd Mitchell, M.D., "Exercise Boosts the Brain," *USA Weekend*, August 1-3, 2008.

[259] Dave Kiefer, *San Jose Mercury News,* November 19, 2006.

[260] *San Jose Mercury News*, July 22, 2009.

[261] *San Jose Mercury News*, April 14, 2006.

[262] Carla K. Johnson, Associated Press, September 4, 2007.

[263] Christopher Gardner, "Eat well for less," *Stanford Medicine News*, Summer 2009.

[264] April Dembosky, *San Jose Mercury News*, July 22, 2009.

[265] *San Jose Mercury News*, October 6, 2008.

[266] National Epidemiological Survey on Alcohol and Related Conditions, published in the Archives of General Psychiatry.

[267] Shari Roan, "Study: Psychiatric disorders plague young adults," *Los Angeles Times,* 2008.

[268] "Mahjong epilepsy named in new medical study," *San Jose Mercury News,* August 5, 2007.

[269] *San Jose Mercury News*, September 4, 2007.

[270] Tedd Mitchell, M.D., "HealthSmart", *USA Weekend,* August 28-30, 2009.

[271] Donna St. George, "8.5 percent of U.S. youths addicted to video games, study finds," *The Washington Post*, April 20, 2009.

[272] Edward M. Hallowell, CrazyBusy: overstretched, overbooked, and about to snap, quoted by Los Angeles Times, March 2006.

[273] Julie Sevrens Lyons, "Shopping bug bites men, too," *San Jose Mercury News*, October 1, 2006.

[274] *San Jose Mercury News*, August 25, 2009.

[275] Laura Casey, Bay Area News Group, September 26, 2009.

[276] Marilynn Marchione, Associated Press.

[277]   Ronald Kotulak, "New vaccines could help people shake bad habits," *Chicago Tribune,* October 1, 2006.

[278]   Marilynn Marchione and Mike Stobbe, Associated Press, August 13, 2009.

[279]   Josephine Marcotty, "Mysticism Meets Medicine," *McClatchy-Tribune,* November 25, 2006.

[280]   John MacIntyre, "Sick at Work," *San Jose Mercury News*, October 22, 2006.

[281]   Chen May Yee, *McClatchy Newspaper*, March 4, 2007.

[282]   *San Jose Mercury News*, March 9, 2004.

[283]   Alicia Chang, Associated Press, April 27, 2008.

[284]   Thomas H. Maugh II, "Cancer deaths decline first time since 1930," *Los Angeles Times*, February 9, 2006.

[285]   Marilynn Marchione, "So-called vaccine kept lymphoma in check for a year," Associated Press, June 1, 2009.

[286]   Karen Kaplan, "Study finds humans still evolving, and quickly," *Los Angeles Times*, December 11, 2007.

[287]   Gina Kolata, "Human Health Gains Amaze Scientists," *The New York Times*, July 30, 2006.

[288]   The size of the human brain's frontal lobe is that which most separates humans from other animals. The frontal lobe enables us to develop higher consciousness, the unique role of humanity.

—CHAPTER 9—

[289]   Rep. Eleanor Holmes Norton, District of Columbia.

[290]   "Value of Abstinence Sex Programs Debated," *San Jose Mercury News*, April 24, 2008.

[291]   Kevin Freking, Associated Press, "No change found in sexual behavior," *San Jose Mercury News,* April 14, 2007.

[292]   Chuck Shepherd, "New ideas for modern education," *San Jose Mercury News*, April 27, 2009.

[293]   March 2007.

[294]   Matt King, *MediaNews*, March 18, 2007.

[295]   The Sun (online) 2007.

[296]   American actress, best known for her role in TV series "Profiler."

[297]   Charlie McCollum, blog, Mercurynews.com, July 2007.

[298]   "The Science of Romance," Physics Forums (online), February 15, 2009.

[299] Seth Borenstein, Associated Press, *San Jose Mercury News*, February 12, 2009.

[300] Dennie Hughes, "RelationTips," *USA Weekend*, July 17-19, 2009.

[301] Research director at the Guttmacher Institute in New York, a private think tank that studies sexual and reproductive issues.

[302] David Crary, Associated Press, *San Jose Mercury News*, December 20, 2006.

[303] Linda Goldston, "More sex allegations against swim coach," *San Jose Mercury News*, June 6, 2009.

[304] Alexei Barrionuevo.

[305] Alexei Barrionuevo, "In tangle of young lips, a sex rebellion in Chile," *The New York Times*, September 12, 2008.

[306] Chuck Shepherd, "Health tips," *San Jose Mercury News,* August 29, 2009.

[307] Jeffrey Fleishman and Amro Hassan.

[308] Jeffrey Fleishman and Amro Hassan, "Gadget to help women feign virginity angers many in Egypt," *Los Angeles Times,* October 7, 2009.

[309] Associated Press, "Actress found guilty of adultery," *San Jose Mercury News,* December 18, 2008.

[310] John Boudreau, "Globalization's ugly side," San Jose Mercury News, June 4, 2009.

[311] Professor at American University Washington College of Law.

[312] Nancy D. Polikoff, "Let's Leave 'Marriage' at the Altar," *The Washington Post,* February 24, 2008.

[313] Stephanie Coontz, teacher of history at Evergreen State College in Olympia, Washington, in an article written for the Hartford, Connecticut *Courant*, "Marriage changes with the culture," March 18, 2007.

[314] Mike Swift, "Growing research suggests being gay is not 'a choice'," *San Jose Mercury News*, November 30, 2008.

[315] David Crary, The Associated Press, August 6, 2009.

[316] Sue Martinez of San Jose, California.

[317] Sue Martinez in "Letters to the Editor," *San Jose Mercury News*, October 30, 2008.

[318] "Former New Jersey governor says coming out was painful," *San Jose Mercury News*, March 18, 2007.

[319] Rachel Zoll, The Associated Press, July 15, 2009.

[320] Tim Craig, "Archdiocese plunges deeper into fight against legalizing gay marriage in D.C.," *The Washington Post*, September 2, 2009.

[321] Norma Love, The Associated Press, June 4, 2009.

[322]   Lisa Leff and David Sharp, The Associated Press, November 7, 2009.

[323]   Chosen by the American Association of Political Consultants.

[324]   Lisa Leff and David Sharp, The Associated Press, November 7, 2009.

[325]   Ibid.

[326]   Mike Swift, "Census identifies more same-sex couples in S. J.," *San Jose Mercury News*, January 2, 2007.

[327]   Jennifer Agiesta and Alec MacGillis, "Poll: Rising U.S. support for social issues, such as gay marriage," *The Washington Post*, May 1, 2009.

[328]   Paula Ettelbrick (executive director of the International Gay and Lesbian Human Rights Commission) in an article written for the *Los Angeles Times*, December 4, 2006.

[329]   Jose Luis Rodriguez Zapatero, quoted by Paula Ettelbrick (executive director of the International Gay and Lesbian Human Rights Commission) in an article she wrote for the *Los Angeles Times*, December 4, 2006.

[330]   Howard Bragman

[331]   Mireya Navarro, "Out in Hollywood: starring roles are rare," *The New York Times*, September 28, 2008.

[332]   Don Thompson, The Associated Press, May 12, 2006.

[333]   Howard Mintz, "Court hears fertility treatment denial case," *San Jose Mercury News*, May 29, 2008.

[334]   The Courts later overturned Mayor Gavin Newsom's decision.

[335]   President Barack Obama has expressed his view that this law is discriminating and should be changed.

[336]   Mike Swift, "Legislation puts off deportation," *San Jose Mercury News*, April 24, 2009.

[337]   Robert Epstein (visiting scholar at University of California-San Diego and a former editor in chief of "Psychology Today") in an article written for the *Los Angeles Times,* December 7, 2008.

[338]   Ibid.

[339]   "Cheney's daughter expecting a child," *San Jose Mercury News*, December 6, 2006.

[340]   Mike Stobbe, Associated Press, November 22, 2006.

[341]   Mike Stobbe, Associated Press, May 14, 2009.

[342]   Mike Stobbe, Associated Press, November 22, 2006.

[343]   Mike Stobbe, Associated Press, May 14, 2009.

[344]   "Mail-order embryos offered commercially," *San Jose Mercury News*, January 6, 2007.

[345]   M.R. Kropko, Associated Press, November 12, 2008.

[346]   David Brown, "Study examines toll of preterm birth," *The Washington Post*, October 5, 2009.

[347]   Michael J. Norton.

[348]   Kirk Johnson, "Proposal in Colorado would give legal rights to fertilized eggs," *The New York Times*, November 18, 2007.

[349]   Robert Barnes, "Late-term abortion provider George Tiller killed in Wichita church," *The Washington Post*, June 1, 2009.

[350]   Susan Fitzgerald of New England.

[351]   Rob Stein, "Slaying of George Tiller focuses attention on late-term abortions," *The Washington Post*, June 5, 2009.

[352]   Sharon Camp, president of Guttmacher Institute, which supports abortion rights and is a leading source of data on abortion-related trends.

[353]   David Crary, Associated Press, October 14, 2009.

[354]   Tracy Wilkinson, "Nicaragua's total abortion ban draws fire," *Los Angeles Times*, July 28, 2009.

[355]   Juan Forero, "Colombian court legalizes some abortions," *The New York Times*, May 12, 2006.

[356]   Boys are seen as breadwinners who will support their parents in old age. Girls cost the family money, jewelry, clothing and perhaps even a car to marry her off.

[357]   Estimates by Mari Bhat, director of the International Institute for Population Sciences in Mumbai.

[358]   Ken Moritsugu, Knight Ridder, June 17, 2006.

[359]   Margie Mason, Associated Press, November 1, 2007.

[360]   "Conductor, wife end their lives together," *San Jose Mercury News*, July 15, 2009.

[361]   Sarah Lyall, "TV broadcast of an assisted suicide intensifies a contentious debate in Britain," *The New York Times*, December 11, 2008.

[362]   "House of Lords rejects debated right-to-die bill," *San Jose Mercury News*, May 13, 2006.

[363]   Steve Geissinger, MediaNews, March 26, 2007.

[364]   Tim Jones, "Resistance to death penalty growing," *Chicago Tribune*, April 8, 2007.

[365]   Adam Liptak, *The New York Times*.

[366]   Ibid.

[367]   Adam Liptak, "Does death penalty save lives? A new debate," *The New York Times*, November 18, 2007.

—CHAPTER 10—

[368]   Isabel Sawhill, an expert on marriage.

[369]   Blaine Harden, "Numbers Drop for the Married With Children," *The Washington Post*, March 7, 2007.

[370]   Associated Press (online), July 1, 2007.

[371]   Suzanne Bianchi.

[372]   Donna St. George, "Despite 'Mommy guilt,' time with kids increasing," *The Washington Post*, March 21, 2007.

[373]   Conducted by the Associated Press and MTV.

[374]   Jocelyn Noveck and Trevor Tompson, Associated Press, *San Jose Mercury News*, August 20, 2007.

[375]   Rob Stein, "Happiness Can Spread Among People Like a Contagion, Study Indicates," *The Washington Post*, December 5, 2008.

[376]   Study conducted by the Josephson Institute of Ethics, which reports on the ethics of American high school students.

[377]   Carla Rivera, "Colleges in crisis," *Los Angeles Times*, November 1, 2009.

[378]   Ruth Marcus, *The Washington Post.*

[379]   Ruth Marcus, "Camping Alone," *The Washington Post*, July 19, 2006.

[380]   Karin Klein, "Big Mother Is Watching," *Los Angeles Times*, March 2, 2009.

[381]   L. J. Williamson, *Los Angeles Times.*

[382]   L.J. Williamson, "Let Kids Outdoors," *Los Angeles Times*, March 29, 2007.

[383]   Hope Yen, Associated Press, *San Jose Mercury News*, June 29, 2009.

[384]   Mike Swift, "Generation gap still there, but it's gentler," *San Jose Mercury News*, August 12, 2009.

[385]   Dawn Klingensmith, Bay Area News Group, *San Jose Mercury News*, January 3, 2010.

[386]   Muhammed Chaudhry, CEO of the Silicon Valley Education Foundation, in an article written for the *San Jose Mercury News*, December 28, 2009.

[387]   According to a government financed survey.

[388]   As every high-school student applying for college knows, colleges today are seeking students with a specific passion.

[389]   As well as other places in the world.

[390]   Sam Dillon, "Foreign Languages Fade in Class — Except Chinese," *The New York Times*, page A-18, January 21, 2010.

[391]   According to Trevor Packer, a vice president at the College Board.

[392]   Grace Rauh, MediaNews, January 2, 2007.

[393]   Brett Zongker, Associated Press, October 10, 2009.

[394]   Karen Gabay, principal dancer, on San Jose Ballet blog site.

[395]   Castilleja School in Palo Alto, California.

[396]   Julia Prodis Sulek, "Going to the head of the class," *San Jose Mercury News*, May 2, 2008.

[397]   Becky Bartindale, "First virtual high school for the gifted," *San Jose Mercury News*, April 12, 2006.

[398]   Dana Hull, "Districts join charter school bandwagon," *San Jose Mercury News*, November 25, 2007.

[399]   Sharon Noguchi, "Charter schools taking off," *San Jose Mercury News*, April 20, 2009.

[400]   Christina Hernandez, *Newsday*, January 21, 2008.

[401]   Mike Antonucci, John Boudreau and Troy Wolverton, "Books, Web can co-exist in kids' world," *San Jose Mercury News*, June 14, 2008.

[402]   Anne Keisman, "When Words Become Endangered," National Wildlife Foundation website, October 1, 2009.

[403]   Soy Tech, Intel, Applied Materials, Lam Research, Advantest, Air Products and Ultra Tech.

[404]   Thirii Myint, "High-Tech Orientation," *San Jose Mercury News,* December 5, 2006.

[405]   "Gender gap narrows for doctorate studies," *San Jose Mercury News*, May 14, 2007.

[406]   Larry Magid.

[407]   Larry Magid, "Technology could aid student learning," *San Jose Mercury News*, June 22, 2009.

[408]   This makes one wonder: Why should information necessarily be stored in our brain rather than in a mobile device, as long as it is readily accessible? With information complexifying so rapidly in today's world, perhaps a better use of our brains would be to think about information, evaluate it, and utilize it, rather than to store it. After all, we store overflow information from our computers on external drives or CDs or thumb drives, or in "clouds." It may well be possible to trigger that information from the Internet as easily as we trigger it from brain storage. Researchers are already studying how our brain accesses information stored in our brain's memory bank, and contrasting it to

how our brain accesses information stored on the Internet. Unless specifics are called to our attention, we may not be using the most efficient method to access information from the Internet. (Of course, if we wait long enough, a computer chip inserted in our brain may totally revolutionize information access.)

[409]   *San Jose Mercury News*, May 13, 2006.

[410]   Becky Bartindale, "High court to get exam case," *San Jose Mercury News*, May 19, 2006.

[411]   Dan Walters, columnist for the *Sacramento Bee*, September 20, 2009.

[412]   Rosalind Chait Barnett.

[413]   Must there be a dividing line between "pass" and "fail" on the high school exit exam? Would it serve society better to present data without evaluation, awarding a diploma for having successfully completed the required courses of high school, and noting on each diploma the score received on the exit exam? Each constituency needing this information for employment or other purposes could rate that score according to their own standards.

[414]   Caryl Rivers and Rosalind Chait Barnett, "Latest crisis, about boys, is manufactured," article written for *The Washington Post*, April 2006.

[415]   Tamar Lewin, "At colleges, women are leaving men in the dust," *The New York Times*, July 9, 2006.

[416]   During the past few decades, women have outpaced men in education. For the first time in U.S. history more women than men now have college degrees, according to David Crary, Associated Press, January 2010.

[417]   In the Fall 2006 issue of Wellesley College's alumnae magazine, Wellesley's female president observed that high-velocity change is shifting the task of education toward preparing students to see with new eyes. Astute assessments by female college presidents of educational needs in the 21st century, as well as the rising stature of women college students, may have prompted an unusual donation of millions of dollars to a dozen or more colleges across the country. The anonymous donor awarded the money only to colleges led by women (Justin Pope, Associated Press, April 24, 2009).

[418]   Tamar Lewin, "At colleges, women are leaving men in the dust," *The New York Times*, July 9, 2006.

[419]   Lisa Black, *Chicago Tribune*, September 12, 2009.

[420]   The rate among youth ages 15 to 24 is considerably lower.

[421]   The Globalist Quiz, an online feature service, "Measuring illiteracy around the globe."

[422]   "$4.5 billion pledged for global education," *San Jose Mercury News*, September 26, 2008.

—CHAPTER 11—

[423]   Dean Takahashi, *San Jose Mercury News*, December 25, 2006.

[424]   Quoted by George F. Will, columnist for *The Washington Post*, December 2006.

[425]   In his book, *Radical Theology*, Don Cupitt says the real "radical theology" today is your own voice, if you can find it.

[426]   Associate professor at San Diego State University and lead author of an analytic study titled "Egos Inflating Over Time," published in 2006.

[427]   George F. Will, *The Washington Post*, December 2006.

[428]   Ruben Navarrette, Jr., columnist for the San Diego *Union-Tribune, "Hung up on themselves,"* May 3, 2009.

[429]   Larry Gordon and Louis Sahagun, *Los Angeles Times*, December 2006.

[430]   Graduate of Menlo School, a private school in Menlo Park, California.

[431]   Erik Klingbeil, student body president (2008-2009) at Palo Alto High School in Palo Alto, California.

[432]   Chris Kenrick, "Voices of '09," Palo Alto *Weekly*, June 12, 2009.

[433]   Ruben Navarrette, columnist for the San Diego *Union-Tribune*, May 18, 2008.

[434]   Vicki Leon, in an article written for *Los Angeles Times*, January 28, 2008.

[435]   Samantha Critchell, Associated Press, *San Jose Mercury News*.

[436]   Gwendolyn Wright, professor of architecture at Columbia University in an article written for *The Washington Post.*

[437]   Jessie Mangaliman, *San Jose Mercury News*, April 16, 2009.

[438]   Amy Green, "Home trends: easier access to laundry, kitchens," Associated Press, *San Jose Mercury News.*

[439]   Palo Alto *Weekly,* Palo Alto, California.

[440]   Sybil Wartenberg

[441]   Elise Ackerman, *San Jose Mercury News*, June 10, 2008.

[442]   Rasha Madhour, "19-year-old's suicide is broadcast live via webcam," Associated Press, *San Jose Mercury News*, November 22, 2008.

[443]   According to Nielsen BookScan.

[444]   Julia Moskin, "Food for the people, whipped up by the people," *The New York Times*, December 27, 2006.

[445]   This is but one of many ways the media includes their users. Another common practice is to invite submission of pictures or videos of breaking news.

[446]   Charlie McCollum, *San Jose Mercury News*, May 21, 2006.

[447]   Karen D'Souza, *San Jose Mercury News*, February 11, 2009.

[448]   Fred Shuster, MediaNews, *San Jose Mercury News*, January 3, 2007.

[449]   Michele Chandler, *San Jose Mercury News*, January 31, 2007.

[450]   "YouTube creates awards, lets community pick winners," *San Jose Mercury News*, March 19, 2007.

[451]   Shay Quillen, *San Jose Mercury News*, March 21, 2007.

[452]   Joe Gross, Cox News Service, *San Jose Mercury News*, February 11, 2007.

[453]   Scott Kirsner, "Free agents, or infomercials?" *San Jose Mercury News*, February 4, 2007.

[454]   Brian Bergstein, Associated Press, *San Jose Mercury News*.

[455]   Brian Bergstein, Associated Press, *San Jose Mercury News*, January 27, 2007.

[456]   *Los Angeles Times*, June 6, 2009.

[457]   According to Jim Kochanski, vice president at Sibson Consulting, a human resources firm.

[458]   Tammy Joyner, Cox News Service, *San Jose Mercury News*, December 3, 2006.

[459]   Jessica Mintz, Associated Press, *San Jose Mercury News*, December 8, 2006.

[460]   Ben Dobbin, Associated Press, *San Jose Mercury News*, March 12, 2007.

[461]   Nicholas Kristof, "The age of ambition," *The New York Times*, January 27, 2008.

[462]   Kate Folmar, MediaNews Sacramento Bureau, *San Jose Mercury News*, January 6, 2007.

[463]   Mary Anne Ostrom, "YouTube, CNN partner for presidential debate," *San Jose Mercury News*, May 17, 2007.

[464]   *San Jose Mercury News*, November 29, 2007.

[465]   Frank Davies, MediaNews Washington Bureau, *San Jose Mercury News*, June 2007.

[466]   Elise Ackerman, "Web-savvy campaigning: Sen. Clinton taps into Internet tools to talk with voters, get message out," *San Jose Mercury News*, January 26, 2007.

[467]   Richard Fausset, *Los Angeles Times*, November 24, 2006.

—CHAPTER 12—

[468]   "She is not the oldest member of the extended human family, but she is by far the most complete of the early hominids." The discovery of "Lucy" had already confirmed that "upright walking [which includes Ardi, and is the standard for being a hominid] evolved long before hominids began using stone tools . . . and *before* their brains began to expand dramatically." Ardi's brain was roughly the same size as a chimpanzee's. "Ardi represents an early stage of human evolution when an ancient ape body plan was being remodeled to live in two worlds—in the trees and on the ground." Ardi represented the "shift to life on the ground, upright-walking and social cooperation." (Ann Gibbons, "Our Earliest Ancestors," *Smithsonian* magazine, March 2010, pp. 35-40.)

[469]   Spencer Wells, *The Journey of Man,* Random House, 2003.

[470]   Ibid., 149.

[471]   Ibid.

[472]   "Hot Spots for 2008," *San Jose Mercury News*, January 6, 2008.

[473]   Bay Area Council is a federation of the CEO's of hundreds of the largest employers in the San Francisco Bay Area.

[474]   Jim Wunderman, "Going global poses challenge for valley," an article written for the *San Jose Mercury News*, December 19, 2006.

[475]   "Global Trade is Lifeblood of SV150," company reports of Bloomberg Financial, *San Jose Mercury News*, April 13, 2008.

[476]   Justin Pritchard, "Your city's news—from India," Associated Press, *San Jose Mercury News*, May 11, 2007.

[477]   James MacPherson, editor and publisher of Pasadena.com.

[478]   Justin Pritchard, "Your city's news—from India," Associated Press, *San Jose Mercury News,* May 11, 2007.

[479]   Nicole C. Wong, "Offshoring gives way to nearshoring to cut costs, customer complaints," *San Jose Mercury News*, February 25, 2007

[480]   "Craigslist—in 4 more languages," Bloomberg News, *San Jose Mercury News,* March 25, 2008.

[481]   Tony Elison.

[482]   Viacom offers its own Japanese-language, social networking service in Tokyo.

[483]   Yuri Kageyama, "In Japan, MySpace up against culture," *San Jose Mercury News*, February 20, 2007.

[484]   Les Blumenthal, "Pollution from Asia reaching western U.S., researchers find," McClatchy Newspapers, *San Jose Mercury News,* February 21, 2010.

[485]   Matt Nauman, "Great leap for Japanese car sales," *San Jose Mercury News,* December 23, 2006.

[486]   Mike Swift, "Other tongues overtaking English as language spoken in majority of Santa Clara County homes," *San Jose Mercury News*, March 4, 2007.

[487]   Jessie Mangaliman, "Earthquake readiness taught in Mandarin," *San Jose Mercury News,* May 4, 2008.

[488]   Joe Bel Bruno, Associated Press, "E-trade opening foreign stocks to traders," *San Jose Mercury News*, February 20, 2007.

[489]   John Boudreau," Chinese firm wins U.S. suit," *San Jose Mercury News,* December 29, 2006.

[490]   Wes Killingbeck and Karl Kahler, "Imports fill rail cars," *San Jose Mercury News*, February 25, 2007.

[491]   Tim Johnson, McClatchy Washington Bureau, "Wealthy Chinese scout housing deals in U.S.," *San Jose Mercury News*, March 25, 2009.

[492]   Gilda L. Ochoa, associate professor of sociology and Latino studies.

[493]   Jennifer Steinhauer, "I'll have a Big Mac, serenity on the side," *The New York Times*, March 2, 2008.

[494]   "Hispanics are nearly one-quarter of the working-age population—five times their percentage of the computer work force." (Mike Swift, "The Diversity Decline," *San Jose Mercury News*, February 14, 2010.)

[495]   Mike Swift, "The Diversity Decline," *San Jose Mercury News*, February 14, 2010.

[496]   Wadhwa researches at Duke, Harvard and the University of California—Berkeley.

[497]   Mike Swift, "The Diversity Decline," *San Jose Mercury News*, February 14, 2010.

[498]   Ibid.

[499]   Andrew Lam, editor at New America.

[500]   Spencer Wells, *The Journey of Man*, p. 63.

[501]   Donald K. Emmerson, "Obama's international background an asset, not a flaw," an op-ed piece written for the *San Jose Mercury News*, February 1, 2007.

[502]   Andrew Lam, editor at New America, in an article written for Pacific News Service, "Celebration of diversity is the wave of the future," *San Jose Mercury News.*

[503]   Andrew Lam, editor at New America. As of August 2011, gay marriages are legal in Massachusetts, Iowa, New Hampshire, Connecticut, Vermont, New York, plus Washington D.C. and the Coquille and Suquamish Indian tribes.

[504]   The fertility rate of Hispanics in Silicon Valley in 2008 was nearly 10 births for every death, according to the Census Bureau. Mike Swift, "Forecast: By 2050, 439 million Americans," *San Jose Mercury News*, August 14, 2008.

[505]   Mike Swift, "Rising population of children who are citizens," *San Jose Mercury News*, April 15, 2009.

[506]   Ken McLaughlin and Mike Swift, "Valley continues to draw Asians, Latinos," *San Jose Mercury News*, May 14, 2009.

[507]   U.S. Census Bureau, cited by *San Jose Mercury News*, January 1, 2006.

[508]   Mike Swift, "Data show nearly even mix in county," *San Jose Mercury News*, August 7, 2008.

[509]   Dave Montgomery, Knight Ridder, "A bid to make English official," *San Jose Mercury News*, May 19, 2006.

[510]   Julia Preston, "Work force fueled by highly skilled immigrants," *The New York Times*, April 16, 2010.

[511]   Dudley L. Poston Jr. and Peter A. Morrison, "Next wave of illegal immigration will be from China," *San Jose Mercury News*, August 19, 2011. (Dudley Poston directs the Asian Studies Program at Texas A&M University. Peter Morrison is an applied demographer and president of Morrison and Associates.)

[512]   Jessie Mangaliman, "Success shows immigrants blending into American life faster, experts say," *San Jose Mercury News*, December 28, 2006.

[513]   Jessie Mangaliman, Joe Rodriguez and Sandra Gonzales, "Festive crowd joins nationwide rallies for illegal immigrants," *San Jose Mercury News*, April 11, 2006.

[514]   *San Jose Mercury News*, January 5, 2007.

[515]   Raman Nelakanti, Lynbrook High School, San Jose, California; David Liu, Lynbrook High School, San Jose, California; Namrata Anand, The Harker School, San Jose, California; and Lynnelle Ye, Palo Alto High School, Palo Alto, California.

[516]   Lynnelle Ye.

[517]   Sharon Noguchi, "Lynbrook High notches first double in Intel science contest," *San Jose Mercury News*, January 28, 2010.

[518]   James Gerstenzang, *Los Angeles Times.*

[519]   James Gerstenzang, "Bush visits border, urges Senate action," *Los Angeles Times*, May 19, 2006.

[520] Jessie Mangaliman, "Report illegal migrants, suit says," *San Jose Mercury News*, April 5, 2007.

[521] "Intel splits off separate China market region," *San Jose Mercury News*, December 21, 2006.

[522] Associated Press and Bloomberg News, "BlackBerry maker to offer China service," *San Jose Mercury News*, May 12, 2006.

[523] John Murrell, "Good morning, Silicon Valley," *San Jose Mercury News*, June 21, 2007.

[524] Matt Slagle, Associated Press, "Dell unveils computer to be sold only in China," *San Jose Mercury News*, March 26, 2007.

[525] "World Region," Table 1, *Global Financial Insight*, December 2006.

[526] "Apple deal to sell iPhone in China," *San Jose Mercury News*, August 15, 2009.

[527] Bloomberg News, "China market gains," *San Jose Mercury News*, May 28, 2009.

[528] Rob Elder, "How China changed in 20-year build-up to Beijing Olympics," *San Jose Mercury News*, August 13, 2008.

[529] Don Lee, "In rural China, a bumper crop of new car owners," *Los Angeles Times*, May 31, 2009.

[530] D'arcy Doran, Associated Press, "Great leap for China: from manufacturer to designer," *San Jose Mercury News*, March 22, 2008.

[531] Thomas L. Friedman, "Who's sleeping now?" *The New York Times*, January 10, 2010.

[532] Tim Johnson, Knight Ridder, "China's huge dam nears completion," *San Jose Mercury*

[533] John Boudreau, "China's big power play," *San Jose Mercury News*, February 2, 2010.

[534] Quoted by Patrick Buchanan, syndicated columnist, "Dictators ride prosperity's tide," *San Jose Mercury News*, August 8, 2008.

[535] Patrick Buchanan, syndicated columnist, "Dictators ride prosperity's tide," *San Jose Mercury News*, August 8, 2008.

[536] Frank Davies, MediaNews Washington Bureau, "Impact of information technology touted," *San Jose Mercury News*, March 14, 2007.

[537] "Gates warns senators on U.S. competitiveness," *San Jose Mercury News*, March 8, 2007.

[538] Lisa M. Krieger, "Stanford president: Research rules too restrictive," *San Jose Mercury News*, January 16, 2010.

[539]   Wirt M. Cook, IBM vice president, in an article written for the *San Jose Mercury News*, "Patent Reform Act best way to protect, foster innovation," June 22, 2007.

[540]   Ian King, Jeff Green and Susan Decker, Bloomberg News, "Patent lawyers are latest hot hires," *San Jose Mercury News*, August 16, 2011.

[541]   Pete Carey and Patrick May, "Valley reinvents itself—again," *San Jose Mercury News*, August 13, 2009.

[542]   Steve Johnson, "'Brain drain' threatening biotech firms, report warns," *San Jose Mercury News*, December 6, 2006.

[543]   William Foreman, Associated Press, "Hong Kong is No. 2 at launching IPO's," *San Jose Mercury News*, January 2, 2007.

[544]   David Barboza, "Former peasant joins ranks of China's richest," *The New York Times*, April 20, 2007.

[545]   "Global Economy?" *San Francisco* magazine, April 2008.

[546]   *San Jose Mercury News*, April 8, 2008.

India has, indeed, gotten closer. By 2011 India's outsourcing strategy had taken a dramatic turn. Instead of gathering large numbers of cheap engineers in India to be the help desk for the U.S., they began hiring thousands of costly engineers in Silicon Valley. This shift was necessitated by the growing complexity of outsourced work, which now requires a higher level of expertise not readily available in India.

[547]   "The G-20's fast growers," The Globalist Quiz, *San Jose Mercury News*.

[548]   "U.S. share of the world economy," The Globalist Quiz, April 11, 2010.

[549]   Frank Davies, "Survey: U.S. losing its edge in innovation," *San Jose Mercury News*, (Washington Bureau), June 16, 2009.

[550]   James Mann, author of *The China Fantasy*, in an article written for *The Washington Post*.

[551]   "Washington Consensus" refers to the free-market, pro-trade and globalization policies promoted by the U.S.

[552]   Thomas L. Friedman, *The New York Times* columnist, "U.S. gridlock making world uneasy," *San Jose Mercury News*, January 31, 2010.

[553]   Rey Ramsey, CEO of TechNet, in an article written for the *San Jose Mercury News*, February 8, 2010.

[554]   Jay Thorwaldson, "Disturbing trends darken Silicon Valley outlook," Palo Alto *Weekly*, February 12, 2010.

[555]   Janice Shriver, Employment Development Department of California.

[556]   Pete Carey, "Region leads recovery with surge in hiring," *San Jose Mercury News*, August 20, 2011.

[557] The U.S. non-proliferation treaty with Russia, signed by President Obama in 2010, is a prime example of this.

[558] Moisis Namm, "Borders more fluid in complex world," *San Jose Mercury News*, May 28, 2006.

[559] Teresa Watanabe, "Area's dual citizens on the increase," *Los Angeles Times*, September 11, 2008.

[560] "International accounting rules allowed for foreign companies," *San Jose Mercury News*, June 21, 2007.

[561] James Green.

[562] Mike Swift, "After 36 years, the moon beckons again," *San Jose Mercury News*, July 26, 2008.

[563] Ralph Vartabedian and W.J. Hennigan, "Obama looks to deeper space as NASA's mission," *Los Angeles Times*, April 16, 2010.

CHAPTER 13-

[564] Peter S. Goodman and Jack Healy, "Grim toll: 651,000 lost jobs," *The New York Times*, March 7, 2009.

[565] Mike Zapler, "250,000 tech jobs lost last year," *San Jose Mercury News*, April 28, 2010.

[566] Peter S. Goodman and Jack Healy, "Grim toll: 651,000 lost jobs," *The New York Times*, March 7, 2009.

[567] Matt Apuzzo and Brett J. Blackledge, Associated Press, "AP analysis: stimulus bill fails to halt unemployment," *San Jose Mercury News*, January 12, 2010.

[568] "Jobless rate hits 10% in euro nations," *San Jose Mercury News*, January 9, 2010.

[569] Ibid.

[570] The unhappiest workers were under age 25.

[571] Jeannine Aversa, Associated Press, "Job dissatisfaction in steady rise in U.S.," *San Jose Mercury News,* January 5, 2010.

[572] Dan Leckrone, "'Patent reform' would destroy incentive to innovate," *San Jose Mercury News*, March 9, 2009. (Dan Leckrone is chairman and chief executive of The TPL Group.)

[573] Amy Bloom, "Coffee, Tea, Then Equality," book review of *When Everything Changed: The Amazing Journey of American Women From 1960 to the Present* by Gail Collins, October 18, 2009.

[574] Gail Collins, *When Everything Changed: The Amazing Journey of American Women from 1960 to the Present.* (Gail Collins is a columnist for *The New York Times* Op-Ed page.)

[575] Amy Bloom, "Coffee, Tea, Then Equality," October 18, 2009.

[576] Gail Collins, *When Everything Changed: The Amazing Journey of American Women from 1960 to the Present.*

[577] Amy Bloom, "Coffee, Tea, Then Equality," October 18, 2009.

[578] Ellen Goodman, *Boston Globe*, December 29, 2009.

[579] Ibid.

[580] Amy Bloom, "Coffee, Tea, Then Equality," October 18, 2009.

[581] Ellen Goodman, *Boston Globe*, December 29, 2009.

[582] Europe has seen an uptrend in its share of women in the workforce. "A key reason . . . is a choice to provide considerably higher levels of public spending on family benefits. These policies include funds for generous maternity leave and child care, which enable women to balance career and family interests by having more flexible working hours." ("Women at work," The Globalist Quiz, *San Jose Mercury News*, February 14, 2010.)

[583] Amy Bloom, "Coffee, Tea, Then Equality," October 18, 2009.

[584] "Women at Work," The Globalist Quiz, *San Jose Mercury News*, February 14, 2010.

[585] Hewlett-Packard, Intel, Cisco Systems, eBay, AMD, Google, Apple, Yahoo, Oracle and Applied Materials.

[586] Mike Swift, "The Diversity Decline," *San Jose Mercury News*, February 14, 2010.

[587] "Women at Work," The Globalist Quiz, *San Jose Mercury News*, February 14, 2010.

[588] U.S. Bureau of Labor Statistics (data from 2005-2006), "Occupations often split by gender," *San Jose Mercury News*, March 12, 2007.

[589] Ibid.

[590] Ibid.

[591] Ibid.

[592] "Pelosi takes gavel, starts historic run," Staff and wire reports, *San Jose Mercury News,* January 5, 2007.

[593] Julie Watson, Associated Press, "Mayan candidate seeks Guatemalan presidency," *San Jose Mercury News*, April 1, 2007.

[594] Ruth Marcus, "Nominating Elena Kagan," *The Washington Post*, May 11, 2010.

[595]   Ibid.

[596]   Christina Boyd, Lee Epstein and Andrew Martin, in a study of female appellate judges published in the *American Journal of Political Science,* 2010.

[597]   Ruth Marcus, "Nominating Elena Kagan," *The Washington Post*, May 11, 2010.

[598]   "Women Lawyers and Obstacles to Leadership," produced by the MIT Workplace Center in conjunction with several bar associations.

[599]   Rikleen is author of Ending the Gauntlet: Removing Barriers to Women's Success in the Law.

[600]   Sacha Pfeiffer, "Law track still rocky for women." *Boston Globe*, May 2, 2007.

[601]   Ibid.

[602]   Jessica Yadegaran, "Breaking Wine's Glass Ceiling," *San Jose Mercury News*, November 18, 2009.

[603]   Bill Cormier, Associated Press, "A new wave of female defense chiefs," *San Jose Mercury News,* January 30, 2007.

[604]   Ibid.

[605]   Ibid.

[606]   Ibid.

[607]   Ibid.

[608]   Ibid.

[609]   Best-selling author and international lecturer on women's issues.

[610]   Joan Chittester, "The great discovery: It's a human issue, not a woman's issue," *National Catholic Reporter*, October 27, 2009.

[611]   "Freddie Mac on Thursday launched a program that makes it possible for people facing eviction because of foreclosure to remain in their homes as renters." ("Foreclosed? Rent your house back," *San Jose Mercury News*, March 6, 2009.) In biblical times the trigger for foreclosure was, for the most part, a bad year of drought. Today's "drought" may be losing one's job.

[612]   "The Globalist Quiz," *San Jose Mercury News*, August 16, 2009.

[613]   Professor at the University of Durham in Great Britain.

[614]   Brian Murphy, Associated Press, *San Jose Mercury News*, December 3, 2009.

[615]   Dave Johnson, fellow at Commonweal Institute of San Francisco, in an article written for the *San Jose Mercury News*, November 19, 2009.

[616]   Dave Johnson, in an article written for the *San Jose Mercury News*, November 19, 2009.

[617]   Ibid.

[618]   "Senate passes tax-relief bill to ease burden on investors and above-average earners," *San Jose Mercury News*, May 12, 2006.

[619]   Dave Johnson, in an article written for the *San Jose Mercury News*, November 19, 2009.

[620]   Thomas L. Friedman, "The inflection is near?" *The New York Times*, March 8, 2009.

[621]   "Consumer debt falls sharply," *San Jose Mercury News*, January 9, 2010.

[622]   Author of *Future Shock, The Third Wave*, and (with Heidi Toffler) *Revolutionary Wealth*.

[623]   Alvin Toffler, in a program hosted by the World Affairs Council on May 16, 2006.

[624]   Ibid.

[625]   Ibid.

[626]   "5 ½ tons of cocaine seized from Venezuelan plane," *San Jose Mercury News*, April 12, 2006.

[627]   As early as 2006, $80 billion were paid for gift cards. "They rank as the second-most given gift by consumers in the United States (2006) and the most-wanted gift by women, and the third- most wanted by males." –Wikipedia

        Despite the rush to give gift cards, many people fail to cash them in. According to Kit Yarrow, a professor of psychology and marketing at Golden Gate University in San Francisco, the reason for failure to cash them in is "they're not perceived to be money."

[628]   Meghan Daum, "The gift card shuffle," *Los Angeles Times*, December 29, 2007.

[629]   "Sober salute for new Dow high," *San Jose Mercury News*, October 4, 2006.

[630]   Joe Bel Bruno, Associated Press, *San Jose Mercury News*.

[631]   A regional business organization in the San Francisco Bay Area.

[632]   John Boudreau of the *San Jose Mercury News*.

[633]   Ibid.

[634]   Jim Wunderman, president and CEO of the San Francisco Bay Area Council

[635]   Bernard Condon, Associated Press, *San Jose Mercury News*, April 10, 2010.

[636]   Mark Williams, Associated Press, *San Jose Mercury News*, February 2009.

[637]   Bernard Condon, Associated Press, *San Jose Mercury News*, January 9, 2010.

[638]   Bernard Condon, Associated Press, *San Jose Mercury News*, April 10, 2010.

[639]   David M. Herszenhorn, "Administration is seeking $700 billion for Wall Street," *The New York Times*, September 21, 2008.

[640] Jennifer Steinhauer, "A Race to be the first to use stimulus money," *The New York Times*, March 17, 2009.

[641] A complicated process in which home owners sell for less than what they owe after getting approval from lenders.

[642] Sue McAllister, "Short sales (and headaches) on rise," *San Jose Mercury News*, April 28, 2010.

[643] "Disconnect between Obama, CEOs," *San Jose Mercury News*, December 17, 2009.

[644] Marcy Gordon and Alan Ziebel, Associated Press, *San Jose Mercury News*, April 27, 2010. As of June 2011 Goldman was still challenging those findings

[645] Columnist for *The New York Times*.

[646] Thomas L. Friedman, "Invent, invent, invent," *The New York Times*, June 28, 2009

[647] Ibid.

[648] Pierluigi Oliverio, member of the San Jose City Council, in an article written for the *San Jose Mercury News*, May 14, 2007.

[649] "Supervisors consider raising revenue through corporate sponsorship and marketing," *San Jose Mercury News*, March 1, 2007.

[650] Truong Phuoc Khanh, "Your ad here: *on* county property," *San Jose Mercury News*, March 4, 2007.

[651] Ibid.

[652] Ibid.

[653] Ashraf Laidi, currency analyst for MG Financial Group, a currency trading firm.

[654] Vikas Bajaj, "U.S. trade deficit narrowed in February," *The New York Times*, April 13, 2006.

[655] The deficit represents the amount the United States must borrow from foreigners to cover the shortfall between exports and imports.

[656] "The Globalist Quiz," The Globalist, *San Jose Mercury News*.

[657] Martin Crutsinger, Associated Press, *San Jose Mercury News*, September 19, 2006.

[658] Intelligence Report, "Who America Owes," Parade.com, November 9, 2008.

W"The U.S. government owes $2.67 trillion to foreign governments and investors—20% of our total GDP. And that number has grown rapidly. 'In 2001, China held $61.5 billion in U.S. debt. Now it has $541 billion,' says James Ludes of the bipartisan American Security Project in Washington, D.C. 'In 2001, we owed Russia less than $10 billion. Now it's $74.4 billion.' The debt is sold to other countries in the form of U.S. Treasury securities.

'We also have to pay interest on those securities,' adds federal budget expert Doug Elmendorf. In coming years, a big chunk of our country's wealth will leave our economy and go overseas to pay back the loans. Will this outflow of cash affect our standing in the world? "The U.S. emerged as a major global power after World War I, and the U.K. declined in part because we owned so much British debt. Ironically, today the U.K. is our third largest creditor."

[659]   "US Overseas Loans and Grants: Obligations and Loan Authorizations," published by US Agency for International Development (USAID), 2006.

[660]   "Foreign investment in U.S. drops in December," *San Jose Mercury News*, February 16, 2007.

[661]   "The Globalist Quiz," The Globalist, *San Jose Mercury News*.

"The U.S. national debt has risen by 69 percent since 2000. This is the largest increase in the G7, above the UK's 58 percent and France's 51 percent. In contrast, fiscal discipline during the Clinton administration held debt growth to 24 percent from 1992 to 2000. Overall U.S. national debt rose from 54 percent of GDP in 2000 to 63 percent in 2008. The impending bailout of theU.S. financial industry will further increase the U.S. debt. At $700 billion, as currently proposed, the plan is equal to about 8 percent of the country's $9 trillion debt. It would cause the U.S. national debt to increase by 82 percent since 2000—and would add more than five percentage points to the U.S. debt-to-GDP ratio."

[662]   Lori Montgomery, "Presidential Commission to address rising national debt," *The Washington Post*, April 27, 2010.

[663]   Trudy Rubin, "Word from Davos: Denial," *The Philadelphia Inquirer*, February 4, 2009.

[664]   Stern's analysis appeared in the "Proceedings of the National Academy of Sciences," December 2006.

[665]   Barry Schweid, Associated Press, "Iran oil revenues dwindle," *San Jose Mercury News*, December 26, 2006.

[666]   Martin Crutsinger, Associated Press, "Higher oil prices push trade deficit to record," *San Jose Mercury News*, December 19, 2006.

[667]   Chris Kahn, Associated Press, "Oil stored, in hope for a rainy day," *San Jose Mercury News*, March 4, 2009.

[668]   "Forest services rejects oil-, gas-drilling appeal," *San Jose Mercury News*, April 12, 2006.

[669]   *Houston Chronicle*, May 16, 2010.

[670]   Juliet Eilperin, "Obama administration reimposes offshore oil drilling ban," *The Washington Post*, December 1, 2010.

[671]   A giant power company in Texas.

[672]   Kohlberg Kravis Roberts and Texas Pacific Group.

[673]   Thomas L. Friedman, "Marching with a mouse," *The New York Times*, March 16, 2007.

[674]   "Silicon Valley experts see California's green regulation as a benefit to economy," *San Jose Mercury News*, May 29, 2009.

[675]   John Woolfolk, "US stimulus funds for energy startups," *San Jose Mercury News*, January 9, 2010.

[676]   Thomas L. Friedman, "Tea Party with a difference," *The New York Times*, April 25, 2010.

[677]   In North America, Europe, India and China.

[678]   Gennady Sheyner, "Riding Palo Alto's clean-tech revolution," *Palo Alto Weekly*, April 16, 2010.

[679]   Janis Mara, BayAreaNewsGroup.com, "Fueling the Future," *San Jose Mercury News*, July 23, 2009.

[680]   Corn ethanol makes up 10 percent of every gallon pumped in California.

[681]   Grasses or shrubs that grow on marginal land.

[682]   Janis Mara, BayAreaNewsGroup.com, "Fueling the Future," *San Jose Mercury News*, July 23, 2009.

[683]   This center is part of the National Renewable Energy Laboratory in Golden, Colorado.

[684]   Suzanne Bohan, Bay Area News Group, "Biofuel market gaining steam," *San Jose Mercury News*, May 9, 2009.

[685]   Mike Cassidy, "OK, oil 'er up," *San Jose Mercury News*, May 12, 2006.

[686]   Matt Nauman, "PG&E begins tapping into cow power today," *San Jose Mercury News*, March 4, 2008.

[687]   James Tisch, "The Answer's in the Wind—and Sun," *The Washington Post*, June 20, 2008. (Tisch is CEO of Loews Corp.

[688]   Alysia Patterson, Associated Press, "McDonald's in N. Carolina will feed hungry electric cars," *San Jose Mercury News*, July 18, 2009.

[689]   Lisa Fernandez, "University launching car-sharing program," *San Jose Mercury News*, January 9, 2010.

[690]   Erica Werner and Ken Thomas, Associated Press, *San Jose Mercury News*.

[691]   The coalition includes Yahoo, Wal-Mart, Environmental Defense, U.S. Environmental Protection Agency, U.S. Energy Department, U.S. mayors, retailers, religious organizations and conservation groups.

[692]   Associated Press.

[693]   Associated Press, "Coalition launching campaign to urge Americans to switch to energy- efficient lighting," *San Jose Mercury News*, February 22, 2007.

[694]   James Tisch, "The Answer's in the Wind—and Sun," *The Washington Post*, June 20, 2008. (Tisch is CEO of Loews Corp.)

[695]   Marla Dickerson, "Big solar projects light up critics," *Los Angeles Times*, December 7, 2008.

[696]   Geothermal technology (cover story), *San Jose Mercury News*.

[697]   One megawatt of electricity is usually enough to power 750 to 1,000 homes.

[698]   *Masdar* is Arabic for "source."

[699]   Hassan M. Fattah, "Exploring energy alternatives," *The New York Times*, March 18, 2007.

[700]   Suzanne Bohan, Bay Area News Group, "New chapter opening for Livermore Lab," *San Jose Mercury News*, May 29, 2009.

[701]   Nicole C. Wong, "Tech pioneer weighs future of energy," *San Jose Mercury News*, July 1, 2007.

[702]   Brigitte Egger, in the newsletter of The Jung Society of Washington, September 5, 2008. Egger is a Jungian training analyst and ecologist in Zurich. She concentrates on the psychic and symbolic dimensions of collective issues, building up the field of psychecology.

—CHAPTER 14—

[703]   Max Lucudo, "The Woodcutter's Advice," *Worldwide Challenge*, September/ October 1995.

[704]   Brian Swimme and Thomas Berry, *The Universe Story*, p. 51.

[705]   Ibid., 52.

[706]   Michael Slackman, "Voices of peace muffled by rising mideast strife," *The New York Times*, July 14, 2006.

[707]   Brian Swimme and Thomas Berry, *The Universe Story*, p. 51.

[708]   Ibid., 56.

[709]   L. Robert. Keck, evolutionary theologian, "Transforming the Root Causes of Violence" (speech), 2001.

[710]   Ibid.

[711]   Ibid.

[712]   Ibid.

[713]   The Purity Code was of utmost importance in New Testament times. Jesus, who tried to eradicate all boundaries, was denounced for violating the Purity

Code by eating with sinners, for allowing a menstruating woman to touch him, for touching a leper, plus other violations. He was reprimanded not just for personal reasons, but for the sake of the community, which they felt had been made impure by his boundary-breaking actions.

[714]   Based on the thinking of L. Robert Keck, evolutionary theologian. As long as people continue to worship a hierarchical God, and see themselves as primarily different from others and from God—not as one with them—violent acts to remain pure (i.e. set apart) will continue. However, even though violence is instinctual, in that human beings have a natural propensity for differentiation and fulfillment of their own inner nature, humans also have the capacity through consciousness to choose how to work with those tendencies in a creative way. The way will involve destruction at some level, but it must be destruction acted out consciously. If you know what you are doing and why, and you consider your choice as having the highest value in the situation, the choice is acceptable, *with* its destructive part.

[715]   Brian Swimme, "Starburst."

[716]   Hitler fell into this line of thinking with regard to Jews, gypsies and homosexuals.

[717]   Wolfgang Giegerich, *The Soul's Logical Life: Towards a Rigorous Notion of Psychology*, p. 236.

[718]   Ibid., 234-246.

[719]   One day in the early sixties, before "black" became "beautiful," I was wandering through an open market in Ghana, looking at the array of fruits and vegetables. A week earlier, my family and I had arrived for an extended stay. I had made no friends at that time, so I spent most of my days wandering around alone, familiarizing myself with new surroundings. Often I would see no other white person until my family came home from work and school.

One day, when I reached out for a succulent-looking pineapple, my eyes suddenly became glued to my extended white arm. "How anemic-looking my white arm looks compared to the beautiful, shiny black skin of the people around me!" I thought. Quickly I realized what a radical thought had come up in me. Black skin more beautiful than white skin? Wow! The mere idea of a black "other" had been killed and was now dissolved within me. It just happened.

[720]   Rita Nakashima Brock and Rebecca Ann Parker, Saving Paradise: How Christianity Traded Love of This World for Crucifixion and Empire, Chapter 10.

[721]   Author of *A Complex Delight: The Secularization of the Breast, 1350-1750.*

[722]   Margaret R. Miles, "God's love, mother's milk," *Christian Century*, January 29, 2008, p. 23.

[723]   Ibid., 24.

[724]   Gertrude Huntington, researcher and expert on children in Amish society.

[725]   Michael Rubinkam, Associated Press, "Amish mourners turn to faith," *San Jose Mercury News*, October 5, 2006.

[726]   Molly Moore, "Virginia killings widely seen as reflecting a violent society," *The Washington Post* Foreign Service, April 18, 2007.

[727]   Deborah Hastings, Associated Press, "Limits on gun use in U.S. being rolled back," *San Jose Mercury News*, April 8, 2009.

[728]   Carol Morello, "An unexpected result for some census takers: the wrath of irate Americans," *The Washington Post*, June 20, 2010.

[729]   "Detained son 'squeaky clean,' father says," *San Jose Mercury News*, April 28, 2010.

[730]   Brian Murphy, Associated Press, "Navy captures suspected pirates," *San Jose Mercury News,* May 2010.

[731]   Neil Irwin and Peter Whoriskey, "Greece's debt pain sparks violence," *The Washington Post*. May 6, 2010.

[732]   Chris Blake, Associated Press, "Unrest spreads in Thailand," *San Jose Mercury News*, May 17, 2010.

[733]   "Another Foxconn worker makes suicide attempt," *San Jose Mercury News*, May 28, 2010.

[734]   Richard Schickel, film critic, in an article written for the *Los Angeles Times*, December 8, 2006.

[735]   American Psychological Association, June 2010.

[736]   Deborah Hastings, Associated Press, "Limits on gun use in U.S. being rolled back," *San Jose Mercury News*, April 8, 2009.

[737]   Ibid.

[738]   Josh Meyer, "North Africa attacks put West on alert," *Los Angeles Times*, April 15, 2007.

[739]   Ibid.

[740]   Michael Slackman, "Voices of peace muffled by rising Mideast strife," *The New York Times*, July 14, 2006.

[741]   Mark Magnier, "Tweet lands Indian official in hot water," *Los Angeles Times*, January 3, 2010.

[742]   Mark Magnier, *Los Angeles Times*.

[743]   Mark Magnier, "Tweet lands Indian official in hot water," *Los Angeles Times*, January 3, 2010.

[744]   Thomas L. Friedman, "Still not tired," *The New York Times*, October 4, 2009.

[745] Jean-Louis Bruguiere, liaison to the U.S. Treasury Department on terrorist financing.

[746] Edward Cody, "In Europe, human-focused counterterrorism," *The Washington Post,* May 13, 2010.

[747] Alan Cowell, "Britain arrests 9 suspects in terrorist kidnapping plot," *The New York Times*, February 1, 2007.

[748] Second director of national intelligence under former president George W. Bush.

[749] "Plots developing faster, warns intelligence chief," *San Jose Mercury News*, February 21, 2007.

[750] Political theorist, Yaron Ezrahi.

[751] Thomas L. Friedman, www.jihad.com, *The New York Times*, December 17, 2009.

[752] Dana Milbank, "The NRA, standing up for terrorists' rights," *The Washington Post,* May 6, 2010.

[753] Alexandra Olson, Associated Press, "Cancun mayor linked to cartels," *San Jose Mercury News*, May 27, 2010.

[754] Ibid.

[755] Dan Eggen, "Violent crime is up for 2nd straight year," *The Washington Post*, December 19, 2006.

[756] Pete Yost, Associated Press, *San Jose Mercury News*, May 25, 2010.

[757] Richard Cohen, "Were liberals wrong on crime?" *The Washington Post*, June 2, 2010. Bad times may not make bad people, but recent studies suggest that bad places (i.e. a person's environment) do.

[758] Tim Talley, Associated Press, "Man faces murder charge after he wounds holdup suspect, then fires five fatal shots," *San Jose Mercury News*, May 30, 2009.

[759] Tim Talley, Associated Press.

[760] Tim Talley, Associated Press, "Man faces murder charge after he wounds holdup suspect, then fires five fatal shots," *San Jose Mercury News*, May 30, 2009

[761] "City Council OKs new handgun restrictions," *San Jose Mercury News*, July 3, 2010.

[762] P. Solomon Banda, Associated Press, "Unit's soldiers connected to 11 slayings in U.S.,"*San Jose Mercury News*, July 16, 2009.

[763] Ibid.

[764] Martha Mendoza, Associated Press, "Order on border: Crime rates fall," *San Jose Mercury News*, June 4, 2010.

[765] Wellesley College symposium on "Globalization," June 2002.

[766] Daniel Wagner, Associated Press, "Holder: white collar crime a top priority," *San Jose Mercury News*, January 15, 2010.

[767] Gregory Reyes, a rising star in the tech industry of Silicon Valley.

[768] Brandon Bailey, "Brocade ex-CEO gets fine, prison," *San Jose Mercury News*, June 25, 2010.

[769] Ibid.

[770] David G. Savage, "Supreme Court has given firms a stronger hand," *Los Angeles Times*, June 25, 2010.

[771] "Report on which states most likely to jail women," *San Jose Mercury News*, May 21, 2006.

[772] Linda McFarlane, deputy executive director.

[773] Just Detention International seeks to end sexual abuse of detainees.

[774] Devlin Barrett and Dena Potter, Associated Press, "Youth center abuses widespread," *San Jose Mercury News*, January 8, 2010.

[775] Shaun Bishop, Bay Area News Group, *San Jose Mercury News*, "Inmates help rehabilitate dogs," February 13, 2010.

[776] "California should abolish death penalty," *San Jose Mercury News*, January 8, 2010.

—CHAPTER 15—

[777] Max Boot, Senior Fellow for National Security Studies at the Council on Foreign Relations, "The Changing Face of Warfare." a program hosted by the World Affairs Council on November 6, 2006.

[778] Ibid.

[779] Ibid.

[780] Ibid.

[781] Lolita C. Baldor, Associated Press, "U.S. faces Afghan war dilemma," *San Jose Mercury News*, October 25, 2009.

[782] Hajji Muhammad Ehsan, a member of the Kandahar provincial council.

[783] Richard A. Oppel Jr. and Taimoor Shah, "A killing further erodes Afghan faith in leaders,"*The New York Times*, April 21, 2010.

[784] *San Jose Mercury News*, October 4, 2009.

[785] This is opposite to the problem of World War II, in which stunted growth and inadequate nutrition caused the rejection of many recruits.

[786]   "Surge in suicide bombs worries military analysts," *San Jose Mercury News*, April 18, 2008.

[787]   Elisabeth Bumiller, "Gates says Taliban must take legitimate Afghan role," *The New York Times*, January 22, 2010.

[788]   Stephen Hunter, "The sniper is the go-to guy for military operations," *San Jose Mercury News,* April 17, 2009.

[789]   "Scientists take step toward 'invisibility cloak'," *San Jose Mercury News*, August 12, 2008.

[790]   Gordon Johndroe.

[791]   Marc Kaufman and Dafna Linzer, "China criticized for anti-satellite missile test," *The Washington Post*, January 19, 2007.

[792]   John Schwartz, "When computers attack," *The New York Times*, June 24, 2007.

[793]   According to the 2007 Defense Department annual report to Congress.

[794]   Scenarios like those spelled out at length in the documentary "Countdown to Zero."

[795]   John Schwartz, "When computers attack," *The New York Times*, June 24, 2007.

[796]   David E. Sanger, John Markoff and Thom Shanker, "U.S. steps up effort on digital defenses," *The New York Times*, April 28, 2009.

[797]   Ibid.

[798]   RBS WorldPay.

[799]   Mike Baker, Associated Press, "Hacker's trial reveals growing scope, complex nature of crimes," *San Jose Mercury News*, August 7, 2010.

[800]   John Markoff and Thom Shanker, "Halted '03 Iraq plan illustrates U.S. fear of cyberwar risk," *The New York Times*, August 2, 2009.

[801]   David E. Sanger, John Markoff and Thom Shanker, "U.S. steps up effort on digital defenses," *The New York Times*, April 28, 2009.

[802]   Christopher Drew and John Markoff, "Contractors vie for plum work, hacking for U.S.," *The New York Times*, May 31, 2009.

[803]   John Markoff and Thom Shanker, "Halted '03 Iraq plan illustrates U.S. fear of cyberwar risk," *The New York Times*, August 2, 2009.

[804]   Karin Laub, Associated Press, "Abbas tells U.S. to impose peace," *San Jose Mercury News*, April 25, 2010.

[805]   Janine Zacharia, "Palestinians turn to boycott of Israel in West Bank," *The Washington Post*, May 16, 2010.

[806]   Ibid.

[807] Columnist for *The New York Times*.

[808] Recep Tayyip Erdogan.

[809] Thomas L. Friedman, "When friends fall out," *The New York Times*, June 3, 2010.

[810] Nicholas D. Kristof, "Our fantasy nation?" *The New York Times*, June 4, 2010.

[811] Meir Dagan, chief of Mossad, Israel's national intelligence agency.

[812] Nicholas D. Kristof, "Our fantasy nation?" *The New York Times*, June 4, 2010.

[813] David E. Sanger and Thom Shanker, "Pentagon plans new arm to wage cyberspace wars," *The New York Times*, May 29, 2009

[814] Ibid.

[815] Thom Shanker and David E. Sanger, *The New York Times*.

[816] Thom Shanker and David E. Sanger, "Privacy may be a victim in cyberdefense plan," *The New York Times*, June 13, 2009.

[817] Stephen Whitlock and Michael Kessler, *The Washington Post*, May 8, 2010.

[818] Charles J. Hanley, Associated Press, *San Jose Mercury News*, May 3, 2010.

[819] Karen DeYoung, "President Obama's national security strategy looks beyond military might," *The Washington Post*, May 27, 2010.

[820] Maura Reynolds and Doyle McManus, "Iraq report gets mixed reception in Congress,"*Los Angeles Times*, December 8, 2006.

The Iraq Study Group viewed the conflict at a deeper level than Congress, seeing the relationship of all its parts to a greater whole. By nitpicking the report, praising some parts and condemning others, Congress distorted its truth.

[821] Elaine Ganley, Associated Press, "Undercurrent of resentment as world mourns," *San Jose Mercury News*, September 12, 2006.

[822] The average cost per service member in Iraq was more than ten times the cost of a soldier deployed in World War II.

[823] The lower cost of wars is largely due to the reduced number of troops required for today's type of warfare.

[824] The Globalist quiz, "The U.S. in Afghanistan," *San Jose Mercury News*, August 1, 2010.

[825] Tom Andrews, former Maine congressman who heads Win Without War, a coalition of 40 different groups.

[826] Frank Davies, "$83.4B spending bill criticized," *San Jose Mercury News*, May 13, 2009.

[827]   Clifford L. Stanley.

[828]   Stephen Whitlock, *The Washington Post*, May 8, 2010.

[829]   Rep. Susan A. David (D-California), chairperson of the military personnel subcommittee of the House Armed Services Committee.

[830]   Stephen Whitlock, *The Washington Post*, May 8, 2010.

[831]   David Brown, "Up to 250,000 Gulf War veterans have 'unexplained medical symptoms',"*The Washington Post*, April 10, 2010.

[832]   Ronald Glasser, "The Hidden Wounds of the Iraq war," *San Jose Mercury News*, April 15, 2007.

[833]   During the Vietnam War the ratio was 2.6 to 1.

[834]   Ronald Glasser, "The Hidden Wounds of the Iraq war," *San Jose Mercury News*, April 15, 2007.

[835]   Tim Jones and Jason Grotto, "Costs soar for compensating veterans with mental disorders," *Chicago Tribune*, April 18, 2010.

[836]   Lizette Alvarez, "Suicides of soldiers reach high of nearly 3 decades," *The New York Times*, January 30, 2009

[837]   Murthada Abdel Rashid.

[838]   Nancy A. Youssef, Knight Ridder, "Iraqis numb to civilian deaths," *San Jose Mercury News*, May 29, 2006.

[839]   "Iraqi civilian death data released," *San Jose Mercury News*, April 24, 2009.

[840]   Special Operations forces were steadily on the rise after 9/11. As of June 2010, they were deployed in about 74 countries, compared with 60 at the beginning of 2009.

[841]   Karen DeYoung and Greg Jaffe, "U.S. 'secret war' expands globally as Special Operations forces take larger role," *The Washington Post*, June 4, 2010.

[842]   Anne Flaherty, Associated Press,"Special Ops HQ in Afghanistan to grow," June 5, 2010.

—CHAPTER 16—

[843]   This fall-off was due to women's wages rising as more women continued to work outside the home after the war.

[844]   Paul Krugman, "King of pain," *The New York Times*, September 18, 2006.

[845]   Thomas L. Friedman, "Vote for ( )," *The New York Times*, October 2, 2008.

[846]   Martin Crutsinger and AlanZibel, Associated Press, "Construction spending, manufacturing pick up," *San Jose Mercury News*, June 2, 2010.

[847]   Chris O'Brien and Jack Davis, "Tech fortunes rebound—even as number of public companies drops," *San Jose Mercury News*, August 26, 2010.

[848]   Troy Wolverton, "Major merger in chip industry," *San Jose Mercury News*, December 5, 2006.

[849]   Elliot Spagat, Associated Press, "Yahoo open to deal," *San Jose Mercury News*, May 28, 2009.

[850]   Rachel Metz, Associated Press, "AOL to be spun off," *San Jose Mercury News*, May 29, 2009.

[851]   Scott Duke Harris, "Facebook, AOL enter partnership," *San Jose Mercury News*, February 10, 2010.

[852]   Mae Anderson, Associated Press, "FAO Schwarz R Us," *San Jose Mercury News,* May 28, 2009.

[853]   Andrew Wolf, an analyst who follows drugstores for BB&T Capital Markets.

[854]   Andrea Chang, "Big chains give small drugstores headaches," *Los Angeles Times*, October 13, 2008.

[855]   "BBC news, entertainment clips debut on YouTube," *San Jose Mercury News*, March 3, 2007.

[856]   "Citigroup to make bid for Japanese brokerage," *San Jose Mercury News*, March 7, 2007.

[857]   Pete Carey, "Tata Group buying Jaguar, Land Rover," *San Jose Mercury News*, March 27, 2008.

[858]   John Boudreau, "Instant cities for sale," *San Jose Mercury News*, June 2, 2010.

[859]   "To gain and hold high office, candidates of both parties depend on the contributions of a monied elite, whose salaries, bonuses, stock options and golden parachutes depend on a rising share price, which means constantly cutting costs by moving production out of the United States and getting rid of high-wage American workers." (Patrick J. Buchanan, syndicated columnist).

[860]   Patrick J. Buchanan, syndicated columnist, *San Jose Mercury News*, February 18, 2007.

[861]   Subhash Dhar.

[862]   John Boudreau, "Microcosm," *San Jose Mercury News*, December 5, 2006.

[863]   John Boudreau, "Valley entrepreneurs invest millions in pollution-cutting ideas," *San Jose Mercury News*, June 18, 2007.

[864]   Dibya Sarkar, Associated Press, "U.S. tech imports soar, as trade gap hits record," *San Jose Mercury News*, July 17, 2007.

[865]   Patrick May, "Behind the valley's blue-collar job drain," *San Jose Mercury News*, July 24, 2009.

[866]   John Boudreau, "More tech firms innovate here but sell overseas," *San Jose Mercury News*, February 23, 2009.

[867]   The trip was won by William Temple of Sacramento, a computer technician.

[868]   The walls of the National Gallery in London and the palace of Fine Arts in San Francisco.

[869]   Dean Takahashi.

[870]   Dean Takahashi, "Playing now: a game that wants you," *San Jose Mercury News*, February 12, 2007.

[871]   Candice Choi, Associated Press, "Employers, hotels catering to mix of work, leisure," *San Jose Mercury News*, November 4, 2007.

[872]   Mark Boslet and Katherine Conrad, "Valley companies dump the cubicle in push for efficiency, teamwork," *San Jose Mercury News*, December 3, 2007.

        This movement from private offices, to individual cubicles within community space, to open community space is interesting, as it is mimicked by the movement from e-mail, to MySpace, to Facebook.

[873]   Apple, Hewlett Packard, Procter and Gamble, IBM.

[874]   Behnam Fabrizi, professor of management science and engineering, Stanford School of Engineering.

[875]   Brandon Bailey, "Stanford professor's lesson: Change should be rapid," *San Jose Mercury News*, May 13, 2009.

[876]   Brandon Bailey, "HP cuts jobs as it looks to future of IT," *San Jose Mercury News*, June 2, 2010.

[877]   Larry Magid, "Yahoo-Facebook deal brings lofty implications," *San Jose Mercury News*, December 7, 2009.

[878]   Applebee's, Aflac and Home Depot were among them.

[879]   Joseph Buckley.

[880]   Rachel Beck, Associated Press, "Companies open up to compromise with insistent investors," *San Jose Mercury News*, February 16, 2007.

[881]   Craig Timberg, "Banker sees a rich market in the poor," *The Washington Post*, May 14, 2008.

[882]   Mike Swift, "Students use technology to promote public good," *San Jose Mercury News*, April 29, 2010.

[883]   George Will, "The case for conservatism," *The Washington Post*, May 31, 2007.

[884]   Tim Craig, "In D.C., 'progressive' isn't what it used to be," *The Washington Post*, May 14, 2010.

[885] Denise Gellene, "Study suggests link between DNA and political persuasion, "*Los Angeles Times*, September 19, 2008.

[886] Nicholas D. Kristof, "Global weirding is here," *The New York Times*, February 17, 2010.

[887] Keith Ellison, a criminal defense attorney who converted to Islam as a college student.

[888] "Lawmaker: Muslim colleague a threat," *San Jose Mercury News*, December 21, 2006.

[889] Marc Hetherington of Vanderbilt University and Jonathan Weiler of the University of North Carolina-Chapel Hill.

[890] Nicholas D. Kristof, "Global weirding is here," *The New York Times*, February 17, 2010.

[891] A conservative commentator and three-time presidential candidate.

[892] Ron Fournier, Associated Press, "GOP departure offers microcosm," *San Jose Mercury News*, April 30, 2010.

[893] Francis Fukuyama, "Making a case for political shift on war in Iraq," *San Jose Mercury News*, April 12, 2006.

[894] Michael Finnegan, *Los Angeles Times*, January 30, 2007.

[895] Matthew Mosk, *The Washington Post*, March 11, 2007.

[896] "Campaign: Web helps many make splash in fundraising," *San Jose Mercury News*, September 30, 2008.

[897] Mary Anne Ostrom, *San Jose Mercury New*

[898] Nick Spaeth, an Iowa resident.

[899] Mary Anne Ostrom, "'Democracy in action' in Iowa," *San Jose Mercury News*, January 4, 2008.

[900] "Election: Mail-in voting saves money, official says," *San Jose Mercury News*, January 21, 2008.

[901] Nearly 40 percent of Obama's votes were from minorities.

[902] Mary Anne Ostrom, *San Jose Mercury News*.

[903] Mary Anne Ostrom, "Ethnically diverse voters value government action, shun divisive politics," *San Jose Mercury News*, November 8, 2008.

[904] Those born between 1982 and 2005.

[905] Mary Anne Ostrom, "Ethnically diverse voters value government action, shun divisive politics," *San Jose Mercury News*, November 8, 2008.

[906] Matt Bai, "Voter insurrection turns mainstream, creating new rules," *The New York Times*, May 20, 2010.

[907]   Companies of all sizes are obsessed with secrecy, even in this age of growing transparency. They desperately push back against the information age they themselves are enabling. (Chris O'Brien, "Hacking Twitter," *San Jose Mercury News*, July 22, 2009.)

[908]   K. Oanh Ha, "Silicon Valley leaders outraged by idea of calls being examined," *San Jose Mercury News*, May 12, 2006.

[909]   "In general [before the new legislation], U.S. companies pay taxes to a foreign country on income generated within its borders, but foreign rates are often lower. If U.S. companies bring the revenue home, they must pay U.S. taxes, although they can deduct foreign tax payments from the amount they owe here." (Brandon Bailey, *San Jose Mercury News*.) Under the new legislation, U.S. taxes must be computed on foreign earnings *before* deducting foreign tax payments.

[910]   Brandon Bailey, "Obama, tech titans clash over tax policy," *San Jose Mercury News*, May 3, 2009.

[911]   Louise Story, "U.S. said to open criminal inquiry into Goldman," *The New York Times*, April 30, 2010.

[912]   Robert Lee Hotz, "Across the U.S., public parks are landing private operators," *Los Angeles Times*, February 11, 2007.

[913]   Ibid.

[914]   Joshua Goodman, Associated Press, "Conservative wins in Colombia, bucking trend to left in region," *San Jose Mercury News*, May 29, 2006.

[915]   Brother of the ailing Fidel Castro.

[916]   Gary Marx, "Raul Castro offers look at his leadership style," *Chicago Tribune*, December 22, 2006.

[917]   Molly Moore and John Ward Anderson.

[918]   Molly Moore and John Ward Anderson, "Sarkozy, royal head to presidential runoff," *The Washington Post*, April 23, 2007.

[919]   Karl Vick, "Iran derides incentive bid to resolve nuclear dispute," *The Washington Post*, May 18, 2006.

[920]   Joby Warrick, "Iran speeding up nuclear program, inspectors say," *The Washington Post*, September 2, 2011.

[921]   "30,000 rally in Seoul against U.S. trade pact," *San Jose Mercury News*, November 26, 2006.

—CHAPTER 17—

[922]   Hewlett-Packard, Intel, IBM, Microsoft and Cisco.

[923]   Steve Johnson, "Dow Jones list replaces GM with Cisco," *San Jose Mercury*

News, June 2, 2009.

[924] Mike Feibus, "Company-created info sites deliver blow to print media," *San Jose Mercury News*, March 20, 2008.

[925] Becky Trout, "Newspapers face tough times but will survive, experts predict," *San Jose Mercury News*, May 18, 2007; "Chicago Tribune trims 14% of its staff," *San Jose Mercury News*, August 15, 2008.

[926] Mac Tully, "1,150,000 strong—and growing," *San Jose Mercury News*, November 1, 2009.

[927] "Mercury News wins 5 awards for journalism," *San Jose Mercury News*, November 14, 2008.

[928] Deepti Hajela, Associated Press, "Pulitzers honor newspapers' government watchdog role," *San Jose Mercury News*, April 21, 2009.

[929] Ibid.

[930] "Further circulation losses for newspapers," *San Jose Mercury News*, April 29, 2008.

[931] "Weekly to combine print editions, launch new 'e-daily'," Palo Alto *Weekly*, August 15, 2008.

[932] The *New York Post*, the *Times* of London, the *Sun* and the *Daily Telegraph*.

[933] *The Wall Street Journal* could get away with charging because its financial content is unique.

[934] Paul Rogers, "Universities form 'wire service'," *San Jose Mercury News*, September 16, 2009.

[935] Associated Press, "Newspaper ad revenue decline slows," *San Jose Mercury News*, May 28, 2010.

[936] "British Library to digitize millions of newspapers," *San Jose Mercury News*, May 19, 2010.

[937] Larry Magid.

[938] Larry Magid, "Newspapers need to find a new model," *San Jose Mercury News*, November 16, 2009.

[939] "Time Inc. cuts jobs as readers move to Internet," *San Jose Mercury News*, January 19, 2007.

[940] E-ink is the same substance used in Amazon's Kindle electronic-book reader.

[941] Andrew Vanacore, Associated Press, "Esquire animates magazine's cover for December with 3-D," *San Jose Mercury News*, November 2, 2009.

[942] Sal Pizarro, "New festival celebrates comic books," *San Jose Mercury News*, January 9, 2010.

[943] Kyle Petersen.

[944] Laura Copeland, "Writer finds hottest new thing in publishing," *San Jose Mercury News*, June 28, 2010.

[945] Liz Perl, publisher of Rodale Books.

[946] Hillel Italie, Associated Press, "Consumers show allegiance to printed word as publishers grapple with digital age," *San Jose Mercury News*, December 18, 2006.

[947] Richard Cohen, "The book on the shelf," *The Washington Post*, August 5, 2008.

[948] Michael Pocock, publisher of Books By You.

[949] This is similar to a concept used for years by one or more children's book publishers.

[950] Sarah Skidmore, "Publisher finds ardent niche personalizing romance novels," *San Jose Mercury News*, February 6, 2009.

[951] John Woolfolk, "Need to know? Just text your local librarian," *San Jose Mercury, News,* August 17, 2009.

[952] Larry Magid, "It's getting easier to borrow e-books," *San Jose Mercury News*, August 31, 2009.

[953] Lisa M. Krieger.

[954] Lisa M. Krieger, "Librarians pack up the past," *San Jose Mercury News*, May 19, 2010.

[955] "Flexible libraries or rigid book warehouses?" *Palo Alto Weekly*, November 19, 2010.

[956] Azam Ahmed and Michael J. de la Merced, "To lift stock, McGraw–Hill will split in two," *The New York Times*, September 12, 2011.

[957] Quoted by Don Kazak, Palo Alto *Weekly*.

[958] Don Kazak, "Tough time for scribes," Palo Alto *Weekly*, May 28, 2008.

[959] Larry Magid.

[960] Larry Magid, "Journalism today—here and abroad," *San Jose Mercury News*, April 27, 2009.

[961] Don Kazak, "Tough time for scribes," Palo Alto *Weekly*, May 28, 2008.

[962] According to Accenture's annual report for 2009, "Baby boomers are embracing popular consumer technology applications nearly 20 times faster than the younger generation."

[963] "Obama plans weekly address on YouTube," *San Jose Mercury News*, November 14, 2008; Chris O'Brien, "Tech-savvy in middle age," *San Jose Mercury News*, April 19, 2009; and Richard Perez-Pena, "Washington Post wins 4 Pulitzers, New York Times gets 3," *The New York Times*, April 13, 2010.

[964]   Aston Carey of San Jose, California.

[965]   Sharon Noguchi, "E-mail: Teens' use is dropping as networking sites explode," *San Jose Mercury News*, June 13, 2006.

[966]   Troy Wolverton, "Awash in tidal wave of e-mail," *San Jose Mercury News*, November 16, 2009.

[967]   Pamela Constable, "Demise of the Foreign Correspondent," *The Washington Post,* February 18, 2007; "Watchdog group reports risks of journalism trend," *San Jose Mercury News*, March 12, 2007.

[968]   *San Jose Mercury News*, May 24, 2008.

[969]   Reed Tucker, "Are you ready for Internet TVs?" USA *Weekend*, August 21-23, 2009.

[970]   Troy Wolverton, "TVs learning a whole bag of new tricks," *San Jose Mercury News*, January 7, 2010.

[971]   Eric Schmidt, (former) CEO of Google.

[972]   Mike Swift and Troy Wolverton, "Google, allies aim to marry TV, Web," *San Jose Mercury News*, May 21, 2010.

[973]   Christopher Liam Moore, from playbill notes for the Oregon Shakespeare Festival's production of *Dead Man's Cell Phone* by Sarah Ruhl, 2008.

[974]   The New York Times, May 16, 2010.

[975]   James London of De Anza College in California.

[976]   John Boudreau, "Your phone, your life," *San Jose Mercury News*, March 15, 2009.

[977]   Jill Colvin, "You've got voice mail, but do you care?" *The New York Times*, April 1, 2009.

[978]   Ian Shapira, "Texting generation doesn't share boomers' taste for talk, "*The Washington Post*, August 8, 2010.

[979]   Pew Internet and American Life Project.

[980]   Julie Sevrens Lyons, "Texting shorthand showing up in schoolwork," *San Jose Mercury News*, April 25, 2008.

[981]   Damon Darlin, "Staying connected more costly, convoluted," *The New York Times*, September 13, 2010.

[982]   Hillel Italie, Associated Press, "A new page for e-books?" *San Jose Mercury News*, April 21, 2008.

[983]   Brad Stone and Motoko Rich, *The New York Times*, December 29, 2008;Rachel Metz, Associated Press, "E-readers jockey for market position," *San Jose Mercury News*, January 8, 2010; and Elise Ackerman, "Written any good e-books lately? Smashwords founder can help," *San Jose Mercury News*, January 11, 2009.

[984]   Natasha Robinson, Associated Press, "Scanning a million books page by page for Google," *San Jose Mercury News*, April 26, 2008.

[985]   Hiawatha Bray, *The Boston Globe*, September 1, 2008.

[986]   Hillel Italie, Associated Press, "Lord of the e-book," *San Jose Mercury News*, April 29, 2009.

[987]   Brad Stone and Motoko Rich, *The New York Times*, December 29, 2008.

[988]   Dawn Chmielewski, "Publishers brace for selling bits of books online," *San Jose Mercury News*.

[989]   Lisa M. Krieger, "Britannica opens its online pages," *San Jose Mercury News*, June 16, 2008; and Hiawatha Bray, "Enter Britannica," *The Boston Globe*, March 31, 2009.

[990]   Novelist and entrepreneur in the publishing industry.

[991]   Elise Ackerman, "Written any good e-books lately? Smashwords founder can help," *San Jose Mercury News*, January 11, 2009; and Hillel Italie, Associated Press, "Lord of the e-book," *San Jose Mercury News*, April 29, 2009.

[992]   Alfonso Castiglia, "Kids in remote Uruguay hamlet eager to connect," *San Jose Mercury News*, May 19, 2007.

[993]   Ryan Blitstein, "Parlez-vous YouTube?" *San Jose Mercury News*, June 20, 2007.

[994]   "YouTube opens global dialogue," *San Jose Mercury News*, January 25, 2008.

[995]   Henry Chu, "In India, newspapers are likely to be a long story," *Los Angeles Times*, May 20 2007.

[996]   Shashi Tharoor, "India's great leveler: cell phones," *San Jose Mercury News*, February 2, 2007.

[997]   Joel Garreau, *The Washington Post*.

[998]   Joel Garreau, "Our cells, ourselves," *The Washington Post*, February 27, 2008.

[999]   In addition, it had become obvious that the prevailing structure was creating security issues through hackers. Other nations wanted to cede oversight of computers that control Internet traffic to an organization independent of the U.S. government.

[1000] Bloomberg News, "Loosen grip on Web, U.S. urged," *San Jose Mercury News*, May 6, 2009.

[1001] Kelly Olsen, Associated Press, "Non-Latin domain names for Web OK'd," *San Jose Mercury News*, October 31, 2009.

[1002] Dheepthi Namasivayam, Associated Press, "Saving world's vanishing languages," *San Jose Mercury News*, February 19, 2009.

[1003] Bloomberg News, "English translation service for Amazon," *San Jose Mercury News*, May 20, 2010.

[1004] Skype is an Internet phone program.

[1005] Frank Davies, MediaNews Washington Bureau, "Internet censors growing globally," *San Jose Mercury News*, May 18, 2007.

[1006] Wen Yunchao.

[1007] Edward Cody, "Text messages giving voice to Chinese," *The Washington Post*, June 28, 2007.

[1008] Ibid.

[1009] John Boudreau, "Tech group: Challenge China on censorship," *San Jose Mercury News*, June 13, 2009; Christopher Bodeen, Associated Press, "China shuts down Twitter ahead of 20th Tiananmen anniversary," *San Jose Mercury News*, June 5, 2009; and Gillian Wong, Associated Press, "China requires PC makers to include filtering software," *San Jose Mercury News*, June 9, 2009.

[1010] Twitter (and Facebook) was used in Iran mostly by the affluent, the young and liberal, and city-dwellers. They were supporting Mir Hossein Mousavi, reformist challenger to the presidency. Poorer, low-educated voters were flocking to President Mahmoud Ahmadinejad. (Rebecca Santana, Associated Press, "Demonstrators in Iran turn to Twitter," *San Jose Mercury News*, June 16, 2009.) The Web site was named after Neda Agha Soltan, who became a global symbol of the post election protest movement after videos of her death by gunfire were posted on Web sites.

[1011] The Web site was named after Neda Agha Soltan, who became a global symbol of the post election protest movement after videos of her death by gunfire were posted on Web sites.

[1012] Shaya Tayefe Mohajer, Associated Press, "Iran protest effort has moved online," *San Jose Mercury News*, June 28, 2009; and Robert F. Worth and Nazila Fathi, "Defiance grows as Iran's leader sets vote review," *The New York Times*, June 15, 2009.

[1013] Austin Heap, a software developer.

[1014] John Boudreau, "Computer-savvy S.F. man helps activists get past filters in Iran," *San Jose Mercury News*, February 16, 2010.

[1015] Mike Swift, "Google tool tracks biggest Web censors by country," *San Jose Mercury News*, April 21, 2010.

—CHAPTER 18—

[1016] "Nanotechnology is the study of manipulating matter on an atomic and molecular scale." (Wikipedia)

[1017]   Drew Hall and Richard Gaster.

[1018]   From the Institute of Electrical and Electronic Engineers for technological solutions to societal problems.

[1019]   Devin Banerjee, "Stanford students win tech award," *San Jose Mercury News*, June 25, 2009.

[1020]   Bill Kaczor, Associated Press, "Nanotechnology may yield new extra-strong material," *San Jose Mercury News*, October 18, 2008.

[1021]   Molecular machines, which would build new products atom by atom, "could spit out a pair of new blue jeans bit by bit the way today's computer printers push out documents," said Arden Pennell, in writing about Mike Treder of the Center for Responsible Nanotechnology.

[1022]   Arden Pennell, "Small scale, big potential," *Palo Alto Weekly*, March 26, 2008.

[1023]   The Pentagon's Defense Advanced Research Projects Agency (DARPA) is under a congressional deadline to have one-third of its military ground combat vehicles unmanned by 2015. The Agency is pushing for development of unmanned vehicles to make warfare safer through use of self-thinking machines that could fight in war zones with no need for remote control.

[1024]   Associated Press, "Robotic vehicles take to the streets," *San Jose Mercury News*, November 5, 2007.

[1025]   Two robotic dune buggies, operated by the Jet Propulsion Laboratory (JPL) from Pasadena, have been patrolling Mars since 2003, taking photographs and collecting information. However, Google's requirement of high-definition images and video will be a first.

[1026]   Elise Ackerman, "Google aims for 3-D world," *San Jose Mercury News*, May 19, 2007.

[1027]   Terence Chea, Associated Press, "Driverless cars come a long way: Herbie, meet Shelley," *San Jose Mercury News*, April 10, 2010.

[1028]   Gary Richards, "Fast, direct, and you'd never have to tip the driver," *San Jose Mercury News,* May 25, 2010.

[1029]   Abu Dhabi, South Korea and Sweden.

[1030]   Hiroko Tabuchi, Associated Press, "Who'll help you when you're old?" *San Jose Mercury News*, October 5, 2007.

[1031]   Benedict Carey and John Markoff, "Students, meet your new teacher, Mr. Robot," *The New York Times,* July 11, 2010.

[1032]   Troy Wolverton, "Robots invade the workplace," *San Jose Mercury News*, August 26, 2010.

[1033]   Campbell Robertson and Clifford Krauss, "Robots work to stop leak of oil in Gulf," *The New York Times*, April 27, 2010.

[1034] Lisa M. Krieger, "Harvard scientist to lead Stanford's Bio-X program," *San Jose Mercury News*, March 21, 2007.

[1035] "Court backs stem-cell agency," *San Jose Mercury News*, April 22, 2006.

[1036] "State's stem cell initiative already paying big dividends," *San Jose Mercury News*, December 21, 2006.

[1037] Geron in Menlo Park, California.

[1038] Steve Johnson, "1st human embryo-cell test," *San Jose Mercury News*, July 31, 2010.

[1039] Steve Johnson, *San Jose Mercury News*.

[1040] Steve Johnson, "1st human embryo-cell test," *San Jose Mercury News*, July 31, 2010.

[1041] Lauran Neergaard, Associated Press, "Scientists say they made world's first synthetic cell," *San Jose Mercury News*, May 21, 2010.

[1042] Lisa M. Krieger, "Creating life from scratch moves one step closer," *San Jose Mercury News,* January 25, 2008.

[1043] Scott Duke Harris, "A 'double' helix," *San Jose Mercury News*, August 17, 2010.

[1044] Ibid.

[1045] Ibid.

[1046] Scott Duke Harris, "New technology provides deeper look into building blocks of life,"*San Jose Mercury News*, September 27, 2009.

[1047] Matt Nauman, "Biotech deal for clean fuel," *San Jose Mercury News*, April 24, 2008.

[1048] John Schwartz, "PETA's latest tactic: $1 million for fake meat," *The New York Times*, April 21, 2008.

[1049] Andrew Pollack, "Genetically altered salmon get closer to the table," *The New York Times*, June 26, 2010.

[1050] Nicholas Wade, "Wider use of DNA lists is urged in fighting crime," *The New York Times*, May 12, 2006.

[1051] Rachel L. Swarns, *The New York Times*, April 16, 2007.

[1052] Some countries in Africa are matrilineal societies, that is, legal inheritance comes through the mother's line.

[1053] Matthew Lee, Associated Press, "DNA tests ahead for some refugees?" *San Jose Mercury News*, November 6, 2009.

[1054] Samantha Young, Associated Press, "Interactive feature shows effects of altered weather," *San Jose Mercury News*, December 3, 2009.

[1055] Seth Borenstein and Michael Casey, Associated Press, "Can Google help enforce a climate change accord?" *San Jose Mercury News*, December 18, 2009.

[1056] Cryptic species are two closely related species that look the same but are genetically distinct.

[1057] San Jose Mercury News, June 2, 2010.

—CHAPTER 19—

[1058] Bill Gates of Microsoft and Steve Jobs of Apple represent two distinctive approaches to technology. Microsoft strives for ubiquity, not uniqueness, whereas Apple focuses on path- breaking design.

[1059] Troy Wolverton, "One stage, two titans of tech," *San Jose Mercury News*, May 30, 2007.

[1060] Larry Magid, "Competitors take their cue from Apple's innovations," *San Jose Mercury News*, August 9, 2010.

[1061] Microprocessor chips are sometimes smaller than a micron. To put it in perspective, a human hair is 100 microns thick.

[1062] Chris O'Brien, "Avatar attraction," *San Jose Mercury News*, August 8, 2010.

[1063] William Saletan, "We've Made our Match," *The Washington Post,* May 13, 2007. Saletan covers science and technology for *Slate*, an online magazine

[1064] Ibid.

[1065] At the center of a black hole is a point called a "singularity" where the laws of physics become useless. They no longer make sense.

[1066] Ray Kurzweil was a pioneer in speech recognition and artificial intelligence.

[1067] Brandon Bailey, "Team's brainchild: PCs like us," *San Jose Mercury News,* November 18, 2009.

[1068] Marcus Wohlsen, "Artificial intelligence subject of conference," *San Jose Mercury News*, September 9, 2007.

[1069] Thomas H.Maugh II, "New procedure lets prosthetic arms listen to the brain," *Los Angeles Times*, February 14, 2009.

[1070] Steve Johnson, *San Jose Mercury News*.

[1071] A neuroscientist at the Mayo Clinic in Florida.

[1072] Steve Johnson, "Just think," *San Jose Mercury News*, January 17, 2010.

[1073] Scott Kirsner, "Why can't Silicon Valley make it simple?" *San Jose Mercury News*, January 7, 2007.

[1074] Troy Wolverton, "U.S. consumers splurged on video games in 2007," *San Jose Mercury News*, January 18, 2008.

[1075] "Tech Notebook," *San Jose Mercury News*, June 14, 2008.

[1076] Troy Wolverton, "In a losing economy, video game industry wins," *San Jose Mercury News,* December 12, 2008.

[1077] The number of fans connecting to the Wi-Fi network each game jumped from 94 in 2004 to more than 1600 in 2009.

[1078] John Boudreau, "Ballpark tech: It's a hit!" *San Jose Mercury News*, July 20, 2009.

[1079] Ibid.

[1080] John Boudreau, "Ballpark tech: It's a hit!" *San Jose Mercury News*, July 20, 2009.

[1081] Beth J. Harpaz, "Our Future: Told by dreamers and realists," *San Jose Mercury News*, May 22, 2010.

[1082] Ann Livermore, former Executive Vice President of Hewlett Packard. In June 2011 she was relieved of her duties and elected to the HP board of directors.

[1083] Brandon Bailey, *San Jose Mercury News*, June 2, 2010.

[1084] Tracey Kaplan, "County court upgraded to handle major case," *San Jose Mercury News*, June 7, 2010.

[1085] Bruce Mehlman and Larry Irving, "Bring On The Exaflood!" *Washington Post*, May 24, 2007.

[1086] "Informing communities: Sustaining Democracy in the Digital Age," a report of the Knight Commission on the Information Needs of Communities in a Democracy.

[1087] Chris O'Brien, "Digital gap is isolating citizens," *San Jose Mercury News*, October 4, 2009.

[1088] Peter Svensson, Associated Press, "Internet access growing," *San Jose Mercury News*, June 22, 2009.

[1089] Joelle Tessler, Associated Press, *San Jose Mercury News*, October 12, 2009.

[1090] Georganne Greene, public health administrator in Curry County, Oregon.

[1091] Michelle Quinn, *San Jose Mercury News*.

[1092] Michelle Quinn, "Technology came up short against weather, terrain," *San Jose Mercury News*, December 6, 2006.

[1093] Dean Takahashi, "Computer executives to converge on CES," *San Jose Mercury News*, January 1, 2007.

[1094] Smartphones are handheld computers disguised as cellphones. Though they can make simple phone calls, purchasers usually buy them for their computer functions, such as downloading e-mail, surfing the Web and keeping track of expenses.

[1095]   Troy Wolverton, "Smart-phone evolution," *San Jose Mercury News*, June 1, 2009.

[1096]   Chris O'Brien, "Where in the world," *San Jose Mercury News*, May 25, 2009.

[1097]   Rose Hanson, Associated Press, "Modern rattler," *San Jose Mercury News*, May 25, 2009.

[1098]   Chris O'Brien, "Microsoft bows to inevitable," *San Jose Mercury News*, February 17, 2010.

[1099]   Cameras count the wrinkles on a customer's face to determine their age.

[1100]   Cameras count the motorist's blinks.

[1101]   Steve Johnson, "Pin-size camera?" *San Jose Mercury News*, May 11, 2009.

[1102]   Beth J. Harpaz, "Our Future: Told by dreamers and realists," *San Jose Mercury News*, May 22, 2010.

[1103]   Image sensors are the light-sensitive computer chips inside digital cameras.

[1104]   John Boudreau, "Cameras count the motorist's blinks," *San Jose Mercury News*, July 6, 2009.

[1105]   China, France, Germany, India, Japan, Singapore, and Malaysia.

[1106]   92 percent vs. 95 percent.

[1107]   86 percent vs. 95 percent.

[1108]   Jean-Laurent Poitou and Kumu Puri, from an article they wrote for the *San Jose Mercury News*, April 15, 2010. Poitou and Puri are managing directors at Accenture.

[1109]   The Pew Internet and American Life Project conducted the survey.

[1110]   Larry Magid, "Technology as a uniter, not a divider," *San Jose Mercury News*, October 27, 2008.

[1111]   Ibid.

[1112]   Ibid.

[1113]   Larry Magid, *San Jose Mercury News*.

[1114]   Larry Magid, "Technology as a uniter, not a divider," *San Jose Mercury News*, October 27, 2008.

[1115]   Larry Magid, "Look behind the data on kids' media use," *San Jose Mercury News*, January 25, 2010.

[1116]   Steve LeBlanc, Associated Press, "Study: Video game play sharpens skills of students— and surgeons," *San Jose Mercury News*, August 18, 2008.

[1117]   The report, "Generation M2: Media in the Lives of 8- to 18-Year–Olds," compares data from 2009 with similar studies done in 2004 and 1999.

[1118] Larry Magid, "Look behind the data on kids' media use," *San Jose Mercury News*, January 25, 2010.

[1119] "Australian Diabetes, Obesity and Life-style Study."

[1120] Dr. David Dunstan, head of the Physical Activity Laboratory at the Baker IDI Heart and Diabetes Institute in Victoria, Australia.

[1121] Jeannine Stein, "All aboard for Michelle Obama's childhood obesity campaign," *Los Angeles Times*, February 11, 2010.

[1122] Loren Frank, assistant professor in the department of physiology at UCSF.

[1123] Matt Richtel, "Recharge your brain by unplugging technology!" *The New York Times*, August 26, 2010.

[1124] Steve Johnson, "Survey: users irked by gadget gaffes," *San Jose Mercury News*, June 18, 2009.

[1125] Harris Interactive conducted the survey for Intel.

[1126] Steve Johnson, "Survey: users irked by gadget gaffes," *San Jose Mercury News*, June 18, 2009.

[1127] Frank Eltman, Associated Press, "High-tech eyes in the sky have civil libertarians concerned," *San Jose Mercury News*, August 15, 2010.

[1128] Columnist for *The New York Times*.

[1129] Thomas L. Friedman, "Really unusually uncertain," *The New York Times*, August 19, 2010.

[1130] Joelle Tessler, Associated Press, "Deal would mandate FM in phones," *San Jose Mercury News*, August 19, 2010.

[1131] Brandon Bailey, "Fighting online thieves," *San Jose Mercury News*, July 11, 2009.

[1132] Mike Swift, "Google good to go in government data storage," *San Jose Mercury News*, July 27, 2010.

[1133] Sgt. Chuck Violette of the Tucson police department.

[1134] Robert O'Harrow Jr. and Ellen Nakashima, *The Washington Post*, March 6, 2008.

[1135] Brandon Bailey, "Obama makes his choice for CTO post," *San Jose Mercury News*, April 18, 2009.

[1136] Pauline Jelinek, Associated Press, "Pentagon plans cybercommand," *San Jose Mercury News*, April 22, 2009.

[1137] Ellen Nakashima, "NSA director confirmed to head cyber-command," *The Washington Post,* May 11, 2010.

[1138] Ellen Nakashima, "WikiLeaks releases CIA paper on U.S. as 'exporter of terrorism,'"*The Washington Post*, August 26, 2010.

[1139]   Julian Assange, founder of Wikileaks.org.

[1140]   Ellen Nakashima and Joby Warrick, "WikiLeaks takes new approach in latest release of documents," *The Washington Post*, July 27, 2010.

[1141]   According to the Cyberstates 2009 report.

[1142]   Elise Ackerman, "As jobs vanish, tech is hiring," *San Jose Mercury News*, March 31, 2009.

[1143]   Transistors are the tiny switches that manage the flow of electronic data.

[1144]   Problems that this density caused have led to building chips with multiple computing engines (cores) that boost performance by processing streams of data simultaneously and provide greater energy efficiency. Even more is in store for the future when the current four cores expand to 48 cores or more.

[1145]   Sean Koehl, technology evangelist for Intel.

[1146]   Steve Johnson, "Evolution of the chip," *San Jose Mercury News*, December 28, 2009.

[1147]   Lisa Krieger, "Researchers find possible heir to silicon," *San Jose Mercury News*, June 16, 2009.

[1148]   Chris O'Brien, *San Jose Mercury News*.

[1149]   Chris O'Brien, "Share more online and do some good," *San Jose Mercury News*, June 20, 2010.

—CHAPTER 20—

[1150]   Patrick May, "Tech tools foster larger, more diverse networks, study says," *San Jose Mercury News*, November 5, 2009.

[1151]   Mike Cassidy, "Not music to some ears," *San Jose Mercury News,* February 23, 2007.

[1152]   Troy Wolverton, "Video games won't need Xbox, Wii or PS3, startup's founder says,"*San Jose Mercury News*, April 19, 2009.

[1153]   "Digital downloads fuel music-sales surge," *San Jose Mercury News*, January 5, 2007.

[1154]   Diane Stafford, McClatchy Newspapers, "Resumes going extinct," *San Jose Mercury News*, April 1, 2007.

[1155]   Jim Buchta, "Focus shifts to firm's data-heavy Web site, alternative media ads," *San Jose Mercury News*, February 10, 2007.

[1156]   Sue McAllister, "Realtors get specific about web selling," *San Jose Mercury News*, April 21, 2007.

[1157]   Michael Barbaro, "Less risk seen in purchasing clothes online," *The New York Times*, May 14, 2007.

[1158]   "Online advertising up 36 percent in 2006," *San Jose Mercury News*, March 8, 2007.

[1159]   Bloomberg News and Associated Press, "Internet advertising soared 35% in 2006," *San Jose Mercury News*, May 29, 2007.

[1160]   "White Pages phone books fading away," AARP *Bulletin*, October 2009.

[1161]   Caitlin McDevitt, "Communities seek routes to save post offices from being stamped out," *The Washington Post*, June 28, 2009.

[1162]   Deborah Yao and Ryan Nakashima, Associated Press, "Comcast's goal: content," *San Jose Mercury News*, December 6, 2009.

[1163]   Scott Duke Harris, "Gore's Current Media files for IPO," *San Jose Mercury News*, January 29, 2008.

[1164]   Chris O'Brien.

[1165]   Chris O'Brien, "Blogging's a-ha moment was more of an evolution," *San Jose Mercury News*, November 4, 2009.

[1166]   Richard Lardner, Associated Press, "Pentagon listens in to online postings," *San Jose Mercury News*, August 10, 2009.

[1167]   The *New York Times* now charges for online subscriptions. The Wall Street Journal has been able to charge for online subscriptions since it first went online because of its unique financial news.

[1168]   Richard Perez-Pena and Tim Arango, "They pay for cable, music and extra bags. How about news?" *The New York Times*, April 8, 2009.

[1169]   Published by Collins Business, 2009.

[1170]   Critic at "TV Guide" and founding editor of "Entertainment Weekly."

[1171]   Jarvis said: "Google creates a virtuous circle: The more we click on search results, the smarter Google gets, the better its results are, and the more we use Google."

Google's vision is reflective of what scientists already know about the natural world in terms of non-local morphic fields, complexity and expansion. "Virtuous circles" function similarly to non-local *morphic fields*; yielding control directly to customers invites *complexity* (as you must deal with millions of people); and charging as little as possible (which draws millions more people) translates into *expansion*.

[1172]   Bruce Manuel, *San Jose Mercury News*.

[1173]   Bruce Manuel, "We've seen the future, and it is Google," *San Jose Mercury News*, March 15, 2009.

[1174]   A headline from the Business Section of the *San Jose Mercury News* is a sign of the increasing importance of speed today: "Google speeds up search engine: Company says Google Instant saves two to five seconds." (September 9, 2010).

[1175] Elise Ackerman, "Google shares speed secrets," *San Jose Mercury News*, June 25, 2009.

[1176] Stephen Ohlemacher, Associated Press, "Americans increasingly plugged in," *San Jose Mercury News*, December 15, 2006.

[1177] San Jose State University associate professor and author of *City Ubiquitous: Place, Communication and the Rise of Omnitopia.*

[1178] Mike Cassidy, "Can we talk? Well, yes, but why bother?" *San Jose Mercury News*, March 16, 2009.

[1179] A few of the most visited websites as of August 2011, according to Google (which did not rank itself), were: Facebook #1, YouTube #2, Wikipedia #5 and Twitter #16.

[1180] David Bank.

[1181] Information for outsiders: Facebook is like an online social gathering. People who sign up for the free service invite people to join their Facebook social circle. Whoever accepts becomes a Facebook "friend," a word that is used loosely. Facebook users have their own home page, where they can share messages with their "friends." Facebook also offers online games and the ability to purchase virtual goods, such as digital flowers for friends. (Scott Duke Harris, "A guide for the Facebook novice," *San Jose Mercury News*, June 27, 2010.)

[1182] Brian Stelter and Tim Arango, *The New York Times*, May 11, 2009.

Two-directional conversation is relationship, the very heart of creation, whereas expressing yourself may be nothing more than that— no response, no give and take.

[1183] Michiko Kakutani, *The New York Times*.

[1184] David Kirkpatrick, author of *The Facebook Effect*.

[1185] Its popularity may be due, in part, to the Web site's minimalist look and the company's decision in 2005 to add photo hosting to the site.

[1186] Michiko Kakutani, *The New York Times*, June 27, 2010.

In its earliest days, Facebook drew primarily whites and Asians. Four years later the number of black and Latino users had surged to 20 percent of its 100 million U.S. members.

[1187] Paul Saffo, Silicon Valley futurist.

[1188] Mike Swift, "Twitter chirps about growth at first developers conference," *San Jose Mercury News*, April 15, 2010.

[1189] David Sarno, *Los Angeles Times*, February 22, 2009; Patrick May, "Twitter," *San Jose Mercury News*, October 5, 2009; and Mike Swift, "Twitter chirps about growth at first developers conference," *San Jose Mercury News*, April 15, 2010.

[1190] Jason Straziuso, Associated Press, "Tweets from the front: War reporting upgrade," *San Jose Mercury News*, June 2, 2009.

[1191] Historian and author of *Presidential Courage.*

[1192] Monica Hesse, "Historians applaud Twitter-post archive," *The Washington Post*, May 16, 2010.

[1193] Claire Cain Miller, "Tracking the national mood through Twitter, "*The New York Times*, July 22, 2010.

[1194] *The Tipping Point: How Little Things Can Make a Big Difference*, page 70.

[1195] The average user on Facebook has 130 "friends."

[1196] John Flesher, Associated Press, "Social-network sites raise funds, but not much," *San Jose Mercury News*, April 27, 2009.

[1197] Stephanie Clifford, *The New York Times*, June 1, 2009.

[1198] Wiki is a type of Web site, such as Wikipedia, that can be updated and edited by any of its participants, encouraging collaboration.

[1199] Larry Magid, "Don't fight students' thirst for technology," *San Jose Mercury News*, July 6, 2009.

[1200] David Reilly, age 37.

[1201] Matt Richtel, "Growing up digital, wired for distraction," *The New York Times*, November 21, 2010.

[1202] Darleen Pryds teaches Christian Spirituality and History.

[1203] Elizabeth Drescher, "Three views on the rise of social media in religious education," GTU *Currents,* Spring 2010.

[1204] Dr. Drescher currently teaches at Santa Clara University.

[1205] Elizabeth Drescher, "Three views on the rise of social media in religious education," GTU *Currents,* Spring 2010.

[1206] Brian Pokorny, CEO of DailyBooth.

[1207] Brad Stone, "For Web's new wave, sharing details is the point," *The New York Times*, April 25, 2010.

[1208] Surveys by Hoofnagle and the Pew Center for the Internet and Society.

[1209] Cecilia Kang, "Internet privacy could be priority in next Congress," *The Washington Post*, November 4, 2010.

[1210] Lolita C. Baldor, Associated Press, "White House urges Net ID system," *San Jose Mercury News,* June 27, 2010.

[1211] The term "applications" (or "apps") refers to a software application that allows people to do something on the Internet (like play games, check their bank balance or look at sport scores) without needing a browser and the Web.

[1212]   As of 2011 the Apple App store had more than 500,000 apps, the Android Market more than 200,000, and over 7 million apps and websites were integrated with Facebook.

[1213]   Mike Swift, "Appetite for apps: the smart, rich, young," *San Jose Mercury News*, September 15, 2010.

[1214]   Patrick May, "New shopping apps blur the line between online, offline," *San Jose Mercury News*, November 23, 2010.

[1215]   Anick Jesdanun, Associated Press, "Americans turn to Net for political fix, study finds," *San Jose Mercury News*, June 15, 2008.

[1216]   Troy Wolverton, "From travel planning to real-time carpools," *San Jose Mercury News*, September 10, 2008.

[1217]   Tina Susman, *Los Angeles Times*, June 6, 2009.

[1218]   Ben Southall from Britain was hired.

[1219]   Tina Susman, *Los Angeles Times*, June 6, 2009.

[1220]   Arian Smedley, Associated Press, "4food reinvents dining by adding social networking," *San Jose Mercury News*, September 23, 2010.

[1221]   Multiple users had previously been able to share documents among themselves, but they were limited in having two or more people work together on the same project at the same time.

[1222]   Mike Swift, "Google Docs' new prescription," *San Jose Mercury News*, April 13, 2010.

[1223]   Scott Duke Harris, "Service connects scientists worldwide," *San Jose Mercury News*, September 9, 2010.

[1224]   Lisa M. Krieger.

[1225]   Lisa M. Krieger, "For math website, proof is in the collaboration," *San Jose Mercury News*, August 9, 2010.

[1226]   April Dembosky, "Wash your hands and text me later," *San Jose Mercury News*, July 20, 2009.

[1227]   "Living and Learning with New Media," a study led by Mizuko Ito, a professor at the University of California-Irvine.

[1228]   Sharon Noguchi, "Chill out, Parents," *San Jose Mercury News*, November 20, 2008.

[1229]   The study was conducted at Stanford University's Communication Between Humans and Interactive Media Lab.

[1230]   Lisa Fernandez, *San Jose Mercury News*.

[1231]   Lisa Fernandez, "Stop scanning the page. Focus!" *San Jose Mercury News*, August 27, 2009.

[1232] Michael Rich, who is also an associate professor at Harvard University.

[1233] Matt Richtel, "Growing up digital, wired for distraction," *The New York Times*, November 21, 2010.

[1234] Jackie Burrell, "Teens choose to text, perchance to sleep," *San Jose Mercury News*, September 13, 2009.

[1235] Christine Handy-Collins, principal of Gaithersburg High School in Gaithersburg, Maryland.

[1236] "Hey, Kid. Don't make me text you twice," *The Washington Post*, September 6, 2009.

[1237] Melissa Healy, "Teenage social media butterflies may not be such a bad idea," *Los Angeles Times*, May 18, 2010.

[1238] Frank Davies, "More Americans turn to Web for political news," *San Jose Mercury News*, April 17, 2009.

[1239] Deborah Tindell and Robert Bohlander, psychology professors at Wilkes University, conducted the survey.

[1240] Michael Rubinkam, Associated Press, "In class, texting a top distraction," *San Jose Mercury News*, November 27, 2010.

[1241] One in five teenagers shares online passwords as a way to build trust and foster romance, according to the Internet and American Life Project at the Pew Research Center.

[1242] Liz Perle, co-founder of Common Sense Media, a non-profit watchdog group that studies families and media.

[1243] Sally Che, a medical student at George Washington University.

[1244] Laura M. Holson, "Breaking up in a digital fishbowl," *The New York Times*, January 6, 2010.

[1245] "The American Way—Working on Vacation," *San Jose Mercury News*, June 2, 2007.

[1246] John Boudreau, "Cloud communication," *San Jose Mercury News*, April 20, 2009.

[1247] Melissa Healy, *Los Angeles Times*.

[1248] Melissa Healy, "Internet use may help you search and find . . . a healthier mind," *Los Angeles Times*, October 29, 2009.

[1249] Miss Manners, "Arriving via e-mail: birth announcements," *San Jose Mercury News*, June 29, 2008.

[1250] Alex L. Goldfayn, *Chicago Tribune*.

[1251] Chris O'Brien, "Debate shows interactive TV's potential," *San Jose Mercury News*, October 30, 2008.

[1252] Julie Chang, "@Disaster: Alert system reaches out," *San Jose Mercury News*, July 9, 2010.

—CHAPTER 21—

[1253] Jeremy N. Bailenson, Director of the Virtual Human Interaction Lab at Stanford University.

[1254] The scientists were from Stockholm's renowned Karolinska Institute.

[1255] Henrik Ehrsson, leader of the project.

[1256] Karl Ritter, Associated Press, "How's this for an out-of-body experience?" *San Jose Mercury News*, December 2, 2008.

[1257] The movie is "Virtuality," a Fox production.

[1258] Glenn Garvin, "'2001' meets reality TV in 'Virtuality'," *San Jose Mercury News*, June 26, 2009.

[1259] Second Life is an online virtual world.

[1260] "Stella McCartney's online fur protest," *San Jose Mercury News*, June 29, 2007.

[1261] Associated Press, "Safe-deposit box for online records," *San Jose Mercury News*, March 19, 2008.

[1262] Larry Rosen, professor at California State University-Dominguez Hills and author of *Me, MySpace, and I: Parenting the Net Generation*.

[1263] Pamela Roberts, professor at California State University-Long Beach.

[1264] Jaweed Kaleem, "Morbid curiosity or natural interest?" *Miami Herald*, March 10, 2008.

[1265] Alana Semuels, "Online services deliver mail without the paper," *Los Angeles Times*, March 12, 2009.

[1266] "Bay Area Virtual Job Fair," *San Jose Mercury News*, April 22, 2007.

[1267] "Ticketmaster goes paperless to reap resale ticket profits," *San Jose Mercury News*, September 18, 2009.

[1268] Claudia Girrbach, "Taking steps toward the paperless office, at last," *San Jose Mercury News*, February 3, 2010.

[1269] Claudia Girrbach, "Taking steps toward the paperless office, at last," *San Jose Mercury News*, February 3, 2010

[1270] Sid Kirchheimer, "Hacked in the parking lot," AARP *Bulletin*.

[1271] Gained by hacking into databases.

[1272] State of Sao Paulo.

[1273] According to a poll made by a Mexican citizens' group.

[1274] Lisa J. Adams, Associated Press, "'Virtual kidnappings' pose real risks in Latin America," *San Jose Mercury News*, May 25, 2007.

[1275] Felicia Anderson.

[1276] Mitchell Confer.

[1277] Dick Scott.

[1278] "Streetwise," *Palo Alto Weekly*, July 23, 2008 Countries from Singapore to Great Britain have considered making Second Life an integral part of their secondary education.

[1279] Sue Dremann, *Palo Alto Weekly*.

[1280] Sue Dremann, "The (not so) real world," *Palo Alto Weekly*, July 23, 2008.

[1281] Sue Dremann, *Palo Alto Weekly*.

[1282] Sue Dremann, "The (not so) real world," *Palo Alto Weekly*, July 23, 2008.

[1283] Kara Andrade, "The virtual university," *San Jose Mercury News*, November 23, 2007.

[1284] Sue Dremann, "The (not so) real world," *Palo Alto Weekly*, July 23, 2008. Second Lifers begin by creating an avatar (an online identity), choosing a body (human, android, or animal), an outfit, and a name.

[1285] Sue Dremann, "The (not so) real world," *Palo Alto Weekly*, July 23, 2008 and Lisa Selin Davis, "Click here to Create a Better World," *OnEarth*, Spring 2007.

[1286] According to Jeremy Bailenson, director of Stanford University's Virtual Human Interaction Lab.

[1287] Sue Dremann, "The (not so) real world," *Palo Alto Weekly*, July 23, 2008 and Lisa Selin Davis, "Click here to Create a Better World," *OnEarth*, Spring 2007.

[1288] Lisa Selin Davis, "Click here to Create a Better World," *OnEarth*, Spring 2007.

[1289] Patricia Levinson, a senior technical writer at Sun Microsystems, Inc.

[1290] Sue Dremann, Palo Alto *Weekly*.

[1291] Sue Dremann, "The (not so) real world," *Palo Alto Weekly*, July 23, 2008.

[1292] "Second Life affair ends real-life marriage," *San Jose Mercury News*, November 15, 2008.

[1293] Rachel Konrad, Associated Press, "'Second Life' bans gambling," *San Jose Mercury News*, August 2, 2007.

[1294] Second Life's users must be at least 18 years old.

[1295] William Thewise Goodman is the avatar's name.

[1296] There is no master planning in SL.

[1297] Lisa Selin Davis, "Click here to Create a Better World," *OnEarth*, Spring 2007.

[1298] Mike Musgrove, "Virtual presents, virtual tress and very real cheer," *The Washington Post*, December 21, 2006.

[1299] Stefanie Olsen, "Storefronts in virtual worlds bringing in real money, "*The New York Times*, December 7, 2008.

[1300] Michele Chandler, "1-800-FLOWERS sells virtual bouquets to 'Second Life' users," *San Jose Mercury News*, June 23, 2007.

[1301] "EBay won't allow virtual items on site," *San Jose Mercury News*, February 3, 2007.

[1302] Sue Dremann, "The (not so) real world," *Palo Alto Weekly*, July 23, 2008.

[1303] David Barboza, "In China, new limits on virtual currency," *The New York Times*, July 1, 2009.

[1304] Edward Castronova at Indiana University Bloomington.

[1305] David Barboza, "In China, new limits on virtual currency," *The New York Times*, July 1, 2009.

[1306] Barbara Orutay, Associated Press.

[1307] Barbara Ortutay, Associated Press, "Kwedit seeks to help creditless buy virtual goods on the Internet," *San Jose Mercury News*, February 6, 2010.

[1308] Credits are sold in India, Australia, New Zealand, Malaysia, Thailand, Singapore, Indonesia and the Philippines.

[1309] Julia Zappei, Associated Press, "Facebook, MOL to sell currency for games," *San Jose Mercury News*, July 10, 2010.

[1310] Facebook had already been signing long-term deals for several months with game makers such as Zynga to use its virtual credits.

[1311] According to Inside Network, which publishes the Inside Facebook blog.

[1312] Frank Michael Russell, "Target to sell Facebook Credits gift cards to buy virtual goods," *San Jose Mercury News*, September 2, 2010.

[1313] http://techpresident.com/blog-entry/hillary-clinton-second-life.

[1314] Frank Davies, "Congressional hearing in two worlds," Mercury News Washington Bureau, *San Jose Mercury News*, April 2, 2008.

[1315] Ibid.

[1316] Ibid.

[1317] Sue Dremann, "The (not so) real world," *Palo Alto Weekly*, July 23, 2008.

[1318] Kara Andrade, "The virtual university," *San Jose Mercury News*, November 23, 2007.

[1319] Among them were Adidas, Dell, IBM, General Motors, Sun Microsystems, Inc., 20th Century Fox, Intel and Warner Bros.

[1320] Sue Dremann, "The (not so) real world," *Palo Alto Weekly*, July 23, 2008.

[1321] Alex Veiga, Associated Press.

[1322] Alex Veiga, Associated Press, "Companies build their brands in 'Second Life' virtual world," *San Jose Mercury News*, February 26, 2007.

[1323] Mark Boslet, "Virtual worlds creating new sales opportunities," *San Jose Mercury News*, June 23, 2007.

[1324] Alana Semuels, "You in back, yes you, the half-lynx," *Los Angeles Times*, May 10, 2008.

[1325] Rachel Konrad, "IBM digs in to virtual worlds," *San Jose Mercury News*, July 27, 2007.

[1326] Alana Semuels, "You in back, yes you, the half-lynx," *Los Angeles Times*, May 10, 2008.

[1327] Alan Sipress, "Where real money meets virtual reality, the jury is still out," *The Washington Post*, December 26, 2006.

[1328] Tech columnist for the *San Jose Mercury News*.

[1329] Dean Takahashi, "The reality of virtual worlds," *San Jose Mercury News*, October 18, 2007.

[1330] Ibid.

[1331] O'Reilly, Cary and Jef Feeley, Bloomberg News, "CBS wins right to NFL player names, stats in fantasy football leagues," *San Jose Mercury News*, April 30, 2009.

[1332] Alex Pham, *Los Angeles Times*.

[1333] Alex Pham, "Sports fields become a virtual world," *Los Angeles Times*, September 22, 2008.

[1334] Konstantin Guericke, co-founder of LinkedIn.

[1335] Dean Takahashi, tech columnist, describing Trip Hawkins' theory.

[1336] Dean Takahashi, tech columnist, *San Jose Mercury News*.

[1337] Dean Takahashi, "It takes a (virtual reality online) village," *San Jose Mercury News*, March 12, 2007.

[1338] Barbara Ortutay, Associated Press, "Kwedit seeks to help creditless buy virtual goods on the Internet," *San Jose Mercury News*, February 6, 2010.

[1339] The top ten Facebook games (in order of popularity) in 2011 were: FarmVille, Texas HoldEm, FrontierVille, Mafia Wars, Cafe World, Treasure Isle, Pet Society, Millionaire City, MindJolt and Bejeweled Blitz.

[1340] Scott Duke Harris, *San Jose Mercury News*.

[1341] Melanie Earhart.

[1342] Scott Duke Harris, "Web Playground for Millions," *San Jose Mercury News*, December 3, 2009.

—CHAPTER 22—

[1343] James Gleick, "Have Meme, Will Travel," *Smithsonian,* May 2011.

[1344] William Saletan, "We've made our match," *The Washington Post*, May 13, 2007.

[1345] Anita Silvers of the philosophy department at San Francisco State University.

[1346] Elizabeth Drescher, "Three views on the rise of social media in religious education," GTU *Currents*, Spring 2010.

[1347] "Pets, family, escape bedroom blaze," *San Jose Mercury News*, June 19, 2009.

[1348] Dean Takahashi, "Playing now: a game that wants you," *San Jose Mercury News*, February 12, 2007.

[1349] Christopher Drew and John Markoff, "Contractors vie for plum work, hacking for U.S.," *The New York Times*, May 31, 2009.

[1350] David Ignatius, "Breaking down the Situation Room," *The Washington Post*, May 5, 2011.

[1351] Max Boot, Council on Foreign Relations, "War made new: technology, warfare and the course of history: 1500 to today," IntelliBriefs, June 9, 2007.

[1352] Yaron Ezrahi, "Behind the masks," *The New York Times*, June 20, 2007.

[1353] Patrick J. Buchanan, "Auto graveyard," FreeRepublic.com, February 16, 2007.

[1354] Brigitte Egger, in the newsletter of The Jung Society of Washington, September 5, 2008. Egger is a Jungian training analyst and ecologist in Zurich. She concentrates on the psychic and symbolic dimensions of collective issues, building up the field of psychology.

[1355] Associated Press, December 17, 2008.

[1356] Thomas L. Friedman, "The inflection is near?" *The New York Times*, March 7, 2009.

Printed in the USA
CPSIA information can be obtained
at www.ICGtesting.com
BVHW041333300723
667919BV00001B/2